The Mountainous West

The Mountainous West

EXPLORATIONS IN HISTORICAL GEOGRAPHY

EDITED BY WILLIAM WYCKOFF AND LARY M. DILSAVER

UNIVERSITY OF NEBRASKA PRESS   LINCOLN AND LONDON

The paper in this book meets the minimum
requirements of American National Standard
for Information Sciences—Permanence of
Paper for Printed Library Materials, ANSI
z39.48-1984.

Library of Congress Cataloging-in-
Publication Data
The mountainous west : explorations in
historical geography / edited by William
Wyckoff and Lary M. Dilsaver.
p. cm.
Includes bibliographical references and index.
ISBN 0-8032-4757-5 (cloth). —
ISBN 0-8032-9759-9
1. Mountains—West (U.S)   2. West (U.S.)—
Historical geography.
I. Wyckoff, William.   II. Dilsaver, Lary M.
F721.M65   1995
978—dc20
94-31183
CIP

Contents

Preface

The idea for a collection of essays on the Mountainous West began several years ago amongst an informal network of like-minded historical geographers who realized that they stood on common yet little-explored ground. The Historical Geography Specialty Group of the Association of American Geographers proved to be a congenial and fertile meeting place, and this book grew from their many discussions and paper sessions. The volume also developed from the collective experiences and wisdom of the contributors, whose varied research careers have taken them to diverse corners of the Mountainous West. What they have brought back with them to share in this volume should be seen not as a culmination, but rather as a beginning, an attempt to deepen our understanding and appreciation for that distinctive American subregion we have called the Mountainous West. For nongeographers reading this volume—and our hope is that there will be many—our distinctive perspective should be clear from the outset as we focus upon landscape change, spatial patterns, and the interconnections between people and environment.

In addition to the contributors, we have many people to thank, including anonymous reviewers for the University of Nebraska Press. Thanks also go to Chris Exline, Leonard Guelke, Theron Josephson, Paul Kay, Roy Ryder, Rob Bonnichsen, John Callahan, James Muhn, Paul Andrews, Steve Bicknell, Amy Morin, Marilyn Denton, and Joanne Needham for their assistance. We especially would like to acknowledge the sharp eye and thoughtful suggestions of Fritz Gritzner. Ann Parker proved to be a wizard in the intricacies of word processing, and Lee Murray contributed his cartographic expertise and ink to many of the base maps in the volume. Portions of Victor Konrad's research were supported by Montana Historic Preservation Office grants 5430-12244-6 and SP 30-12332-3, and by the University of Maine. Finally, we express our special appreciation to Linda and Robin for their constant patience and support as we wandered off amidst the sometimes rarefied terrain of the Mountainous West.

The Mountainous West

1 / Defining the Mountainous West

WILLIAM WYCKOFF and LARY M. DILSAVER

Generations of historians and geographers have pondered the regional character of the American West. Traditional interpretations have often centered on the West's widespread aridity as a common theme. Indeed, the West's dry corners have been amply and eloquently probed by Walter Prescott Webb, Wallace Stegner, Donald Worster, and many others. But this dominant historical perspective, while perhaps appropriate at a continental scale, begins to suffer upon closer inspection. Strewn everywhere across the West's vastness are mountains that belie our stereotyped views of a single "western" region. Any physiographic map of the West suggests the pattern (figure 1). The central problem is this: both the *physical* and *human* geographies of these mountain zones have conspired to create a very different West than that encountered in the coastal lowlands, desert valleys, and arid plains below. And even though the western mountains are a fragmented and discontinuous collection of separate ranges that extend from the Rockies to the Pacific Slope, these seemingly isolated places share a special character and coherence which binds them together as a distinctive American subregion. The collection of essays in this volume focuses upon this other West, the green islands of the Mountainous West that have witnessed patterns of settlement and development quite different from their lowland neighbors. This West is defined not only by its elevation and slope, but also by its peculiar diversity of environments, by its hoards of concentrated resources, and by a unique convergence of historical events which occurred in these settings during the past 150 years. Our volume, from the perspective of historical geography, explores the ways in which the special nature of the Mountainous West stands in sharp contrast to the dust bowls, irrigation canals, and parched cattle skulls of the other American West. These essays remind us, as well, that one cannot appreciate one West without recognizing the significance of the other. Inevitably, of course, the Mountainous and Arid Wests *are* tied together by proximity,

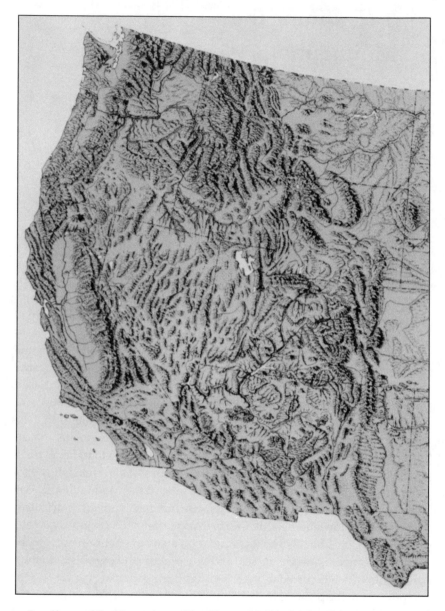

1. Landforms of the Mountainous West (Source: National Atlas of the United States of America, Washington, D.C.: U.S. Geological Survey, 1970, Sheet 59).

history, and resources. Still, they remain conspicuous realms, each with its own character, history, and geography.

Five characteristics define the Mountainous West as a distinctive American subregion. Two of these emphasize unifying elements of physical geography across the Mountainous West. As landform features, the western mountains have served as enduring *barriers* to easy movement and communication across the region. Indeed, their complex topography, steep slopes, and tangled drainages have complicated the exploration, development, and settlement of much of the larger American West. From the horrors of the Donner Party in the snowbound Sierra to the modern-day costs associated with living in remote mountain settings, the Mountainous West has isolated its residents from easy access to the outside world. Mountains also create their own climates; this second element of their physical geography contributes, as well, to the distinctive character of the Mountainous West. Prevailing westerly winds across the region are forced upward by the mountains. The air cools, and the moisture produced creates dramatic *islands of moisture* which clothe much of the region in a forest cover quite unlike the vegetation patterns found at lower elevations. Diverse local plant and animal communities thrive in these complex environmental settings. Most importantly, the water surpluses characteristic of these highland zones stand in sharp contrast to the perennial moisture deficits in many of the adjacent lowlands. The result is that these distinctive western "islands" become pivotal economic and political entities in the allocation of water resources in the West.

A third unifying factor in defining the Mountainous West is economic: it is a *zone of concentrated resources* in which extractive activities are traditionally focused. Indeed, this attribute of the Mountainous West is an outgrowth of how European and American cultures assessed and used the special environments that they encountered in the region. Tectonic processes contributed to the concentration of mineral resources, often in linear belts or "veins" that ran along entire mountain systems. Similarly, the increased orographic rainfall of the region resulted in the intensification of vegetation, focusing the commercial forests of the West into mountain belts from the Coast Ranges to the Rockies. These same forests provided homes for fur-bearing animals, and where the forests parted in meadows, good summer pastures could be found. Each of these attributes of the Mountainous West became a "resource," especially to the Americans who peopled the region by the nineteenth century. The subsequent development of these resources has shaped the urban and transportation geography of the greater American West and has left an enduring signature on the human landscape. Surely the most dramatic contemporary visual examples of these concentrated impacts include the open-pit copper and gold mines that dot the region as well as the efficient devastation marked by commercial clear-cuts on formerly timbered hill slopes.

A fourth unifying theme of the Mountainous West is political and temporal. The accelerated and formative changes focused upon in this volume date from a convergence of events associated with the Anglo-American presence in the region, dating roughly from the middle of the nineteenth century. This ushered in a period, continuing today, in which the region became an enduring *area of government control*. Thus, even though the human occupance of the western mountains obviously extends back in time for thousands of years, we argue that the emergence of the Mountainous West as a distinctive subregion is a much more recent phenomenon, essentially associated with the Anglo-American experience in the region and the overwhelming role played by the federal government in its exploration, development, and management. Although all of the West can cite the importance of government influences, government institutions and expenditures are especially focused upon the mountains themselves. Indeed, the federal government manages approximately 90 percent of the region today and thus becomes a pivotal factor in mitigating and, in some cases, creating conflicts between a variety of public and private interest groups.

Further complicating this federal role undoubtedly has been the emergence of an American cultural attitude that sees much of the Mountainous West as a *restorative sanctuary*. This fifth attribute of the region is an outgrowth of late nineteenth-century Romanticism, which envisaged many western mountain settings as healthy and idyllic retreats from the increasingly urbanized and fast-paced world beyond. Also contributing to this image of the Mountainous West has been the increasing ability of Americans to make weekend and seasonal retreats to the high country. Not surprisingly, the aesthetic appeal of the region often stands in sharp contrast to its image as a storehouse of concentrated natural resources, thus breeding a seemingly endless series of conflicts. Adding complexity to the picture is the fact that the sanctuary seekers themselves have split into many factions, ranging from the hiker desiring the solitude of pristine wilderness to the snowmobiling or speedboating family enjoying a weekend of outdoor recreation.

In the remainder of this chapter we explore how the conceptual region—the Mountainous West—compares to current and past debate over western identity, we review the literature from historical geography and western history to establish its base, and we offer definitive discussions of each theme, again grounded in the literature to demonstrate our case for the uniqueness of this important region.

The Mountainous West within a Larger West

Defining the "West" is an old historiographic problem, often further muddled by that equally confounding notion of the "frontier."[1] One school of thought, well articulated by Frederick Jackson Turner and Ray Allen Billington, defines the West as any place experiencing the "frontiering process," whether it be the wilds of Wyoming or the lower Connecticut Valley.[2] Another school of thought has emphasized the West as a particular place with a well-defined set of characteristics which bind it together as a region. This areal definition of the West usually locates the region somewhere beyond the Mississippi or, even more appropriately, the Missouri, and it extends, with varying conviction and interpretations, to the Pacific. Broadly defined, the characteristic most often linked to this geographical West is its abiding aridity, the forested valleys of the Pacific Coast sometimes excepted. The lineage of this tradition is clear. It includes John Wesley Powell's 1879 *Report on the Lands of the Arid Region* as well as Walter Prescott Webb's *Great Plains* and his other essays on the challenges of coping with the western desert.[3]

Much of the recent writing on the American West has also defined it as a "place" rather than a "process." Certainly Wallace Stegner's essay, appropriately titled "Living Dry," states the West's presumed geographical unity in straightforward fashion: "The West is defined, that is, by inadequate rainfall, which means a general deficiency in water."[4] Works by Marc Reisner and Donald Worster on western water management and manipulation also emphasize the peculiar climatic and political environments of the region.[5] Worster has written further on western unity, suggesting that "the region derives its identity primarily from its ecologically adapted modes of production."[6] In other words, the West's special environments have shaped its political economy in ways fundamentally different than in the East. Similarly, historian Patricia Limerick's West is clearly a definable region that shares the challenge of aridity and that bears the scars of centuries of external "conquest."[7]

But even as historians have struggled with new ways to unify the West, they are also uneasy with their task. The dialogue over precise western borders continues, and the discussion helps us to understand the boundaries of the Mountainous West as well. For example, Robert Athearn's musings over the "Mythic West" lead him to conclude that both the challenges of environment and a unique state of mind tend to locate the "real West" in the intermountain region, while at the same time excluding the Pacific coastal zone.[8] Athearn's traditional "Intermountain West" bears some superficial resemblance to the Mountainous West as we define it, but there are clear differences as well. Most importantly, the intermountain region typically *focuses* on the interior basins and valleys between the Sierra Nevada and Rockies, rather than on the mountains themselves. In addition, as Athearn notes, the "Intermountain West" usually fails to contain the coastal ranges of the Pacific states, and yet this zone shares many attributes with the mountains of the interior.

Traditional northern and southern borders are worth considering as well. Charles Wilkinson's definition of the West acknowledges the complexities involved: clearly, western Canadian and northern Mexican environments and settlement histories share a great deal with their neighboring American districts.[9] In the end, however, Wilkinson argues for bounding his "West" at the international borders, suggesting that unique American processes have contributed to a regional experience distinct from those both to the north and south. Wilkinson's definition aids in locating the Mountainous West as well, because we argue that the region evolved the way it did because of the special course of *American* settlement and the shaping impact of *American* political, economic, and cultural institutions.

Other historians have also recognized the issue of the West's internal complexities. Richard White, still unwilling to disassemble the West, does acknowledge that "if simple geography determined regions, the West, open to the outside and divided within, would not exist."[10] Howard Lamar fears that the West may be "a conglomerate of so many regions that it is impossible to cover their history in a single course," and Michael Malone acknowledges that the "West is a sprawling amalgamation of diverse subregions."[11] Significantly, all of these historians still conclude their probing with a conviction expressed for a larger western unity. Elliott West is less sanguine, however, and brings us even closer to the rationale behind our focus on the Mountainous West. In his search for a western identity, he writes, "Complicating things has been a growing appreciation for the region's geographical and historical diversity. The Willamette Valley and Tucson, the Texas panhandle and the Wind River Mountains—these places have less in common than, say, the Tennessee hills and the Green Mountains of Vermont. Does it make sense, then, to speak of 'the West' as a region at all?"[12]

Indeed, two leading western historical geographers anticipate Elliott West's dilemma, asking that we look at the region in fresh ways. Donald Meinig's 1972 article, significantly titled "American Wests: Preface to a Geographical Interpretation," demonstrates how the perspective of historical geography is ideally suited to inquire into the West's evolution "as a set of dynamic regions."[13] Rather than focusing upon the unique attributes of mountainous western places, Meinig prefers to organize his regional scheme around discrete centers of historical power and influence, such as Denver, Salt Lake City, and San Francisco. David Hornbeck's overview of the West echoes the theme of diversity as well. He argues that the "Far West was a series of regional frontiers in which solutions to environmental problems required new methods that, in turn, created distinct and often unique differences among places."[14]

We agree that the West is indeed an aggregate of distinctive subregions, and we further submit that the Mountainous West is precisely one of those different kinds of places that, through a combination of environment and history, emerges as something clearly unique. As the five themes of the Mountainous West suggest, wherever those characteristics converge, there is often a common story to be told. Disparate western localities share the complexities of the Mountainous West. Geology begins the definition of the Mountainous West on the steep slopes of the Coast Ranges and then even more dramatically across the densely forested and almost continually elevated spine of the Cascades and Sierra Nevada. These mountain regions stand in sharp contrast both to the urban and agricultural lowlands toward the Pacific and to the arid and sparsely settled basins situated to the east. Far inland, over a score of individual uplifts define the Rockies, and these mountains as well display the characteristic physical and cultural landscapes of the Mountainous West. Finally, even in the heart of the western deserts, numerous smaller ranges from the Blue Mountains of northeastern Oregon to the Chiricahuas of southeastern Arizona reveal distinctive fragments of the subregion.

However, it is the human or, more specifically, the American experience that fully differentiates the Mountainous West. The early peopling of the western mountains occurred between ten and fifteen thousand years ago as Paleo-Indian hunters and gatherers arrived in the region from the northwest.[15] Many Paleo-Indian sites remain in western North America, including hunting camps and temporary settlements in rugged mountain settings.[16] Mountains also served as major trailways between more densely populated lowlands. But for one practice, Indian impacts were modest and included local use of rock and mineral resources, the selective gathering of wild plants, and the hunting of preferred game animals. However, their widespread use of fire created substantive ecological change.[17] Mountain forests were burned to drive game, to select preferred wild plant species, to harvest tree moths, and to promote rain.

Roughly a half dozen "culture areas" are traditionally used to define patterns of subsistence and adaptation across the West, and these subregions provide clues to how mountain environments contributed to Native American survival.[18] The Coastal California and Northwest Coast zones served as homes for relatively large native populations who made use of many foothill plants and game.[19] The "Plateau" culture area in the inland Pacific Northwest was also linked to mountain environments through a dependence on fish populations in the major rivers as well as a secondary reliance on wild plants and game.[20] South of the Plateau tribes, the "Great Basin" culture area supported even fewer Native Americans in the western interior of modern-day Nevada, Utah, and portions of Wyoming and western Colorado.[21] The Paiute, Ute, and Shoshone peoples typical of this region subsisted on a limited resource base which usually depended upon the relative abundance of nuts and small game in the mountains. The "Plains" culture area extended along the eastern base of the Rocky Mountains and was home to a diverse and changing population which survived through a mix of small-game hunting, gathering, and small-scale valley horticulture.[22] Agricultural adaptations culminated, however, in the valleys of the modern-day Southwest, while many of the higher mountain areas of that region served as strongholds and game reserves for the more nomadic Apaches in the period immediately preceding European contact.[23]

The emergence of the Mountainous West as a distinctive region is directly linked to the destruction of these traditional Native American patterns. The arrival of Europeans in the sixteenth century signals a key and often devastating transition from one world to another. Initially, the Native American occupants of the region became intimately intertwined with varied European powers.[24] This temporary and transitional "common world" shared by Native Americans and Europeans featured a panoply of key cultural and technological exchanges which had direct consequences for the formation of the Mountainous West. European diseases often began the demographic decline of native populations long before shots were fired and restrictive reservation boundaries imposed. Various native populations also acquired the horse, which differentially empowered particular tribal groups.[25] Native guides also proved pivotal in providing the functional outlines of the West's mountainous geography to Lewis and Clark and others.[26] Ironically, the information provided by these early native guides accelerated the very processes of settlement doomed to overwhelm their own peoples. Similarly, the advantages involved in engaging in the fur and pelt trade with the Europeans proved painfully temporary.[27] Eventually, European and American trappers largely replaced the Native Americans, and the increased knowledge of the Mountainous West that the trappers gained in the process set the stage for even more dramatic changes in the middle nineteenth century.

The first permanent European settlements on the border of the Mountainous West were Spanish movements into the valleys of northern New Mexico.[28] Both the sedentary Pueblo groups and the nomadic Apaches, Utes, and Navajos felt the impact of these Spanish settlements.[29] Pueblo villages were severely disrupted as the Spanish incorporated the land and labor of the native inhabitants into a new colonial economic system. In a different fashion, the Spanish also had to deal with the surrounding nomadic tribes that periodically both raided and traded with the Europeans. Over time, the Spanish settlements increasingly intruded upon the mountains and plateau country to the west, north, and northeast as Spanish grazers expanded their use of mountain pastures and as explorers probed the high country for precious metals.[30]

Spanish intrusions into the Mountainous West were only the first of several European arrivals. By the eighteenth century, French and British interests vied for control of the eastern borderlands of the Mountainous West. It was not until the arrival of the Americans, however, that the Mountainous West was to come into its own as a distinctive region. William Goetzmann suggests that the aims of American exploration, as contrasted with earlier European efforts, reveal why the pace of change was destined to accelerate as it did in the nineteenth century. Goetzmann argues that the American exploration of the Mountainous West featured a broad view focused not just on the exigencies of short-term resource finds or trade, but on longer-term goals of permanently occupying and settling the region.[31] We concur and further submit that recognition of the region as one containing moisture islands, concentrated resources, and restorative sanctuary came with American perception and occupation, as did government control.

The high country that came to constitute the Mountainous West fell into American control through four key territorial acquisitions in the first half of the nineteenth century.[32] A large collection of still unknown western ranges was included in the Louisiana Purchase from the French in 1803. Little did President Jefferson realize that he had acquired most of the Colorado Rockies, Wyoming's Bighorn and Wind River Ranges, much of Yellowstone Park, and a potpourri of Montana mountains in his singular deal with the French! Forty-two years later the American annexation of a newly independent Texan republic added more to the Mountainous West from central New Mexico into southern and central Colorado. A year later, a negotiated agreement with the British solidified much of the Pacific Northwest and brought the mountains of western Montana, Idaho, Oregon, and Washington into American control. Finally, a fruitful American war with Mexico resulted in the 1848 cession of much of the Southwest, including all of California. The southern Coast Ranges, the Sierra Nevada, the Wasatch Range, and the high country of the Colorado Plateau thus passed into American hands.

Its political foundation thus guaranteed and its physical lineaments in place, the resource base of the Mountainous West was now open to exploitation, transformation, and conflict under American dominance. No one could have predicted the magnitude and scope of the changes which followed in the later nineteenth and twentieth centuries. The era saw the creation of a new human geography and a pace of landscape change that swept away the relatively modest imprints of native cultures in a deluge of new settlers and settlements.

The Literature of the Mountainous West

In this volume we seek to define, explain, and demonstrate the significance of this distinctive American subregion—the Mountainous West. Yet this is not an unnoticed or an undescribed portion of the North American landscape. In both historical geography and western history, many have pondered how people have adapted to the diverse mountainous settings of the American West. What is more important, both historical geography and the "new western history" offer critical pathways to further research on this dynamic human-environment interface.

Historical Geography

As Meinig and Hornbeck suggest, the field of historical geography pro-vides an appropriate perspective for examining the Mountainous West. In addition to the historical geographer's sensitivity to regional differences, two other emphases are especially noteworthy. First, historical geography focuses on the significance and distribution of spatial patterns and how varied cultural groups and economic institutions organize areas in distinc-tive ways.[33] Here the emphasis is on how strategies for developing re-source opportunities produced distinctive settlement geographies across the Mountainous West. Mapping key centers and linkages in such spatial systems is an integral part of such an approach: it reconstructs networks of activity and attempts to explain the origin and evolution of such patterns. The flow of mineral and forest products out of the Mountainous West, for example, established an entirely new geography of towns, wagon roads, and rail lines which reorganized the region's human geography into an area ever more closely tied to the national economy.

These changing geographies ultimately reshape the visual scene itself. This second emphasis in the field of historical geography is focused on the making of the cultural landscape.[34] In such an approach, the emphasis is on how people have created and then altered particular places. There is also an abiding sensitivity to the complex interactions between people and their environment. The landscape becomes a valuable source of evidence that displays the concrete impact of cultural and economic forces upon specific localities. Diverse signatures have been left upon the Mountainous West which reveal the varied influence of miners, merchants, ranchers, lumberers, government bureaucrats, and tourists, among others. These impacts are a rich and accessible record of past geographical change. In particular, the cultural landscapes of the Mountainous West often high-light the sharply divided visions of what the region should be. For exam-ple, the Mountainous West is replete with scenes which juxtapose an al-pine wilderness, a plush resort area, a mine shaft, and a herd of grazing cattle. Each component of this landscape potentially stands in conflict with other visions of the region.

Some historical geographical research on the Mountainous West has fo-cused on Native Americans and how these diverse peoples lived in and modified western mountains before Americans tied the high country to-gether in a distinctive Mountainous West subregion.[35] Other cultural and historical geographers have been especially active contributors to the grow-ing literature on Hispanic influences in the West. Many of these studies consider how Hispanics settled and changed mountain environments, both before and after the arrival of the Anglos. Donald Meinig outlines how distinctive Hispanic human geographies evolved over several centuries of change in the Southwest.[36] Richard Nostrand describes how patterns of Hispanic expansion included significant portions of the mountainous zones of northern New Mexico and southern Colorado.[37] Alvar Carlson also has contributed to our understanding of how the landscape of the region has been shaped by Hispanic settlement.[38] Of particular relevance to the Mountainous West is his detailed reconstruction of how long-time Hispanic ranchers came into increasing conflict with the National Forest bureaucracy in the twentieth century. To the west, David Hornbeck has focused his efforts on reconstructing elements of Hispanic settlement in Alta California.[39] Hornbeck shows how portions of California's Coast Ranges became an integral part of the regional economy prior to the Anglo invasions of the 1840s.

The period of initial Anglo exploration and exploitation is highlighted by other historical geographers.[40] The monumental *Atlas of the Historical Geography of the United States*, edited by Paullin and Wright, is a lasting contribution in the field that provides excellent historical and cartographic detail on the exploration and settlement of the Mountainous West.[41] David Wishart's review of the western fur trade is a classic example of how European influences impose a radically new spatial system across the Rockies.[42] Wishart clearly maps the creation and evolution of the Rocky Mountain fur trade system and also reconstructs the seasonal cycle of operations and impacts across the Mountainous West. Another growing list of contributions from John Allen is focused upon the nineteenth-century exploration, mapping, and imagemaking of the Mountainous West. His *Passage through the Garden* offers an in-depth portrait of how the Lewis and Clark expedition shaped an emerging picture of the early nineteenth-century West.[43] Allen has also reviewed changing conceptions of the continental divide and the invention of a Romantic West based on pastoral and sublime images of the region's landscape.[44]

Landscape perceptions and images operate as central themes for several other historical geographers in the Mountainous West. Valerie Fifer reviews the development of nineteenth-century tourism in the West through the guidebooks and the regional images created by George Crofutt.[45] In a related fashion, Stanford Demars explores the tourist experience in Yosemite and highlights the impacts of Romanticism and the changing nature of outdoor recreation on the evolution of the park.[46] More generally, Kenneth

Thompson assesses changing nineteenth-century images of nature and relates these to the restorative properties perceived to be a part of wilderness landscapes.[47] Finally, recent books by Thomas and Geraldine Vale make creative use of two major highway transects, US40 and US89, to examine the changing western American landscape.[48] They ponder the dominant images encountered along the western roadscape and provide an abundance of visual evidence that suggests the complex nature of the Mountainous West today.

The concentrated resources of the Mountainous West and the interplay of public and private interests in managing those resources provide other major themes for historical geographers working in the region. Lary Dilsaver, Richard Francaviglia, and Randall Rohe each examine the impacts of metals mining in a variety of western mountain settings.[49] Michael Williams's monumental overview of American forests provides a general context for assessing the evolving spatial systems and landscape changes associated with commercial lumbering in the region.[50] The history of western grazing on public and private lands and its role in the Mountainous West are touched upon in Bret Wallach's Wyoming example and in William Wyckoff and Katherine Hansen's case study from southwestern Montana.[51] The guiding hand of public resource management in the Mountainous West is also exemplified in Lary Dilsaver and William Tweed's study of Sequoia and Kings Canyon National Parks.[52]

Other more general regional works by western historical geographers are not set specifically in the Mountainous West, but nevertheless they detail the creation of spatial systems and landscapes that touch upon the region. Donald Meinig's assessments of the Mormon culture area, the inland Northwest's Great Columbia Plain, and the Southwest are primarily focused on valley and lowland settings.[53] Still, Meinig's regional scale of observation inevitably leads to a broader view that includes how nearby examples of the Mountainous West fit into the historical evolution of his subregions. A number of valuable state geographies and historical atlases contain assessments of how the Mountainous West evolved in a variety of settings.[54] In particular, Samuel and Emily Dicken's *The Making of Oregon: A Study in Historical Geography*, David Hornbeck's *California Patterns: A Geographical and Historical Atlas*, and James Scott and Roland DeLorme's *Historical Atlas of Washington* exemplify patterns of spatial evolution and landscape change that include important components of the Mountainous West.[55]

Other important work by western historical geographers is focused even more explicitly on valley and lowland settings, but even these case studies are often linked to activities and resources in nearby mountain zones. Although William Bowen's Oregon study is aimed at reconstructing the settlement history of the Willamette Valley, his detailed maps show how lowland settlers soon encroached upon Cascade foothill locales in their search for additional land and superior mill sites.[56] Kenneth Thompson reconstructs past perceptions of California's Central Valley and suggests how images of the region contrasted with those elsewhere in the state.[57] To the east, Marshall Bowen and Robert Sauder have both examined struggling settlements in the mountain-rimmed Great Basin from the Owens Valley to northeastern Nevada.[58] In addition to Meinig's work on Mormon settlement, Richard Francaviglia, Richard Jackson, Jeanne Kay, and Craig Brown have provided other perspectives on the experience of the Latter-day Saints in Utah.[59]

Finally, historical human impacts in western American mountains have also been studied by an affiliated group of mainly physical geographers. These "mountain geographers" have produced an important and relevant literature set in the Mountainous West which represents part of an expanding look at mountain systems worldwide.[60] Typically, these studies measure the extent to which people have modified natural ecosystems, and often they contain a strong landscape component in their analyses. Sixty-nine historical photographs are matched with the modern views in Thomas Veblen and Diane Lorenz's *The Colorado Front Range: A Century of Ecological Change*.[61] Their volume documents the extent of landscape change in one of the most heavily utilized subregions of the Mountainous West. Often, the early photographs reveal the extensive disturbances coincident with nineteenth-century mining, lumbering, and settlement while the more recent views reveal the ways in which the landscape has recovered from and adapted to these century-old scars. Conrad Bahre's *A Legacy of Change* takes a similar approach in its examination of human impacts on vegetation in southern Arizona.[62] Studies by Stephen Arno and George Gruell and by David Butler use historical livestock-grazing records to measure the impacts of grazing on montane and subalpine forests and rangelands of the northern Rockies.[63] Similar impacts in the mountain environments of California and Oregon are studied by biogeographers Alan Taylor, J. L. Vankat and Jack Major, and Thomas Vale.[64] Fluvial geomorphologists also have developed approaches to determine the extent of historical human impacts on stream and slope erosion across the West. Grazing, lumbering, and mining activities have received attention.[65] Taken together, these studies of the Mountainous West link the traditional archival methodologies of historical geography with a keen eye for detailed changes in the physical landscape.

The New Western History

A new generation of western American historians also has produced a growing literature essential to our study of the historical geography of the Mountainous West. Two approaches are of special importance. First, the penchant of the new historians to focus on the essentially unequal economic and political relationships between the West and the world beyond well articulates some of the driving forces shaping the economic and spatial systems of the Mountainous West. Second, the study of environmental history, very much a part of this new emphasis, often bears a close relationship to the geographer's traditional interest in cultural landscape evolution. Indeed, many of the settings for these studies of the western environment are in the Mountainous West.

Most economic and political decisions historically affecting the Mountainous West have originated far beyond its boundaries. Indeed, the concentrated resources and the federally controlled lands of the Mountainous West traditionally have been managed by nonresidents. Thus, the Mountainous West emerges as a classic peripheral region in larger national and global systems. Indeed, the spatial connections of roads, communications links, and capital flows which help to define the region's economic geography often reflect the needs and policies of outside interests. Surely the defining statement articulating this perspective is Bernard DeVoto's "Plundered Province" essay of the 1930s.[66] DeVoto emphasizes the colonial nature of the economic relationship between the western economy and eastern capitalists. William Robbins recently suggests that DeVoto's perspective still has relevance for the modern West as well.[67] In Montana history, K. Ross Toole's biting critiques of the mining, rail, and lumber industries in the state are a reminder of the variety of ways in which the resources of the Mountainous West have been controlled and decimated from beyond the bounds of the region.[68] Other historians point out how the federal presence in the Mountainous West has sometimes worsened its colonial predicament. Richard White suggests that much of the West's long territorial status within the United States imbued it with a truly colonial mentality, and others argue that sympathetic bureaucrats within the federal government aided the economic colonialism fostered by outside corporate investors.[69] In fact, Patricia Limerick declares that such relationships continue today, plaguing the West with an ongoing inability to control its own destiny or adjust to the vagaries of the boom-and-bust economies inevitably tied to the extraction of western resources.[70]

Debate and discussion continue concerning the precise geographies entailed in these core-periphery relationships. Departing from DeVoto's argument that the West is a colonial outpost of the East, Gerald Nash and Earl Pomeroy suggest that the post-1945 era has brought a new independence and self-control to western destinies.[71] Their suggestion that the West is not quite the periphery it once was has not gone unchallenged, however. Yet another view holds that the West itself can now be divided into a series of regional cores and peripheries. Donald Worster and others argue that western power is concentrated in its major cities and in the public and private institutions which control its resources.[72] Never the meek critic, Worster takes direct aim at these dominant corporate economic and political institutions in the West, arguing that they have conspired to dim the potential of many western communities and to degrade the quality of innumerable western environments. Although Worster concentrates his efforts on the "agrarian" and "hydraulic West" of the arid lowlands and plains, many of the public and private institutions that he examines maintain a major presence in the Mountainous West as well. Rural areas of the West, including much of the Mountainous West, remain a hinterland, perhaps to be mined or vacationed in, but lacking the power to control their own resource base.

Whether one accepts all of these current misgivings about the West's peripheral status, the perspective adopted by these new western historians does offer geographical insights for the Mountainous West. In particular, William Robbins suggests that the Mountainous West is largely a dependent periphery in a world economic system anchored beyond the mountains.[73] Similarly, in describing the history and importance of extractive industries in the West, Michael Malone suggests that the region's globally peripheral status is apparent when reconstructing the commodity linkages between the West and the world beyond.[74] Both Malone and Robbins echo themes among geographers who have utilized Immanuel Wallerstein's world-systems theory to discuss the evolution of space economies and landscapes over time.[75] D. W. Meinig's geographical analysis of imperialism provides a related context in which he outlines how localities are transformed in the process of imperial conquest.[76] The implications for the

Mountainous West are clear: as an enduring part of the periphery, from the era of initial European exploration until today, many of its landscapes and much of its economic and political geography have been created from a distance. Several essays in our volume describe how westerners historically struggle to adapt to their peripheral status, often finding themselves in conflict, not only with the world beyond, but with one another as well.

A second theme in the new western history focuses directly on how people have modified the environment of the region. This growing interest in environmental history shares a great deal with traditions in cultural and historical geography and has much to contribute to our understanding of the Mountainous West. Much common ground is found in the study of cultural landscapes, in reconstructing patterns of resource use and management, and in assessing changing human perceptions and attitudes toward the environment.[77] This growing literature typically highlights the fragility and vulnerability of the western landscape: its vast spaces and resources are often illusory, initially masking limitations that are becoming ever more apparent in the late twentieth century. Such studies also often emphasize how the ecological complexities of the Mountainous West and the character of political and economic interests peculiar to the region combine to create a unique history.

Many contributions in the field of environmental history have broad applicability to the Mountainous West. Native American impacts on the environment have been examined.[78] Other historians provide useful perspectives on Anglo-European impacts across the West and include reviews of resource management strategies and shortcomings in the Mountainous West.[79] In particular, a plethora of books focus on the role of conservation and preservation in the Mountainous West and ponder the inherent conflicts as varied public and private interests vie for control of the region's resources. Samuel Hays's study of the conservation movement, Roderick Nash's review of the wilderness concept, and Alfred Runte's assessment of the evolution of the national parks stand as major and representative contributions.[80]

A growing number of environmental historians have completed more detailed case studies that are focused on varied local examples of the Mountainous West. Douglas Strong assesses the historical evolution of the Lake Tahoe region, illustrating how recreational and urban demands have impacted the area's environment and how they continue to pose challenges to the planning process today.[81] Barbara Vatter's forest history of Douglas County, Oregon, retraces the nineteenth-century evolution of a region that spanned the Coast and Cascade Ranges and that witnessed accelerating changes as agricultural and lumbering interests modified the landscape.[82] Carlos Schwantes's recent histories of the Pacific Northwest and of Idaho both devote considerable attention to the theme of environmental history.[83] Schwantes vividly reconstructs the opening of these corners of the Mountainous West to lumbering and mining interests and offers a penetrating, often harsh critique of the federal role in managing the public lands of the region.

Examples from the interior reaches of the Mountainous West further illustrate the growing contribution of environmental historians. James Young and Jerry Budy investigate the depletion of Nevada's pinyon-juniper woodlands in the mountains of Nevada and relate these landscape changes to huge demands for fuel in nineteenth-century refining mills in the mining districts of the central Great Basin.[84] An even broader array of human impacts is considered by Philip Fradkin in his book *Sagebrush Country: Land and the American West*.[85] Much of the volume is focused on the Uinta Mountains of eastern Utah and southern Wyoming. Fradkin uses the Uinta example to assess the impact of Native American occupance, fur trapping, railroads, livestock grazing, conservation, federal agencies, and recreation in the Mountainous West. Fradkin effectively relates historical patterns and problems to the modern resource management dilemmas facing the Mountainous West. To the east, Duane Smith focuses on mineral resource development in the Colorado Rockies, reminding twentieth-century observers that despite the dangers and the pollution, most Colorado mining communities ignored the environmental hazards of the time.[86] Smith also argues that the environmental costs of mining need to be seen in the context of the human benefits and wealth produced in nineteenth-century Colorado.

The dramatic Sangre de Cristo Range in southern Colorado and northern New Mexico has also witnessed rapid human modification in a pattern of human impacts which have accelerated since the Spanish first arrived in the region. William DeBuys's environmental history of the Sangre de Cristo, suggestively titled *Enchantment and Exploitation*, reviews how people have transformed this portion of the Mountainous West.[87] The volume reflects not only a command of the archives, but also an intimacy with the land that is typical of the best of this genre. Hal Rothman's northern New Mexico case study of the Pajarito Plateau west of Santa Fe echoes many of DeBuys's themes.[88] Rothman's narrative reconstructs the evolution of an isolated fragment of the Mountainous West from a common hunting and grazing ground used by Native Americans and Hispanics to a commercialized landscape of lumber camps and overgrazed pastures.

A final research theme in environmental history emphasizes the study of changing perceptions and place images. This well-developed tradition in historical geography explores how people perceived the character of particular places or landscapes in the past and how those perceptions shaped attitudes and behavior.[89] Historians have utilized both written and visual sources to reconstruct past images and perceptions of the West. Henry Nash Smith's *Virgin Land: The American West as Symbol and Myth* is the classic example of this approach.[90] Although much of Smith's work is devoted to agrarian images in the West, he also examines the lineage of wilderness adventure heroes from Leatherstocking to Buffalo Bill. Roderick Nash grapples, as well, with the evolution of wilderness images and ideas that have often been central to perceptions of the Mountainous West.[91] Other historians have delved into how works of imaginative literature reflect vivid landscape images and experiences.[92] Indeed, the growing corpus of contemporary western American essays, novels, short stories, and poetry often is strongly grounded in the distinctive, often dramatic environments of the Mountainous West.[93]

Landscape paintings, sketches, and historical photographs are another rewarding source of evidence in the reconstruction of past images of the Mountainous West. William Truettner's edited volume for the National Museum of American Art challenges many of the traditional interpretations of western landscape painting.[94] The book suggests that many depictions of nature and mining activities in the Mountainous West misrepresented the limitations of the western environment and the real challenges of western life. Another recent overview by Anne Hyde argues that the western landscape demanded a new aesthetics and that it took artists and writers several decades to come to terms with the fantastic environments they found in the West.[95] The distinctive landscapes of the interior Mountainous West from Karl Bodmer to Charles Russell are effectively displayed and assessed in Patricia Trenton and Peter Hassrick's *The Rocky Mountains: A Vision for Artists in the Nineteenth Century*.[96] Farther west, William Goetzmann reviews the artistic landscapes of the Pacific Northwest in his *Looking at the Land of Promise*.[97] Individual artists of the Mountainous West are also reviewed in Gordon Hendricks's book on the grand canvases of Albert Bierstadt, in Joni Kinsey's survey of Thomas Moran, and in David Weber's volume on expeditionary artist Richard H. Kern.[98] Given the timing of settlement and development in the Mountainous West, photographers offer another important source of historical landscape images. Recent examples that consider the photographs of John K. Hillers, William H. Jackson, and J. E. Stimson all include varied views of the Mountainous West and considerations of how chosen scenes reflect different images and perceptions of the region's environment.[99]

Five Themes

This abundance of research in historical geography and in western American history has explored many of the distinctive characteristics of the Mountainous West and, indeed, differentiates the subregion from the larger West as it is usually defined. We now assess the five themes that we have chosen to define the Mountainous West in greater detail, suggesting how each theme contributes to our understanding of the region and how geographers and historians have traditionally incorporated these themes in earlier treatments of the West.

Barriers

> I felt a secret pleasure in finding myself so near the head of the heretofore conceived boundless Missouri; but when I reflected on the difficulties which this snowy barrier would most probably throw in my way to the Pacific, and the suffering and hardships of myself and party in them, it in some measure counterbalanced the joy I had felt in the first moments in which I gazed on them.
>
> Meriwether Lewis, in central Montana, 1804[100]

Meriwether Lewis's sobering words as he gazed upon the northern Rockies suggest a persisting theme in the Mountainous West: the numerous ranges and uplifts which define the region have in fundamental ways shaped its cultural landscapes and its spatial systems of transportation and interaction. Indeed, the settlement history of all of the American West, both lowlands and highlands, has been molded by the presence of these barriers. What roads and rails cross the ranges of the Mountainous West are like narrow channels through a tortuous reef, weaving around smaller uplifts and funneling into the few significant passes which breach the high country (figure 2). As Charles Wilkinson notes in his recent assessment of the larger West, the fact that "the terrain is variously chopped up by rugged mountains" has contributed a pivotal element to the West's identity.[101]

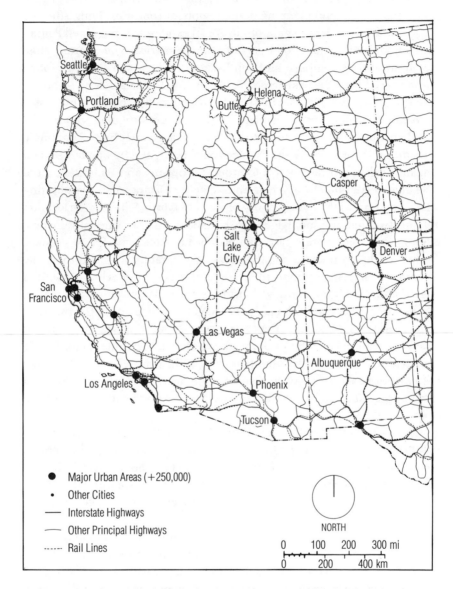

2. *Transportation in the Mountainous West (Sources: National Atlas, 2–3, and "Major Highways, 1987," National Atlas, 1988 update).*

The highland barriers of the Mountainous West complicated the European exploration and mapping of the region for centuries. Long after the region first fell under the gaze of European explorers, it remained a little-known and little-understood part of North America. The Spanish clustered around its southern and southwestern edges, the French probed from the east, and the British established an isolated presence on its northern fringes. Only slowly did this vast terra incognita give way to more systematic exploration and settlement. Early explorers struggled with several fundamental challenges of complicated physical geography.[102] The simple breadth of the interior West, characterized as it is not by one but several major north-south ranges, confounded Europeans and Americans until the time of Alexander McKenzie and Lewis and Clark. Also complicating the situation was the hydrography of western North America: the location of the twisting continental divide remained unclear, and a stubborn, though incorrect, notion of a common headwaters zone for all western rivers continued to obfuscate the region's geography well into the nineteenth century. An accurate appreciation of the central Rockies—south of Lewis and Clark's route and well north of the Spanish settlements—kept that subregion beyond the pale of detailed knowledge until the fur trade era of the 1820s. Making matters worse was the fact that a large portion of the West featured an interior drainage system with no outlet to the Pacific or Atlantic. Indeed, a clear understanding of the precise lineaments of the Mountainous West did not emerge until the late nineteenth century, and it represented the combined efforts of decades of European and American exploration.

As Americans moved into the West, the region's transportation geography continued to be shaped by the presence of mountains.[103] Overland travel across the Oregon, California, and Santa Fe/Old Spanish Trails was made more uncertain by the dual challenges of mountains and deserts. A large historical literature documents the challenges of rugged terrain for these early travelers. John Evans's *Powerful Rockey: The Blue Mountains and the Oregon Trail, 1811–1883* reviews the vast number of journals and diaries of those who crossed the range in the nineteenth century.[104] Evans found that the Blue Mountains emerged as a vivid feature for those making the journey west because the mountains were the principal physical obstacle along the way. Oscar Winther also assesses the human and economic costs involved in creating the Oregon Trail.[105] In addition, he reviews the larger network of early routes in the Pacific Northwest from the Mullan Road across the northern Rockies to the Barlow Road through Oregon's Cascades. Further south, the California Trail has also received attention from historians. George Stewart's general reconnaissance of the trail's history is complemented by his vivid reconstruction of the Donner Party disaster on the snowbound slopes of the Sierra.[106] His *Ordeal by Hunger* is the quintessential account of how western mountains conspired with human miscalculation to produce disaster. Further east, Rocky Mountain trail and road construction is highlighted in Marshall Sprague's *The Great Gates*.[107] The volume focuses on how the Rockies influenced the transportation geography of the West, encouraging settlement along and near accessible passes while isolating other portions of the region. Michael Kaplan's biography of toll-road-builder Otto Mears offers a more specific case study of how one man's entrepreneurial vision contributed to overcoming the barriers of the Colorado Rockies.[108] Public road building was also of critical importance; W. Turrentine Jackson's *Wagon Roads West* reviews how government surveyors were challenged by the presence of western mountain barriers.[109]

The Mountainous West also played a pivotal role in railroad construction. As in previous frontiers, various towns competed among themselves to attract railroad lines. However, the Mountainous West shaped this competition in ways the eastern plains never did. The experience of central California provides an apt example. In 1859, as the excitement of the gold rush waned, Californians began exploring opportunities for a transcontinental railroad. They selected reputable engineer Theodore Judah to find a pass through the Sierra Nevada—unquestionably the most difficult barrier along the 2,100-mile route. Judah studied a variety of options, including Beckwourth, Henness, Donner, Emigrant, and Carson Passes. Each pass descended the western slope of the Sierra through fading gold towns where disgruntled former miners struggled on miserable mountain farms disparagingly likened to those of the Appalachians. Thereafter, the various routes glided into the broad Central Valley to the aggressive agricultural centers of Marysville, Sacramento, and Stockton. Each route had its boosters who lobbied San Francisco, the state legislature, and Judah himself. All knew what this lifeline meant. Judah finally recommended the Donner Pass route (modern Interstate 80) through Auburn and Sacramento. For the next decade, amid recriminations and legal challenges, continued lobbying and corporate finagling, the Donner Pass advocates defended the route. Indeed, when the railroad was completed in 1869, a sustained economic corridor was galvanized across the Sierra. Nearby farms prospered, new rail towns such as Colfax appeared, gold-town decay was reversed, and Sacramento exploded past its rivals as the queen city of the Central Valley.[110]

Similar stories of the interplay between mountain barriers, railroad investments, and patterns of subsequent economic development have been written all across the Mountainous West.[111] They form a central chapter in linking the region to the developing national and world economy and illustrate the special costs of doing so in the setting of the Mountainous West.[112] Each of the major transcontinental routes has been assessed by historians.[113] The real drama of railroad construction in rugged mountain terrain is most clearly exemplified in histories of the short, often narrow-gauge lines that deeply penetrated the high country. These rail corridors were almost always related to the mineral resources found in these isolated regions. Robert Athearn's *Rebel of the Rockies* is a colorful history of the Denver and Rio Grande Railroad and the role played by William Palmer in breaching the high passes of the region in pursuit of commercial opportunities.[114] Similarly, John Lipsey's history of the Colorado Midland line to Leadville and Aspen highlights the vision of its principal promoter, James Hagerman.[115] A burgeoning literature, propelled both by professional historians and amateur railroad buffs, also has contributed to our understanding of many other construction efforts across the rugged terrain of the Mountainous West.[116]

Clearly, the presence of mountain barriers dramatically shaped the spatial systems of transportation and interaction across all of the American West. Indeed, even the twentieth century continues to illustrate the pattern, with the arrival of the automobile in the West. The challenges of early transcontinental travel often focused on the primitive state of mountain roads.[117] The more recent creation of the interstate system has repeated the boom-and-bust syndrome of the railroad era: a town bypassed by the freeway often suffers a long, slow death, while an interchange several miles away thrives in a new strip development of gas stations, franchise restaurants, and motels. Once again, mountain barriers have been pivotal in the dispensation of these costs and benefits because the economics of interstate route construction make the crossing of rugged terrain extraordinarily expensive. Finally it can be argued that even the placement of major airports across the West has been significantly impacted by mountains: although modern jets can soar across the highest peaks, they must still take off and land in weather conditions often shaped by nearby peaks.

Islands of Moisture

Yesterday and to-day we have had before our eyes the high mountains which divide the Pacific from the Mississippi waters; and entering here among the lower spurs, or foot hills of the range, the face of the country began to improve with a magical rapidity. . . . The bottoms of the streams and level places were wooded with aspens; and as we neared the Summit, we entered again the piney region. . . . The country had now become very beautiful—rich in water, grass, and game . . .

John Charles Frémont, in northern Colorado, 1844[118]

Just as the barriers of the Mountainous West have shaped the human geography of both highland and lowland, the fact that the region collects a relative abundance of moisture inexorably binds the snowbound peaks of the high country with the thirsty lands below. As Frémont suggests, the facts of physical geography are simple enough: the ranges of the Mountainous West generally lay astride a belt of winds which sweep off the Pacific Ocean in an eastbound flow across the land. Almost at the coastline the winds are forced upward by the mountains, cooling and losing their capacity to hold the vast moisture collected over the ocean. Much of the resulting precipitation falls in the higher elevations as snow, creating a natural snowpack reservoir, the first and most important water distribution mechanism across the West. Beyond the coast, the prevailing winds pass over scores of other mountain masses, enveloping isolated peaks and funneling through canyons and passes, to scatter the ocean's moisture in a discontinuous pattern (figure 3). Complex islands of moisture lay upon the westward tilting slopes, creating diverse local vegetation and animal communities that range from foothill woodlands to alpine tundra. These same islands cast long rain shadows eastward across a succession of lower, drier basins and plains. The result is that the uplands provide the overwhelming proportion of surface runoff for all the West as they act as headwaters for the region's major rivers. These drainage patterns also have a great impact on agricultural and urban activity in the surrounding valleys (figure 4).

Much of the West's historical geography of settlement and its resulting cultural landscapes have involved the manipulation and reallocation of the moisture found in the mountains. An elaborate infrastructure of dams, catchment reservoirs, canals, and irrigation ditches is the complex expression of this human response and has transformed the visible scene, both within the Mountainous West itself and in the surrounding lowlands. A growing literature, much of it quite critical of the politics and economics behind these manipulations, has focused on the water history of the West. Marc Reisner's *Cadillac Desert* details the historical saga of water consumption across all of the West, with special emphasis on the extensively mod-

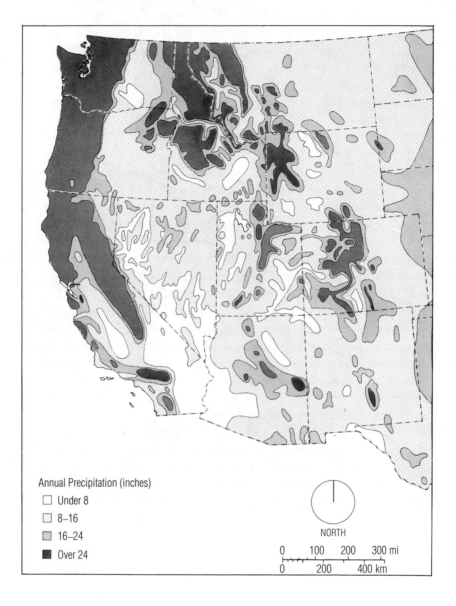

3. Annual Precipitation in the Mountainous West (Source: National Atlas, 97).

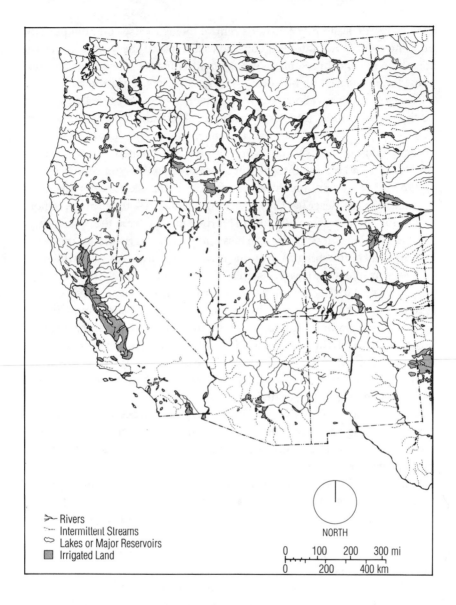

4. Drainage Patterns and Irrigated Lands of the West (Source: National Atlas, 2–3, 158–59).

ified Colorado system.[119] Reisner's central theme focuses on how political and entrepreneurial interests conspired to capture the West's water for their own benefit. In a similar vein, Donald Worster's *Rivers of Empire* also provides an excoriating historical overview. Worster argues that the reallocation of western water has created a distinctive society oriented around "a sharply alienating, intensively managerial relationship with nature."[120] His critique further suggests that a western power elite, composed of bureaucrats, agribusinesses, and corporations, has created its own empire oriented around maintaining power over the region's water resources.

Worster vividly summarizes the key role of the Mountainous West in this empire as he describes the harvesting of water resources in the region:

It drips endlessly from the roof of North America, from the cordillera of the Rockies, down from its eaves and gables and ridges, its mossy slates and piney shingles, running this way and that, running whichever way offers the least resistance. Put a barrel where it drips, and a second next to that one, and so on until the yard is full of barrels. . . . Barrel after barrel, each with a colorful name but all looking alike, quickly becoming an industry in their manufacture . . . everywhere barrels filling in the spring, barrels emptying out again in the dry season. . . . So the rooftop of the Rockies, in a matter of thirty or so frantic years, was ringed about with the means to capture and hoard all the falling, dripping mountain waters.[121]

Indeed, in Worster's eyes, the Mountainous West has been held hostage to this burgeoning and voracious empire because key decisions affecting water supplies in the mountains have typically been made from beyond the borders of the region.

Other historians have concentrated their efforts on individual river systems. The Rivers of America series, published in the 1940s and 1950s, though lacking in recent commentary, still contains valuable historical interpretations that focus on the character of particular western rivers. Specifically, Stewart Holbrook's *The Columbia*, Dale Morgan's *The Humboldt*, and Frank Waters's *The Colorado* all represent lasting contributions which include important components of the Mountainous West.[122] Paul Horgan's multivolume *Great River*, a detailed historical and geographical sojourn down the Rio Grande, also remains a valuable contribution that highlights the relationship between mountain moisture and patterns of human settlement downstream.[123] Elsewhere in the West, the green island of the Sierra Nevada has received considerable attention because of its important mois-

ture surpluses both on its eastern and western slopes.[124] Abraham Hoffman and William Kahrl have completed important histories of the Owens
Valley water controversy in which powerful southern California interests
tapped into major Sierra water resources. In similar fashion, Robert de
Roos and Erwin Cooper have contributed studies assessing the Central
Valley Project on the western slope. Each of these volumes focuses on valley manipulations of mountain water, demonstrating the close relationship between the islands of moisture in the Mountainous West and the arid
lands which surround them. Finally, the Colorado River has received a
great deal of attention. Both Reisner and Worster highlight the Colorado
system in their broader discussions of western water, and Philip Fradkin's
A River No More: The Colorado River and the West offers a book-length synthesis on the entire length of the river.[125]

Zones of Concentrated Resources

Leaving nature for the material, beauty for booty, fancy for fact, I
come to speak of the mineral wealth and development of this section
of the Rocky Mountains. . . . This whole vast range of mountains,
that divides our Continent, seems indeed crowded with veins of rich
mineral ore. . . . There is no end to them in number; there is no apparent limit to their depth.

Samuel Bowles, near Central City, Colorado, 1861[126]

One of the fundamental historical ironies of the Mountainous West is
that it has functioned as both barrier and goal. While the high country inhibited travel and communication, the concentrated resources in these
same mountains also served as the primary initial draw for westbound pioneers. It is important to understand the special properties of these mountain zones that contribute to the spatial concentration of resources in these
regions. Recently alpine scholars have used the term *geoecology* to study
and describe the total environment of the mountains. It refers to the interaction between topography, climate, soils, and biota. To this we can add
the subsurface geology that produces both the topography and the mineral
resources of the mountain regions. The resulting geoecology of the Mountainous West created a condition of resource concentration that was even
more fully exploited upon the arrival of the Europeans and Americans. As
well as precious water, the highlands contained furs, minerals, forests,
and forage. These resources drew European explorers into the region, attracted the first waves of settlement, stimulated subsequent corporate in-

vestments, spawned many of the surviving towns, and shaped the design of the region's transportation infrastructure.

The tectonic processes that buckled and warped the earth's crust into mountain ranges also heated the subsurface rock beyond the melting point. This molten material expanded and cooled as it pressed into the dense rock above. At the same time water in the magma was expelled, or "precipitated," carrying with it mineral elements. These elements collected in fissures and along the contact zones with surrounding rock, forming linear belts or "veins" of economic ores. Which chemical elements precipitated depended on the temperature, pressure, and duration of liquidity. Gold, silver, zinc, copper, lead, and other valuable elements thus aligned along and within mountain systems, the foci of tectonic activity (figure 5).

The story of the Mountainous West's frenzied exploration in search of precious metals, the boom towns and busts, and the evolution to externally funded corporate mining is a familiar one to all who know the region. Yet the significance of these rushes for the long-term historical geography of the Mountainous West is hard to overstate. In California, the discovery of gold inflated the population from 10,000 non-Indians to 200,000 in two years. San Francisco, Sacramento, and other cities swelled to prominence as financial and supply entrepôts. Roads and rails carpeted the state to move men, machinery, and money. Tens of thousands of frustrated would-be millionaires reverted to agriculture to feed the miners and eke out a living, creating the foundations of the state's agribusiness. Embryonic lumber, construction, commercial, and transport businesses were also established. In the process, the Indians and the lower-elevation forests were all but obliterated, and much of the landscape was changed forever. More than anything else, wherever a boom appeared in the Mountainous West, mining vastly accelerated the settlement process, shrinking twenty years of change into a period of a few months. Almost instantly, entirely new settlement geographies were created, and places such as southwest Montana and the Colorado Front Range were altered in fundamental and lasting ways.

The presence of orographic rainfall provides for the intensification of vegetation as well. Mountains in the West boast the vast majority of the commercial timber west of the hundredth meridian (figure 6). Initially sought for mine timbers, fuel, and housing construction, the forests became the principal target of the nation's lumber industry after 1890. Animals in these same western forests were also harvested as the expanding North American fur trade moved out of the Great Lakes and Great Plains regions. In

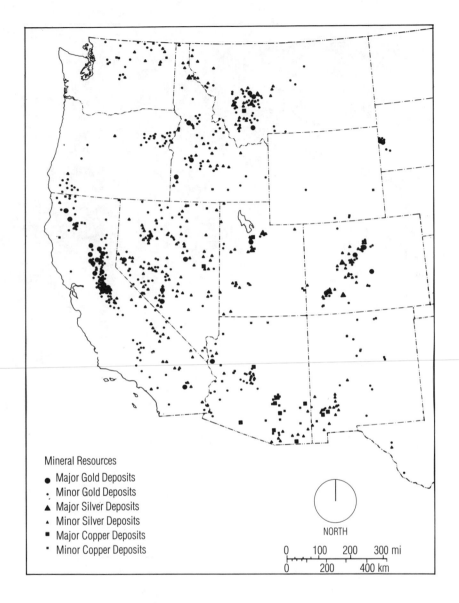

Mineral Resources
- ● Major Gold Deposits
- · Minor Gold Deposits
- ▲ Major Silver Deposits
- ▴ Minor Silver Deposits
- ■ Major Copper Deposits
- · Minor Copper Deposits

NORTH

0   100   200   300 mi
0   200   400 km

5. *Selected Mineral Resources of the Mountainous West (Source: National Atlas, 178–79).*

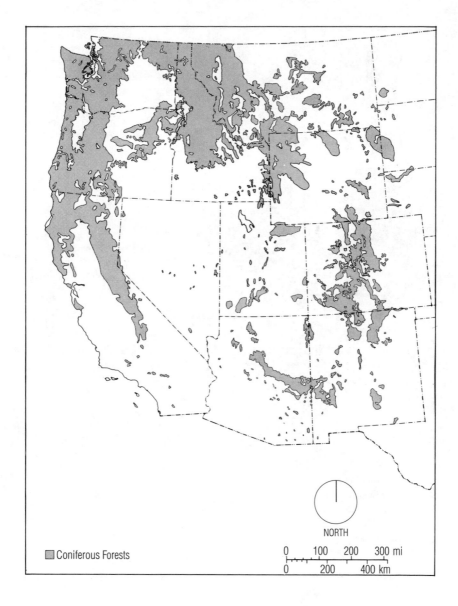

NORTH

Coniferous Forests

| 0 | 100 | 200 | 300 mi |
| 0 | 200 | 400 km |

6. Forests of the Mountainous West (Source: "Major Forest Types," 1987 National Atlas, 1989 update).

addition, rich mountain grasslands and meadows provided forage for domesticated livestock.

As the new western historians remind us, the presence of these concentrated resources in the Mountainous West has combined with an evolving national and global economy to produce a region still dependent upon unpredictable extractive industries. Michael Malone persuasively argues that this is an essential characteristic of the entire West and, indeed, that the focus of extractive industries in the mountainous zones themselves is even more pronounced than for the larger region.[127] Patricia Limerick and William Robbins echo Malone's sentiments with their emphases on the continuity between nineteenth-century "frontier" economies and the often uncertain predicaments of the modern West.[128] Among more popular treatments of the West, Joel Garreau's essay on the resource-based "Empty Quarter" in his Nine Nations of North America provides a parallel perspective that stresses the boom-and-bust nature of western extractive economies.[129]

Historians have contributed a large literature detailing how the Mountainous West has served as a zone of concentrated resources since European and American occupance. The fur trade represented the initial imposition of a truly global commercial system across the region as it spread from the Great Lakes and Missouri Basin into the high country of the West during the early nineteenth century.[130] Biographical studies of major participants such as Jedediah Smith dramatize the human experience of penetrating and surviving in the Mountainous West during this era.[131] Other historians have offered detailed subregional explorations of fur trade operations. For example, David Weber's The Taos Trappers paints a clear picture of how Taos became a focal point for fur-trading operations across all of the mountains of the Southwest.[132] Close on the heels of the beaver harvest in the Mountainous West came the even more dramatic transformation in which concentrated reserves of precious metals drew thousands to the region and radically reshaped the landscape almost overnight. Perhaps this story more than any other has been highlighted in earlier historical treatments of the Mountainous West. William Greever, David Lavender, and Rodman Paul have written some of the most useful and enduring overviews of the impact of mining on the region.[133] More specialized mining histories also abound. John Reps and Duane Smith describe the peculiarly urban nature of the settlement patterns associated with mining.[134] Others have completed detailed case studies on specific mining towns, such as Aspen, Leadville, Ten Mile, and Cripple Creek.[135] California's Sierra Nevada mining rushes have produced a sizable literature that summarizes the development of particular mining districts, reconstructs the experiences of those who came to the Mother Lode, and assesses the evolution of the area's economy and society once boom times ebbed.[136] Nevada's varied gold and silver strikes, which stretched from the 1850s into the twentieth century, also illustrate how the isolation and harshness of remote mountain environments were overcome in the name of potential riches.[137] The pivotal role of mining in directing the settlement history of the northern Rockies and much of central and western Colorado has been assessed as well.[138] Finally, both historians and geographers have contributed to the growing literature on the landscape impacts of mining across the Mountainous West and in nearby lowland regions.[139]

The timber resources of the Mountainous West have also been extensively exploited during the era of American occupancy. A number of major studies have examined the use and abuse of western forests over the past century and have highlighted the concentration of these resources in the Mountainous West.[140] These studies emphasize the special regional importance of commercial forests in the Pacific Northwest and the ongoing and often controversial interplay between public and private institutions in the management and use of western forest resources. They suggest that timber management across the Mountainous West historically has failed to satisfy either the needs of the lumber industry or conservationists. One theme, however, is clear: the landscape changes resulting from the modifications of the past century have forever altered the forest resources of the region, often in destructive ways.

Domestic livestock grazing has received attention as well. As with timber, this activity is closely intertwined with the theme of government control in the Mountainous West.[141] Traditionally, domestic livestock in the region make extensive use of high-country pastures during the summer, returning to lower valley settings in the winter. Often, the mountain pastures are public lands managed for such seasonal use. Specific studies have examined this pattern in many settings across the Mountainous West. James Young and B. Abbott Sparks tell the tough story of livestock grazing in the Great Basin in their *Cattle in the Cold Desert*.[142] The impacts of overgrazing and the role of public institutions in altering mountain grazing patterns are reviewed by Dan Flores in the case of Utah's Wasatch Range and by Wyckoff and Hansen in their assessment of southwest Montana's Madison Range.[143] J. Orin Oliphant's broader regional overview of cattle ranching in the Pacific Northwest also details the interplay of highlands and lowlands.[144]

An Area of Government Control

> I fought for the conservation of the public domain under federal leadership because the citizens were unable to cope with the situation under existing trends and circumstances. The job was too big and interwoven for even the states to handle with satisfactory coordination.
>
> Representative Edward I. Taylor,
> author of Taylor Grazing Act, 1934[145]

A fourth identifying theme of the Mountainous West is a function of historical circumstance: the region came under the effective control of the United States during the nineteenth century, and its initial acquisition was followed by a still-evolving set of relationships that forever wed the region's identity with the presence and actions of the federal government. In this sense, the Mountainous West as a peculiar national region did not exist prior to the imposition of American control. This special role of government in shaping the Mountainous West's character is widely recognized by historians. The theme forms a central chapter in Limerick's "conquest" of the larger West as she critically assesses the role of government land disposal and land management policies since the mid-nineteenth century.[146] Richard White also organizes a major portion of his western synthesis around the importance of the federal government.[147] Similarly, Michael Malone suggests that the West has always been especially and uncomfortably dependent upon institutions based in Washington.[148] Indeed, if the entire West shares this special tie to government, it is certainly doubly true for the Mountainous West in which nearly 90 percent of the land is managed directly by a panoply of federal bureaucracies.

Historically, the federal government played a central role in every step of settling the Mountainous West. Explorations of western mountains and passes often had government sponsorship. William Goetzmann's *Exploration and Empire* ably reviews these contributions, which extend from initial forays by Lewis and Clark, Pike, and Frémont to later and more detailed expeditions during the Pacific Railroad Surveys of the 1850s and the scientific surveys of Powell, Hayden, and King in later decades.[149] The huge task of settling these western public lands is another important chapter in federal involvement. General assessments of the land laws used to dispose of the public domain in the Mountainous West identify the importance of the Homestead, Timber Culture, and Desert Land Acts, as well as the roles played by railroad grants and individual states.[150] These overviews are also full of tales of the abuse and mismanagement often associated with these disposal policies. Other volumes have focused on disposal patterns in specific states. Jerry O'Callaghan's summary of Oregon, for example, points out the importance of wagon road grants, the Timber and Stone Act, and railroad grants in the mountainous regions of that state; Victor Westphall produces a parallel assessment for New Mexico.[151]

Much of the Mountainous West, however, has remained part of the public domain. The issues of water allocation and the protection of limited forest and forage, as well as the rise of the preservation ethic, all propelled Congress to suspend various land alienation programs and to create permanent reserves across large portions of the Mountainous West. Yellowstone National Park, established in 1872, was the first major withdrawal. The following century witnessed a dizzying series of federal moves, under a variety of often contested motivations, which placed much of the region under long-term federal management. As agencies evolved to shape the public domain of the Mountainous West, there was a predictable stratification of bureaucracies by elevation (figure 7). The foothill zones of the Mountainous West, including many sagebrush-dominated desert slopes, fall to the Bureau of Land Management. Being the successor to the General Land Office, it is left holding all the lands too undesirable for early alienation or subsequent reservation for park or forest. In the middle elevations, where the commercial forests of the region prevail, as do many mining and recreational sites, the U.S. Forest Service holds sway. Finally, beginning at the middle elevations but containing principally lands at high elevations, are the isolated national parks and specially managed wilderness areas.

Because of their significance and size, the national parks of the Mountainous West have generated a large historical literature. Alfred Runte's *National Parks: The American Experience* offers an interpretive overview of the system which explores the still-unfolding tension between the twin park ideals of preservation and recreation.[152] Craig Allin, Hans Huth, and Roderick Nash also put the park concept into the larger context of wilderness preservation.[153] A growing number of individual park studies highlight examples from the Mountainous West and provide the historical details of changing federal management policies over time. The Sierra parks of Sequoia and Kings Canyon have been examined by Lary Dilsaver and William Tweed.[154] Two recent books by Alfred Runte and Stanford Demars focus on Yosemite, one of the most heavily utilized of all the parks in the Mountainous West.[155] Further north, Arthur Martinson has produced another valuable photo history of Mount Rainier in the northern Cascades.[156] High-country parks in the Rockies are also associated with book-length histories: the stories of federal involvement in the creation of Mesa Verde,

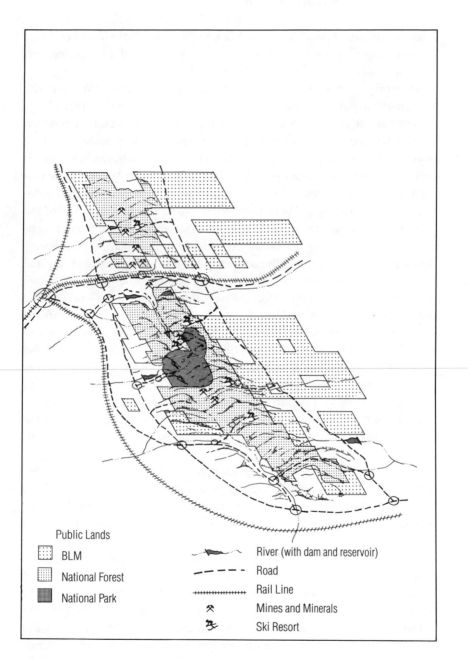

Public Lands

⬚ BLM

▦ National Forest

▧ National Park

🪶 River (with dam and reservoir)

- - - - Road

+++++++++ Rail Line

⚒ Mines and Minerals

⛷ Ski Resort

7. *A Settlement Model of the Mountainous West.*

Rocky Mountain, Grand Teton, and Glacier National Parks have been well documented.[157] Not surprisingly, given its age, size, and importance, Yellowstone has received the most attention.[158]

Of even greater areal importance across the Mountainous West was the inauguration of the national forests in 1891. Some 187 million acres, a huge majority in the region, were so designated over the next quarter century. Within these conserved lands the government has tried to satisfy as many users as possible including loggers, miners, recreationists, ranchers, hunters, and downstream farmers. These Forest Service lands are also associated with a diverse historical literature that provides insight into the evolution of the Mountainous West. General works review the evolution of the agency and how its management policies have changed over the past century.[159] Others focus on particular aspects of resource planning on Forest Service lands. For example, the controversial Mining Law of 1872 has had tremendous consequences for the Mountainous West, and its impact across the region has generated considerable interest.[160] Federal grazing policies have also come under scrutiny.[161] In addition, the use and abuse of timber resources on Forest Service lands continue to spark discussion and debate.[162] The challenge of integrating the Forest Service's multiple use ethic with a rising demand for wilderness acreage has received attention as well.[163] Finally, a growing number of Forest Service studies examine the history of a particular region or administrative unit; these overviews include large portions of the Mountainous West, illustrating in great detail how the federal presence in the region has shaped its settlement and landscape.[164]

The third of the great federal agencies was created to protect the remaining rangelands of the West. Suspension of homesteading and other land alienation statutes, as well as inauguration of the Taylor Grazing Act, confirmed the beliefs of people inside and outside the government that western resources were too diffused and fragile and the environment too susceptible to damage to allow private exploitation. In 1947 the Bureau of Land Management (BLM) was formed, combining the functions of the General Land Office and the Grazing Service. Today the agency manages some 270 million acres, the vast majority in the West, including many sites typically in the lower and drier portions of the Mountainous West. The history of the BLM is reviewed by Paul Culhane in *Public Lands Politics* and by James Muhan and Hanson Stuart in *Opportunity and Challenge: The Story of BLM*.[165] As with the Forest Service lands, there is also a considerable literature which examines the impact of grazing policies on BLM acreage and which vividly reconstructs the historical animosity between western ranchers and the Washington bureaucracy.[166]

Undoubtedly, the past century has witnessed a tremendous increase in the level of federal involvement in the Mountainous West. Nineteenth-century policies of disposal shifted late in the century to policies of conservation and evolved further in the twentieth century to an increasingly active role in land management and economic development. Histories of the modern West chronicle this ever-growing federal largesse.[167] The rapid expansion of government involvement during the critical New Deal era also deserves attention because many of Roosevelt's policies had a direct impact on the region.[168] No better example exists than the Civilian Conservation Corps (CCC), whose roads, trails, campgrounds, dams, and lookout towers still blanket the high country of the Mountainous West.[169] More recent federal expenditures and policies continue to display Washington's signature across the landscape.[170] Indeed, it is a mark which shall always remain indelibly etched across the region's human geography and one which shall continue to spark conflict as a variety of public and private pressure groups lobby for influence on lands under federal control.

A Restorative Sanctuary

There is no end of wholesome medicine in such [a mountain] experience. That morning we could have whipped ten such people as we were the day before—sick ones at any rate. But the world is slow, and people will go to "water cures" and "movement cures" and to foreign lands for health. Three months of camp life on Lake Tahoe would restore an Egyptian mummy to his pristine vigor, and give him an appetite like an alligator. I do not mean the oldest and driest mummies, of course, but the fresher ones. The air up there in the clouds is very pure and fine, bracing and delicious. And why shouldn't it be?—it is the same the angels breathe.

Mark Twain, from *Roughing It*, 1906[171]

Twain's words echo a growing voice across the Mountainous West over the past century. Increasingly, the region's isolation and its relatively pristine character have sparked a sympathetic response in an America ever more industrial and urban. The roots of this theme in the Mountainous West also lie in the blossoming of nineteenth-century Romanticism, first in Europe and then in America. Mountains played a particularly central role in American Romanticism because they became associated with spiritual regeneration and because Americans, lacking the historical and cultural icons to match those of Europe, identified strongly with the wonders of their natural landscape. Adding to these sentiments was the growing late-nineteenth-century belief that mountain environments exerted a curative influence on invalids and consumptives.[172] All of these attitudes recognized an inherent value in wilderness and generated moves to enjoy and preserve such settings across the Mountainous West. Inevitably, these same attitudes also conflicted with other conceptions of the region, particularly those which emphasized the extractive economic value of its concentrated resource base. Indeed, as Richard White argues, it is this peculiar convergence of conflicting ideologies and institutions that give the region its special character.[173]

The evolution of a wilderness aesthetics, its articulation as an ethic of preservation, and its changing political expression constitute an important chapter in the making of the Mountainous West. Much of the national energy and controversy sparked by the preservation movement centered on lands within the region. Roderick Nash's *Wilderness and the American Mind*, as well as his more recent *The Rights of Nature: A History of Environmental Ethics*, provides historical perspective on these issues.[174] Hans Huth's *Nature and the American: Three Centuries of Changing Attitudes* and Anne Hyde's *An American Vision* are valuable as well because they suggest how the landscape of the Mountainous West interacted with nineteenth-century experiences to produce new responses to the natural world.[175] Biographers have also produced sketches of many of the key historical figures who found their own lives intertwined with the landscapes of the Mountainous West. Recent works by Douglas Strong and Peter Wild show how individuals such as John Muir, Stephen Mather, Enos Mills, and William O. Douglas were both shaped by and shapers of the Mountainous West.[176] Undoubtedly, Muir emerges as the spiritual leader for the conception of a preserved Mountainous West; both Muir's Sierra ramblings and his political activism have garnered considerable attention.[177]

Americans, however, were hardly unified when it came to appreciating the natural charms of the Mountainous West. One set of conflicts surrounded the preservation versus the conservation forces, personified by the schism which developed between Muir and Chief American Forester Gifford Pinchot.[178] Pinchot's multiple-use philosophy advocated substantial forest resource development, an approach that ran counter to Muir's purist views. Another occurrence that conflicted with the preservation ethic was the growth of the tourism and recreation industry in the Mountainous West. Here was a set of activities which prospered from the West's restorative properties and yet ultimately challenged the image of the region as a sanctuary. Colorado's foothill and mountain resorts of the late nineteenth century illustrate the phenomenon: as the Pikes Peak/Colorado Springs, Estes Park, and Glenwood Springs regions blossomed into popular and accessible pleasure grounds, thousands of tourists and invalids came to revel in the pure air and outdoor enjoyments of the region. California became another popular destination, with both valley and mountain settings serving as tourist and sanitarium sites. The general history of this early tourism in the Mountainous West can be traced through works by Robert Athearn, Valerie Fifer, and Earl Pomeroy.[179] The particulars of tourist development in Colorado Springs and Yosemite have been explored in even greater detail.[180] Alfred Runte has also sketched the special role of the railroads in promoting tourism in the national parks of the Mountainous West.[181] The impact of dude ranching, typically focused in the high country, has received attention as well.[182]

The present century has seen a further fragmentation of the restorative-sanctuary theme across the Mountainous West. The majority of the U.S. population, three out of four from urban places, are satisfied with luxurious winter resorts, recreation-focused reservoirs, summer cabins, and roadside sightseeing. They often bristle at the suggestion that more areas should be denied them and their comfortable enjoyments. But another group—louder, often better organized, better educated, and brandishing scientific rationales—demands closure of large areas both to extractive economic activities and to many popular recreational pursuits.[183] Indeed, the often close juxtaposition of major alpine ski resorts and existing federal park and wilderness areas epitomizes these different visions of the Mountainous West which had their roots in the nineteenth century (figure 8). Ultimately, the region possesses a finite number of prized areas containing crucial transport corridors, surplus waters, other extractive resources, scenes of inspiration, and arenas for recreation. Indeed, as the twenty-first century nears, the forces of preservation and recreation increasingly demand ever larger amounts of the remaining Mountainous West.

Clues to a Western Diversity

Thus born from a convergence of physical setting and historical circumstance, the special character of the Mountainous West has created a distinctive setting for a rapidly changing human geography. Many western places,

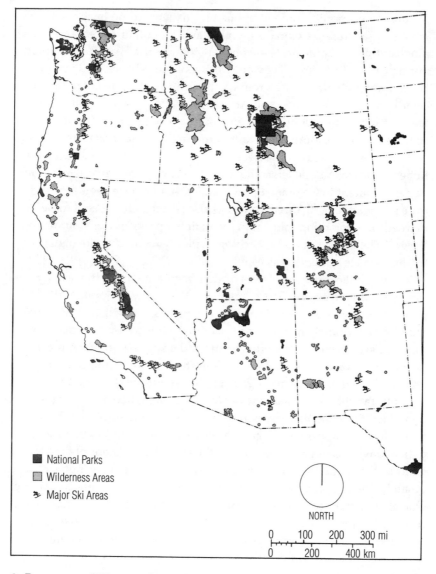

Legend:
- ■ National Parks
- ▨ Wilderness Areas
- ⤳ Major Ski Areas

NORTH

| 0 | 100 | 200 | 300 mi |
| 0 | 200 | 400 km |

8. Preserves and Pleasure Grounds of the Mountainous West (Sources: "The National Wilderness Preservation System, 1964–1989," map by the Wilderness Society, 1989; "National Park System," map by the National Park Service, U.S. Department of the Interior, 1989; and Mobil Road Atlas and Trip Planning Guide, New York: H. M. Gousha, 1991).

9. *A Landscape of the Mountainous West: Georgetown, Colorado, in the 1860s. (Courtesy Colorado Historical Society, no. F4961.)*

both in the nineteenth century and today, bear the mark of the five themes we have described (figure 9). These themes come together across the disparate reaches of the Mountainous West from the Cascades to the Chiricahuas and form a complementary yet different sort of West than the region encountered elsewhere in valley and lowland settings. Without rejecting the notion of a western unity, these clues to a western diversity become useful ways to assess the peculiar character of that portion of the West where mountains matter and often dominate the story of recent human occupancy.

The essays that follow illustrate some of the ways in which the practice of historical geography can focus on these themes of the Mountainous West. They are by no means intended to be a kind of regional synthesis of the Mountainous West—that, in itself, would likely be a multivolume undertaking. Rather, they are historical snapshots in which each touches upon themes and settings central to understanding the evolution of the region. Although the editors have grouped the contributions by theme, it is readily apparent that all of the authors touch upon multiple themes in their work. That is the nature of the Mountainous West.

From California's Sierra Nevada to Washington's Coast Ranges and from Colorado's San Juan Range to Montana's Pryor Mountains, the contributors paint rich and dynamic portraits of this important American region. Their case studies span the era from initial European contacts with native peoples to twentieth-century resource and land-use conflicts. They display a rapidly changing and often unpredictable settlement geography which forever transformed the Mountainous West. In the process, these changes produced a spatial system and a cultural landscape that richly reflect the values and inherent conflicts of a conquering civilization as it encountered, adapted to, and altered the region over the past 150 years.

Notes

1. John T. Juricek, "American Usage of the Word 'Frontier' from Colonial Times to Frederick Jackson Turner," *Proceedings of the American Philosophical Society* 110 (1966): 10–34; Patricia Nelson Limerick, *The Legacy of Conquest: The Unbroken Past of the American West* (New York: W. W. Norton, 1987), 17–32.

2. Ray Allen Billington and Martin Ridge, *Westward Expansion: A History of the American Frontier* (New York: Macmillan, 1982); Frederick Jackson Turner, *The Frontier in American History* (New York: Henry Holt, 1947).

3. John Wesley Powell, *Report on the Lands of the Arid Region of the United States* (Washington, D.C.: Government Printing Office, 1879); Walter Prescott Webb, *The Great Plains* (New York: Grosset and Dunlap, 1931); Webb, "The American West: Perpetual Mirage," in *The Montana Past: An Anthology,* ed. Michael P. Malone and Richard B. Roeder (Missoula: University of Montana Press, 1969), 1–12.

4. Wallace Stegner, *The American West as Living Space* (Ann Arbor: University of Michigan Press, 1987), 6.

5. Marc Reisner, *Cadillac Desert: The American West and Its Disappearing Water* (New York: Viking Press, 1986); Donald Worster, *Rivers of Empire: Water, Aridity, and the Growth of the American West* (New York: Pantheon Books, 1985); Worster, "New West, True West: Interpreting the Region's History," *Western Historical Quarterly* 18 (1987): 141–56.

6. Worster, "New West, True West," 149.

7. Limerick, *Legacy of Conquest*.

8. Robert Athearn, *The Mythic West in Twentieth-Century America* (Lawrence: University Press of Kansas, 1986), 10–22.

9. Charles Wilkinson, *The American West: A Narrative Bibliography and a Study of Regionalism* (Niwot: University Press of Colorado, 1989), 5.

10. Richard White, *"It's Your Misfortune and None of My Own": A New History of the American West* (Norman: University of Oklahoma Press, 1991), 3.

11. Howard Lamar, "Much to Celebrate: The Western History Association's Twenty-Fifth Birthday," *Western Historical Quarterly* 17 (1986): 404; Michael P. Malone, ed., *Historians and the American West* (Lincoln: University of Nebraska Press, 1983), 1.

12. Elliott West, "A Longer, Grimmer, but More Interesting Story," in *Trails: Towards a New Western History*, ed. Patricia Nelson Limerick, Clyde A. Milner II, and Charles E. Rankin (Lawrence: University Press of Kansas, 1991), 104.

13. Donald W. Meinig, "American Wests: Preface to a Geographical Interpretation," *Annals of the Association of American Geographers* 62 (1972): 159–84.

14. David Hornbeck, "The Far West," in *North America: The Historical Geography of a Changing Continent*, ed. Robert D. Mitchell and Paul A. Groves (Totowa, N.J.: Rowman and Littlefield, 1987), 279.

15. Karl Butzer, "The Indian Legacy in the American Landscape," in *The Making of the American Landscape*, ed. Michael P. Conzen (Cambridge, Mass.: Unwin Hyman, 1990), 27–50; Harold E. Driver, *Indians of North America* (Chicago: University of Chicago Press, 1961).

16. James B. Benedict, "Early Occupation of the Caribou Lake Site, Colorado Front Range," *Plains Anthropology* 19 (1974): 1–4; Ronald L. Ives, "Early Human Occupation of the Colorado Headwaters Region: An Archeological Reconnaissance," *Geographical Review* 32 (1942): 448–62; Joel C. Janetski, *Indians of Yellowstone Park* (Salt Lake City: University of Utah Press, 1987).

17. Stephen W. Barrett and Stephen F. Arno, "Indian Fires as an Ecological Influence in the Northern Rockies," *Journal of Forestry* 80 (1982): 647–53; Stephen J. Pyne, *Fire in America: A Cultural History of Wildland and Rural Fire* (Princeton: Princeton University Press, 1982).

18. Joseph G. Jorgensen, *Western Indians* (San Francisco: W. H. Freeman, 1980); Donald J. Ballas, "Historical Geography and American Indian Development," in *A Cultural Geography of North American Indians*, ed. Thomas E. Ross and Tyrel G. Moore (Boulder: Westview Press, 1987), 15–31.

19. David Hornbeck, "The California Indian before European Contact," *Journal of Cultural Geography* 2, no. 2 (1982): 23–39; Ballas, "Historical Geography"; Jeff Zucker, Kay Hummel, and Bob Hogfoss, *Oregon Indians: Culture, History, and Current Affairs* (Portland: Oregon Historical Society Press, 1983).

20. Ballas, "Historical Geography"; Alvin M. Josephy Jr., *The Nez Perce Indians and the Opening of the Northwest* (New Haven: Yale University Press, 1965); Zucker, Hummel, and Hogfoss, *Oregon Indians*.

21. Robert Harold Brown, *Wyoming: A Geography* (Boulder: Westview Press, 1980); Janetski, *Indians of Yellowstone*; Martha C. Knack and Omer C. Stewart, *As*

Long as the River Shall Run: An Ethnohistory of Pyramid Lake Indian Reservation (Berkeley: University of California Press, 1984); Brigham D. Madsen, *The Northern Shoshoni* (Caldwell, Idaho: Caxton Printers, 1980); Wilson Rockwell, *The Utes: A Forgotten People* (Denver: Sage Books, 1956).

22. Ballas, "Historical Geography"; George Hyde, *Indians of the High Plains: From the Prehistoric Period to the Coming of Europeans* (Norman: University of Oklahoma Press, 1959).

23. D. C. Cole, *The Chiricahua Apache* (Albuquerque: University of New Mexico Press, 1988); Malcolm L. Comeaux, *Arizona: A Geography* (Boulder: Westview Press, 1981); Richard J. Perry, *Western Apache Heritage: People of the Mountain Corridor* (Austin: University of Texas Press, 1991).

24. White, *New History*, 27–53. For a classic overview of this process in the Southwest, see Edward H. Spicer, *Cycles of Conquest: The Impact of Spain, Mexico, and the United States on the Indians of the Southwest, 1533–1960* (Tucson: University of Arizona Press, 1962).

25. Hyde, *Indians of the High Plains*; Rockwell, *Utes*; Frank G. Roe, *The Indian and the Horse* (Norman: University of Oklahoma Press, 1955).

26. John L. Allen, *Passage through the Garden: Lewis and Clark and the Image of the American Northwest* (Urbana: University of Illinois Press, 1975); James P. Ronda, *Lewis and Clark among the Indians* (Lincoln: University of Nebraska Press, 1984).

27. Calvin Martin, *Keepers of the Game: Indian-Animal Relationships and the Fur Trade* (Berkeley: University of California Press, 1978); David J. Wishart, *The Fur Trade of the American West, 1807–1840* (Lincoln: University of Nebraska Press, 1979).

28. Donald W. Meinig, *Southwest: Three Peoples in Geographical Change, 1600–1970* (New York: Oxford University Press, 1971); Richard L. Nostrand, "The Spanish Borderlands," in *North America*, ed. Mitchell and Groves, 48–64.

29. Jack D. Forbes, *Apache, Navaho and Spaniard* (Norman: University of Oklahoma Press, 1971); Thomas D. Hall, *Social Change in the Southwest, 1350–1880* (Lawrence: University Press of Kansas, 1989).

30. Alvar Carlson, *The Spanish-American Homeland: Four Centuries in New Mexico's Rio Arriba* (Baltimore: Johns Hopkins University Press, 1990); William DeBuys, *Enchantment and Exploitation: The Life and Hard Times of a New Mexico Mountain Range* (Albuquerque: University of New Mexico Press, 1985); Richard Nostrand, "The Century of Hispano Expansion," *New Mexico Historical Review* 62 (1987): 361–86.

31. William H. Goetzmann, *Exploration and Empire: The Explorer and the Scientist in the Winning of the American West* (New York: Vintage Books, 1966).

32. Charles O. Paullin and John K. Wright, *Atlas of the Historical Geography of the United States* (Washington, D.C.: Carnegie Institution, 1932); White, *New History*, 61–84.

33. This theme is developed in Donald W. Meinig, "The Continuous Shaping of America: A Prospectus for Geographers and Historians," *American Historical Review* 77 (1978): 1186–205. Applications of the theme are found in Meinig, *The Shaping of America: A Geographical Perspective on 500 Years of History*, vol. 2, *Continental America, 1800–1867* (New Haven: Yale University Press, 1993), and in Mitchell and Groves, *North America*.

34. The landscape theme is developed and illustrated in Conzen, *Making of the American Landscape*; Meinig, *Shaping of America*; and Carl O. Sauer, *Land and Life* (Berkeley: University of California Press, 1965).

35. For general perspectives, see Sauer, *Land and Life*, 45–52; Ballas, "Historical Geography"; Butzer, "Indian Legacy." For specific examples, see Hornbeck, "California Indian"; Ives, "Early Human Occupation"; Stephen C. Jett, "The Origins of Navajo Settlement Patterns," *Annals of the Association of American Geographers* 68 (1978): 351–62; Jerry N. McDonald, "La Jicarilla," *Journal of Cultural Geography* 2, no. 2 (1982): 40–57.

36. Meinig, *Southwest*.

37. Nostrand, "Spanish Borderlands"; Nostrand, "Century of Hispano Expansion"; Nostrand, *The Hispano Homeland* (Norman: University of Oklahoma Press, 1992).

38. Carlson, *Spanish-American Homeland*.

39. David Hornbeck, "Land Tenure and Rancho Expansion in Alta California," *Journal of Historical Geography* 4 (1978): 371–90; Hornbeck, *California Patterns: A Geographical and Historical Atlas* (Palo Alto: Mayfield Publishing, 1983).

40. A useful conceptual overview of the exploration process is provided in J. D. Overton, "A Theory of Exploration," *Journal of Historical Geography* 7 (1981): 53–70.

41. Paullin and Wright, *Atlas*.

42. Wishart, *Fur Trade*.

43. Allen, *Passage through the Garden*.

44. John L. Allen, "Division of the Waters: Changing Concepts of the Continental Divide, 1804–1844," *Journal of Historical Geography* 4 (1978): 357–70; Allen, "Horizons of the Sublime: The Invention of the Romantic West," *Journal of Historical Geography* 18 (1992): 27–40.

45. Valerie Fifer, *American Progress* (Chester, Conn.: Globe Pequot Press, 1988).

46. Stanford E. Demars, *The Tourist in Yosemite: 1855–1985* (Salt Lake City: University of Utah Press, 1991).

47. Kenneth Thompson, "Wilderness and Health in the Nineteenth Century," *Journal of Historical Geography* 2 (1976): 145–61.

48. Thomas R. Vale and Geraldine R. Vale, *US 40 Today: Thirty Years of Landscape*

Change in America (Madison: University of Wisconsin Press, 1983); Vale and Vale, *Western Images, Western Landscapes: Travels along U.S. 89* (Tucson: University of Arizona Press, 1989).

49. Lary M. Dilsaver, "Food Supply Regions for the California Gold Rush," *California Geographer* 23 (1983): 36–50; Dilsaver, "After the Gold Rush," *Geographical Review* 75 (1985): 1–18; Richard V. Francaviglia, "Copper Mining and Landscape Evolution: A Century of Change in the Warren Mining District, Arizona," *Journal of Arizona History* 23 (1982): 267–98; Francaviglia, *Hard Places* (Iowa City: University of Iowa Press, 1991); Randall Rohe, "The Geography and Material Culture of the Western Mining Town, " *Pioneer America* 16 (1984): 99–120; Rohe, "Man and the Land: Mining's Impact in the Far West," *Arizona and the West* 28 (1986): 299–338.

50. Michael Williams, *Americans and Their Forests: A Historical Geography* (Cambridge: Cambridge University Press, 1989).

51. Bret Wallach, "Sheep Ranching in the Dry Corner of Wyoming," *Geographical Review* 71 (1981): 51–63; William Wyckoff and Katherine Hansen, "Settlement, Livestock Grazing, and Environmental Change in Southwest Montana, 1860–1990," *Environmental History Review* 15 (1991): 45–71.

52. Lary M. Dilsaver and William C. Tweed, *Challenge of the Big Trees: A Resource History of Sequoia and Kings Canyon National Parks* (Three Rivers, Calif.: Sequoia Natural History Association, 1990).

53. D. W. Meinig, "The Mormon Culture Region: Strategies and Patterns in the Geography of the American West, 1847–1964," *Annals of the Association of American Geographers* 55 (1965): 191–220; Meinig, *The Great Columbia Plain: A Historical Geography, 1805–1910* (Seattle: University of Washington, 1968); Meinig, *Southwest*.

54. Warren A. Beck and Ynez D. Haase, *Historical Atlas of California* (Norman: University of Oklahoma Press, 1974); Beck and Haase, *Historical Atlas of New Mexico* (Norman: University of Oklahoma Press, 1969); Brown, *Wyoming*; Comeaux, *Arizona*; Henry P. Walker and Don Bufkin, *Historical Atlas of Arizona* (Norman: University of Oklahoma Press, 1979).

55. Samuel N. Dicken and Emily F. Dicken, *The Making of Oregon: A Study in Historical Geography* (Portland: Oregon Historical Society, 1979); Hornbeck, *California Patterns*; James W. Scott and Roland L. DeLorme, *Historical Atlas of Washington* (Norman: University of Oklahoma Press, 1988).

56. William A. Bowen, *The Willamette Valley: Migration and Settlement on the Oregon Frontier* (Seattle: University of Washington Press, 1978).

57. Kenneth Thompson, "Insalubrious California: Perception and Reality," *Annals of the Association of American Geographers* 59 (1969): 50–64.

58. Marshall Bowen, "A Backward Step: From Irrigation to Dry Farming in the Nevada Desert," *Agricultural History* 63 (1989): 231–42; Robert Sauder, "Sod Land

versus Sagebrush: Early Land Appraisal and Pioneer Settlement in an Arid Intermountain Frontier, " *Journal of Historical Geography* 15 (1989): 402–19.

59. Richard Francaviglia, *The Mormon Landscape* (New York: AMS Press, 1978); Richard H. Jackson, ed., *The Mormon Role in the Settlement of the West* (Provo: Brigham Young University Press, 1978); Jackson, "Mormon Perception and Settlement," *Annals of the Association of American Geographers* 68 (1978): 317–34; Jeanne Kay and Craig Brown, "Mormon Beliefs about Land and Natural Resources, 1847–1887," *Journal of Historical Geography* 11 (1985): 253–67.

60. Larry W. Price, *Mountains and Man* (Berkeley: University of California Press, 1981).

61. Thomas T. Veblen and Diane C. Lorenz, *The Colorado Front Range: A Century of Ecological Change* (Salt Lake City: University of Utah Press, 1991).

62. Conrad J. Bahre, *A Legacy of Change: Historical Human Impact on Vegetation in the Arizona Borderlands* (Tucson: University of Arizona Press, 1991).

63. Stephen F. Arno and George F. Gruell, "Douglas Fir Encroachment into Montana Grasslands in Southwestern Montana," *Journal of Range Management* 39 (1986): 272–76; David R. Butler, "Conifer Invasion of Subalpine Meadows, Central Lemhi Mountains, Idaho," *Northwest Science* 60 (1986): 166–73.

64. Alan H. Taylor, "Tree Invasion in Meadows of Lassen Volcanic National Park, California," *Professional Geographer* 42 (1990): 457–70; J. L. Vankat and Jack Major, "Vegetation Changes in Sequoia National Park, California," *Journal of Biogeography* 5 (1978): 377–402; Thomas R. Vale, "Forest Changes in the Warner Mountains, California," *Annals of the Association of American Geographers* 67 (1977): 28–45; Vale, "Tree Invasion of Montane Meadows in Oregon," *American Midland Naturalist* 105 (1981): 61–69.

65. Robert C. Balling Jr. and Stephen G. Wells, "Historic Rainfall Patterns and Arroyo Activity within the Zuni River Drainage Basin, New Mexico, " *Annals of the Association of American Geographers* 80 (1990): 603–17; William L. Graf, "Mining and Channel Response," *Annals of the Association of American Geographers* 69 (1979): 262–75; Yi-fu Tuan, "New Mexican Gullies: A Critical Review and Some Recent Observations," *Annals of the Association of American Geographers* 56 (1966): 573–97.

66. Bernard DeVoto, "The West: A Plundered Province," *Atlantic* 169 (August 1934): 255–64.

67. William G. Robbins, "The 'Plundered Province' Thesis and Recent Historiography of the American West," *Pacific Historical Review* 55 (1986): 577–97.

68. K. Ross Toole, *Twentieth-Century Montana: A State of Extremes* (Norman: University of Oklahoma, 1972).

69. White, *New History*, 155–78.

70. Limerick, *Legacy of Conquest*.

71. Gerald Nash, *The American West in the Twentieth Century: A Short History of an Urban Oasis* (Englewood Cliffs, N.J.: Prentice-Hall, 1973); Earl Pomeroy, *The Pacific Slope: A History* (New York: Alfred A. Knopf, 1965), 372–97.

72. Worster, *Rivers of Empire*; Worster, "Beyond the Agrarian Myth," in *Trails*, ed. Limerick, Milner, and Rankin, 3–25; Robbins, "Plundered Province"; Peter Wiley and Robert Gottleib, *Empires in the Sun: The Rise of the New American West* (New York: G. P. Putnam's Sons, 1982).

73. Robbins, "Plundered Province," 596–97; Robbins, "Western History: A Dialectic on the Modern Condition," *Western Historical Quarterly* 20 (1989): 429–49.

74. Michael P. Malone, "Beyond the Last Frontier: Toward a New Approach to Western American History," *Western Historical Quarterly* 20 (1989): 409–27.

75. Gary L. Gaile and Cort Wilmott, eds., *Geography in America* (Columbus, Ohio: Merrill, 1989), 160–62.

76. Donald W. Meinig, "Geographical Analysis of Imperial Expansion," in *Period and Place: Research Methods in Historical Geography*, ed. A. R. H. Baker and Mark Billinge (Cambridge: Cambridge University Press, 1982), 71–78.

77. For useful overviews and themes, see Craig Colten and Lary Dilsaver, "Historical Geography of the Environment: A Preliminary Literature Review," in Dilsaver and Colten, eds., *The American Environment: Historic Geographic Interpretations of Impact and Policy* (Savage, Md.: Rowman and Littlefield, 1992); Donald Worster, ed., *The Ends of the Earth* (Cambridge: Cambridge University Press, 1988), 289–307; William L. Lang, "Using and Abusing Abundance: The Western Resource Economy and the Environment," in *Historians and the American West*, ed. Malone; John Opie, "The Environment and the Frontier," in *American Frontier and Western Issues: A Historiographical Review*, ed. Roger L. Nichols (New York: Greenwood Press, 1986), 7–25; Joseph M. Petulla, *American Environmental History* (Columbus, Ohio: Merrill, 1988); Richard White, "American Environmental History: The Development of a New Historical Field," *Pacific Historical Review* 54 (1985): 297–335.

78. Christopher Vecsey and Robert W. Venables, eds., *American Indian Environments: Ecological Issues in Native American History* (Syracuse: Syracuse University Press, 1980); Richard White, "American Indians and Their Environment," *Environmental Review* 9 (1985): 101–3.

79. Limerick, *Legacy of Conquest*; Petulla, *American Environmental History*; White, "American Environmental History."

80. Samuel P. Hays, *Conservation and the Gospel of Efficiency* (Cambridge, Mass.: Harvard University Press, 1959); Roderick Nash, *Wilderness and the American Mind* (New Haven: Yale University Press, 1982); Alfred Runte, *National Parks: The American Experience* (Lincoln: University of Nebraska Press, 1984).

81. Douglas H. Strong, *Tahoe: An Environmental History* (Lincoln: University of Nebraska Press, 1984).

82. Barbara Vatter, *A Forest History of Douglas County, Oregon to 1900* (New York: Garland Press, 1989).

83. Carlos A. Schwantes, *The Pacific Northwest: An Interpretive History* (Lincoln: University of Nebraska Press, 1989); Schwantes, *In Mountain Shadows: A History of Idaho* (Lincoln: University of Nebraska Press, 1991).

84. James A. Young and Jerry D. Budy, "Historical Use of Nevada's Pinyon-Juniper Woodlands," *Journal of Forest History* 23 (1979): 113–21.

85. Philip L. Fradkin, *Sagebrush Country: Land and the American West* (New York: Alfred A. Knopf, 1989).

86. Duane A. Smith, "My Profit, Your Land: Colorado Mining and the Environment, 1858–1900," in *A Taste of the West: Essays in Honor of Robert G. Athearn*, ed. Duane A. Smith (Boulder: Pruett, 1983), 87–108.

87. DeBuys, *Enchantment and Exploitation*.

88. Hal Rothman, "Cultural and Environmental Change on the Pajarito Plateau," *New Mexico Historical Review* 64 (1989): 185–211.

89. Colten and Dilsaver, "Historical Geography of the Environment"; Ralph H. Brown, *Mirror for Americans* (New York: American Geographical Society, 1943); David Lowenthal and Martyn Bowden, eds., *Geographies of the Mind: Essays in Historical Geosophy* (New York: Oxford University Press, 1976); John K. Wright, "Terra Incognitae: The Place of Imagination in Geography," *Annals of the Association of American Geographers* 37 (1947): 1–17.

90. Henry Nash Smith, *Virgin Land: The American West as Symbol and Myth* (New York: Vintage Books, 1950).

91. Nash, *Wilderness*.

92. Western American literature can be explored in further detail through Richard W. Etulain, *A Bibliographical Guide to the Study of Western American Literature* (Lincoln: University of Nebraska Press, 1982), and J. Golden Taylor and Thomas J. Lyon, eds., *A Literary History of the American West* (Fort Worth: Texas Christian University Press, 1987).

93. A short, selective, but representative, list of these contributions would certainly include Edward Abbey, *Journey Home: Some Words in Defense of the American West* (New York: E. P. Dutton, 1977); Ivan Doig, *This House of Sky: Landscapes of a Western Mind* (New York: Harcourt Brace Jovanovich, 1978); Doig, *English Creek* (New York: Atheneum, 1984); Gretal Ehrlich, *The Solace of Open Spaces* (New York: Viking, 1985); Richard Ford, *Rock Springs Stories* (New York: Atlantic Monthly Press, 1987); Patricia Henley, *Friday Night at Silver Star* (St. Paul: Graywolf Press, 1986); Wil-

liam Kittredge, *Owning It All* (St. Paul: Graywolf Press, 1987); Kittredge and Annick Smith, eds., *The Last Best Place: A Montana Anthology* (Helena: Montana Historical Society Press, 1988); Larry McMurtry, *Lonesome Dove* (New York: Simon and Schuster, 1985); Russell Martin and Marc Barasch, eds., *Writers of the Purple Sage: An Anthology of Recent Western Writing* (New York: Penguin Books, 1984); Wallace Stegner, *Angle of Repose* (Garden City, N.Y.: Doubleday, 1971); George R. Stewart, *Storm* (New York: Random House, 1941); Stewart, *Fire* (New York: Random House, 1948).

94. William H. Truettner, ed., *The West as America: Reinterpreting Images of the Frontier, 1820–1920* (Washington, D.C.: Smithsonian Institution Press, 1991).

95. Anne Farrar Hyde, *An American Vision: Far Western Landscape and National Culture, 1820–1920* (New York: New York University Press, 1990).

96. Patricia Trenton and Peter H. Hassrick, *The Rocky Mountains: A Vision for Artists in the Nineteenth Century* (Norman: University of Oklahoma Press, 1983).

97. William H. Goetzmann, *Looking at the Land of Promise: Pioneer Images of the Pacific Northwest* (Pullman: Washington State University Press, 1988).

98. Gordon Hendricks, *Albert Bierstadt: Painter of the American West* (New York: Harry N. Abrams, 1973); Joni L. Kinsey, *Thomas Moran and the Surveying of the American West* (Washington, D.C.: Smithsonian Institution Press, 1992); David J. Weber, *Richard H. Kern: Expeditionary Artist in the Far Southwest, 1848–1853* (Albuquerque: University of New Mexico Press, 1985).

99. Don D. Fowler, *The Western Photographs of John K. Hillers: Myself in the Water* (Washington, D.C.: Smithsonian Institution Press, 1989); Peter B. Hales, *William Henry Jackson and the Transformation of the American Landscape* (Philadelphia: Temple University Press, 1988); Mark Junge, *J. E. Stimson: Photographer of the West* (Lincoln: University of Nebraska Press, 1985).

100. Meriwether Lewis, quoted in Bernard DeVoto, ed., *The Journals of Lewis and Clark* (Boston: Houghton Mifflin, 1976), 118.

101. Wilkinson, *American West*, 1.

102. Many of the geographical complexities of the West are explored in depth by Goetzmann, *Exploration and Empire;* and Carl I. Wheat, *Mapping the Trans-Mississippi West, 1540–1861,* 5 vols. (San Francisco: Institute of Historical Cartography, 1957–63).

103. General sketches of the West's transport infrastructure can be gleaned from Billington and Ridge, *Westward Expansion;* Meinig, "American Wests"; and Oscar Osburn Winther, *The Transportation Frontier: Trans-Mississippi West, 1865–1890* (New York: Holt, Rinehart and Winston, 1964).

104. John W. Evans, *Powerful Rockey: The Blue Mountains and the Oregon Trail, 1811–1883* (La Grande: Eastern Oregon State College, 1990).

105. Oscar Osburn Winther, *The Old Oregon Country: A History of Frontier Trade, Transportation, and Travel* (Bloomington: Indiana University, 1939).

106. George R. Stewart, *Ordeal by Hunger: The Story of the Donner Party* (Boston: Houghton Mifflin, 1969); Stewart, *The California Trail, an Epic with Many Heroes* (New York: McGraw-Hill, 1962).

107. Marshall Sprague, *The Great Gates: The Story of Rocky Mountain Passes* (Boston: Little, Brown, 1964).

108. Michael Kaplan, *Otto Mears: Paradoxical Pathfinder* (Silverton, Colo.: San Juan County Book Co., 1982).

109. W. Turrentine Jackson, *Wagon Roads West* (Berkeley: University of California Press, 1952).

110. Ward M. McAfee, *California's Railroad Era, 1850–1911* (San Marino, Calif.: Golden West Books, 1973).

111. The story of western railroading can be traced through Billington and Ridge, *Westward Expansion;* and Winther, *Transportation Frontier.*

112. White, *A New History,* 246–58.

113. Examples of research on the major lines include Robert G. Athearn, *Union Pacific Country* (Chicago: Rand McNally, 1971); Keith L. Bryant Jr., *History of the Atchison, Topeka and Santa Fe Railway* (New York: Macmillan, 1974); John C. Hudson, "Main Streets of the Yellowstone Valley," *Magazine: The Magazine of Western History* 35, no. 4 (Autumn 1985): 56–67; Richard C. Overton, *Burlington Route: A History of the Burlington Lines* (New York: Alfred A. Knopf, 1965).

114. Robert G. Athearn, *Rebel of the Rockies: A History of the Denver and Rio Grande Western Railroad* (New Haven: Yale University Press, 1962).

115. John J. Lipsey, *The Lives of James John Hagerman: Builder of the Colorado Midland Railway* (Denver: Golden Bell Press, 1968).

116. For example, see Ted Wurm and H. W. Demoro, *The Silver Short Line: A History of the Virginia and Truckee Railroad* (Glendale, Calif.: Trans-Anglo Books, 1983).

117. For general background on early automobiling in the West, see W. Turrentine Jackson, "Transportation in the American West," in *Historians and the American West,* ed. Malone, 123–47. Travel descriptions that detail the challenges of cross-country travel include Winifred Hawkridge Dixon, *Westward Hoboes: Ups and Downs of Frontier Motoring* (New York: Charles Scribner's Sons, 1921); and Emily Post, *By Motor to the Golden Gate* (New York: D. Appleton, 1917).

118. John Charles Frémont, quoted in Donald Jackson and Mary Lee Spence, eds., *The Expeditions of John Charles Fremont,* vol. 1 (Urbana: University of Illinois Press, 1970), 709–11.

119. Reisner, *Cadillac Desert.*

120. Worster, *Rivers of Empire,* 5.

121. Worster, *Rivers of Empire,* 266–67.

122. Stewart Holbrook, *The Columbia* (New York: Rinehart, 1956); Dale L. Mor-

gan, *The Humboldt: High Road of the West* (New York: Rinehart, 1943); Frank Waters, *The Colorado* (New York: Rinehart, 1946).

123. Paul Horgan, *Great River: The Rio Grande in North American History*, 2 vols. (New York: Rinehart, 1954).

124. Erwin Cooper, *Aqueduct Empire* (Glendale, Calif.: Arthur H. Clark, 1968); Abraham Hoffman, *Vision or Villainy: Origins of the Owens Valley–Los Angeles Water Controversy* (College Station: Texas A and M University Press, 1992); Norris Hundley Jr., *The Great Thirst: Californians and Water, 1770's–1990's* (Berkeley: University of California Press, 1992); William L. Karhl, *Water and Power: The Conflict over Los Angeles' Water Supply in the Owens Valley* (Berkeley: University of California Press, 1982); Robert de Roos, *The Thirsty Land: The Story of the Central Valley Project* (New York: Greenwood Press, 1968).

125. Philip L. Fradkin, *A River No More: The Colorado River and the West* (Tucson: University of Arizona Press, 1968).

126. Samuel Bowles, *Across the Continent: A Summer's Journey to the Rocky Mountains, the Mormons and the Pacific States* (Springfield, Mass.: Samuel Bowles and Co., 1865), 33.

127. Malone, "Beyond the Last Frontier."

128. Limerick, *Legacy of Conquest*; Robbins, "Western History."

129. Joel Garreau, *The Nine Nations of North America* (Boston: Houghton Mifflin, 1981).

130. P. Nick Kardulias, "Fur Production as a Specialized Activity in a World System: Indians in the North American Trade," *American Indian Culture and Research Journal* 14 (1990): 25–60; Wishart, *Fur Trade.*

131. LeRoy Hafen, ed., *The Mountain Men and the Fur Trade of the Far West: Biographical Sketches of the Participants*, 10 vols. (Glendale, Calif.: Arthur H. Clark, 1965–72); Dale Morgan, *Jedediah Smith and the Opening of the West* (Lincoln: University of Nebraska Press, 1953); John H. Sunder, *Bill Sublette, Mountain Man* (Norman: University of Oklahoma Press, 1959).

132. David J. Weber, *The Taos Trappers: The Fur Trade in the Far Southwest, 1540–1846* (Norman: University of Oklahoma Press, 1971).

133. William S. Greever, *The Bonanza West: The Story of the Western Mining Rushes, 1848–1900* (Norman: University of Oklahoma Press, 1963); David Lavender, *The Rockies* (New York: Harper and Row, 1968); Rodman W. Paul, *Mining Frontiers of the Far West, 1848–1880* (New York: Holt, Rinehart and Winston, 1963).

134. John W. Reps, *Cities of the American West: A History of Frontier Urban Planning* (Princeton: Princeton University Press, 1979); Duane A. Smith, *Rocky Mountain Mining Camps: The Urban Frontier* (Lincoln: University of Nebraska Press, 1967).

135. Stanley Dempsey and James E. Fell Jr., *Mining the Summit: Colorado's Ten Mile District, 1860–1960* (Norman: University of Oklahoma Press, 1986); Malcolm J. Rohrbough, *Aspen: The History of a Silver Mining Town, 1879–1893* (New York: Oxford University Press, 1986); Marshall Sprague, *Money Mountain: The Story of Cripple Creek Gold* (Boston: Little, Brown, 1953); Stephen M. Voynick, *Leadville: A Miner's Epic* (Missoula: Mountain Press Publishing, 1984).

136. Dilsaver, "Food Supply Regions"; Dilsaver, "After the Gold Rush"; J. S. Holliday, *The World Rushed In: The California Gold Rush Experience* (New York: Simon and Schuster, 1981); Ralph Mann, *After the Gold Rush: Society in Grass Valley and Nevada City, California, 1849–1870* (Stanford: Stanford University Press, 1982); Rodman Paul, *California Gold* (Lincoln: University of Nebraska Press, 1947).

137. Donald R. Abbe, *Austin and the Reese River Mining District* (Reno: University of Nevada Press, 1985); Russell R. Elliott, *History of Nevada* (Lincoln: University of Nebraska Press, 1987); W. Turrentine Jackson, *Treasure Hill: Portrait of a Silver Mining Camp* (Tucson: University of Arizona Press, 1963).

138. Larry Barsness, *Gold Camp: Alder Gulch and Virginia City, Montana* (New York: Hastings House, 1962); Dempsey and Fell, *Mining the Summit*; Phyllis Flanders Dorset, *The New Eldorado: The Story of Colorado's Gold and Silver Rushes* (London: Macmillan, 1970); John Fahey, *Hecla: A Century of Western Mining* (Seattle: University of Washington Press, 1990); Michael P. Malone and Richard B. Roeder, *Montana: A History of Two Centuries* (Seattle: University of Washington Press, 1988), 50–69; Duane A. Smith, *Song of the Hammer and Drill: The Colorado San Juans, 1860–1914* (Golden: Colorado School of Mines, 1982); William Wyckoff and David Lageson, "Retrograde Mineral Exploration and Settlement of Western and Central Montana During the Late 19th Century," *Centennial Field Conference Guidebook* (Billings: Montana Geological Society, 1989), 5–18.

139. Francaviglia, *Hard Places*; Robert L. Kelley, *Gold vs. Grain: The Hydraulic Mining Controversy in California's Sacramento Valley* (Glendale: Calif. Arthur H. Clark, 1959); Rohe, "Man and the Land"; Duane A. Smith, *Mining America: The Industry and the Environment, 1800–1980* (Lawrence: University Press of Kansas, 1987); Veblen and Lorenz, *Colorado Front Range*; Stephen M. Voynick, *Colorado Gold: From the Pike's Peak Rush to the Present* (Missoula: Mountain Press, 1992).

140. David A. Clary, *Timber and the Forest Service* (Lawrence: University Press of Kansas, 1986); Thomas Cox, Robert S. Maxwell, Phillip Drennon Thomas, and Joseph J. Malone, *This Well-Wooded Land: Americans and Their Forests from Colonial Times to the Present* (Lincoln: University of Nebraska Press, 1985); Robert Ficken, *The Forested Land: History of Lumbering in Western Washington* (Seattle: University of Washington Press, 1987); William Robbins, *American Forestry: A History of National, State,*

and Private Cooperation (Lincoln: University of Nebraska Press, 1985); Robbins, Hard Times in Paradise: Coos Bay, Oregon (Seattle: University of Washington Press, 1988); Williams, Americans and Their Forests.

141. Phillip O. Foss, Politics and Grass: The Administration of Grazing on the Public Domain (Seattle: University of Washington Press, 1960); William L. Graf, Wilderness Preservation and the Sagebrush Rebellions (Savage, Md.: Rowman and Littlefield, 1990); G. D. Libecap, Locking Up the Range: Federal Land Controls and Grazing (Cambridge, Mass.: Ballinger, 1981); William D. Rowley, U. S. Forest Service Grazing and Range-lands: A History (College Station: Texas A and M University Press, 1985); William Voight Jr., Public Grazing Lands: Use and Misuse by Industry and Government (New Brunswick, N.J.: Rutgers University Press, 1976).

142. James A. Young and B. Abbott Sparks, Cattle in the Cold Desert (Logan: Utah State University Press, 1985).

143. Dan L. Flores, "Agriculture, Mountain Ecology, and the Land Ethic: Phases of the Environmental History of Utah," in Working the Range: Essays on the History of Western Land Management and the Environment, ed. John R. Wunder (Westport, Conn.: Greenwood Press, 1985), 157–86; Wyckoff and Hansen, "Settlement, Live-stock Grazing."

144. J. Orin Oliphant, On the Cattle Ranges of the Oregon Country (Seattle: University of Washington Press, 1968).

145. Edward I. Taylor, quoted in Dyan Zaslowsky, These American Lands (New York: Henry Holt, 1986), 131.

146. Limerick, Legacy of Conquest.

147. White, New History, 55–178, 392–533.

148. Malone, "Beyond the Last Frontier."

149. Goetzmann, Exploration and Empire.

150. Vernon Carstensen, ed., The Public Lands: Studies in the History of the Public Domain (Madison: University of Wisconsin Press, 1963); Paul Wallace Gates, History of Public Land Law Development (Washington, D.C.: Government Printing Office, 1968); Roy M. Robbins, Our Landed Heritage: The Public Domain, 1776–1970 (Lincoln: University of Nebraska Press, 1976).

151. Jerry A. O'Callaghan, The Disposition of the Public Domain in Oregon (New York: Arno Press, 1979); Victor Westphall, The Public Domain in New Mexico, 1854–1891 (Albuquerque: University of New Mexico Press, 1965).

152. Runte, National Parks.

153. Craig W. Allin, The Politics of Wilderness Preservation (Westport, Conn.: Greenwood Press, 1982); Hans Huth, Nature and the American: Three Centuries of Changing Attitudes (Berkeley: University of California Press, 1957); Nash, Wilderness and the American Mind.

154. Dilsaver and Tweed, *Challenge of the Big Trees.*

155. Demars, *Tourist in Yosemite;* Alfred Runte, *Yosemite: The Embattled Wilderness* (Lincoln: University of Nebraska Press, 1990).

156. Arthur D. Martinson, *Wilderness above the Sound: The Story of Mount Rainier National Park* (Flagstaff: Northland Press, 1986).

157. C. W. Buchholtz, *Rocky Mountain National Park: A History* (Boulder: Colorado Associated University Press, 1983); Warren L. Hanna, *Stars over Montana: Men Who Made Glacier National Park History* (West Glacier, Mont.: Glacier Natural History Association, 1988); Robert W. Righter, *Crucible for Conservation: The Creation of Grand Teton National Park* (Boulder: Colorado Associated University Press, 1982); Duane A. Smith, *Mesa Verde National Park: Shadows of the Centuries* (Lawrence: University Press of Kansas, 1988).

158. Richard A. Bartlett, *Yellowstone: A Wilderness Besieged* (Tucson: University of Arizona Press, 1989); Alston Chase, *Playing God in Yellowstone: The Destruction of America's First National Park* (Boston: Atlantic Monthly Press, 1986); Aubrey L. Haines, *The Yellowstone Story: A History of Our First National Park,* 2 vols. (Yellowstone National Park, Wy.: Yellowstone Library and Museum Association, 1977).

159. Harold K. Steen, *The United States Forest Service: A History* (Seattle: University of Washington Press, 1976); Steen, ed., *The Origins of the National Forests: A Centennial Symposium* (Durham, N.C.: Forest History Society, 1992); Charles F. Wilkinson and H. Michael Anderson, *Land and Resource Planning in the National Forests* (Washington, D.C.: Island Press, 1987).

160. Carl J. Mayer and George A. Riley, *Public Domain, Private Dominion: A History of Public Mineral Policy in America* (San Francisco: Sierra Club Books, 1985); White, *New History,* 395–430; Wilkinson and Anderson, *Land and Resource Planning.*

161. Foss, *Politics and Grass;* Graf, *Wilderness Preservation;* Libecap, *Locking Up the Range;* Rowley, *U.S. Forest Service;* Voight, *Public Grazing Lands.*

162. Clary, *Timber and the Forest Service;* Robbins, *American Forestry;* Williams, *Americans and Their Forests.*

163. Nash, *Wilderness and the American Mind;* Dennis M. Roth, *The Wilderness Movement and the National Forests: 1964–1980* (Washington, D.C.: U. S. Department of Agriculture, 1984); Zaslowsky, *These American Lands,* 203–40.

164. Thomas Alexander, *The Rise of Multiple-Use Management in the Intermountain West: A History of Region 4 of the Forest Service* (Washington, D.C.: U. S. Department of Agriculture, 1987); Robert D. Baker, Robert S. Maxwell, Victor H. Treat, and Henry C. Dethloff, *Timeless Heritage: A History of the Forest Service in the Southwest* (Washington, D.C.: U. S. Department of Agriculture, 1988); Wayne K. Hinton, *The Dixie National Forest: Managing an Alpine Forest in an Arid Setting* (Washington, D.C.: U. S. Department of Agriculture, 1987).

165. Paul J. Culhane, *Public Lands Politics* (Washington, D.C.: Resources for the Future, 1981), 75–109; James Muhan and Hanson R. Stuart, *Opportunity and Challenge: The Story of BLM* (Denver: Bureau of Land Management, 1988).

166. Foss, *Politics and Grass;* Graf, *Wilderness Preservation;* Voight, *Public Grazing Lands.*

167. Michael P. Malone and Richard W. Etulain, *The American West: A Twentieth-Century History* (Lincoln: University of Nebraska Press, 1989); Charles F. Wilkinson, *Crossing the Next Meridian: Land, Water, and the Future of the West* (Washington, D.C.: Island Press, 1992).

168. John Braeman, Robert Bremner, and David Brody, eds., *The New Deal,* vol. 2, *The State and Local Levels* (Columbus: Ohio State University Press, 1975); Richard Lowitt, *The New Deal and the West* (Bloomington: Indiana University Press, 1984).

169. Perry H. Merrill, *Roosevelt's Forest Army: A History of the Civilian Conservation Corps, 1933–1942* (Montpelier, Vt.: Perry Merrill, 1981); John Salmond, *The Civilian Conservation Corps* (Durham, N.C.: Duke University Press, 1967).

170. Malone and Etulain, *American West;* Elmo R. Richardson, *Dams, Parks, and Politics: Resource Development and Preservation in the Truman-Eisenhower Era* (Lexington: University Press of Kentucky, 1973); Shanks, *This Land Is Your Land;* Wilkinson, *American West.* For ongoing perspective on the federal role in the West, see the *High Country News,* published in Paonia, Colo.

171. Mark Twain, from an excerpt quoted in Robert L. Reid, ed., *A Treasury of the Sierra Nevada* (Berkeley: Wilderness Press, 1983), 135.

172. Kenneth Thompson, "Wilderness and Health."

173. Richard White, "Trashing the Trails," in *Trails,* ed. Limerick, Milner, and Rankin, 37–38.

174. Nash, *Wilderness and the American Mind;* Nash, *The Rights of Nature: A History of Environmental Ethics* (Madison: University of Wisconsin Press, 1989).

175. Huth, *Nature and the American;* Hyde, *American Vision.*

176. Douglas H. Strong, *Dreamers and Defenders: American Conservationists* (Lincoln: University of Nebraska, 1988); Peter Wild, *Pioneer Conservationists of Western North America* (Missoula: Mountain Press, 1979).

177. Stephen Fox, *John Muir and His Legacy* (Boston: Little, Brown, 1981); Frederick Turner, *Rediscovering America: John Muir in His Times and Ours* (New York: Viking Press, 1985).

178. Petulla, *American Environmental History;* Strong, *Dreamers and Defenders;* Wild, *Pioneer Conservationists.*

179. Athearn, *Mythic West;* Fifer, *American Progress;* Earl Pomeroy, *In Search of the Golden West: The Tourist in Western America* (New York: Alfred A. Knopf, 1957).

180. Demars, *Yosemite;* Marshall Sprague, *Newport in the Rockies* (Chicago: Swallow Press, 1980).

181. Alfred Runte, *Trains of Discovery: Western Railroads and the National Parks* (Flagstaff: Northland Press, 1984).

182. L. R. Borne, *Dude Ranching: A Complete History* (Albuquerque: University of New Mexico Press, 1983).

183. Many of these controversies can be followed in recent issues of the *High Country News.*

Barriers

The Mountainous West served both as a barrier and a goal to nineteenth-century Europeans and Americans. The three chapters in this section focus specifically on this interplay, emphasizing both the complexities of the region and the dynamic responses of the encroaching civilizations. At a truly continental scale, John Allen offers a penetrating analysis of the role of the fur trade in contributing to the evolution of nineteenth-century cartography. Before the Lewis and Clark expedition, many politicians and theoreticians actually minimized the potential role of the western mountains as barriers to transcontinental movement. They envisioned the mountainous interior as being draped along a single western uplift that could be readily traversed. Allen suggests how Lewis and Clark complicated matters with their sobering discoveries of tangled, seemingly endless mountains and unnavigable rivers. He then reconstructs how fur traders, especially the wide-wandering mountain men between 1823 and 1840, pierced these alpine barriers and rapidly pieced together an accurate geographical picture of the Mountainous West which was gradually represented in the published cartography of the period. The search for furs and, more generally, the fur traders' regional reconnaissance of the West contributed to a new and more accurate image of western mountains which facilitated further explorations and, ultimately, the rush for western resources.

Duane Smith and Cathy Kindquist then take much more detailed looks at a single uplift within the Mountainous West and assess how its rugged character contributed special challenges to the settlement of the region and the development of its concentrated mineral resource base. Southwestern Colorado's San Juan Mountains provide the setting for both Smith's and Kindquist's related essays. Smith recounts how the region's isolation made its initial promotion more difficult. He describes the high costs associated with developing trail, road, and railroad networks in the San Juans, even after vast mineral resources of gold and silver were uncovered. He also chronicles how tramway technologies and electricity provided creative human responses to the mountain barriers encountered. Finally, Smith reconstructs how exploitation of the area's timber, forage, and recreational resources shaped its settlement geography in the present century. Kindquist, in a more focused analysis, takes a single pass and meticulously demonstrates its impact on the flow of people, goods, and information into a portion of the San Juans in the first generation of American settlement. Her assessment of evolving spatial patterns dramatically reveals the potent role played by Stony Pass in creating and limiting opportunities in the early mining era of the San Juans. She then shows how changing technologies of transportation and communication further altered the region's human geography and rendered obsolete the originally valuable pass.

2 / Maps and the Mountain Men: The Cartography of the Rocky Mountain Fur Trade

JOHN L. ALLEN

A historical convention of long standing holds that the trappers and traders—the "mountain men"—of the Rocky Mountain fur trade did not contribute significantly to either geographical knowledge or cartography of the Rocky Mountains of western North America during the first half of the nineteenth century.[1] This conventional wisdom is based upon the assumption that the mountain men did not make maps, that the mountains themselves served as barriers to the transmission of geographical data, and that the trappers and traders of the Rockies were so bent upon exploitation of the rich fur resource of the region that they consciously withheld geographical data in order to maintain the security of their own hunting grounds. Such assumptions, however, depend upon a definition of geographical knowledge that is restricted to the "formal" geographical knowledge in atlases and gazetteers and obtained through official, government-sponsored exploration.[2]

Contrary to the conventional wisdom, however, the fur traders and trappers of the American West *did* make many noteworthy additions to the geographical awareness of the Rocky Mountain system prior to the formal exploration and mapping of the Rockies by the U.S. Army Corps of Topographical Engineers in the 1840s and 1850s. For the most part, these fur trade contributions can best be understood as falling into the category of "informal" geographical lore—that which was available in the river-front taverns of St. Louis and in the newspapers of the frontier and border towns but not necessarily in the published gazetteers, atlases, and geographies of the eastern cities. Bernard DeVoto has suggested that "geographers did not read the newspapers";[3] it might be added that neither did most geographers or cartographers frequent the river-front taverns. Had they done either, had they read the letters from fur traders and trappers to friends and family in St. Louis or a score of other frontier communities, or had they listened to the tavern-told tales of trappers returned from the mountains, they might have produced maps that were a great deal more accurate than many of the ones generally accepted by the literate American public between 1800 and 1840 as the best representations of western North America.

But just because most geographers and cartographers did not explicitly absorb the informal lore emanating from the fur trade does not mean that fur trade information was excluded from all formal sources of geographical information. Some of those who wrote the geographies and drew the maps (including some prominent government officials) did incorporate the experiences of the mountain men; they produced some of the most accurate, if not the most influential, maps of the Rocky Mountains prior to those of John C. Frémont and his cartographer, Charles Preuss, in the 1840s. The purpose of this essay is to contradict the conventional wisdom regarding the integration of the informal geographical data of the fur trade into formal sources and to trace the process whereby fur trade information did find its way—often without anyone being aware of the process of incorporation—into the more formalized geographical lore of the American West, particularly the Rocky Mountain system. As this information was assimilated into lore, geographical images or patterns of belief about the nature and content of the Mountainous West began to take shape, and two processes critical to the development of that region took place: by providing details on the *nature* of the region (the structure of the Rockies and the passes across them), the fur trade significantly reduced the actual and conceptual role of the mountains as a barrier to interaction; by providing data on the *content* of the region (the resource base of the Rockies, particularly the wealth in beaver and other furs), the fur trade helped to develop early an impression of the mountains as a zone of concentrated resources.

To understand the process through which the informal lore of the mountain men became absorbed into the greater store of American geographical knowledge of the Rocky Mountains during the first half of the nineteenth century, it is necessary to view five distinct stages of the fur trade enterprise in the Rocky Mountains and Farther West:

- an initial phase that began with the first entry of Canadian-based British and French fur traders into the Canadian West and the upper Missouri in the eighteenth century and that continued through the period of French and Spanish activities between St. Louis and the upper Missouri, ending with the United States purchase of Louisiana Territory in 1803

- a second phase that began with the Lewis and Clark expedition of 1804–6 and that concluded with the abortive ventures of Manuel Lisa's St. Louis–based Missouri Fur Company on the Upper Missouri in 1807–11
- a third phase that incorporated the travels of the participants in John Jacob Astor's visionary but premature attempt to establish his northwestern fur trade empire of Astoria between 1811 and 1813 and the first penetrations of the southern Rockies by Santa Fe–based trappers
- a fourth phase, between the mid-1820s and the 1840s, when the British fur trade, particularly the brigades of the Hudson's Bay Company, was active in the Columbian and Great basins
- a fifth phase temporally conterminous with the fourth, between 1823 and the 1840s, during the heyday of the St. Louis–based American fur trade of the Rocky Mountains (1823–39)

During each of these stages and in distinctive ways, certain prevalent cartographic images of the Rocky Mountains, generated largely out of fur trade lore, became consequential images presented in even the most formal sources of geographical information available to the general public.[4] In these images, the Rockies were invariably presented as a zone of concentrated resources rather than scarcity; as such, the mountains were the goal of the fur trade, and for the mountain men, the role of the mountains as a barrier was largely absent. Even in the broader scale, the fur trapper tended to view the mountains as an area through which communication as far as the Pacific shore was reasonably easy. Although the images of the mountains grew more sophisticated with the passage of time, that central belief would not change. The West would pose barriers to transcontinental travel, but these barriers were more often viewed as those of desert or "savages" or scanty food supply rather than of terrain.

Before Lewis and Clark

Even before the opening of the nineteenth century, before the great "official" (meaning government-sponsored) expeditions of Lewis and Clark, Zebulon Pike, and Stephen Long, there existed a body of geographical and cartographic lore regarding the form, location, extent, and character of the Rocky Mountains that was largely derived from the activities of the fur trade in western North America. These images were the product of the

Hudson's Bay Company and the Northwest Company, based in British North America; of French and Spanish partisans of the great merchant houses of the St. Louis–based fur trade; and even of the loosely organized and largely unofficial fur trade operating out of the Spanish outpost city of Santa Fe.[5] Of the maps during this period, by far the most significant were those produced by the London cartographic firm of Aaron Arrowsmith between 1795 and 1802.[6] In addition, there were a small number of early French maps of Louisiana Territory which at least hinted at the presence of the Rocky Mountains, and an even smaller number of Spanish maps produced during the years when Spain controlled Louisiana Territory.[7]

Fortunately, there exists one manuscript map, drawn by Nicholas King in 1803 and intended for the use of Meriwether Lewis during his transcontinental journey, that is a superb compilation of these British, French, and Spanish maps.[8] On his 1803 map (figure 1), King synthesized what was believed to be the best and most accurate information on the American West and on the "Stoney Mountains" on the eve of the Lewis and Clark expedition. While there were some variations between the British, French, and Spanish views of the Rockies available to King, there was general agreement on the salient features of the geography of the American West in general and of the Rocky Mountains in particular.[9] Perhaps the most important area of agreement between the fur trade explorers and the European theoretical geographers who translated fur trade lore into maps was their view of the symmetry of continental geography: it was known that the rivers flowing west from the Appalachian system into the Mississippi Basin had sources relatively close to the Atlantic Ocean where they interlocked with the source streams heading east to the Atlantic; the same set of conditions should exist on the western margins of the continent. This sweeping and teleological view of North America offered an enthusiastic assessment of the cardinal elements of western geography—the mountains and river systems—as offering easy commercial accessibility to the interior portions of the continent and as facilitating the possibility of commercial transcontinental communication by water.[10] People like Thomas Jefferson, viewing the King map, understood this "Passage to India" to be providential; rather than serving as a barrier to trade, the western mountains would facilitate the easy development of trade connections between Atlantic and Pacific.

There were five significant features of the conceptual geography of the Rockies as represented by the King map: (1) the Rocky Mountains formed the core of continental symmetry west of the Mississippi and, as such, acted as a continental divide which parted the Atlantic from Pacific streams;

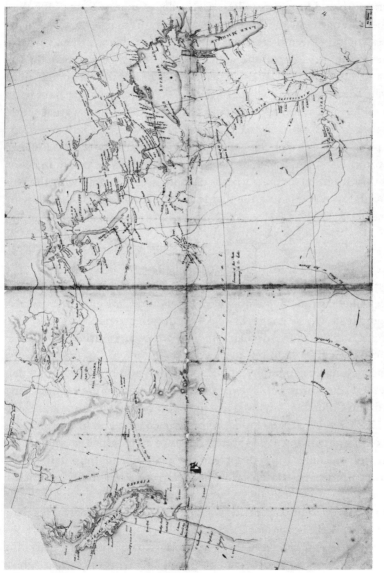

1. *The Trans-Mississippi West before Lewis and Clark. Nicholas King, 1803. (Courtesy Geography and Maps Division, Library of Congress.)*

(2) although the mountains served as a divide between Atlantic and Pacific streams, that divide was not necessarily a long, linear one but may have been a pyramidal height-of-land or core drainage region where, between the forty-fifth and fiftieth parallels of latitude, all major rivers of the West had their sources; (3) the Rockies were configured as a narrow, single-ridged structure, extending from north to south and being extensive in neither height nor breadth; (4) the sources of the navigable waters of the Columbia and the Missouri lay on opposite sides of this narrow, single ridge and were connected by a short portage; and (5) the Rockies may have had a southern terminus around 45 degrees north latitude where a great southern branch of the Columbia had its source. The Lewis and Clark expedition of 1804–6 would examine the geographical suppositions of the King map and would seek "the most direct & practicable water communication across this continent for the purposes of commerce"[11] by following the Missouri to its source, crossing the divide, and following westward-flowing streams to the Pacific.

From Lewis and Clark to Manuel Lisa

Between May 1804 and September 1806, Lewis and Clark and their Corps of Discovery tested these images of Rocky Mountain geography as presented by King. Over the course of their two-year westward journey of 1804 and 1805, and their six-month return in 1806, the Corps of Discovery learned that the optimistic geography of Nicholas King and his source materials was faulty. There was not, between the headwaters of the Missouri and those of the Columbia, anything like the short portage that had been suggested by King. What they found, rather, was a long and tortured mountain crossing, involving at its shortest distance an overland journey of approximately 140 miles through some of the most difficult mountain terrain in North America. The Rockies were not a narrow, single-ridge system like the Blue Ridge of Virginia; they were a formidable mountain barrier to the attainment of the transcontinental water communication that had been the central objective of Lewis and Clark.

Shortly upon the return of the Corps of Discovery, William Clark, the expedition's cartographer, began preparing a manuscript map which would reflect the results of their journey for the cartographic image of the Rocky Mountains. This manuscript map, which Clark completed in 1810 or 1811, has been referred to as a "master map" (one from which many others were derived); it was ultimately redrafted by Samuel Lewis of Philadelphia for inclusion as a large and beautifully engraved map in Nicholas Biddle's *History of the Expedition*, published in 1814.[12] A master map it was—but it was not all Lewis and Clark data. Much of the data on Clark's map was derived from the fur trade after the expedition; the extent to which this "unofficial" or informal geographical knowledge from the fur trade was used by Clark in drafting major portions of his map is not widely known. Clark's map was, indisputably, the product of an official government-sponsored expedition undertaken by officers and enlisted men in the U.S. Army. But it was equally undeniably the result of contributions by the fur trade. After his service as co-commander of the Corps of Discovery, William Clark became superintendent of Indian affairs, stationed in St. Louis, the center of the Missouri River fur trade and soon to be the center of the fur trade of the Rocky Mountains as well. From his St. Louis location, Clark was in a perfect position to obtain the informal lore of returning fur traders and trappers, most of whom sought out the popular Clark when they were in town. From them he obtained the geographical lore which, when added to the information obtained during his journey to the Pacific and back, became the base data for his manuscript map and, hence, for the published map that would continue to represent for many Americans the most precise view of the American West until the 1840s.

Clark's reception of fur trade lore began almost as soon as the expedition returned to St. Louis in 1806. On their way down the Missouri in the late summer of that year, Lewis and Clark met two Illinois trappers heading upstream to trap beaver.[13] A member of the Lewis and Clark force, John Colter, received permission from the captains to accompany the Illinois trappers back into the mountains.[14] Little is known of Colter's first venture into the mountain region, but it is virtually certain that whatever he learned was relayed to Clark upon Colter's return to St. Louis in 1807. Shortly thereafter, Colter again headed up the Missouri for the mountains, this time as a member of a fur-trading party organized by Manuel Lisa, a Spaniard from New Orleans who had moved to St. Louis, who had been attracted to the fur business by the reports of Lewis and Clark of the rich fur resource of the Rocky Mountains, and who was to play a pivotal role in the early fur trade.[15] Accompanying Colter on Lisa's venture was another Lewis and Clark veteran, George Drouillard.[16] Over the next few years, Colter and Drouillard would contribute significant information to William Clark, which he put to good use in his cartographic representation of the "new" pyramidal height-of-land or core drainage area of the Rocky Mountains.

The Lisa party traveled up the Missouri to its junction with the Yellow-stone and then up that river to the mouth of the Big Horn River. Here they built a crude fort which served as the base of fur trade exploration of the northern Rockies during the next few years. In 1807–8 Colter made an extraordinary solitary journey into the Big Horn Basin, across the continental divide into Jackson's Hole and what is now Yellowstone National Park, then crossing the mountains east of Yellowstone to the Shoshone River and down that stream to the Big Horn and Lisa's fort. In 1808, also traveling alone, Drouillard covered the eastern flank of the mountains in the same area explored by Colter—from the Pryor Mountains of Montana to the Wind River Range of Wyoming. And in 1810, a party of Lisa's men led by Andrew Henry (probably following recommendations by Colter) crossed the continental divide between the upper Yellowstone and the Snake River in eastern Idaho, establishing the first American trading post west of the divide.[17] Although Lisa's venture failed and his post on the Big Horn was abandoned in 1811, the returning Lisa men—particularly Colter, Drouillard, and Henry—provided significant geographical information to William Clark, still in the process of completing his manuscript master map. Drouillard even provided Clark with a map of the upper Big Horn that he had drawn on the basis of his and Colter's travels (figure 2), showing the proximity of its headwaters with the source region of a "Spanish river"—either the Colorado or the Rio Grande. This was the core of the information provided Clark by these mountain men: the rivers on which they had traveled—the Big Horn, the Shoshone, and the Snake—all had their sources close to the headwaters of the "Spanish" rivers of the Rio Grande and Colorado.

Clark's published map (figure 3) accurately showed the country through which the expedition passed, clearly delineating the easiest route across the Rockies between the upper Missouri and the westernmost reaches of the Columbia system. Most of the Missouri and Columbia drainage basins were faithfully shown, and the northern Rocky Mountains, although shown in parallel north-south ridges that marched across the map, were represented in their proper location and extent. To the south of the captains' crossing of the continental divide in Montana, however, accuracy was thrown to the winds, and Clark's major remaining misunderstanding of a single source region for western rivers produced a geography as fanciful as it was fundamental to American images of the Rockies during the first half of the nineteenth century. A relatively small tributary of the Columbia, the Willamette, was elevated to the status of a great continental river, the "Multnomah," and was depicted as draining the vast area be-

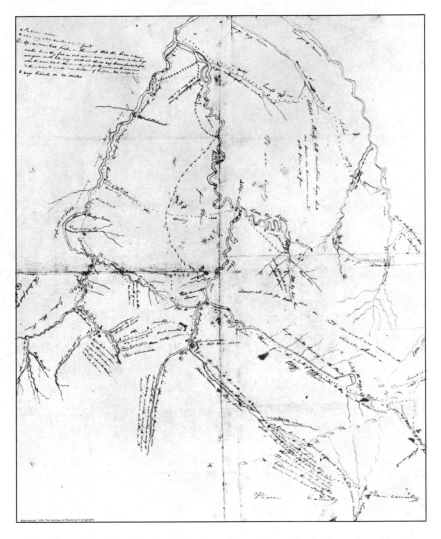

2. The Upper Big Horn Drainage Region. George Drouillard, circa 1810. (Courtesy Missouri Historical Society.)

tween its debouchment into the Columbia (near where Portland, Oregon, now stands) and the western slope of the Rockies opposite the source region of the Rio Grande. In the form of its major eastern tributary, the "Rio de San Clementi," the Multnomah headed with not only the "Rio del Norte" (Rio Grande) and the Arkansas, but also with the Platte, Yellowstone, Missouri, and Snake: the pyramidal height-of-land still existed.

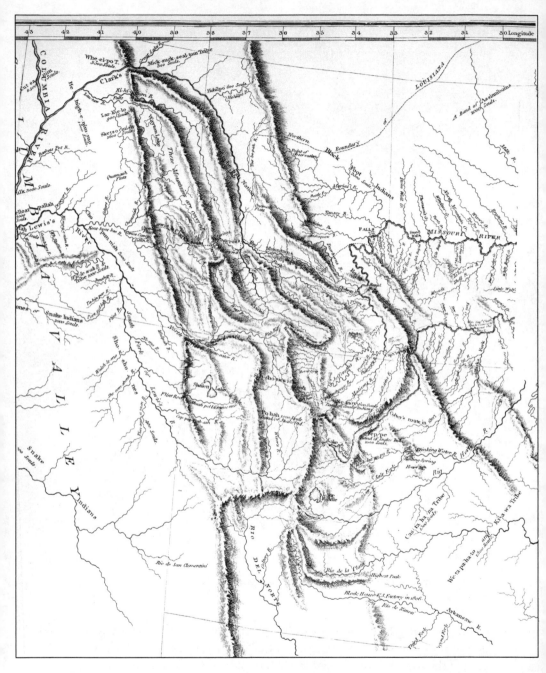

3. *A Map of Lewis and Clark's Track. . . . Engraved by Samuel King, 1814. Reproduced from Nicholas Biddle, A History of the Expedition under the Command of Captains Lewis and Clark . . ., 2 vols. (Philadelphia: Bradford and Inskeep, 1814.)*

Clark's conception of a core drainage region south of his and Lewis's transcontinental crossing was confirmed by mountain men lore, and this hypothetical core region of approximately four hundred square miles within which lay the headwaters of nearly all major western rivers (including the mythical Multnomah) was "a remarkable exercise in fictional geography."[18] After the publication of Clark's map in 1814, the pyramidal height-of-land continued to confuse the American image of the Rocky Mountains for another thirty years. The Jeffersonian concept of the Passage to India persisted in American images of the Rockies, and the mountains were still viewed more as a mechanism to effect the dream of transcontinental commerce than as a barrier to the Passage.

Astoria and Santa Fe

The second phase of fur trade contributions to geographical and cartographic lore began even before the failure of Manuel Lisa's attempt to establish a permanent fur-trading post near the junction of the Big Horn and Yellowstone Rivers. Stimulated, as had been Lisa, by the first reports from Lewis and Clark, a New York fur merchant named John Jacob Astor established the Pacific Fur Company to "exploit the commerce of the Pacific Coast."[19] While Astor's venture was primarily a Pacific Northwest operation and his primary trading post of "Astoria" was located near the mouth of the Columbia River, two parties of Astor's men, traveling overland to and from Astoria, crossed the Rocky Mountain region and provided geographical lore on the Rockies to an entire generation of commercial cartographers. In 1811, while Astoria itself was being built by a party which Astor had sent by ship around Cape Horn, an overland party left St. Louis for the mouth of the Columbia, originally intending to follow the Lewis and Clark route up the Missouri to the Columbia.[20] Upon learning of the travels of Lisa's men in the region south of the Lewis and Clark traverse, Wilson Price Hunt, the leader of the westbound Astorians, was determined to make his crossing of the Rockies using the passes discovered by John Colter and Andrew Henry. Guided by veterans of Henry's 1810 party, Hunt and his men crossed the continental divide at Union Pass in west-central Wyoming, traveled across Jackson's Hole, and then proceeded across the southern end of the Teton Range via Teton Pass to the Snake River to the fort built and abandoned by Henry the year before. From this point, the westbound Astorians followed (more or less) the course of the Snake River to the Columbia and then down that river to the fort which was being built at its mouth. While the portion of their journey from the Snake River to Astoria was far from uneventful, the key part of Hunt's journey from the standpoint of geographical knowledge of the Rockies was his confirmation of Henry's discovery of the pass across the continental divide between the Missouri and Columbia Basins (Union Pass) and the pass across the Teton Range (Teton Pass). Both passes were to play key roles during the heyday of the American fur trade of the next generation. Union Pass, in particular, figured prominently in the continuing cartographic representation of the core drainage region inasmuch as Hunt, like Henry, had concluded that the headwaters of the Missouri Basin (the Wind River of Wyoming), which he followed westward to the continental divide, rose close to the sources of the "Spanish River." Somehow, this information was also conveyed to William Clark; the published version of his map contains the hint of Union Pass and its proximity to the pyramidal height-of-land.

The most significant of the Astorian overland ventures, however, was the eastbound or return journey made in 1812–13.[21] Led by Robert Stuart, this journey commenced even before the surrender of Astoria to the British in the War of 1812 and the end of Astor's imperial venture on the Pacific. Stuart led his men back to St. Louis via what would later become the Oregon Trail. From the Pacific, Stuart retraced most of Wilson Price Hunt's route two years earlier as far as the crossing of Teton Pass. But from Jackson's Hole, Stuart led his men up the Hoback River (a tributary of the Snake) to the low pass between the Hoback and the Green River (the upper Colorado). He followed the Green River downstream, along the western flank of the Wind River Mountains, and then turned eastward, crossing the continental divide at what must have been South Pass—the easiest way across the divide in the Central Rockies—following the Sweetwater River east to the Platte and then the Platte down to the Missouri and St. Louis. That Stuart's crossing of the divide via South Pass did not go unnoticed is evidenced by the following report in a St. Louis newspaper in May 1813: "a journey across the continent of N. America, might be performed with a waggon, there being no obstruction in the whole route that any person would dare call a mountain."[22] The rhetoric was, perhaps, a bit extreme; but it provided ample evidence of the continuing American faith in the Rocky Mountains as holding the key to the transcontinental commercial route. It was also a powerful indication that fur trade lore *was* a part of the geographical information on the Rockies available to the literate public. There are even more abundant manifestations of this process in the commercial cartography which followed the Astorian venture.

While the Astorians were active in the American Northwest, other groups of adventurous Americans were operative in the fur trade of the Southwest.[23] As early as 1807, a few American trappers had moved from St. Louis into the region of New Mexico; by 1809 they had penetrated into the upper waters of the Red River, and by 1814, American trappers had reached the upper Arkansas River in the Colorado Rockies and had discovered the passes between the Arkansas and the still-Spanish settlements of Taos and Santa Fe. Although the geographic lore which came out of the early southwestern fur trade was sketchy and inconsequential at best, at least some of it appeared on crucial maps before 1820. If nothing else, the Santa Fe trappers aided in the transmission to cartographers of Spanish geographical lore—some of it dating to the sixteenth century—on the configuration of the southern Rockies.

The best known American representative of the commercial maps of this early period was the "Map of the United States with the contiguous British and Spanish possessions" by John Melish of Philadelphia. An advertisement for this map appearing in the Niles Weekly Register in 1816 indicated the cartographer's reliance on the "researches" of Lewis and Clark, Zebulon Pike, and "others" (almost certainly the Astorians and possibly Santa Fe trappers as well).[24] Melish was a well-known travel writer whose 1812 work Travels in the United States of America had contained maps that extended only to the Mississippi Valley. In his 1816 map, however, he expanded his horizons to include most of North America between the fifty-fifty and thirtieth parallels and to include a level of mythical geography that was significant for the American image of the Rockies. Running into San Francisco Bay, for example, were dotted lines that represented, according to the map caption, the "Supposed course of a river between the Buenaventura and the Bay of San Francisco which will probably be the communication from the Arkansas to the Pacific Ocean." The Buenaventura itself was shown in the western interior running into a large lake from the core drainage region where it arose near the "principal sources of the Red River of California" (the Colorado), the Multnomah, the Rio Grande, the Arkansas, the Platte, the Big Horn, and the Snake. The "highest peak" of the Rockies was shown in the proximity of this core drainage region and, west of it, a blank "Unexplored Country" broken only by an apocryphal stream (Melish's version of the Buenaventura) that flowed toward the Pacific. No less a geographical authority than Thomas Jefferson wrote to Melish, commending him on the execution and scale of the map of 1816 and noting that Melish had given "a luminous view of the comparative possessions of different powers in our America."[25] Jefferson also must have been intrigued by the continuing representation of the pyramidal height-of-land and what it promised for his continuing dream of transcontinental commerce.

Hudson's Bay Company Maps

Even before Melish's map was published, the mapping efforts of the British fur trade in the Columbia Basin, followed shortly by those of American trappers and traders ranging the Rockies from Taos to the upper Missouri, began to generate geographical data based on firsthand observation and informed extrapolation. These mapping efforts seldom, if ever, created maps that were published; hence, they played an indirect role in the creation of geographical images of the West. But because some of the information on British fur trader manuscript maps did eventually work its way onto maps published in both Europe and America, these manuscript maps are part of formal cartographic history. The first and most active of the mapping efforts related to the fur trade were those carried out by the representatives of the British fur trade interests in the Columbia and Snake Basins. The British fur trade maps were of greater import for cartographic development than their American counterparts because, unlike the American fur trade maps, the British were immediately and formally utilized by such cartographers as Aaron Arrowsmith, who had ready access to the collections of the Hudson's Bay Company and the Northwest Company, where many of the manuscript maps drawn by such men as David Thompson, William Kittson, and Peter Skene Ogden were deposited and from which they filtered out to become a part of general knowledge.[26]

Of all the members of the British fur trade who drew maps of the western interior, David Thompson, "Official Geographer and Explorer to the Northwest Company," was arguably the most important.[27] Trained in astronomical and geographical observation and one of the most able explorers of the eighteenth and nineteenth centuries, Thompson spent over two decades (1784–1812) exploring the reaches of both the Columbia and Missouri drainage systems and was the first explorer to traverse the entire course of the Columbia River from its source in the Canadian Rockies to the Pacific. Among his maps, which fed directly into the commercial productions of Aaron Arrowsmith, two were of greatest significance: his large manuscript of "The Oregon Territory," probably drawn in or about 1818, after Thompson had left the West, and another manuscript, probably drawn about the same time, that illustrated the southern portions of the Columbian system.[28] The precision with which Thompson illustrated the northern half of the Columbian Basin and, therefore, the southern Canadian Rockies, on the first of these two maps is incontestable. Of more importance for the geographic image of the American Rockies, however, was his second map of the southern portions of the Columbia Basin. On this map Thompson, like nearly everyone else of the time, ran afoul of geographical misinformation and misunderstanding. Near the Columbia itself, Thompson's map was quite good; most of the Snake system was shown more accurately than on many period maps, although Thompson confused the geography of the upper Snake River in the "3 Guides" or Teton/Jackson Hole area. The waters of the upper Green River were indicated, probably on the basis of information obtained from the Astorian crossings, with the notation that this river was "Supposed to be the Rio Collarado Spanish River." From this point on to the south and east, Thompson's geography was as confused and confusing as that of other cartographers of the time. Just east of the Green River, a small stream was located that was claimed to be a "Branch of the Arkansaw river"; in the same vicinity the Sweetwater River of the North Platte was drawn but was misleadingly labeled as "Sweet water or Chayenne River." Such a confusion between the westernmost streams of the North Platte drainage and the Cheyenne River, a tributary of the Missouri heading far to the east near the Black Hills, was a major error that, like similar errors on other maps, reinforced the concept of the single core drainage area. Thompson's erroneous geography south of the Columbia may be forgiven since he was relying on data other than his own; for the areas he had observed personally, his maps were more accurate than almost any others of the time, a fact that was reflected in the accuracy of the commercial maps of Arrowsmith, who relied heavily on Thompson's information for most of his North American maps produced between 1818 and 1830.

In addition to the maps of Thompson, a Northwest Company employee, the efforts of the Hudson's Bay Company personnel to develop an accurate cartographic picture of the Northwest were crucial in the development of both commercial cartography and American images of the Rocky Mountains. In particular, the maps of Peter Skene Ogden and his clerk, William Kittson, were fundamental in providing the first accurate geographical details on the Snake River country and the northern end of the

Great Basin.[29] Between 1824 and 1830, Ogden, in six separate expeditions, covered nearly all of the region between the Rockies on the east, the Pacific on the west, the Columbia on the north, and the Humboldt River of Nevada on the south. The delineation of drainage systems by Ogden and Kittson provided new insights into the geography of the Rockies and the Intermountain West. Kittson's map of 1825, for example, drawn to illustrate the first Ogden expedition of 1824–25 into the area south of the Snake River, was an excellent rendering of the geography as it was seen by Ogden's party. Unfortunately, Kittson also chose to make comments upon areas that had not yet been explored, conceiving, for example, of the Bear River as flowing into a "Large Bear Lake"—almost certainly the Great Salt Lake in its first representation as such on a map—and thence west to the Pacific. He also badly confused the northern core drainage region of the upper Green, Snake, and Yellowstone, although he provided reasonable detail on the rivers of the Missouri system east of the "Grand Defile" or continental divide (the Big Horn, Platte, Powder, Cheyenne, and White).

The map drawn by Kittson's chief, Peter Skene Ogden, to illustrate his trek of 1828–29 into the Snake River country and northern Great Basin is even more fascinating. Like Kittson, Ogden showed the Great Salt Lake (which he called by the name it now bears) and its Bear River tributary, minus Kittson's attempt to make the Bear a stream draining to the Pacific. But the most important feature on Ogden's map was his "Unknown River," flowing west across the region west of Salt Lake to its terminus in "Unknown Lake." In 1828 Ogden had traveled down this stream to the "unknown" lake; the river would bear several names on subsequent maps— Mary's River and Ogden's River being the most common—but it was the Humboldt River, and the "Unknown Lake" into which it flowed was Humboldt Sinks. This was the first representation of the ephemeral streams of the Great Basin to appear on a map, and subsequent British (and some few American) maps would begin to improve on the earlier apocryphal drainage systems west of the continental divide by showing such fragmentary streams as Ogden's "Unknown River."

The firm of Arrowsmith utilized the information from the Hudson's Bay Company brigades on its great 1834 map of British North America that carried data from the explorations of Peter Skene Ogden in the "Snake Country." The 1834 Arrowsmith map removed the Multnomah as a continental stream, replacing it with a Willamette River that approximated reality in length and size of drainage basin. The proximal sources of the Snake, Yellowstone, and Big Horn (Wind River) were shown in a nearly correct geographical relationship with no hint of a great southerly extension of the Snake to near the headwaters of the Arkansas and Platte. In the area of the Great Basin, "Youta or Gt. Salt L." was shown (in a curious square shape); heading slightly to the west, there was a detached stream that was unconnected to any other drainage system and that probably represented the Humboldt (an interior drainage stream). Although Arrowsmith's geography was curiously distorted and disoriented (as was Ogden's view of the area south of the Snake), it did represent another step in clarifying the geographical riddle of the vast area between the Rockies and the Pacific. In spite of this increment to valid geographical lore, however, the Arrowsmith map still contained the apocryphal Buenaventura that had haunted maps for more than a half century. West of the Great Salt Lake the northern and southern branches of the Buenaventura had their heads and flowed west across the Great Basin to become the Sacramento River flowing into San Francisco Bay. That the Arrowsmith map and its European progeny continued to represent geography that was as fanciful as it was realistic is prime indication of the state of formal geographical lore before the American fur trade information began to appear on maps. The common source region for the Missouri, Columbia, Colorado, Rio Grande, and Arkansas continued to be featured—but the mythical Multnomah was no longer part of that imaginary geography. This was the major contribution to geographical knowledge of the Rocky Mountain system by the British fur trade in the interior, and it marked the beginning of an important transition in western cartography in that it represented the first serious erosion in the concept of the core drainage region within which *all* western streams had their sources.

Maps and Mountain Men, 1823–40

Between the years 1823 and 1840, the free trappers of the American Fur Company and other St. Louis fur companies carried out a great reconnaissance of the Rocky Mountains from Canada to Mexico and from the Missouri River to the shores of the Pacific. These free trappers have been characterized by William Goetzmann as "expectant capitalists,"[30] meaning they were discoverers who roamed new country for whatever they might find. Unlike their counterparts in the Santa Fe–Taos trade or in the Hudson's Bay Company brigades, these free trappers did not just define the West as a zone of concentrated resources, rich in beaver pelts. They also described the ways to get into the West, across the Rockies, to the Pacific—

and what is more important, they described what could be done with the land once it was settled by people other than trappers. They sought and found routes across the mountains and plains and deserts that could be used not only by the fur trade but by the Missouri farmer enticed by the word *Oregon* or the New York shopkeeper bound for the gold fields of California. It is impossible to offer even the briefest details of their extensive travels here. Suffice it to say that during this fifteen-year period of the free trappers' heyday, men like Jedediah Strong Smith, Joseph Walker, James Bridger, Kit Carson, Thomas Fitzpatrick, James Clyman, William Sublette, and countless and even nameless others "went about the blank spaces of the map like men going to the barn."[31] In doing so, they contributed immeasurably to the cartographic images of the Rocky Mountains. They drew few maps, and those that they drew were not always utilized immediately by the mapmakers in Boston and New York and Philadelphia—or, for that matter, in London or Paris. But their geographic information, informal as it was, became a staple of American lore of the West and the Rockies, and there were few significant maps produced after 1830—either in Europe or the United States—that did not contain at least some flavoring of the geographical data contributed by the mountain men.

The free-trapping system, in which trappers worked the streams and rivers of the plains and mountains for beaver and then met at a rendezvous in the mountains to exchange their winter's catch for equipment and supplies brought out from St. Louis, began in 1823 with the formation of the partnership between William Ashley and Andrew Henry which became the American Fur Company.[32] The system, with a number of different controlling St. Louis interests involved, continued until the final major rendezvous in 1839. While it lasted, major explorations took place: Etienne Provost's and Jim Bridger's discovery of Bear Lake and Great Salt Lake in 1824 (Bridger even thought he had reached an arm of the Pacific because of the brackishness of Salt Lake); Jedediah Smith's magnificent discoveries in the upper Green River valley, his traversing of routes between the Rockies and California, and his circumnavigation of the Great Basin, all during the years 1824–29; and Joseph Walker's pioneering of the Humboldt River route to California in 1833–34.[33] After the heyday of the fur trade was over, many of the mountain men became guides for emigrant wagon trains, for army explorers, or for scientists exploring the West. Others became merchants and established trading posts where they supplied travelers with geographical information as well as with dried beans and salt pork and coffee and calico. Both during and after the great reconnaissance of 1823–40, the mountain men contributed to the basic geographical knowledge of the Mountainous West.

It was nearly a decade after the beginnings of the free-trapping system before the potential accessibility of fur trader lore for cartographic scientists was converted into actual accessibility. A number of significant cartographic productions from both Europe and America in the decade of the 1830s continued to provide still fuzzy—if increasingly detailed—images of the American West. But many of the maps from both Europe and America would contain hints of fur trader information, and as the decade of the 1830s progressed, the trickle of fur trade data became a flood. The European cartographers who began to rely, even peripherally, upon the fur trade for their most current geographical information were led, as usual, by the houses of Brue in Paris and Arrowsmith in London. In 1833 and 1834, for example, two Brue maps were published that were among the first commercial cartographic productions in either Europe or the United States to be heavily dependent upon geographical information from the American fur trade in the Rockies and Plains. The 1833 Brue map carried the now familiar "R. Timpanogos" but made a new claim that it was the principal source water of the Multnomah. And although the Buenaventura was shown, it was a short stream flowing into "Gd. Lac Teguayo" (probably Utah Lake) south of Lake Timpanogos. The map also showed a "R. Ashley," named after William Ashley, that ran into the Colorado from the north. The upper part of this stream was labeled "Seeds Keeder," the name given the Green River by Jedediah Smith, although another nearby river carries the legend "probably the Seeds Keeder of Smith." The appearance of the names of Ashley and Smith, along with the removal of the apocryphal streams flowing across what would later come to be recognized as the Great Basin, is indication that American fur trade lore was beginning, by the early 1830s, to work its way onto maps. The evidence for this is even more clear on the 1834 Brue map that, in addition to the Ashley–Seeds Keeder and Timpanogos-Multnomah streams of its predecessor, showed the 1826 route of Smith from the Green River to San Diego. The 1834 map also clearly labeled one of the two great lakes west of the mountains as "Lac Sale" or Salt Lake. West of this lake no rivers were shown—even as dotted lines—flowing westward to the ocean. It is clear that Brue did not recognize the interior drainage system of the Great Basin (most of the rivers he showed in the region drained south to the Colorado or north to the Multnomah), but he did begin to clear up some of the most fanciful creations that had appeared and would continue to appear on other period maps.

The decade of the 1830s was also critical for American maps of the West. In the opening years of the decade relatively small and not terribly innovative maps characterized the efforts of American cartographers. By 1836, however, a real watershed in American cartography of the West had been reached; in that year there appeared two important maps that established the cartographic precedents for the remainder of the decade and that provided clear examples of the state of American public images of the West prior to the official explorations of John Frémont and others in the 1840s. The first of these maps was the map published in 1836 by Albert Gallatin. A man with a long history of public service and "one of the great savants of his time,"[34] Gallatin had also played a major role in gathering the geographical data which Nicholas King used to complete his 1803 map over three decades before. Gallatin's 1836 map, entitled "Map of the Indian Tribes of North America . . . ," was designed to accompany his "Synopsis of the Indian Tribes . . ." published under the auspices of the American Antiquarian Society[35] and was thus symbolic of the mainstream of American literary opinion. Most of Gallatin's map, like other period maps, was drawn from the traditional formal sources of Lewis and Clark and Pike for the area east of the Rocky Mountains. Gallatin did, however, show "Lorimier's Peak" or Laramie Peak and an unnamed Laramie River in the vicinity of the North Platte, information that only could have come from the fur trade, just then becoming active on the North Platte drainage. And in the Snake-Yellowstone core drainage area, Gallatin showed the trappers' "3 Peaks" of the Tetons although his view of the complex drainage systems of the area was still more primitive than was actual fur trapper lore.

Gallatin left most of the region west of the continental divide blank. Significantly, however, he did show two rivers originating in the mountains east of Great Salt Lake which flowed south to join and become the Colorado. These were clearly the Green and Grand Rivers and represented one of the first instances of the inclusion of Jedediah's Smith's geography in American mapping. The Green River heads in the Wind River Range of west-central Wyoming and flows south to become the Colorado. Near Grand Junction, Colorado, the Green is joined by the river now called the Colorado but known to the trappers as the Grand, with its head in the Colorado Rockies—nearly four hundred miles south of the headwaters of the Green River. Smith's geographical image, and by extension Gallatin's, now recognized (and presented for the first time on a map) the two source areas of western rivers in the Rocky Mountains: the northern source region of Wyoming which gives rise to the Snake, Yellowstone, Big Horn, and

Green, and the southern source region of Colorado from which flow the Grand, Rio Grande, Platte, and the Arkansas. Between the two source areas lie the South Pass, the Continental Divide Basin, and the divide itself. None of this geography (other than the accurate distinction between the Green and Grand branches of the Colorado River) appeared on Gallatin's map; but it was hinted at, which is enough to assume that Gallatin probably had this complex geography reasonably well figured out. Certainly Jedediah Smith (and hundreds of other mountain men) had done so.

Gallatin's map also showed a line connecting the Colorado and the Pacific coast—but this line was not an apocryphal stream. Rather, it was labeled "J. S. Smith's route 1826." Farther north on the map, east of the Sacramento River (which carries the appellation of "Buenaventura") was another dotted line with the caption "J. S. Smith's route 1827." Between these two representations of Smith's trek across the Great Basin appeared the words "Great Sandy Desert," along with rivers that represented the modern Sevier, Beaver, Virgin, and Mojave Rivers. It is not known how Gallatin came by information from Smith's travels, but in the final analysis it is unimportant. His map represented the beginning of a new geography, one that did not contain large quantities of apocryphal features, but showed only features that had been observed by responsible and aware observers such as Smith. In a very real sense, the Gallatin map was just as important for what it did not show as it is for what it did show.

The second important American map of 1836, and one that also showed evidence of the growing familiarity of American cartographers with lore from the fur trade, was Henry Tanner's large map of North America, published in his New Universal Atlas.[36] In most respects, Tanner's map was very similar to Gallatin's, providing further evidence that both cartographers had relied on a common body of knowledge, probably obtained from Jedediah Smith. There were some differences between Tanner's map and Gallatin's, however, and these differences are intriguing. Tanner, for example, did a much less credible job than Gallatin in showing the Green River, placing the source of that stream farther south than Gallatin's approximately correct location. Nor did Tanner show the Laramie Peak and Laramie River geography on the North Platte, although he showed, as Gallatin had not, both Longs Peak and James (Pikes) Peak in the vicinity of the South Platte. South of Pikes Peak, in the area that Gallatin had labeled as part of the Rocky Mountains, Tanner used the term "Mts. of Anahuac," a trappers' nomenclature that would become increasingly common for the southern Rockies during the next few years. For the region drained by the

Snake River, Tanner's view was much more precise than that of Gallatin, including showing the southern branch of the Snake (the Snake proper) heading into "Snow L." or Jackson Lake, the first time this feature had appeared on any published map. Tanner also presented considerably more detail—and generally accurate detail—on the tributary streams of the Snake. For the areas south of the Snake Basin, the region of the Great Basin, Tanner's map was very similar to that of Gallatin, although Tanner used the term "Sandy Plains" rather than Gallatin's "Great Sandy Desert." Tanner also showed a small "Utau L." south of the Great Salt Lake, an important clarification of those two bodies of water that were combined into one lake on most period maps. Finally, Tanner correctly located, as did Gallatin, the Bear River and its associated (and unnamed) lake to the north of Salt Lake. Viewed together, despite their relatively unimportant differences, the Tanner and Gallatin maps were remarkable cartographic achievements and were indicative of the growing importance and volume of fur trade lore.

Of even greater importance than the 1836 maps of Gallatin and Tanner, largely because of their wide circulation, were those maps published with Washington Irving's *The Rocky Mountains* (1837).[37] This book was widely read and was certainly among the most important literary sources for images of the Rockies and the West prior to Frémont.[38] The two maps from Irving's work were derived from information provided by the travels of Benjamin Bonneville, a West Point graduate and officer in the U.S. Army who was on "detached duty" to engage in fur trade activities in the mid-1830s (it has long been assumed that his real role was to "spy" on the British fur trade west of the Rockies). The first of these maps was of a relatively small area, although carrying the elegant and grandiose title "A Map of the Sources of the COLORADO & BIG SALT LAKE, PLATTE, YELLOWSTONE, MUSCLE-SHELL, MISSOURI; & SALMON & SNAKE RIVERS, branches of the COLUMBIA RIVER" (figure 4). As convoluted as that title might be, it is an apt description for a map that was the first detailed and accurate representation of the northernmost of what fur trappers had learned were the *two* core drainage regions of the Rockies. Lying symbolically in the exact center of the map, near the northern end of the Wind River Range, is the complex and interlocking drainage system that gives rise to the Yellowstone, Wind, Green, and Snake Rivers. Surrounding that core drainage region are the peripheral areas, also shown in considerable and accurate detail: the Big Horn Basin with its mountain ring surrounding it; the southern end of the Wind River Range and the (unnamed) South Pass between the Sweetwater

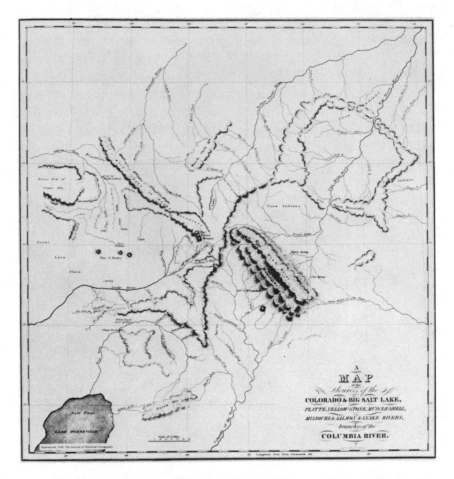

4. *A Map of the Sources of the Colorado & Big Salt Lake. . . . Benjamin Bonneville, 1837. (Courtesy Institute of Historical Cartography.)*

branch of the Platte and the Big Sandy fork of the Green; the Uinta Range and the Bear River draining into the Great Salt Lake or "Lake Bonneville"; the course of the Snake across the "Great Lava Plain" with "The 3 Butes" to the north; the course of the Lemhi and Salmon Rivers across the divide from the westernmost stretch of the upper Missouri system; and the Yellowstone River flowing from its lake a short distance north of Jackson's Hole and the headwaters of the Snake. Only the members of the fur trade had the geographical awareness that could allow this precise a picture of the most complex river and mountain system that exists on the continent.

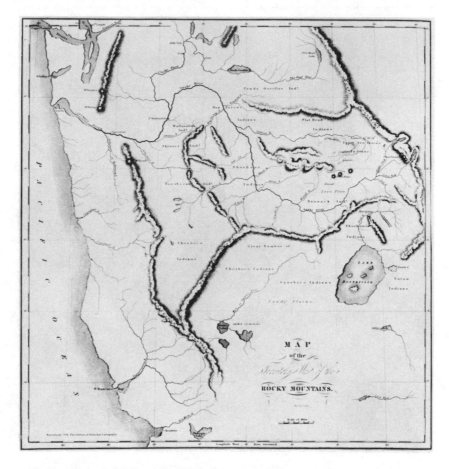

5. *A Map of the Country West of the Rocky Mountains. . . . Benjamin Bonneville, 1837. (Courtesy Institute of Historical Cartography.)*

Even more support for the inclusion of fur trade lore in popular geographical knowledge can be found in the second of the two great maps accompanying Irving's *The Rocky Mountains*. This map (figure 5) illustrated the geography of the country between the northern core drainage region and the Pacific north of the thirty-eighth parallel. On the far eastern verge of the map, where the first map left off, was the "Lake Bonneville" version of Great Salt Lake with its associated Utah Lake, although that lake was shown east rather than south of the Salt Lake. The Snake River and its major tributaries were shown with remarkable accuracy, as were the Willamette entering the Columbia from the south and the Umpqua and the Clamet flowing from the Cascades to the Pacific. The course of the Humboldt ("Mary or Ogden's River") flowing southwest from the area just west of Salt Lake to its terminus east of the Sierra Nevada was depicted with considerable clarity, and in the Humboldt's terminal region there appeared the large freshwater lakes of the Sierra's eastern front. To the west, the Sacramento and San Joaquin Rivers were shown properly penned up by the Sierra to their east, and there was not a hint of any major stream such as the Buenaventura or Timpanogos draining the area east of the Sierra and west of the Rockies. Indeed, there appeared on this map only one geographical feature that was not closely approximated by reality. Linking the westernmost outliers of the Rockies with the Sierra and lying north of Salt Lake and the Humboldt was a great linear range of mountains bearing the legend "Perpetual Snows." This was the imaginary Snowy Range, a fixture in most geographical images of the time and a forgivable error until Frémont's travels defined the nature of the basin and range country of the Intermountain West. As was its companion map, this great map was nearly totally dependent upon fur trader lore, and in the face of the evidence of these maps, it is simply wrong to say, as many have, that the geographical lore of the fur trade did not enter formal American geographical knowledge until Frémont or later.

Just as the maps contributed by Bonneville's geographical information and published in Irving's popular histories confirmed the presence of fur trade lore in the store of common geographical knowledge, so did two maps produced in 1839, at the very end of the free-trapping system. Neither of these maps was produced for public consumption, like those in Irving's works, but both had wide circulation among government circles and could be considered "official maps" and, therefore, part of the body of formal geographical knowledge on the Rockies at the end of the fur trade's heyday.

The first of these two final maps was produced by Captain Washington Hood of the U.S. Army Corps of Topographical Engineers. Hood had obtained fur trade data from "frequent conversations with two highly intelligent trappers, William A. Walker, of Virginia, and Mr. Coates, of Missouri, who belonged originally to Captain Bonneville's party, but subsequently continued to roam the mountains as free trappers for six consecutive years; as also that derived from others who were connected with [fur trade] surveys and expeditions as far to the westward as Santa Fe and Taos."[39] Utilizing this information from the fur trade, he drew the map "exhibiting the practicable passes of the Rocky Mountains," which his superior, Chief of the Topographical Engineers Colonel J. J. Abert, called "far more correct than [any] other extant."[40] This map existed only in manuscript form, but given its origins in the army's Topographical Bureau, it must have been known to a fairly wide segment of the establishment in Washington. On this map, which extends only from the forty-ninth parallel to Great Salt Lake and from the Powder River to the Salmon, Hood laid down routes across the Rockies considered the "most practicable" for wheeled vehicles—essentially the routes used by the fur trappers to cross the mountains. This statement represents not only a validation of the presence of mountain man lore in formal geography but of the continuing American faith in the belief that the Rockies posed no impenetrable barrier to transcontinental travel.

The second map of 1839 which demonstrated the connection between informal fur trade and the formal, "official" geographical images of the West was that produced by David Burr, "Geographer to the House of Representatives."[41] Burr's map was apparently produced from a Jedediah Smith manuscript map, and the West drawn by Burr in 1839 was the West of Jedediah Smith, the most widely traveled of the members of the American fur trade. Smith's routes back and forth across the vast expanse between the Rockies and the Pacific and from the Columbia to Mexico are clearly marked on Burr's map. Most significantly, the Burr map showed the two core drainage regions—the northern one in which the Snake, Missouri, Yellowstone, and Green Rivers head, and the southern one from which rise the source streams of the Platte, Rio Grande, Arkansas, and Colorado or Grand—along with a clear definition of a true continental divide. The correct courses of western rivers were depicted on Burr's map, as was the accurate configuration of the various ranges of the Rocky Mountains which defined the drainage basins of those rivers. Numerous small legends on the map passed along descriptive information on the complex geography of the Rocky Mountain system which could only have come from Smith or some other equally well-informed mountain man of the American fur trade.

The Cartographic Legacy

It cannot be known just what the impact of the geographical lore of the American fur trade would have been upon the cartography of western

North America had that information been accessible immediately and had maps such as Burr's been published a decade earlier, when the information was first available, or had some of the other maps drawn by fur trappers become as convenient to American geographers and cartographers as Smith's data were to Burr. It is conceivable that the mythical western rivers such as the Multnomah and Buenaventura and the single core drainage area of William Clark would have disappeared from the American geographical image much more quickly than they did. It is also possible that had the early discovery of South Pass been fully recognized for what it was, the image of the Rockies as an avenue to the Pacific rather than a barrier would have been strengthened. The fact remains that the masterful maps (mental or otherwise) produced by trappers were not readily accessible to commercial mapmakers. But, in at least some form, they had to be obtainable by some members of the cartographic community by the late 1830s and early 1840s, and as they became available, they began to make an impact on the cartographic image of the American West. Although the impact of fur trade lore was quickly submerged by the documented and widely available maps and accounts of the Frémont expeditions, the fact that geographical data from the American fur trade played a major role in the formation of images of the Rocky Mountains before the resumption of formal exploration in the 1840s can no longer be denied. As they exploited the zone of concentrated resources which the Rockies and adjacent areas represented, the members of the fur trade contributed immeasurably to the American view of the Rocky Mountain system, not as a barrier, but as a gateway to the Pacific.

Notes

1. Cf. Bernard DeVoto, *Across the Wide Missouri* (Boston: Houghton Mifflin, 1947), 1–6; and William H. Goetzmann, *Exploration and Empire: The Explorer and Scientist in the Winning of the American West* (New York: Alfred A. Knopf, 1966), 78.

2. John L. Allen, "An Analysis of the Exploratory Process: The Lewis and Clark Expedition of 1804–06," *Geographical Review* 62 (1972): 13–39.

3. DeVoto, *Across the Wide Missouri*, 3.

4. Carl I. Wheat, *Mapping the Trans-Mississippi West, 1540–1861*, 5 vols. (San Francisco: Institute for Historical Cartography, 1957–63).

5. Hiram M. Chittenden, *The American Fur Trade of the Far West*, 3 vols. (New York:

1902; reprint, 2 vols., Lincoln: University of Nebraska Press, 1986); Paul C. Phillips, *The Fur Trade* (Norman: University of Oklahoma Press, 1961).

6. John L. Allen, *Passage through the Garden: Lewis and Clark and the Image of the American Northwest* (Urbana: University of Illinois Press, 1975), 74–80, 98–105, and passim.

7. Allen, *Passage through the Garden*, 38–45.

8. Allen, *Passage through the Garden*, 97–108.

9. John L. Allen, "To Unite the Discoveries: The American Response to the Early Exploration of Rupert's Land," in *Rupert's Land: A Cultural Tapestry,* ed. Richard C. Davis (Waterloo, Ontario: Wilfred Laurier University Press, 1988), 79–86.

10. John L. Allen, "Division of the Waters: Changing Concepts of the Continental Divide, 1804–44," *Journal of Historical Geography* 4 (1978): 358–59; Allen, "Pyramidal Height-of-Land: A Persistent Myth in the Exploration of Western Anglo-America, " *International Geography* 1 (1972): 395–96.

11. "Jefferson's Instructions to Lewis, June 20, 1803," in Donald Jackson, ed., *Letters of the Lewis and Clark Expedition with Related Documents, 1783–1854* (Urbana: University of Illinois Press, 1962), 61.

12. Nicholas Biddle, ed., *History of the Expedition under the Command of Captains Lewis and Clark . . .*, 2 vols. (Philadelphia: Bradford and Inskeep, 1814).

13. Bernard DeVoto, *Course of Empire* (Boston: Houghton Mifflin, 1952), 491; Allen, *Passage through the Garden*, 363.

14. Burton Harris, *John Colter: His Years in the Rockies* (New York: Scribners and Sons, 1952), chaps. 4 and 5.

15. Richard E. Oglesby, *Manuel Lisa and the Opening of the Missouri Fur Trade* (Norman: University of Oklahoma Press, 1963).

16. M. O. Skarsten, *George Drouillard, Hunter and Interpreter* (Glendale, Calif.: Arthur H. Clark, 1964), 260–70.

17. Allen, *Passage through the Garden*, 379, note 61.

18. Goetzmann, *Exploration and Empire*, 25.

19. Allen, "Division of the Waters," 361; James P. Ronda, *Astoria and Empire* (Lincoln: University of Nebraska Press, 1990).

20. Phillip A. Rollins, ed., *The Discovery of the Oregon Trail: Robert Stuart's Narrative of His Overland Trip Eastward from Astoria in 1812–1813* (New York: Edward Eberstadt, 1935).

21. Rollins, *Discovery of the Oregon Trail.*

22. *Missouri Gazette* (St. Louis), 15 May 1813; Allen, "Division of the Waters," 361.

23. Goetzmann, *Exploration and Empire*, chap. 2.

24. *Niles Weekly Register* (Baltimore), 9 November 1816, sec. 2, 164; see also Wheat, *Mapping the Trans-Mississippi West*, 2:63–64.

25. Thomas Jefferson, cited in Wheat, *Mapping the Trans-Mississippi West*, 2:64.

26. Wheat, *Mapping the Trans-Mississippi West*, 2:117–18.

27. J. B. Tyrrell, ed., *David Thompson's Narrative of His Travels in Western America, 1784–1812* (Toronto: Champlain Society, 1916).

28. Wheat, *Mapping the Trans-Mississippi West*, vol. 2, map no. 329.

29. E. E. Rich, ed., *Peter Skene Ogden's Snake Country Journals*, 5 vols. (London: Hudson's Bay Record Society, 1950–61).

30. William H. Goetzmann, "The Mountain Man as Jacksonian Man," *American Quarterly*, 15 (1963): 402–15.

31. DeVoto, *Across the Wide Missouri*, 5.

32. Harrison Clifford Dale, *The Ashley-Smith Explorations and the Discovery of a Central Route to the Pacific* (Glendale, Calif.: Arthur H. Clark, 1941); Dale L. Morgan, *The West of William Ashley* (Denver: Old West, 1964).

33. Dale L. Morgan, *Jedediah Smith and the Opening of the American West* (Lincoln: University of Nebraska Press, 1953); Charles L. Camp, "Jedediah Smith's First Far-Western Exploration," *Western Historical Quarterly* 4 (1973): 151–70; George R. Brooks, ed., *The Southwest Expedition of Jedediah S. Smith* (Glendale, Calif.: Arthur H. Clark, 1977); Harvey L. Carter, "Jedediah Smith," in *The Mountain Men and the Fur Trade of the Far West*, ed. LeRoy R. Hafen, 10 vols. (Glendale, Calif.: Arthur H. Clark, 1971), 8:331–48; Maurice S. Sullivan, ed., *The Travels of Jedediah Smith* (Santa Ana, Calif.: Fine Arts Press, 1934).

34. Wheat, *Mapping the Trans-Mississippi West*, 2:151.

35. Albert Gallatin, "Synopsis of the Indian Tribes. . . ," *Transactions* (American Antiquarian Society) 2 (1836).

36. Wheat, *Mapping the Trans-Mississippi West*, vol. 2, map no. 422.

37. Washington Irving, *The Adventures of Captain Bonneville* (Norman: University of Oklahoma Press, 1962); originally published as *The Rocky Mountains; or, Scenes, Incidents, and Adventures in the Far West* (Philadelphia, 1837).

38. John L. Allen, "Horizons of the Sublime: The Invention of the Romantic West," *Journal of Historical Geography* 18 (1992).

39. Gouverneur K. Warren, *Memoir to Accompany the Map of the Territory of the United States from the Mississippi to the Pacific Ocean . . .* , 33rd Cong., 2d sess., 1859, Sen. Exec. Doc. 78, 19.

40. J. J. Abert, "Practicable Route for Wheeled Vehicles across the Rocky Mountains," Missouri Historical Society, St. Louis, n.d., manuscript.

41. Wheat, *Mapping the Trans-Mississippi West*, 2:169, map no. 441.

3 / "A Country of Tremendous Mountains": Opening the Colorado San Juans, 1870–1910

DUANE A. SMITH

The rugged, majestic Colorado San Juan Mountains have inspired awe for well over a century (figure 1). Frederic Endlich, geologist in charge for the 1874 Hayden survey, wrote after his late summer visit:

> As a rule, the character of the country is very mountainous, with numerous high and rugged peaks studding the mountain groups. . . . Numerous points of great beauty in detail can be noticed throughout the mountain regions just mentioned. . . . Rugged and steep is the character of the mountain-sides, while numerous subsidences produced amphitheaters, with perpendicular walls, sometimes of considerable extent. . . . Many points of importance must have escaped notice, because of the rugged character of the country is such that much may be hidden to the eye of one who cannot command over an almost unlimited amount of time.[1]

Crowned by thirteen 14,000-foot peaks and a mighty host of those over 13,000 feet, cut by deep canyons and framed by beautiful mountain valleys, the San Juans were, and are, everything that Endlich described (figure 2). They are among Colorado's highest and most spectacular mountain ranges.

A Magnificent Barrier

Initial visitors were awed, while many early prospectors and miners were appalled as they first gazed upon the San Juans. John P. Jones, a California and Comstock mining man and U.S. senator from Nevada, visited the San

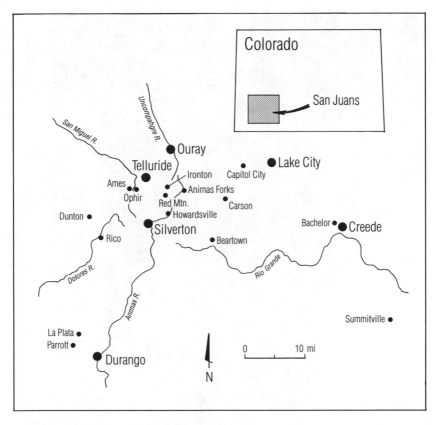

1. Colorado's San Juan Mountains Place-Names.

Juans in 1879 to investigate some mining prospects. He wrote his wife on 6 August from high, isolated Animas Forks: "This place must be the back-bone of the world. So rugged a country, such tremendous mountains, such awful trails I never saw." He went on to say that there was no wagon road to Animas Forks nor a telegraph line, and "no telegraph station within 150 miles. So far as news from the outside world is concerned I might as well be in Africa." Yet Jones appreciated what he saw: "The country we have passed over and the scenery spreading out on every hand all day has been magnificent and grand beyond my powers of description, far surpassing anything I ever saw in the Sierras."[2]

The San Juans represented a challenge which Rossiter Raymond, U.S. commissioner of mining statistics, well understood when he wrote in his 1874 report: "Being located so many hundred miles away from the rest of

2. *Arrastra Gulch near Silverton in 1874. This W. H. Jackson view clearly illustrates the challenges faced by San Juaners. (Courtesy U. S. Geological Survey.)*

the world, and lying under the many disadvantages caused by hard winters and almost impassable mountain barriers, the San Juan mines have as
yet no market for ores."[3]

Raymond in that one sentence described the three main problems facing anyone wishing to settle or develop property in the San Juans—their
regional isolation, the unpredictable climate, and the ruggedness of the
mountains themselves. Each of these factors had to be carefully considered
if would-be San Juaners hoped to make this their home. Of the three, isolation would prove to be the easiest to resolve, but for the other two factors
there was little that the individual could do, except try to adapt. As one
Swedish miner reportedly mumbled as he "went down the hill" looking for
another mine, he did not care to work in a district where "there were three
months of mighty late fall and nine months of winter." The passing of the
years did not ease the toll taken by winter weather. The *Engineering and
Mining Record* reported, for example, that snow hindered mining in 1901,
1902, 1905, 1906, and 1909. Indeed, as a mountainous barrier the San Juans
were unsurpassed in Colorado, and their ruggedness delayed settlement,
hindered the progress of transportation, shaped urban development, and
handicapped mining.

Long before the coming of the Europeans, the Utes had called this land
home, hunting in the mountains, camping in the valleys, and enjoying the
hot springs for their curative powers. Then eighteenth-century Spaniards
marched out of New Mexico looking for gold and silver. But the Spanish
did not stay because the region was too isolated, the Utes too threatening,
and the environment too hostile for them in the waning days of their colonial empire. They left behind only names—La Plata, Rio de las Animas,
and San Juans. They also contributed a multitude of lost mine stories to
tempt those who came after them. A generation into the nineteenth century found the fur trapper walking the rivers, trapping beaver, but no permanent settlement resulted. Indeed, with the waning of the fur trade, the
San Juans returned by the 1840s to their mountainous seclusion, and the
Utes retained their land for a few more decades.

A turning point in San Juan history happened far to the east near the future site of Denver when gold was discovered by the Russell Party in 1858.
The resulting Pikes Peak gold rush of 1859 brought prospectors scurrying
through the mountains, and in 1860 Charles Baker ventured into the heart
of the San Juans, into what is now Baker's Park, where Silverton sits (figure
3). Baker proved more than a miner: he was a promoter. Almost single-
handedly he created the excitement which led to the first mining rush into

3. Part of the Animas Canyon and Baker's Park as They Appeared in 1874. (Courtesy U.S. Geological Survey. Photo by W. H. Jackson.)

the region: "In these mountains, on the waters of the Rio de los Animos [*sic*] are the gold mines discovered by myself and party in August last. They are extensive gulches and bar diggings, and I believe them to be richer than any mines hitherto discovered to the North-East of them."[4] In spite of the objections of *Rocky Mountain News* editor William Byers, who termed the rush "a hasty, rash and ill-advised venture," the late spring of 1861 found prospectors converging onto the San Juans from far away Canon City, Colorado, and Abiquiu, New Mexico.[5]

Despite the gold rushers' optimism that they had discovered another California, Byers's pessimism proved nearer to the truth. The 1861 rush to the San Juans failed, and by the end of the summer the miners had gone. The gold fever had failed to pan out for a variety of reasons, the overriding one being a lack of rich diggings. This district did not abound in placer deposits. Even if the placers had proved lucrative, the very isolation of the region, plus the inhospitable nature of the San Juans and their changeable weather, boded ill for success when the nearest supply points were hundreds of miles away. Nor had the Utes been receptive to this rush into their long-held land.

Miners abandoned the San Juans, but their hopes were not dashed. Rumors still persisted of lost mines and mother lode gold deposits. Indeed, their implicit faith in finding profitable deposits in such a mountain zone would bring them back. Nearly a decade went by before prospectors returned, coming first up the Dolores River valley in 1869 and then into Baker's Park by the following year. Because of Ute objections to these incursions into their land, William Arny, special agent for the Indian Service, visited the area that May. He reported that some miners had been ordered off by the Indians and left; most stayed, and 274 gold and silver claims had been located.[6]

This time the miners had come to stay, although for a couple of years prospecting and mining were carried on seasonally, with abandonment coming as winter returned. One of the first results was protests by both the miners and Utes, trapping the federal government between irate prospectors who wanted access to precious metals and treaty agreements which protected Indian rights. The taxpayers won out. In 1873 the Brunot Agreement was signed, and the Utes gave up territory in the San Juans from the future site of Durango to Ouray.

With the land title cleared, promising discoveries were made, and permanent settlement came to the region. The struggle between settler and this mountainous environment now took a new turn. The battle would be carried forward on several fronts, and the San Juaners would have to "match the mountains," and their isolation, if they planned to stay and prosper.

Early Promotion

Development and settlement came to the San Juans for one reason only: the mineral resources were highly attractive to exploitation. A concentrated resource, such as precious metals, could exert a tremendous force on settling even an isolated region like the San Juans. Gold had provided the initial lure, though silver soon came to the forefront in the 1870s. Eventually this mineral treasure box would yield copper, lead, zinc, tungsten, molybdenum, coal, and uranium. Excitement soared from the very first, and despite the problems of opening an isolated, new district, enthusiasm seldom wavered. The respected *Engineering and Mining Journal* of New York published an editorial 5 May 1877 on "The San Juan Mines." The writer concluded, "In a word, the San Juan is an undoubted success. Its mines are not myths, nor its rich ore solely of the imagination." Colorado mining reporter Frank Fossett described the huge size and "great richness" of the gold and silver lodes in this area of some 15,000 square miles, larger than several eastern states. For him, and other Coloradans, the future appeared only bright.

Such predictions continued. For example, in the early 1880s a reporter for the *Denver Tribune* was moved to say: "we venture to predict that within a short period of time, it [the San Juans] will rank with the leading mining regions of the country in production and reserves." Finally, an 1890 article claimed the district had "never before looked as promising as at the present time."[7]

Glorious predictions were fine; however, for the San Juaners it would take more than that to develop what Frank Fossett also called "terra incognita." Starting in the 1870s, vigorous promotional efforts were undertaken, paralleling what other western and Colorado districts had tried or were doing. E. M. Hamilton published a pamphlet in 1874 describing the region, its mines, and routes to reach the area from Denver. Hamilton based his observations on personal experience, which lent credibility to his comments. An "excellent" map was issued the next year as the San Juaners worked to overcome their geographic isolation. This was followed by exhibits at the Territorial Fair, later at the State Fair, and at the nation's Centennial Exposition in 1876 at Philadelphia. Then the Kansas Pacific Railroad, which had reached Denver in 1870, published two pamphlets promoting the San Juans and providing readers with such interesting tidbits as what to take, how to make money mining, and how to file a claim.

San Juaners themselves contributed their share of information by writing and sending articles to newspapers, some as far away as the *New York Times*. Mayor C. H. McIntyre of Ouray traveled to New York in 1879 to address the Bullion Club on the mines of Ouray and San Juan Counties. Once local newspapers were established, they issued a steady stream of promotional articles and news items. As the *Ouray Times* (11 August 1877) correctly pointed out, "we need men of capital to build roads, put up mills and develop mines." The editor urged "our people" to make the effort to "make known to investors the rare opportunities of our country."[8]

In the following decades the San Juaners continued their advertising and promotion. Unluckily for them, Leadville stole their thunder in 1878–79 when it burst on the scene. The more isolated, undeveloped, and less newsworthy San Juans took a back seat to this new silver queen. Regrouping, the San Juaners pushed ahead and were just making good headway in the mid-1880s when Aspen's silver mines opened. The district remained on the sidelines until the 1890s, when everything critical for success fell into place. Finally, after twenty years, the San Juans came into their own.

A Regional Road Network

Promotion helped overcome the isolation to a degree and certainly made the San Juans and their potential better known to the outside world. The mountains continued as a barrier to interaction, however, and that matter had to be resolved as quickly as possible. Without an adequate transportation system, it would be difficult to ship ore to smelters, bring in needed equipment, reduce the cost of living, or entice investors to come.

Deep canyons, high passes (10,600 to over 13,000 feet), and steep mountainsides were just the beginning of the problems (figure 4). Except for the small farming/ranching community of Animas City fifty miles south of Silverton on the Animas River, other support communities were considerable distances over roads that might better have been described as trails. Nor were the San Juans initially attractive enough to excite the railroads to come the distance from Denver or Pueblo to tap the mines. Writers such as Rossiter Raymond believed that the principal problems facing the San

4. *Smuggler-Union Mine above Telluride. The photo shows how miners had to adapt to the San Juan terrain. (Courtesy Forest Service, National Archives, no. 95-G-19264A. Photo by H. Wheeler.)*

Juans were the inaccessibility of the country and the lack of capital in the region available for investment.

There were two initial gateways to the San Juans. One was a round-about route which took the wayfarer via New Mexico and finally north via the Animas Valley into Baker's Park. As Cathy Kindquist's chapter reveals in detail, this southern route was superseded by another from the east by way of the Del Norte and the Rio Grande drainage over well-named Stony Pass. Either way remained time-consuming and seasonal. When winter came, travel in and out of the San Juans nearly drew to a close for all but determined individuals willing to risk the weather and elevation.

The intradistrict trails were no better, providing tribulations to man and beast. Early day miner Rasmus Hanson testified during a trial that in 1876 the trail from Mineral Point to Ouray, which went along "a very precipitous cliff," was such that a man risked his life on it. It was not safe to ride a horse over the trail, and when slippery, it was "unsafe to walk over." San Juaners were acutely aware of their transportation problems. Lake City to the northeast eventually would provide a third gateway into the district via Engineer and Cinnamon Passes. Its newspaper, the *Silver World*, advocated employing "special energies" to open "communication with more distant and inaccessible camps by good wagon roads."[9] San Juaners throughout the district concurred and quickly set about to create a road system to replace the early trails, while they dreamed about something even better—railroad connections.

Initially, footpaths and trails climbed from valleys into the mountains; narrow and dangerous, they were not sufficient. Pack animals were the only reliable means of transporting goods, a slow, costly arrangement. The *Rocky Mountain News* (22 August 1876) pointed out the obvious: "Just as soon as a good wagon road is opened," new life would be infused into the entire Animas region. Until such time "development of the country must of necessity be slow." Early efforts focused on building the best possible roads to the San Juans. Thereafter, miners could concentrate on the more difficult problem of the mountainous terrain. The new counties of La Plata, San Juan, Hinsdale, and Ouray, created between 1874 and 1877, did not have the finances to underwrite the road construction. As a result, private enterprise stepped in. Toll roads were built, with the peak years being 1875–80. The idea of private road construction became so popular that far more companies were organized and planned roads than ever graded a foot of road.

San Juaners worked hard to develop a road system, but the mountainous terrain, harsh climate, and counties' lack of finances hindered maintenance and construction. It did not slow down complaints. For example, outspoken Ouray editor Dave Day wrote in his *Solid Muldoon* (13 April 1883) that the "wagon? road from Silverton to Chattanooga is pronounced by the Denver drummer to be dangerous even for pedestrians." Even Otto Mears, the famous San Juan toll road builder, was not above criticism. The *Animas Forks Pioneer* (21 February 1885) complained about his "outrageous prices," his "highway robbery prices" on the Ouray-to-Red Mountain road.

Such complaints concerning the high charges and poor maintenance eventually encouraged the counties to take over most of the toll roads. The transportation network slowly improved. Roads over the passes reached the young mining communities and from there fanned out throughout the district. One especially vital road went from Silverton south some fifty miles down the Animas River to tap the agricultural part of the valley. Here

little Animas City sat surrounded by farms and ranches; soon farm products were being freighted into the mountains, a welcome development.
However, as new camps and districts, such as Rico and Telluride, were
opened on the western edge of the San Juans in the late 1870s and early
1880s, those residents found themselves even more isolated and behind
the rest of the region in their transportation system. It would take them a
while to catch up, and meanwhile they had to go through the same problems that their neighbors had experienced earlier.

The major mining towns and camps soon fell to fighting among themselves to dominate the transportation networks in order to funnel trade
and business their way. As early as 1876, Silverton and neighboring Howardsville squared off, with the latter calling a meeting to discuss road construction. Silverton boycotted the meeting and refused to pay its share of
the construction bonds that had been approved. Urban rivalries superseded even the vital matter of road construction.[10]

For all its faults, and oftentimes seasonal use, a road system was developed that connected the urban communities with the nearby mines and
with each other. The roads climbed the valleys and rose up into the high
mountains, some even being good enough to be used by ore wagons during the summer months. The main roads uniting the major towns carried
the majority of the traffic, including regular stage runs and freighters bringing in supplies. An attempt was made to keep these open year around, but
snow and avalanches often closed them for days, sometimes weeks at a
time. While transportation had improved with these early roads, the ultimate answer had not been achieved.

The Significance of the Railroad

Fundamental changes would come with the railroad. It could conquer distance, overcome isolation, and provide the fastest, most comfortable, year-
around transportation (figure 5). San Juaners and other westerners knew it
provided the answer to the region's isolation and fervently believed that
each and every district should have rail connections. The only remaining
question was how to secure this technology.

Only a fleeting moment after settlement had taken root, San Juaners began dreaming of a railroad. A writer who identified himself only as "Southwest" was convinced in December 1874 that "we of the southwest are to
have a railroad before a great lapse of time beyond doubt." Others agreed.

5. Train to Silverton. The problems of winter railroading are demonstrated as this train plows through mountain snow. (Author's collection.)

"That there will be a railroad in this country within two years, hardly anybody who knows anything about the matter doubts, the question being as to the line and direction," concluded the *Lake City Silver World* in September 1876. Three years later the young *Dolores News* believed "pioneers, prospectors and miners" had done their share, and now it was up to the railroads to come and "enhance their [the mines'] value."

Thomas Comstock, San Juan mining engineer and promoter, described what the railroad would do in practical terms. It would cut freight rates, which doubled or more during the winter season, "if indeed one were fortunate enough to secure transportation of goods at any figure." Comstock was correct. Of the three key factors in mining development—year-round transportation, abundant ore, and finances—the San Juaners possessed one and needed only the railroad to solve the other two. Investors would come, they believed, if transportation were only easier. Their assumptions proved correct; almost all of the hard-rock districts of the west reached their peak production in the years after the arrival of the railroad.

San Juaners unendingly dreamed about railroads. Where would be the best route? What railroad company would lay the rail? People even planned their own companies on paper. The problems of financing were staggering because it would be costly both to cross mainly unsettled territory to reach the San Juans and then to build into such a rugged mountainous region. Maintaining operation in the face of San Juan winters and elevations would be another problem. It would not be easy, but from the railroad's viewpoint, the San Juan mines and towns offered tempting profit potential.[11]

A railroad finally came. The Denver and Rio Grande proved to be a pioneer in reaching a number of southwestern Colorado mining districts. As early as 1875, its guiding genius and creator, William Jackson Palmer, had cast longing glances toward what he described as "more rich silver lodes" than had been discovered elsewhere in any western state or territory. San Juaners proved willing to be pursued, only to see the courtship languish temporarily because of Leadville's more glittering attractions, various railroad rivalries, and predictable financial difficulties. Palmer never lost his enthusiasm, and after winning a fight with the Atchison, Topeka and Santa Fe Railroad over access to Leadville, he wrote a friend, "Any peace that stops AT&SF at South Pueblo and gives us Leadville & San Juan, . . . will put D&RG on stock dividend paying basis." While he was a little too enthusiastic about profits, he did come to the San Juans.

Surveys were run in the fall of 1879. The La Plata Miner could not contain itself: "it is impossible to estimate the great advantage in every way the completion of this road will be to our camp." It would start a boom "for this country" that would not "cease growing for a hundred years to come." Meanwhile the railroad was not worrying about a "hundred years to come." The fledgling line had difficulties enough at the moment. Surveyors had to be lowered on ropes down the canyon walls to complete their work, as would railroad workers later when blasting out the now famous "high line" beyond Rockwood. Cold and snow also hampered the surveying, which continued into November.

By July 1881, the railroad had reached the D&RG-created town of Durango, and track-laying crews moved beyond toward Silverton. The tracks reached Rockwood before winter put an end to work for the season. Silverton could hardly wait. A Christmas Eve 1881 editorial in the La Plata Miner expressed the commonly held feeling that the railroad would demonstrate to the world that the San Juans had "more and richer mines" than any other "section of equal extent." Further, it would "give us facilities both for transportation and reduction," allowing the working of low-grade ore, "hitherto lain upon the dumps as not profitable to ship to market." Finally, the railroad would "create a revolution in our mining industry" and make Sil-

verton a "mining town second to none in the state." In July of 1882, the potential for all this came to pass when the first Denver and Rio Grande train
arrived, forty-five mountainous miles and five hours and twenty minutes
out of Durango.[12]

In the years that followed, the D&RG opened Colorado's Western Slope;
towns, farms, and ranches soon appeared to the north of the San Juans.
Then, after a respite, the Denver and Rio Grande, in 1887, added an extension from its main line at Montrose, traveling southward thirty-six miles
into Ouray. This was followed two years later with an extension into Lake
City and, finally, into Creede in 1892. The D&RG had tapped the San Juans
in four places, but it would not have a monopoly on the region's rail transportation. Erstwhile toll road builder Otto Mears built two short rail lines
out of Silverton to Red Mountain and Animas Forks. Another narrow-
gauge line ran to Gladstone; Silverton, with four railroads, had become the
"narrow gauge capital" of Colorado and perhaps the world.

Mears completed the major San Juan railroad construction with his Rio
Grande Southern line which ran northwestward from Durango to Rico and
Telluride before joining the D&RG at Ridgway. While it appeared that all of
these lines challenged the hold of the Denver and Rio Grande, none really
did because all were connected to it as feeder lines. The San Juans had become a private fief of Colorado's "baby railroad."[13]

While the blessings never reached the level anticipated by the *La Plata
Miner*, San Juaners greatly benefited from the coming of the railroad. Indeed, the railroads were the underpinning for the San Juan region to finally become one of Colorado's premier mining districts in the mid-1890s
and first decade of the twentieth century. Clearly the miners could see the
benefits brought by the railroads. The cost of fuel declined as coal was
hauled in from the new fields opened at Durango. With the establishment
of the D&RG-backed San Juan and New York smelter in the same community, a regional reduction works was nearby. The ease of bringing investors
to the region to examine mining properties could not be denied. San Juan
County's production jumped twelve times in its first decade of railroad
connections, and San Miguel's doubled; most amazing was Mineral County's
production, which vaulted six times in the first year. Freight rates for hauling equipment and the variety of goods that mining required dropped
from the days of the wagons and pack trains. The *Engineering and Mining
Record* (21 January 1892) had been right about railroads in general when it
forecast that the completion of the Rio Grande Southern would be of "vast

importance for the southwestern portion of Colorado." Of course, complaints also appeared. The *Silverton Weekly Miner* of 4 January 1890 scolded about the "great drawback to our young mines," the continued "high rate of freight exacted by the railroad."

The railroads, like the miners, faced a continuous struggle with nature. The "winter of the century" (1883–84), for example, blocked the Silverton line for seventy-three days; Telluride was isolated for a month in 1909 by a flood; and the "flood of the century" (1911) cost the Rio Grande Southern fifty miles of track and many bridges and stopped Durango-to-Silverton operations for nine weeks. Otto Mears had intended to operate in the winter with his Silverton and Silverton Northern lines, but generally he found the expense too great and the snow removal too difficult. The best of snow and rotary plows were no match for a San Juan snow slide.

The engineering skills and innovations that these rail lines had to devise and use became legendary. The Corkscrew Gulch turntable above Ironton, which allowed the Silverton Railroad to overcome the vexing problems of mountainside steepness and confined space, and the Ophir Loop, over which the Rio Grande Southern ran on a high curved bridge and then doubled back above itself in an almost "continuous series of trestles," are classic innovations. To adapt to the conditions faced in the San Juans took ingenuity and boldness. While the railroads never completely overcame the San Juans and nature, they did provide the best transportation available and allowed mining and settlement to gain a firmer hold.

The Barriers Challenged: Mining Technology

Miners also had to innovate to match the San Juan challenges. The greatest obstacles that they faced were the elevation, the isolation, and the fuel expenses. Winter weather not only shut down railroad operations; it nearly stopped the entire transportation system and without question raised expenses for all concerned. Isolated in their mines nestled among the peaks, miners worked as best they could. Long trails and pack trains tied them to the lower valleys and the rest of the world; blizzards and avalanches could isolate them for weeks, sometimes months, on end. Even the coming of the railroad did not help during the winter season unless some means could be found to easily reach the tracks year-round. The cost of wood and coal to heat and power operations severely cut into mine profits; managers and stockholders wished that something could be done. Fortunately, several answers appeared.

One solution was the construction of tramways (cables, supported by towers, carrying buckets) that stretched from mine to mill or railroad siding and that offered unmistakable advantages in year-round operation. San Juaners quickly perceived the benefits of trams and pioneered in their use. As the directors of the Cosmopolitan Mining Company happily told stockholders, their new tramway would allow work under all circumstances of weather, run constantly without rest, cross deep gorges, pass around precipitous cliffs, and travel down the most rugged mountains. Their joy could hardly be restrained when it was announced that their tram could also be "constructed and worked cheaper than any other system." Ouray's *Solid Muldoon* concurred in 1887, saying that tramways would "revolutionize" mining in "this section of the country."

The directors were not really overstating their case. With gravity's assistance, trams overcame geographic obstructions and lowered costs; full buckets coming down pulled empty ones back up. The freighter and burro could not compete. Trams could be constructed almost anywhere and could deliver timber, coal, supplies, and even miners to the mines. Swaying to and fro in a bucket, numbed by the cold wind, many a miner might have wondered if it would have been wiser to walk. Mining engineer and writer T. A. Rickard wrote about traveling by tram: "The aerial voyage was made speedily and safely, if not very comfortably." He thought it wise to use them in the winter and spring when the avalanche danger was high. By the early twentieth century, trams stretched around the mountainsides and across the valleys, some running several miles in length.[14]

Tramways solved one major transportation problem, although a snow slide tearing down tram towers left San Juaners with a mess to clean up and repair. Electricity solved yet another problem by reducing the high cost of fuel and light. The impact of mining on the timber resources had been immediate; lumbering came with the miners, and as the forests were depleted, costs rose. The expense of purchasing and hauling coal and wood to the high mountain mines actually stopped operation of some mines. The answer was at hand by the mid-1880s as America entered its electric age.

The San Juans offered an abundance of water, one definite asset in the production of electricity. Streams tumbled down mountainsides, awaiting only a generating plant to harness their potential. In 1890, the Virginius plant was the first to tap this capability with a system utilizing direct current. Within a few years, the *Engineering and Mining Journal* estimated that fuel savings "probably more than repays the cost of the plant every year." Utilizing DC electricity, however, presented some problems, including loss of power when transferred over long distances. In the San Juans this was an important matter, so an ambitious Telluride lawyer-turned-mining man, Lucien Nunn, considered alternating current as an option.

As manager of the Gold King Mine, perched over 12,000 feet in the mountains southwest of Telluride, Nunn saw his operation lose money because of the expense of freighting fuel. An AC system at Aspen, Colorado, transmitted high-voltage electricity more cheaply and easily than DC; that was enough evidence for Nunn, who visited the Westinghouse Electric Company in Pittsburgh to discuss possibilities and examine equipment. Nunn also recruited young college students with exceptional academic talents to work with him in a nineteenth-century version of a "think tank." Experiments followed, and finally construction started on the Ames Plant; in June 1891 the generator was revved up, and electric current raced to the mine and mill. The plant ran thirty days without stopping, proving the success of the idea, although rumor hinted that the operators were afraid to shut down for fear it might not start again. Once operations stabilized on a regular six-day basis, many locals came to watch the novelty of the often sparking, arcing, smoking fireworks that accompanied the machinery's start on Sunday evening.

Nunn's experiment had worked, and he proved to be a real pioneer. His fellow San Juaners soon came to realize the larger significance of his accomplishments. His plant, which used water power, was the first regional commercial venture and the first in Colorado to transmit alternating current over a long distance. Hailed "for his foresight in introducing this new power," Nunn watched with interest as other San Juan companies quickly moved to tap electricity. Not that electric power was all that cheap. The large Tomboy Mine across the mountain from the Gold King soon spent $1,200 per month for power and light. Still, San Juan towns and camps eagerly accepted electricity. Durango had lights in homes and businesses as early as 1887, with Creede, Ouray, Telluride, Rico, Silverton, and Lake City not far behind.

By 1896 thirty-eight Colorado mining operations were utilizing electricity, and the director of the mint hailed the heart of the San Juan district (San Juan, Ouray, and San Miguel Counties) for having the best examples. Electricity offered a world of benefits for mining, including financial savings, more efficiency, less attendance and repairs than steam or compressed-air engines, easier adaptability, and the "avoidance of the bad effects of steam underground."[15] In everyday life, San Juan miners simply appreciated and respected Nunn for making their existence safer and easier.

A New Vision: Mountains as a Restorative Sanctuary

San Juaners had come for mining and stayed to put down roots in their new homes. While the mountains had been a barrier, they found that the San Juans could also provide them with benefits beyond natural resources—tourists and health seekers. The central Colorado Rockies had long been hailed for their curative and restorative potential. It was not, however, until the railroad reached Denver in 1870 that these facilities could easily be utilized by visitors. The San Juan region developed during that decade, while the reputation of Colorado as a health and tourist mecca grew. By 1882, all barriers were down. With the railroad at Durango and Silverton and with the Utes removed from the region, San Juaners could tap this new potential for profit and publicity.

Ouray, with one of the most beautiful mountain locations for a community anywhere in the country, quickly capitalized on its advantages. Almost from the community's birth, it promoted its local scenery, its fishing and hunting potential, and the curative nature of its hot springs. The *Ouray Times* (14 July 1877, for instance), praised the "grandeur and magnificence" of local scenery and went on to say: "in its vicinity are many hot springs highly charged with medicinal properties."

Colorado became famous for its variety of mineral springs which, if one believed the publicity, could cure almost all known ailments. Mineral springs emerged as popular American attractions in the mid-nineteenth century, and the San Juans had several areas of thermal activity, Ouray being the most famous. What advantages did Ouray have? Its *Solid Muldoon* of 14 May 1880 included its "unequaled climate," mineral springs, excellent society, and "no preachers!" Railroad connections eased the visitors' way (the circle tour brought them from Denver via Durango and Silverton), and a bath house and elegant hotel greeted arrivals. The Beaumont Hotel, when it opened in 1887, was hailed as one of the finest in the state. The Denver and Rio Grande ownership realized such tourism benefits and told potential passengers "the moral of all this is, therefore, for health, wealth and the grandest scenery on earth, visit OURAY."[16]

Ouray was not the only tourist paradise, as the 1885 *Tourist's Hand Book* pointed out. Silverton's surrounding scenery rivaled the "grandest views in Switzerland," and it was well "supplied with hotels." Wagon Wheel Gap, in the eastern San Juans, offered "scenery wonderfully beautiful" and hot springs, and it was the favorite sporting ground for "lovers of rod and gun." The Animas Canyon, where the D&RG rolled to Silverton, offered scenery "solitary, weird and awful" and a river bordered with "flowers, swaying vines, stately trees." But Ouray's chief rival was Durango, where Trimble Hot Springs, with its reasonable rates, baths, and "best attention" for invalids, held sway. Located nine miles north of the city, Trimble Springs advertised itself as "The Favorite Health and Pleasure Resort of the San Juan," with "curative qualities unsurpassed" (figure 6). Its owners "guaranteed" to cure "any case of rheumatism"; another enthusiastic booster went even further, suggesting the waters would "cure all diseases!" Nearby Pinkerton Springs offered soda springs "with the same chemical analysis" as the famous Manitou Springs. Meanwhile, Durango, the "Magic Metropolis," was not shy about promoting its own health and pleasure virtues: "basking in the warm sunlight of the south, overlooked by snow capped mountains, cool in summer, mild in winter, its days inviting to labor or pleasure in the tonic air, its nights full of cool calmness for rest." An 1892 pamphlet praised the clear, dry air "full of ozone" and offered one benefit which Durangoans have echoed down through the years, the "very best climate found in the United States."[17]

Whether these were "the most remarkable medicinal springs in the world" would be debated by every other mineral springs owner in the region. What cannot be debated is the fact that these nineteenth-century and early-twentieth-century San Juaners had taken remarkable advantage of health, tourist, and mineral resources available to them in the San Juan Mountains. They laid the basis for the tourist industry that survived the decline of mining and became the region's paramount economic pillar.

Mining might have waned, but its sites and heritage have become tourist attractions. Jeeping in the San Juans grew into "big business" for Silverton, Ouray, Telluride, and Lake City. At least two mines have reopened for tourists to visit and sense a time and place irretrievably gone. Where once it hauled ore, miners, and mining equipment, the Durango-to-Silverton train now carries tourists (over 207,000 in 1993) admiring the mountains and canyon and vicariously experiencing "a trip into yesteryear." All re-

6. *Trimble Springs Resort North of Durango. The resort opened in the 1880s. (Courtesy Center of Southwest Studies, Fort Lewis College.)*

maining San Juan communities capitalize on their Victorian legacy, none more so than Durango. Even the long discussed and "cussed" snow has proven to be an economic windfall, to which two major San Juan ski areas can testify in recent years.

Conclusion

A generation had slipped away since permanent settlement arrived, and certainly the mountains were still a barrier to transportation, settlement, and development, although the railroad had eased the situation as much as possible. So had tramways and electricity for the mines nestled among those peaks. The San Juaners had done as much as allowed by technology and finances to overcome the natural obstacles that they faced. The abundance of mineral resources had motivated them to challenge the mountain barrier and supported settlement until it took permanent root. Then a new resource, the restorative abilities of hot springs and natural environment, permitted a new mountainous economic benefit which continues to this day. San Juaners matched the mountains as best they could, and neither they nor the region would ever be the same again.

Notes

1. Frederic Endlich Report in F. V. Hayden, *Annual Report of the United States Geological and Geographical Survey* (Washington, D.C.: Government Printing Office, 1876), 185–86.

2. John P. Jones to Georgina F. Jones, 3 and 6 August 1879, Henry E. Huntington Library.

3. Rossiter W. Raymond, *Statistics of Mines and Mining* (Washington, D.C.: Government Printing Office, 1875), 385.

4. *Rocky Mountain News* (Denver), 21 January 1861. For the overall San Juan story, see Allen Nossaman, *Many More Mountains* (Denver: Sundance, 1990); and Duane A. Smith, *Song of the Hammer and Drill* (Golden: Colorado School of Mines Press, 1982).

5. For Byers's objections, see *Rocky Mountain News*, 21 November 1860, and 9 February 1861. The *News* of January–June 1861 covers the rush.

6. W. F. Arny, "Report to Eli Parker, Commissioner of Indian Affairs, July 19, 1870," letters received by the New Mexico Superintendency, 1870; Arny, "Journal of Wm. F. Arny, 1870," Bureau of Indian Affairs Records, Microfilm 557. See also *Daily Central City (Colo.) Register*, 19 April 1870.

7. Frank Fossett, *Colorado* (New York: C. G. Crawford, 1879), 509; *Denver Tribune*, 8 January 1882; *Engineering and Mining Journal*, 12 July 1890, 54.

8. For the preceding section on promotion, see the following: Fossett, *Colorado* 511, 513, and 557; *The San Juan Mines* (Kansas City: Commerce Publishing House, 1876); *Silver-Seeking in the San Juan Mines* (Kansas City: Ramsey, Millett and Hudson, 1878); *Rocky Mountain News*, 25 January 1874, 24 September 1874, 29 April 1875, and 13 December 1879; *New York Times*, 29 May 1876, 3 November 1876, and 8 January 1877.

9. Rossiter Raymond, *Statistics of Mines and Mining* (Washington, D.C.: Government Printing Office, 1877), 324. Rasmus Hanson testimony found in *The Board of County Commissioners of the County of Ouray vs The Board of County Commissioners of the County of San Juan* (Denver: Clark Printing, 1908), 49; *Lake City (Colo.) Silver World*, 20 April 1878.

10. *Ouray (Colo.) Times*, 14 July 1877; *Rocky Mountain News*, 16 September 1874 and 31 October 1877; *Dolores News* (Rico, Colo.), 21 August 1879; *Engineering and Mining*

Journal, 22 December 1877; *Silver World*, 18 September 1875, 31 March 1877, and 22 May 1880; *Saguache (Colo.) Chronicle*, 8 July 1876.

11. *Rocky Mountain News*, 4 January 1875 and 20 April 1876; *Silver World*, 30 September 1876; *Dolores News*, 22 November 1879; *Engineering and Mining Journal*, 30 September 1876 and 20 December 1879.

12. *La Plata Miner* (Silverton, Colo.), 25 October 1879, 1 November 1879, 29 November 1879, 4 December 1880, 20 August 1881, 24 December 1881, and 15 July 1882.

13. For further information on these three lines, see Robert G. Athearn, *Rebel of the Rockies* (New Haven: Yale University Press, 1962); Mallory Hope Ferrell, *Silver San Juan: The Rio Grande Southern* (Boulder: Pruett, 1973); Robert E. Sloan and Carl A. Skowronski, *The Rainbow Route* (Denver: Sundance, 1975).

14. For material on tramways, see *The Cosmopolitan Mining Company* (Portland, Ore.: circa 1883), 10; Horatio Burchard, *Report of the Director of the Mint for 1884* (Washington, D.C.: Government Printing Office, 1885), 236–37; *Ouray (Colo.) Solid Muldoon*, 11 March 1887; J. A. Porter, "The Smuggler-Union Mines, Telluride, Colorado," *Transactions of the American Institute of Mining Engineers*, 1897, 458. In addition, T. A. Rickard, *Across the San Juan Mountains* (New York: Engineering and Mining Journal, 1903), presents numerous insights into trams.

15. Irving Hale, "Electric Mining in the Rocky Mountain Region," *Transactions of the American Institute of Mining Engineers*, 1897, 403, 406–9; George Roberts, *Report of the Director of the Mint* (Washington, D.C.: Government Printing Office, 1898), 113; *Financial and Mining Record*, 4 July 1891, 8, and 20 August 1892, 138; *Engineering and Mining Journal*, 27 February 1892, 259, 12 March 1892, 304, 2 March 1895, 205, 18 July 1896, 61, and 20 May 1898, 598.

16. *Solid Muldoon*, 25 July 1883 and 29 July 1887; William Weston, *Descriptive Pamphlet* (Denver: Republican Publishing, 1882), 31; *Denver and Rio Grande Official Local Time Tables* (Denver, 1888), 105.

17. *Tourist's Hand Book in Colorado, New Mexico and Utah* (Denver, 1885), 41–50; *Durango (Colo.) Daily Herald*, 15 April 1882, 15 May 1883, and 13 December 1883; Richard McCloud, *Durango As It Is* (Durango, Colo.: Durango Board of Trade, 1892), 9–10, 58; *Denver Tribune*, 14 September 1881; *Durango* (Durango, Colo.: Herald, 1883), 3, 8.

4 / Communication in the Colorado High Country

CATHY E. KINDQUIST

This is the story of two passes in the Colorado high country, their rapid rise and demise, and the brief yet critical role they played in the creation of a new historical geography in an important region within the Mountainous West (figure 1).

Down the trickling, reckless rill which later broadens and deepens into the Rio Las Animas . . . leads a trail almost as tumbling and impetuous as itself, along which none but a trained mountain mule would even look; and we dismount from our animals, letting them go on alone, and pick our way after as best we can. . . . The woods are dense and rocks high, so that we cannot see out; but when at last some sort of levelness is reached, we find ourselves in a vast canon. There is another way in here, by which we afterward crawled out. It is called a wagon road; but the only means of using it is to take your wagon to peices [sic] and let it down several steep places by rope.[1]

This is how Ernest Ingersoll, a member of the Hayden Survey, described the route across Cunningham and Stony Passes in the middle of the 1870s. For a decade (1871–81), the passes, collectively known as the Rio Grande or Stony Pass route, were the primary link between the Upper Animas mining region and the outside world (figure 2). Across the two windswept summits flowed the people, goods, capital, and ideas that transformed the region from an incipient mining district into a civilized place. Diamond-tipped drills, Dodge crushers, smelters, cattle, foodstuffs, books, printing presses, dishware, musical instruments, and all manner of goods made their way into the interior valleys of southwestern Colorado's craggy San Juan Mountains by way of the two passes. So did the first mails, initial investments, and the first government agents.

The ascendency of the Rio Grande route was short-lived. In 1881, the extension of the railroad by a southern route to the site of Durango effected a shift in the focus of trade and communication. Attention and activity, pre-

1. *Ledge Trail to the Mines above Cunningham Gulch, 1875. (Courtesy U.S. Geological Survey, no. 06108. Photo by W. H. Jackson.)*

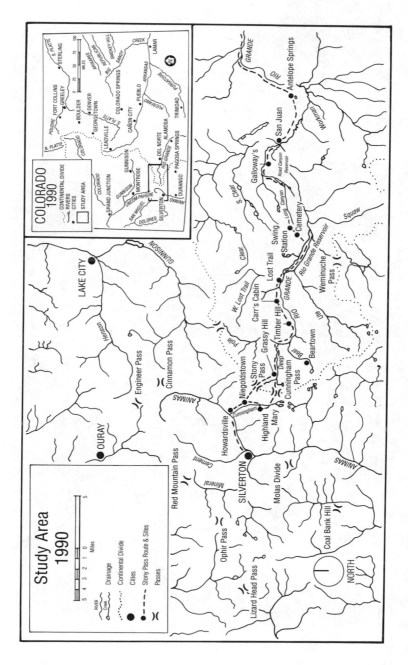

2. *Location Map of the San Juan Mountains.*

viously directed to the east by way of the two passes to the Rio Grande, shifted to the south, where connections to the east could be made through Durango. Settlements that had appeared during the 1870s along the Stony Pass route east of the continental divide disappeared, post offices lost their commissions, and the wagon road and trail fell into disrepair.

Without the tenuous links provided by the Stony Pass route and its pair of 12,000-foot summits, initial development of the San Juan region could not have proceeded. If mountains are barriers to interaction, then passes are critical elements in the process of regional integration. Reliance on high passes, however, is problematic. The rigors of high-country climate impose seasonal patterns on the movement of goods and people, and on the flow of communications.

The nature of transportation and communications shaped the society that was emerging in the San Juans—its patterns, its composition, the scale of activities, and the very character of social life. As transportation and communications were improved, the Upper Animas Valley was transformed and ties to the world economy were strengthened. Change did not progress, however, in an orderly, linear way. Initial frontier development amidst mountains cannot.

Mountain development based on primary resource exploitation can more accurately be described as proceeding in a pattern of undulating warps and woofs in time and space. Population expands and contracts. Development booms and collapses. Time and space stretch and shrink. Improvements in transportation and communications do not produce the relatively consistent pattern of convergence in time and space seen in the flatlands as roads are built and railroads completed.

In mountains links remain tenuous despite technological change, and the rhythms of social life remain intimately linked with the seasons and terrain. The sequencing of social life associated with mechanization and modernization is only partial.[2] The society that emerged in the interior valleys of the San Juan massif was one shaped by the mountainous barriers to interaction that surrounded it and by the concentration of mineral resources within those mountains. Simultaneously zones of concentrated resources and barriers to interaction, mountains provided the region's raison d'être and the single most significant obstacle to economic development.

The pages that follow tell the story of the development of a region in the context of dependence on an unreliable, largely seasonal route. Discussion focuses on the ways in which people communicated from an interior valley, how they transported the materials necessary for development, and the nature and extent of their connectedness with the outside world over the high passes. This colorful local story is set against the backdrop of the late nineteenth century: a time of rapid technological advance in transportation and communications, and a time of rapid development and expansion of the world economy. The Upper Animas Valley, while remote, was not isolated from these developments. It was very much a product of its time and of its place.

The Pass: Initial Exploration and Use

The interior valleys of the San Juan range remained relatively untouched by Europeans until the latter part of the nineteenth century.[3] Sustained exploration and development of the region occurred in the context of the global search for precious metals, a movement which found concrete expression in the rush to Colorado that began in 1858. As Duane Smith recounts, the San Juan region received some short-lived attention in the early 1860s, and while the rush sputtered and soon faded, it established the region in the minds of a number of men who would return at later times.[4] It allowed experimentation with routes in and routes out, and it was in this context that the Stony Pass route was first identified.[5] Its discovery was quite accidental. In 1861, Alonzo Perkins and John Thompson were prospecting near the continental divide.[6] The men became disoriented and wandered down the Rio Grande, subsisting for days on wild onions, roots, and whatever else they could find. They ultimately found themselves in the San Luis Valley and made their way to the military post at Fort Garland. After recovering from their ordeal, the two men parted company. Thompson returned north to the diggings at California Gulch, but Perkins retraced his steps up the Rio Grande to rejoin his party and convey information about the new route. Perkins's party and several other groups left the Upper Animas by way of the Rio Grande that year.[7]

In the aftermath of the Civil War and amidst buoyant optimism about the West and its prospects, interest in the San Juan region was renewed. In 1870, a number of claims were staked, including the Little Giant, a rich gold deposit. There is a certain irony here. The Little Giant was the claim around which development of the region was initially organized. It was an anomoly in a silver-bearing region, yet it was the Little Giant that attracted the first investment of capital, brought the first powers of government authority into the remote reaches of the San Juans, and provided the impetus for construction of the first wagon road across Stony Pass.[8]

To finance work on the Little Giant for the 1871 season, the prospectors who had discovered the lode sold shares and took on three working partners.[9] Additional capital was needed, and so investment was secured from Santa Fe entrepreneur Joshua S. Fuller and the territorial governor of New Mexico, William Pile. In exchange, Fuller and Pile received a half interest in the Little Giant.[10] The deed was originally recorded at Santa Fe, but discovering partner Miles T. Johnson had the foresight to stop and record the deed again in Conejos County, Colorado. Johnson's stop in the sleepy little town of Guadalupe on his way north through the San Luis Valley also served another purpose. He persuaded the clerk and recorder of Conejos County to deputize him, thereby extending the county's and the territory's jurisdiction to the San Juan mines.[11] As Johnson proceeded up the Rio Grande and across Cunningham Pass, he carried the first vestiges of government authority with him.[12]

The Road

The rush to the San Juan high country was on. In 1872, men flooded into the Upper Animas Valley, staking claims, building cabins, and establishing the rudiments of mining district organization. The Rio Grande route was rapidly becoming the dominant access route to the region, but the old route north from Taos and Santa Fe through the settlements of Abiquiu and Tierra Amarilla remained in use, along with approaches from the northwest from the Lake Fork of the Gunnison River.

Each spring miners outfitted themselves at Taos, Santa Fe, Denver, Colorado City, or other centers and set out for the San Juan mines. Most traveled by foot or with pack animals, banded together in parties of varied size. A few hardy and experienced souls, like George Howard, traveled alone.[13] Snow remained on the 12,000- to 14,000-foot summits of the San Juan range well into June and July. Access was difficult, particularly early in the season. Pass crossings were complicated by pack animals breaking through the crust, sometimes requiring the men to unpack them and dig them out. East of the pass, rain and melting snow turned sections of the trail into a mire.[14] Summers were occupied staking and developing claims, and each fall there was an exodus as temperatures plummeted and snows threatened to close the passes leading out of the Upper Animas. In October miners cached their tools where they could be found the next spring and packed out supplies and ore.[15] Wintering in the country was out of the question.

As attention turned from placer mining to lode mining, it became obvious that development of the San Juan mines depended upon the construction of wagon roads. Ore from the Little Giant and other lodes required reduction, and while crude local crushing and processing could accomplish the task, quartz mills and smelters could do so more efficiently. The first wagon road to penetrate the San Juan massif was built over the 12,588-foot summit of Stony Pass in 1872, for the express purpose of transporting machinery for the Little Giant mill (figure 3).[16] The machinery and the road were part of New York–born capitalist E. M. Hamilton's investment in the Little Giant Mine.

Emery M. Hamilton's Little Giant mill came through Loma (the early name for Del Norte) and made its way up the Rio Grande to Baker's Park, a distance of approximately 110 miles. The machinery was transported by ox-drawn wagons. Hamilton's crew constructed the road up the Rio Grande as they went, modifying only those sections necessary to allow wagons to pass. In this sense, the road was not continuous, but rather had sections of bona fide grade interspersed with open meadows crossed by wagon tracks.[17] As the mill approached its site on the Upper Animas, miners stopped their work and gave their time to help with road construction.[18]

Tenuous as it was, the wagon road did much to increase levels of interest and investment in the San Juan mines. Between Del Norte and Baker's Park, ranches and wayside stopping places began to appear. In the Upper Animas Valley log cabin construction accelerated, and incoming population increased exponentially each season. In 1872 alone, it was estimated that over 1,500 claims were staked, despite the fact that it rained and snowed through both August and September.[19]

The Little Giant mill was in operation by July of 1873. Wagons began filtering into the Upper Animas in increasing numbers, some carrying families and their worldly goods, others carrying the machinery necessary for development. Between 1873 and 1879, sawmills, smelters, blacksmithing equipment, diamond-tipped drills, boilers, brick for lining smelters, and even a billiard table and a melodion arrived on the Upper Animas by way of the Stony Pass wagon road. Ore was transported out.

From its inception, the road was a problem. At first the tracks were so faint that travelers lost the road.[20] As the years passed and the rigors of San Juan winters took their toll on the road, the grade deteriorated badly.

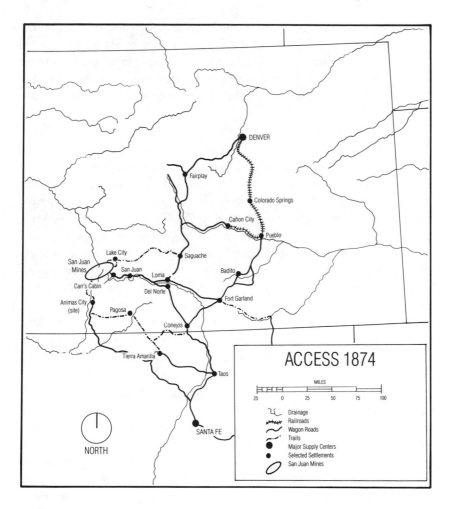

3. Routes to the San Juan Mines, 1874.

Those experienced in the country tended to be oblivious to ruts, bogs, small slide areas, and steep grades. Those new to the country were appalled and intimidated by the road's condition. One irate traveler described the route as

> a fiction and a snare. . . . it is humbug of the first water, and has been the author of more profanity than any other evil we endure. It is paved with the curses of the poor unfortunates who have climbed it, and it is darkened with the shadows of equine ghosts given up on Timber and Grassy Hills. Oh! Sir! It is a develish [*sic*] bad road![21]

George Howard, a man whose experience in the country dated to the Baker's Park excitement, was distinctly unimpressed by Hamilton's wagon road. He wrote in his diary: "About two miles above my camp we turned off from the old trail to try a new one that had been recommended to us, but we found it a most miserable one being very steep and wet. I don't want any more of it."[22]

On the west side of the pass, the road plunged into Cunningham Gulch at a rate of a thousand feet per mile. Methods were adapted to get wagons safely down the precipitous three-mile section. Once timberline was reached, snubbing could be employed. Wagons were tied off by rope to large spruce trees and let gradually down the slope. Rocks were then thrust under the wheels to prevent wagons from careening downhill, while the ropes were quickly moved to a lower tree. Above the timberline other methods were required. Back teaming entailed hitching the wagon team to the rear of the vehicle, with the draft animals acting as the brakes and preventing the wagon from plummeting into the valley below. Another method involved attaching logs to the rear wheels to provide drag.

The Stony Pass route was seasonal at best. Snow often remained on the range from October to late June, impeding transportation and communications. Only the mail carrier and a handful of others crossed the pass in the winter with regularity. They made their way by foot or on snowshoes.[23] In the spring and fall, it was common practice for travelers to proceed in the middle of the night or the early hours of the morning, when the crust on top of the snow was hard and could support their weight.[24]

Though in winter travel over the Rio Grande passes slowed to a trickle, goods could still be moved. The diary of Timothy Plantz documents a five-foot accumulation of snow on the range by 21 November 1875. Three days later Plantz was engaged hauling goods for Greene and Company, which had a storage and commission house at the eastern base of Timber Hill on the Rio Grande side. Plantz and his partner transported the goods by sleigh, a quarter ton at a time. They completed their contract shortly before Christmas, and Plantz earned $126.69 for his efforts.[25]

The poor condition of the 1872 wagon road and its seasonal nature were perceived as retarding development. Between 1875 and 1879, close to a dozen papers were filed at the county level chartering toll road companies that proposed either improving and maintaining the Stony Pass route or using an alternative pass to cross the continental divide (figure 4).[26] Attempts were made to arrange financing of road improvements through joint capitalization. Cooperative efforts failed though. The complexity of

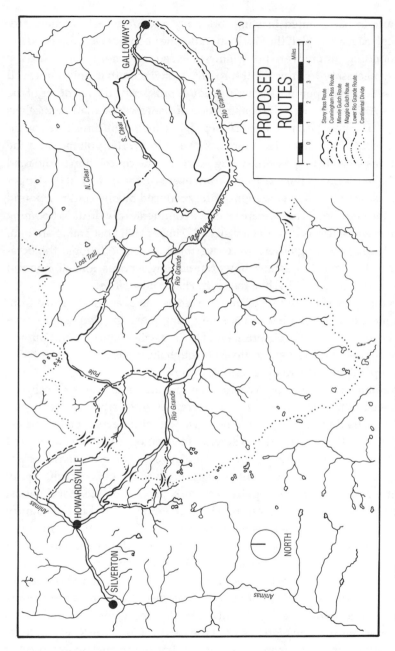

4. *Proposed Routes to the Upper Animas from the Rio Grande, 1872–1879.*

the terrain necessitated blasting, bridging, and continual maintenance. Though eager to exploit the San Juan trade, the people of Del Norte and the surrounding county were not willing to expend the money or secure the bonds necessary to improve the road.[27] Convinced that only improved connections with points east could produce prosperity, the residents of the Upper Animas financed the construction of a new wagon road themselves in 1879. The new road remained seasonal, but during the time it was open, goods could be transported more easily and in greater volume, and the road was suitable for passenger stage service. The completion of the road was hailed as one of the most significant events in the history of the Upper Animas. Freight fares were immediately reduced by one cent per pound from the railhead.[28] The towns east of the continental divide did a booming trade in wayside services. At Grassy Hill, Timber Hill, Lost Trail, San Juan, and Antelope Springs there were overnight accommodations, the occasional saloon or eating establishment, freighting services, and storage and commission houses.[29] Each of the towns had a post office.

In the span of a decade, the Upper Animas had been transformed from an almost primeval state into a bustling mining region. Two major towns had been established at Silverton and Howardsville (figure 5), and numerous other settlements were scattered through the mountains, connected to the Upper Animas by roads and trails (figure 6).

A dominantly male society had been modified into one that included women and families. The year-round population increased as each year passed. The rhythms of life had been worked out: development and exploitation of the mines and movement of technology, material goods, and ore dominated the summers; attraction of investment in the mines, planning, community improvement, and ancillary activities (gear and equipment repair, sewing, darning, leather work, gun repair, etc.) for the most part occupied the winter months. The men who wintered in the country were back at work on their claims by mid-March. By the end of April, miners who wintered elsewhere were returning to the Upper Animas, and in May and June the flow became a flood.[30] The arrival of the first jack train of the season was an important event, noted in local papers and diaries. In 1876, the first jacks loaded with supplies reached the Animas settlements on 10 May, followed five days later by a herd of beef cattle.[31]

Dependence on the high passes at the headwaters of the Rio Grande remained a limiting factor in development, but the region was connected with the nation and the world outside. Capital investment in the region had been secured from Chicago, New York, and Great Britain, and distant

5. Silverton, 1881. Jack trains were a common site in the towns of the Upper Animas. Burros were used to transport ore from the mines and supplies, and to carry goods across the continental divide, especially early and late in the season. (Courtesy Colorado Historical Society, no. F2504.)

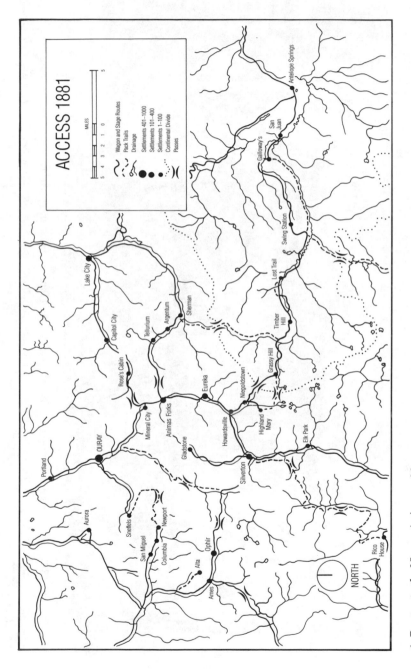

ACCESS 1881

MILES

5 4 3 2 1 0   5

Wagon and Stage Routes
Pack Trails
Drainage
Settlements 401–1000
Settlements 101–400
Settlements 1–100
Continental Divide
Passes

Antelope Springs

San Juan

Galloway's

Swing Station

Lost Trail

Timber Hill

Grassy Hill

Niegoldstown

Highland Mary

Elk Park

Silverton

Eureka

Howardsville

Gladstone

Animas Forks

Mineral City

Sherman

Argentum

Tellurium

Rose's Cabin

Capitol City

Lake City

OURAY

Portland

Aurora

Sneffels

Newport

San Miguel

Columbia

Alta

Ophir

Ames

Rico House

NORTH

6. Routes to the Upper Animas, 1881.

markets developed for San Juan silver. Germans, Austrians, Italians, and Irishmen were employed in the mines of the Upper Animas.[32] County government was well established; Colorado jurisprudence had penetrated the mountains; and agents of the federal government had surveyed and mapped the area.[33] The San Juan high country was connected with national and international postal systems. Tenuous ties, but ties they were.

Postal Communications

The early postal history of the Upper Animas, like the cycles of boom and bust described in the first section of this chapter, and the cycles of road improvement and deterioration described in the second, demonstrates the discontinuous nature of mountain development. Evolution of the postal system in the San Juans was not an orderly, linear progression from informal arrangements to a functioning system which grew ever more efficient.

Indeed, the first mails were privately arranged, informal, and somewhat unreliable, but management of the mails by the U.S. Postal Service was at times even less reliable. Prior to the ratification of the Brunot Agreement in the spring of 1874, the miners on the Upper Animas were trespassers in Ute Indian territory. As such, they had no right to federal protection or federal services. The Brunot Agreement brought the San Juans and the wealth that they contained under U.S. jurisdiction, opening the way for legal development of the region and the extension of federal powers and services into the area. Until the first post office was established at Howardsville, in the wake of Brunot, in June of 1874, the mails were carried by local residents under private arrangements. The nearest U.S. post office was at Loma, later renamed Del Norte, 110 miles distant. During the 1873 season, miners paid between twenty-five and fifty cents per letter to have the post carried between Del Norte and Baker's Park.[34]

Between 1874 and 1882, when the railroad reached Silverton, mail was carried over the wagon roads and trails of the San Juan high country under contract, sometimes with alarming inconsistency and lack of care. Postal communications were frequently the subject of articles and diatribes appearing in the Del Norte and Silverton newspapers.[35]

Postal service to the region was provided under a system of contracts managed by the federal government. Contracts were let to the lowest bidder. People unfamiliar with the territory would underbid the routes and then find themselves unable to provide the service, much to the outrage of local residents. Delivery was further complicated by deep snows and outright chicanery by some of the contractors.

Contracts and routes were subject to change every few months. One of the early contracts made use of a circuitous route through Lake City and Animas Forks. A piece in the Del Norte paper from a resident of the Upper Animas protested the situation:

The subject of the mails is one that interests us more than anything else at present. The Route from Lake City to Animas Forks is desperately bad, and from the Forks down to Eureka is but little better, every time the carrier comes over the route it is at the risk of his life. From Del Norte in, via Jennison's ranch is safe and passable the winter through [the Rio Grande route]. Our people have petitioned strongly for a change. It is our only avenue of supply during the winter.[36]

The route was changed only after the mail carrier was buried in an avalanche, and Animas residents took resolutions and testimony to the governor.[37] By fall of 1876, the mails were described as occasional at best. The Silverton postal route had been sublet to Barlow and Sanderson, a reputable company. It in turn tried to subcontract the route, but could find no one to take the meager pay for the work involved. Despite failure to perform the service, no one was able to underbid the contractor. A special agent from the postal service made an investigation, and service improved somewhat.[38] Under such conditions, informal arrangements persisted. Men traveling to and from Del Norte carried postal communications when they could. Private express services were organized, and communities in the interior found their own carriers upon occasion.[39]

By the winter of 1878–79, the Silverton mails were in the hands of Harry Brolaski, who subcontracted the route from J. B. Price of Jefferson City, Missouri. The triweekly service from Antelope Springs to Silverton and Howardsville was originally bid at $2,840 per year.[40] The contract was one of many held by the flatlander Price. When he discovered that the pay would not cover the expense of winter service, he sublet the contract to Brolaski. On the strength of Brolaski's promises, the carriers provided service well into December without receiving compensation. At that time the carriers and the people of the Upper Animas learned that the larcenous Brolaski had drawn all the money he could from the U.S. Postal Service and quit the area, leaving someone else with the contract.[41] It was a full three months until service was returned to some semblence of regularity.

During the interim, service was sporadic. In February an angry article appeared in the Silverton paper indicating that only one mail delivery had been received in the previous eleven days.[42] A separate piece in the same issue cogently pointed out that regular service was needed for another reason: daily passage of the mail carrier packed the trail across Cunningham Pass, and it was customary for the carrier to make sure stakes marking the route were visible, so people walking, skiing, or snowshoeing out of the Upper Animas would not get lost.[43]

Public outrage grew when four men in a span of four weeks were killed crossing the range. One was the mail carrier, another was a man compelled across Cunningham Pass's 12,090-foot summit by illness in his family back in Iowa, and the other two were men traveling on business that could have been handled by mail had there been reliable service.[44]

Other problems along the route were of a more idiosyncratic nature. In 1880, one of the mail carriers was described as "keeping so full of whiskey that he came near having tremens."[45] Another was characterized as an irresponsible lout who left a bag of mail sitting exposed on top of the continental divide for a week. The editor of the Silverton paper urged that the man be prosecuted.[46] In the winter of 1876–77, the mail carriers had difficulty hauling the mail because of its volume. The *San Juan Prospector* described the situation:

> A lot of demented idiots in town have advertised in some eastern journals, whose circulation is principally in hasheries and other houses of refreshment, for lady correspondents, and they have got them with a vengeance. There are five tons of pink, green and blue enveloped letters now piled up at Alden's, and the place smells of musk and patchouli like a ten cent barber's shop. Mr. O'Bayles fainted the other day on the range from the press of tender recollections of by-gone days called up by the sweet scent from the mail bags.[47]

The mails were an essential link between the people and businesses of the Upper Animas and the outside world. To the men and women of the San Juan settlements, the mails represented the only means of communications with people and places that they had left behind. Timothy Plantz wrote in his journal, "Sunday, dreary blustering day, went to town for the mail, no letters, very much disappointed, feel very blue and lonesome for want of company, nothing to read."[48] Plantz frequently noted that he "answered letters." He watched for the mail carrier, either following or accompanying him to town. He subscribed to two Chicago newspapers. Around the time the mail carrier was buried in an avalanche coming over the Lake City route, Plantz wrote, "I went to Silverton, no mail yet; very anxious, now over a week since we had mail."[49] John Greenhalgh observed several times in letters to his brother Charley that Charley was the only member of his family who ever wrote. Greenhalgh was most grateful, and also appreciative of Maine newspapers which Charley sent.[50] In an unusually wistful passage he wrote, "I should like to draw the lines over a 2.40 horse once more to sleigh and see how it would seem."[51] He stated frequently his intention to return to Maine to visit, but he could rarely find time away from his business endeavors, mining claims (the Portland and the Penobscot), or his responsibilities as sheriff and mail carrier. In an early letter he encapsulated rootlessness in this way: "Sometimes I think I will come home this winter, or East rather, for I have no home. My home is wherever I chance to be."[52] In the same letter, Greenhalgh expressed his love for his family and noted that "although I am wandering around the world away from all that I really love . . . I wish you to inform me in regard to all of the family." Charley's letters were John's most important link to Maine.

The disruption of postal communications had the potential to severely complicate personal relationships and business dealings, and upon occasion it forced people to walk and ride across the divide to conduct their affairs. Railroad service substantially improved the quality and consistency of postal communications, but was not infallible. The heavy snows and concommitant avalanches typical of San Juan winters blockaded the tracks on several occasions, disrupting communications and preventing supplies from reaching the Upper Animas (figure 7).

Route Demise and Space-Time Convergence

The train reached Silverton in 1882, arriving from the south, crossing the mountains along the Colorado–New Mexico border to reach Durango, then ascending the Animas River (figure 8). Its arrival in Durango in 1881 spelled the end of dependence on the high passes to the Rio Grande. Attention and movement were redirected to the south.

Within a matter of months, telegraph and telephone lines followed. The relatively insular, seasonal society of the Upper Animas collided with the technologically sophisticated late-nineteenth-century world. As traffic along the Stony Pass route declined, the residents of the wayside service towns east of the pass moved elsewhere, and the post offices closed. A time-biased society was transformed within a matter of months into a space-biased one capable of instantaneous communications.[53] Seasonal patterns were not erased, but they were muted. Trains carrying supplies,

7. *Tunnel through a Snowslide on the Silverton-Ouray Toll Road, 1888. Taken in July, this photograph illustrates some of the particular difficulties encountered in mountain transportation and communications. (Courtesy Colorado Historical Society, no. F14975. Photo by C. Goodman.)*

machinery, ore, and passengers could move in and out of the Upper Animas year-round. For the first time, schedules of delivery and departure had meaning.

A regularity was imposed on life in the interior of the San Juans that had previously been impossible. Patterns of work, travel, and activity were more closely synchronized with the comings and goings of the train. During the earlier period of reliance on the Rio Grande route, staging systems had been organized with tenative timetables, and mail routes were contracted with specified times for arrival and departure, but they existed on paper, not in reality. Even when communications and material goods or passengers were moved on schedule, it was only occasionally, only seasonally. The pre-rail rhythms of life on the Animas were associated with

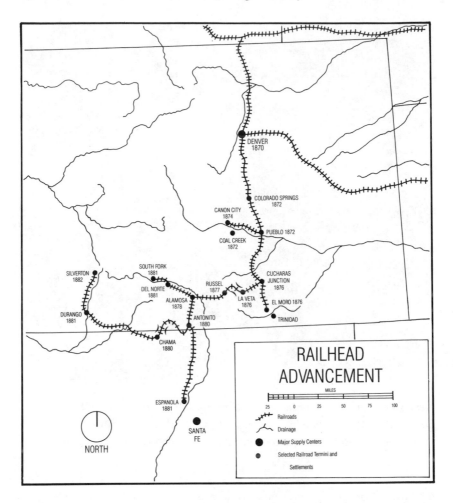

8. *Railhead Advancement, 1870–1882. The map shows the progress of lines related to early San Juan transportation.*

immutable physical realities, such as the length of the day, the weather, the season, the steepness of the slopes. Timothy Plantz would watch from his cabin for the mail carrier at certain times of the day, on certain days of the week, but he would not necessarily see him pass. He could more reliably expect to see the first jack train in mid-May and the last "fancy women" heading from Silverton toward the pass in October or November. The sequencing of social life during the period of the Rio Grande route's dominance was very partial.

9. First Automobile to Reach the Upper Animas, 1910. Driven by D. L. Mechling of Denver, the four-cylinder, thirty-horsepower Croxton-Keeton had to be hauled first up Timber Hill and then the Stony Pass summit—shown here—by a team from San Juan County. Mechling was an ardent supporter of the good roads movement in Colorado. (Courtesy San Juan County Historical Society.)

After the arrival of the train, the population of the Upper Animas changed, becoming more balanced in terms of gender and age. Businesses boomed, amenities increased, and the face of Silverton was transformed until the town appeared much like other American towns of the era. With the railhead at Silverton, routes connecting the center to other corners of the San Juans were improved, and spur lines were constructed to bring ore from the mines. The scale of development and investment expanded. Capitalism and industrialism, once transported into the Upper Animas piece by piece over a tenuous pair of passes, were now linked with national and international systems by a continuous band of steel and two threadlike wires. Industrialism and capitalism emerged during the wagon road era, but they became established and fully functional under the influence of mechanized transportation and communication.

The first automobile to reach Silverton arrived, strangely enough, by way of Stony Pass in 1910 (figure 9). It had to be hauled up the east side of the summit because the driver was unaware of carburetor adjustments. Nonetheless, it signaled the beginning of a new period in San Juan transportation. It proved that automobiles could make it into the most complex of mountain ranges, and by doing so it helped promote the construction of highways in the San Juans and other mountainous sections of Colorado.[54]

Today, Stony Pass is traversed only by a jeep road used for recreation. The train runs only in the summer and carries tourists, not ore. The tracks linking the line with the national rail network have been torn up. Mail arrives in Silverton by truck, as do goods, supplies, and machinery for the few operating mines that remain on the Upper Animas. Ore is trucked out. The road that reaches Silverton does so over passes to the south and north. In winter travel slows to a trickle, and in the summer it accelerates. To the present, mountains remain zones of concentrated resources and barriers to interaction. Mountain development is anything but continuous, and passes are still critical elements in the process of integration, the tenuous links that connect an interior valley with the outside world.

Notes

1. Ernest Ingersoll, *Knocking Round the Rockies* (New York: Harper and Brothers, 1883), 109.

2. The intellectual context for this chapter is provided by the ideas of British sociologist Anthony Giddens in *The Constitution of Society: Outline of the Theory of Structuration* (Berkeley: University of California Press, 1984) (see his concept of time-space distanciation, 377) and *The Nation-State and Violence: Volume Two of a Contemporary Critique of Historical Materialism* (Berkeley: University of California Press, 1987) (see his concepts of sequencing of social life and space-time convergence, 173–81).

3. Pre-1860 exploration and human activity are discussed in more detail in Cathy E. Kindquist, *Stony Pass: The Tumbling and Impetuous Trail* (Silverton, Colo.: San Juan County Book Co., 1987), 10–18.

4. These initial expeditions to the area are discussed in more detail in Kindquist, *Stony Pass*, 19–22.

5. Allen Nossaman, *Many More Mountains: Silverton's Roots* (Denver: Sundance, 1989), 63.

6. Robert J. Bruns, "The First We Know: The Story of the San Juan in Colorado, or The Pioneer History of the San Juan," San Juan County Historical Society Collection, Silverton, Colo., 1927, manuscript.

7. Nossaman, *Many More Mountains*, 68–69.

8. The discovery of Little Giant was also fortuitous in the sense that it provided a

basis for development of the region at a time when federal legislation supporting silver mining (the Sherman Silver Purchase Act) was not yet in place.

9. Bruns, "The First We Know," chapter 5.

10. Deed, *Johnson to Pile and Fuller*, 26 April 1871, Records of the Las Animas Mining District and of La Plata County, Colorado Territory, San Juan County Clerk and Recorder's Office, Silverton.

11. Nossaman, *Many More Mountains*, 98.

12. The importance of the recorder's authority cannot be underestimated. It provided the means of registering claims and preventing claim jumping. Refer to George Howard, "The 1872 Diary of George Howard," San Juan County Historical Society Collection, Silverton, Colo., unpublished diary, typescript, 7 June entry.

13. Howard, "1872 Diary," May and June entries.

14. Howard, "1872 Diary," 6 June and 9 June entries.

15. Howard, "1872 Diary," 7 June and October entries.

16. E. M. Hamilton, *The San Juan Mines: A Brief History of Their Discovery and Development—With Map* (Chicago: C. E. Southard, 1874).

17. Hamilton, *San Juan Mines*.

18. Howard, "1872 Diary," 20 September entry.

19. Hamilton, *San Juan Mines*, 14–18.

20. Lieutenant E. H. Ruffner, *Report on a Reconaissance of the Ute Country, Made in the Year 1873* (Washington, D.C.: Government Printing Office, 1874).

21. *San Juan Prospector* (Del Norte, Colo.), 30 May 1874, 3.

22. Howard, "1872 Diary," 9 September entry.

23. In the San Juans during the 1870s and 1880s, the term *snowshoe* was used to describe both the webbed variety with which we are familiar today and early cross-country skis (also refered to as *skidors*).

24. "Across the Great Divide," unpublished oral history project conducted in co-operation with the Silverton, Colo., Public Library and Fort Lewis College, 1976, 17–18.

25. T. P. Plantz, "T. P. Plantz Diary, 1875–1876," San Juan County Historical Society Collection, Silverton, Colo., unpublished diary.

26. Articles of Incorporation: *Antelope Park and Carr's Cabin Toll Road Company*, 11 July 1878; *Del Norte and Antelope Park Toll Road Company*, 20 December 1875; *Del Norte and San Juan Wagon Road Company*, 26 July 1875; *Rio Grande and Animas Toll Road Company*, 7 October 1875; *Rio Grande and Animas Wagon Road Company*, 30 December 1876; *Rio Grande and Cunningham Gulch Toll Road Company*, 12 October 1876; *San Juan and Silverton Turnpike Company*, 29 January 1876, Hinsdale County Clerk and Recorder's Office (Lake City, Colo.); *Stony Pass Wagon Road Company*, 2 July 1878, San Juan County Clerk and Recorder's Office, Silverton, Colo.

27. *San Juan Prospector,* 9 January 1875, 1.

28. *San Juan Prospector,* 13 September 1879, 1.

29. The towns have a fascinating history, which is beyond the scope of this chapter. They are treated in detail in Kindquist, *Stony Pass,* 43–49. The towns of Howardsville, Niegoldstown and Highland Mary on the Animas side of the pass are also discussed, 49–53.

30. Plantz, "Diary," March, April, May, and June 1876 entries.

31. Plantz, "Diary," 10 May and 15 May 1876 entries.

32. U.S. Bureau of the Census, *The Tenth Census of the United States, 1880,* population schedules, San Juan and Hinsdale Counties, Colo. (Washington, D.C.: National Archives, 1962).

33. Between 1873 and 1876, three government-authorized expeditions were conducted in the area: the Ruffner expedition (1873), which was an Army Corps of Engineers reconnaissance survey; the Hayden survey (1874–76); and the Wheeler survey (1873–75), both of which were scientific surveys.

34. *San Juan Prospector,* 21 March 1874, 3.

35. The *San Juan Prospector* and *La Plata Miner* (Silverton, Colo.) are the sources for most of the information contained in this section of the chapter. Official postal records at the time were rather perfunctory and do little to elucidate the problems associated with postal communications in the San Juan region.

36. *San Juan Prospector* 12 February 1876, 1.

37. Plantz, "Diary," 1 January 1876 entry; *San Juan Prospector,* 29 January 1876, 1. The mail carrier lived.

38. *San Juan Prospector,* 14 October 1876, 4.

39. Greenhalgh Correspondence, 1871–76, San Juan County Historical Society Collection, Silverton, Colo. Also refer to advertisements in the *San Juan Prospector.*

40. *San Juan Prospector,* 15 February 1879, 1.

41. *San Juan Prospector,* 15 February 1879, 2.

42. *La Plata Miner,* 8 February 1879, 4.

43. *La Plata Miner,* 8 February 1879, 1.

44. *La Plata Miner,* 8 February 1879, 4.

45. *La Plata Miner,* 17 January 1880, 1.

46. *La Plata Miner,* 16 October 1880, 1.

47. *San Juan Prospector,* 17 March 1877, 1.

48. Plantz, "Diary," 14 November 1875 entry.

49. Plantz, "Diary," 31 December 1875 entry.

50. Letter, John Greenhalgh to Charles Greenhalgh, 14 December 1875, Greenhalgh Correspondence. John Greenhalgh died on top of Stony Pass in the winter of 1876. He was carrying a twenty-nine-pound pack filled with dispatches be-

tween Carr's Cabin and Howardsville. Greenhalgh died of exhaustion and exposure.

51. Letter, John Greenhalgh to Charles Greenhalgh, 11 December 1874, Greenhalgh Correspondence.

52. Letter, John Greenhalgh to Charles Greenhalgh, 7 July 1872, Greenhalgh Correspondence.

53. For elucidation of the the concepts of time-biased and space-biased societies, refer to Harold A. Innis, *Empire and Communications* (Oxford: Clarendon Press, 1950). The significance of instantaneous communications is explored in Stephen Kern, *The Culture of Time and Space, 1880–1918* (Cambridge, Mass.: Harvard University Press, 1983). Also see Marshall McLuhan, *Understanding Media: The Extensions of Man* (New York: McGraw Hill, 1964).

54. J. A. McGuire, "On Top of the Earth in a Motor Car," *Outdoor Life,* 1911 (April), 45–54.

Islands of Moisture

Watch any western sky on a summer afternoon, and a fundamental geographical fact presents itself—the clouds gather and boil over mountain peaks and plateaus while adjacent lowlands lie parched and baking in the sun. That ubiquitous scene is a microcosm of a larger regional reality, in both summer and winter, that has shaped patterns of precipitation, vegetation, and human adaptation across the West. Clearly, the moisture surpluses of the Mountainous West have made it a different sort of place than the nearby valleys and plains. These islands of highland moisture have also become inextricably wed to the nearby lowlands as people have sought to channel and utilize the precious resource.

Thomas Vale reviews how mountain moisture has contributed to the making of the Mountainous West. He challenges the stereotype of the West as a universally dry region and demonstrates how much of the economic and political culture of the West has derived from an adequate but spatially uneven distribution of moisture. He begins with a set of maps which reveal that the western mountains are often wetter than many areas of the Midwest and East. This evidence in hand, Vale then challenges some of the sweeping generalizations recently posed by the new western historians regarding the development of irrigated agriculture in the West. Vale argues that the local abundance of western water in mountain settings has made the development of nearby agricultural areas an entirely rational and sustainable activity. This utilitarian vision of western water also shaped the passage of the Forest Reserve Act in 1891, and Vale reconstructs how nineteenth-century bureaucrats perceived the interrelationships between watershed protection, forest resources, and agriculture. Integrating the government control and restorative sanctuary themes into his essay, he finally recounts how the presence of abundant water resources contributed to the creation of national parks in the Mountainous West and how recent regional arguments for biodiversity are a recognition of the complex insular nature of western environments.

5 / Mountains and Moisture in the West

THOMAS R. VALE

Even from the height of a commercial jetliner on a cross-continental flight, the summertime West stretches below with tones all its own. In contrast to the hazy green and blue expanses of the eastern United States, the western landscape unfurls its tawny canvas in subdued browns, tans, grays, and sometimes sandy ivories. But occasionally a swath of a different hue is brushed across these vast reaches: a belt of dark jade green, almost black, often dotted by imperfect circles of gleaming reflective light. The aberration, typically masked in places by clouds, sweeps below rather quickly, and the landscape returns to its dominant brownish hues.

The colors tell of a western essence. The extensive lowlands of drying grasses and gray-green shrubs, of bare rock and salt-encrusted playas, are punctuated by narrow banks of mountains, clothed in forests of conifers and, for those ranges which have been glaciated, dotted with shining lakes. Herein lies the quintessence of the West: a juxtaposition of dry lowland and moist mountain. Neither alone is enough to characterize the region. When commentators suggest that aridity is the most basic of western attributes, they are only partly right. The essence of the region and its history of human dramas depend upon localized abundance of water—water from mountains—in an otherwise dry environment. The coupling of these seemingly antithetical characters, moistness and aridity, is the essential feature of the American West.

Moisture in the West

The West is more arid than the rest of the country. The lack of heavy annual precipitation results in smaller volumes of surface water in the West than elsewhere in the lower forty-eight states (figure 1).[1] With about 39 percent of the area of the contiguous states, the West accounts for only 29 percent

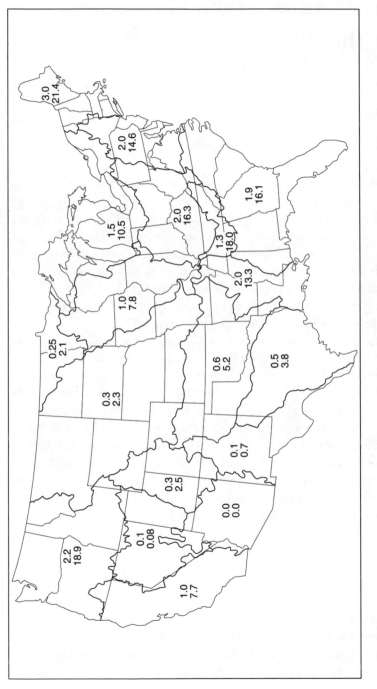

1. Surface Water in the United States by Major Hydrologic Basin. The top number is the ratio of percent of the country's surface water to percent of the country's land area, for each basin. The bottom number is the surface runoff, in inches of water, for the average acre in each basin.

of the surface runoff. These values of water and land may be expressed as a ratio, or 0.74, far lower than comparable ratios for any region east of the Mississippi River. A calculation of surface runoff, derived by dividing the natural streamflow by the area for each major hydrologic basin, produces the same picture. The West generates a runoff of 6.1 inches per acre, lower than most areas in the East, although higher than the central prairies and plains.

Hidden within these aggregated totals for the West as a whole, however, are regional variations. The most striking deviation is the well-known abundance of water in the Pacific Northwest. With 9 percent of the country's area, the drainage of the Columbia River generates 20 percent of the nation's water; the ratio of water to land is 2.2, higher than all areas in the East except New England. The runoff value of 18.9 inches per acre is similarly exceeded only by the region of New England. Even California, often described as a civilization in a "desert," accounts for about 5 percent of both water and land; California's water to land ratio (1.0) and its surface runoff (7.7 inches per acre) equal that of the Upper Mississippi River drainage (1.0 and 7.8 inches), the "garden" of the Upper Midwest. By contrast, much of the Interior West is extremely dry, with much larger percentages of area than of water and with low runoff values.

On a finer scale, the presence of surface water is still more localized (figure 2). Northwestern California, for example, is unusually wet (2.1 percent of water, 0.78 percent of land, ratio of 2.7; runoff of 21.8 inches per acre), whereas the southern part of the state is typical of the dry Interior West (1.2 percent of water, 3.3 percent of land, ratio of 0.4; runoff of 2.8 inches per acre). The Great Basin region is exceedingly dry (ratio of water to land of 0.08; runoff of 0.8 inches per acre), but a portion of that region, the drainages of the Great Salt and Bear Lakes, generates values (ratio of 0.24 and runoff of 2.0 inches per acre) which approach those of the northern plains (ratio of 0.3 and runoff of 2.3 inches per acre). Even more striking is the uneven occurrence of water in the driest hydrologic region, the Lower Colorado drainage: as a whole, this area experiences higher evaporation and transpiration than precipitation and thus generates no net runoff, but in the subregions of the Little Colorado and Gila Rivers (most of eastern Arizona), the ratio of water to land (0.05) and the calculated figure for runoff (0.4 inches per acre) are positive, albeit low.

The primary reason for this variability in surface water in the West is the presence of mountains. Two other factors are secondarily important. Specifically, proximity to the coast enhances precipitation because the Pacific Ocean acts as the major source of moisture. Moreover, latitude alone ex-

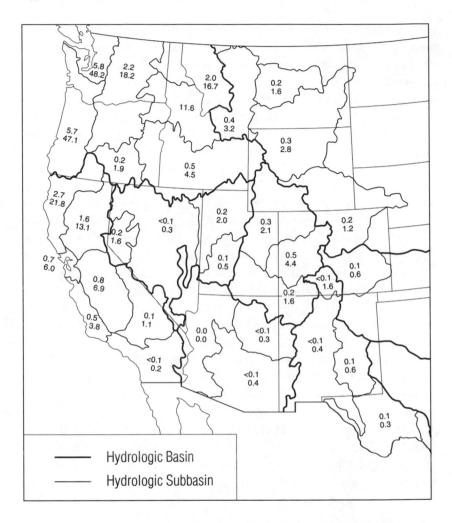

2. *Surface Water in the American West by Major Hydrologic Basin. The top number is the ratio of percent of the country's surface water to percent of the country's land area, for each basin. The bottom number is the surface runoff, in inches of water, for the average acre in each basin.*

plains some of the pattern (the higher the latitude, the higher the frequency of cool season storms, the primary precipitation producers for most of the West). But it is the orographic enhancement of precipitation that dictates most of the spatial pattern in western water.

In order to assess mountains as producers of water in the West, the area

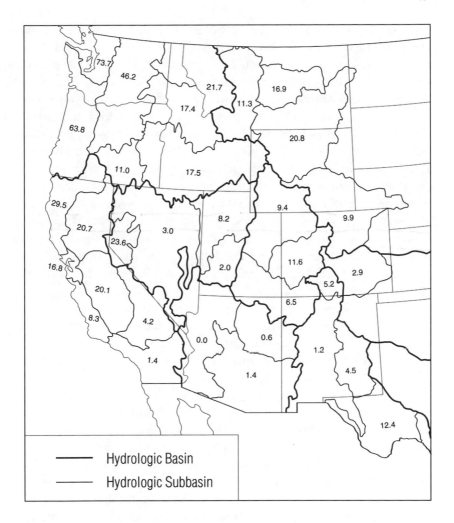

3. Estimated Surface Runoff. The runoff is shown in inches of water per acre, for mountains of the West, by hydrologic basin. For calculation procedure, see text.

in "forest and woodland" can be used as a surrogate for area in "mountains." In most of the West, forest or woodland vegetation is associated with mountains that are at least moderately moist; thus, a figure for forest and wooded cover includes mountainous terrain that generates runoff but excludes dry mountains which do not.[2] Such calculations suggest that water in mountains—and, by implication, in the immediately adjacent lowlands—is not always dramatically meager when compared to the humid East (figure 3).

The mountains in the basins of the Northern Rocky Mountains, for example, generate as much or more runoff (11.3 to 21.7 inches per acre) than most of the hydrologic basins in the East (7.8 to 21.4 inches per acre), and several of those in the Southern Rocky Mountains produce runoff (9.4–11.6 inches per acre) comparable to the Upper Mississippi River Valley and Great Lakes (7.8 and 10.5 inches per acre). Drainages from mountains along the Pacific Slope in the Northwest are much wetter (29.5–73.7 inches per acre) than those anywhere else in the country, and the Sierra Nevada and the southern end of the Cascade Range in California produce runoffs (20.1, 20.7) comparable to the wettest Eastern region of New England (21.4 inches per acre). Even the Bear Lake–Great Salt Lake region of Utah generates runoff values (9.4 inches per acre) higher than the Upper Mississippi River region (7.8 inches per acre). Finally, the mountains in the driest part of the southern Interior West produce meager flows of water (0.6–1.4 inches per acre), although not greatly different from areas of the northern plains (2.1–2.4 inches per acre).

These comparisons involve differing spatial scales, with the western areas more localized. But because the spatial variability of runoff is less in the East than in the West, the comparisons honestly reflect the major point: mountain ranges of the West, then, are by implication as wet or wetter than areas of comparable size in the East.

Lest this perspective be misunderstood as completely lacking the modern environmentalist 3-D viewpoint ("dire and dreadful disaster"), let the conclusion of the assessment be clearly stated: unequivocally, the West is dry, with water generally less available, less evenly distributed, and less dependable than in the East. But western mountains are anything but dry. On their rugged slopes, water is concentrated, in lakes and streams, in summer rains and deep winter snowpacks. As oases, the mountain ranges of the West support verdant bands of forest, conifers rather than palms, that rise above the brush and grass of the surrounding lowlands; as fountains, the rivers and rivulets bubble forth an abundance of water that tumbles into the arid valleys below; as islands of moisture in a sea of desert, western mountains provide landfalls for human hopes and habitations.

Mountain Moisture for an Agricultural Garden

Irrigated Western agriculture was fervently promoted and believed to be boundless a century ago; today, with comparable zeal, it is denigrated and seen as overextended. For example, in his critical evaluation of four recent books, reviewer Tom Wolf finds the various authors either too "fair" and "balanced," or too "human-centered" and too "sentimental"; he at once dismisses the approach of the "free-marketeer" and the "mainline environmental community"; he pleads for revelation of the "dark side of life represented in our literary tradition," the "great forces of history [which] grind down individuals and ideas," the "banality of evil in our time," and the "American pork-and-power pie" of which *everyone* seeks a slab. The end result, a saga of how we have treated the landscape of western water, is a "regional tragedy" and an "environmental disaster," "a tragic story" that makes "you thirst for vengeance."[3] Wolf speaks with anger. But whether expressed gently or with rage, his general position that western water policy has been fundamentally misguided is so common as to be conventional wisdom.

The human activity central to this "tragedy" is agriculture. The evolving image of the agricultural potential of the West from one of unbounded verdure to unforgivable violation is readily documented from a variety of sources. Henry Nash Smith stresses the importance of the American vision of "an agricultural paradise in the West" as a particular expression of a more general image of "the garden of the world," in which "blissful labor in the earth" would create "a happier state of society."[4] Bernard DeVoto also emphasizes a vision, broader than that of Nash and perhaps more focused on individual motivation, to explain the spread of the American empire into the arid West:

> The lodestone of West tugged deep in the blood, as deep as desire . . . . Toward that Western horizon all heroes of all peoples known to history have always traveled . . . the open country, freedom, the unknown. Westward lies the goal of effort.[5]

In emphasizing the "state of society" that federal irrigation projects would create, William Smythe typified the motivations described by Nash:

> The Nation reaches its hand into the Desert, and lo! private monopoly in water and in land is scourged from that holiest of temples. . . .
> That which lay beyond the grasp of the Individual yields to the hand of Associated Man.[6]

Patricia Limerick sees ignoble motivations, specifically individual desires for wealth and property, as prompting the westward "tugging," which, for her, was a desire for "conquest" over the native peoples and the natural world alike. In the same spirit, she characterizes the human reaction to the arid West, conditioned by a more humid and therefore benevolent East, as marked by "a sense of betrayal."[7] Also stressing the capitalist system as a reason for failed environmental and economic relations, Donald Worster, the high priest of the contemporary cynical realism, seems to find little pertaining to the West about which to be positive:

> The hydraulic society of the West . . . is increasingly a coercive, monolithic, and hierarchical system, ruled by a power elite based on the ownership of capital and expertise. Its face is reflected in every mile of the irrigation canal.[8]

The collective conviction common to these commentators is simple: whether dreaming of an egalitarian garden or a noble life, whether dupes of a humid-land mind-set or pawns of an economic system, those who believed in irrigation in the West brought about disaster, particularly ecological disaster, because they tried to create agricultural land in a landscape too arid to support it. After all, the West *is* a desert.

But those who promoted or engaged in irrigated agriculture did not see it as such. Their failure to interpret the "truth" about the arid West says much about the ability of the mind's eye to succumb to longing desire and promoters' cajoling, but it also reflects the spatial unevenness of that truth. No gardens were attempted in California's Panamint Valley, Nevada's Black Rock Desert, Utah's Tule Valley, Arizona's Cabeza Prieta country, or New Mexico's White Sands. The faith of even a William Smythe would be severely tested in such landscapes. But where water was available, attempts to create gardens seem less irrational: beside the San Joaquin River in California and the Salt in Arizona, below the Uinta Mountains in Utah and the Front Range in Colorado, along the Colorado River, the Columbia, the Snake, the Yellowstone, the Truckee, the Sevier, and the Reese. When as astute an interpreter as Donald Worster proclaims that the entire state of Utah is "river-deprived" and therefore too dry for much agriculture, he is partially seduced by his own mythmaking.[9] The fountains of the Wasatch send down a surprising volume of water, making the vision of an agricultural garden believable by the sanest of observers. The early Mormons, who settled the Wasatch Front, were no fools.

In fact, precisely because western water is locally abundant, the belief in a western garden seems rational, at least in certain locales; it is the extrapolation to all of the West that is unreasonable. The seduction of the myth, moreover, is widespread. Perhaps even skeptical reformer John Wesley Powell contributed to the development and persistence of the false belief in the potentials of western agriculture. Something of a folk hero among contemporary critics of western water policy, Powell was nonetheless a booster of the garden image. What he worked toward, unsuccessfully, was a thorough assessment of water availability in the West and settlement adjusted to fit that reality; he promoted farms of eighty irrigated acres, pasture allotments of 2,560 acres per farm, clustering of farmsteads in towns, and common grazing of unfenced rangeland.[10] Powell's popularity in the modern day stems more from his vision of egalitarian communities—he constantly urged the need for "local social organizations and cooperation in public improvements" in order to make irrigation endeavors successful—than from a conviction that the desert West should remain unsettled.[11] In fact, his own assessment of what irrigation was possible in the West is surprisingly similar to what has been accomplished. Powell's estimate that the average irrigated acre would require about six and one-half acre-feet of water allows for about 17,404,000 acres of irrigated land (ignoring the water-rich Snake-Columbia River area of the Pacific Northwest), compared to an actual 19,762,000 acres.[12] For California (the classic "hydrologic empire" and "Cadillac Desert"), Powell's calculations suggest a possible irrigated area of 10,470,000 acres, *more* than the current actual 9,342,000 acres. Powell favored dams ("The greater storage of water must come from the construction of great reservoirs in the highlands where lateral valleys may be dammed and the main streams conducted into them by canals") and a classification of land based entirely on narrow utility ("In providing for a general classification of the lands of the Arid Region, it will, then, be necessary to recognize the following classes, namely: mineral lands, coal lands, irrigable lands, timber lands, and pasturage lands").[13] Powell saw the concentration of water in western mountains and advocated appropriately concentrated development of that water as a utilitarian resource.

The point of examining Powell in this perspective is not to denigrate a conservation hero, but rather to illustrate that the image of a western agricultural garden was hardly the sole domain of soft-headed dreamers and vile capitalists. In a sense, these visionaries share common faiths that people are infinitely clever in their abilities to control nature, that human-dominated landscapes are more desirable than wild ones, and that growth in human numbers is not a threat as long as the physical base for that growth is not exceeded.[14] Such faiths, rather than allegiance to an unattainable utopia or to a particular economic system, are at the root of what angry commentator Tom Wolf bemoans as the threat to the "watery soul" of the West—the wildness of its rivers.[15]

Mountain Moisture and Forest Reserves

A utilitarian vision was not only the basis for attempts to create an agricultural garden in the West, but also a primary motivation for the initial formation of forest reserves in the United States from 1891 to 1906. Western mountains, and particularly water from those mountains, were keys in this major thrust of federal authority into the conservation arena.

The presidential authority to proclaim forest reserves on federal land was the result of an obscure rider attached to a bill which repealed the Timber Culture Laws; Congress approved the bill in 1890, with the rider "almost unnoticed": "From a close reading of the *Congressional Record* one gets the firm impression that Representative Payson, who was in charge of the bill, had steam-rollered it through a distracted and inattentive House, as repeated calls for it to be read, printed, and seen were denied, sidestepped, and evaded."[16] In his history of American forest policy, John Ise is even more emphatic about the role of chance in the creation of this particular presidential power: "no general forest reservation measure, *plainly understood to be such* [Ise's emphasis], . . . would ever have had the slightest chance of passing Congress."[17]

Nonetheless, the power was granted in March of 1891 (usually called the "Forest Reserve Act"), and presidents employed it to create forest reserves. In the first two years of the authority, from September 1891 to September 1893, Presidents Benjamin Harrison and Grover Cleveland proclaimed about 17,500,000 acres of forest reserves. By the time political pressure had mounted to force repeal of the general presidential authority in 1906, over 150 million acres were in forest reserves (to become the "National Forests" in 1907). This episode is typically characterized as "the most important time in the history of American forestry," but its significance is far greater: it made plausible a permanent federal land system serving a variety of purposes, whether for commodity resources such as timber and livestock forage or aesthetic resources such as landscapes and wildlife. Moreover, it legitimized a federal role in natural resource issues, a government control that, in spite of efforts to retard it, would grow with each subsequent decade.[18]

The Forest Reserve Act may have been passed without clear Congressional mandate, but the efforts to authorize permanent federal forestland extend back into at least the 1870s, and through it all, the focus of debate was on the mountains of the West. Forest historians typically portray the argument, usually implicitly, as primarily one over timber supply, with federal management promoted as necessary to maintain forest productivity.[19] Williams, however, comes close to recognizing that the concern over water from western mountains was pivotal in the dialogue over the future of American forests.[20]

A case might be made, in fact, that water, more than timber, was the primary worry that led to the first forest reserves. Recognition of the "interconnectedness" between elements in the environment was increasingly fashionable in the second half of the 1800s (spurred in part by the writings of George Perkins Marsh).[21] Clearly, the links between forests and water in the dry West were a concern for agitators for forest reserves, notably the early chiefs of the Forestry Division in the U.S. Department of Agriculture. Franklin Hough, for example, the first chief (1881–83), included extensive discussions of the interplays among forests, climate, and surface water in his three-volume *Report upon Forestry,* the first major assessment of forests in the United States.[22] These essays on water were combined with treatments of forest fires, timber supplies, wood products, and regional assessments of American forests. Hough, apparently an "avid follower of Marsh," depended upon mostly European examples for illustration.[23] His conclusions were strongly in favor of federal forest reserves in the United States: "We would therefore earnestly recommend that the principal bodies of timber land still remaining in the property of the government (to be specified and described upon particular examination) be withdrawn from sale or grant . . . the title being retained by the Government."[24]

The second chief of the Forestry Division, N. H. Egleston (1883–86), emphasized more than Hough the relationships between forests and water in his annual reports for 1884 and 1885. His essays entitled "Protection of Rivers by Forests," "Influence of Forests upon the Flow of Streams and upon Floods and Droughts," and "Forestry Better Than Dikes" were strongly prescriptive, arguing in favor of public forest ownership.[25] Consistent with this stance of advocacy, Egleston also expressed regret over Congressional failure to establish "a reservation of a forest tract in Montana" in the headwater region of the Missouri and Columbia Rivers, where such a reserve could act as "a regulator of those important streams."[26]

Still more explicit statements about the importance of the links between dense forest cover and healthy streamflow came from B. E. Fernow, Forestry Division chief from 1886 to 1898. In responding to a rhetorical question regarding the "first duty of the general government in regards to the forestry question," Fernow answered with a discussion of the importance of forests in the West for the even delivery of water from mountain rains and snows to the adjoining lowlands: "The forest cover regulates and beneficially influences the rapidity with which these precipitations are carried to the plain for utilization on agricultural lands."[27] Fernow felt, moreover, that the streamflow functions were more important than the timber supply purposes of western forests:

> [T]he forest cover . . . on the Rocky Mountains and the Pacific Slopes subserve a function which makes its material value of only secondary importance. It has become already evident that the denudation of mountain sides in the region . . . has impaired the regularity of waterflow, upon which irrigation in the arid valleys below depends. . . .
> The interest of the nation, therefore, in properly administering this property reaches beyond that of any material advantage.[28]

In his 1888 "Report on the Forest Conditions of the Rocky Mountains," an updated and more explicitly American sequel to Hough's earlier three-volume treatment of forest issues, Fernow would again say that "in the Rocky Mountain region . . . the most important office performed by the forests is the conservation and distribution of moisture."[29] He repeatedly reiterated this position: "the primary object of these [federal forest] reservations is to insure favorable water conditions in the regions which depend for their fertility upon irrigation."[30]

In pressing for federal action, Fernow reported the efforts of local farming groups to protect water supplies; in California, a "convention of citizens of Fresno, Tulare, Kern, and Merced Counties . . . [has] ask[ed] for the permanent protection of the forests lying upon the water-sheds of those counties," and in Colorado "a movement . . . [is working for the] preservation of the forests of a region which is the source of several large streams."[31] Only Congressional action, Fernow felt, could preserve these forestlands:

> If timber lands near the sources of our large rivers are to be carefully guarded by national legislation there is no better place to begin the work than right here at the headwaters of the Yellowstone and Snake, which send their waters from the heart of the continent to both the Atlantic and Pacific.[32]

Even the mountain slopes rising around the Los Angeles basin, mostly covered with brush rather than commercial timber, were seen to need protection because of their water-conserving functions.[33]

Fernow was an especially effective spokesperson, and he, along with Edward Bowers, is credited with drafting the legislation that became the

Forest Reserve Act.[34] The distribution of the first reserves strongly reflects the sense that water conservation was a preeminent consideration, with locations long advocated by Fernow: in the headwater regions of central Colorado and northwestern Wyoming, above the San Joaquin and Willamette Valleys, on the slopes above Los Angeles (figure 4). The reservation in the mountains above Santa Fe was called the Pecos River Forest Reserve and may have been prompted by considerations of watershed protection, although the Grand Canyon and Pacific Forest Reserves (i.e., Mount Rainier) seem to have received attention for aesthetics more than utility. Taken together, the early forest reserves signal a growing role for government control, in the name of conservation, in the Mountainous West. *Conservation of what?*

The arguments in behalf of federal forest reserves made a century ago echo a decidedly contemporary tone. Forests serve functions beyond just the production of wood, this perspective suggests; in fact, the most important functions are those involving "services" rather than "commodities." The modern environmentalist worries about climate changes induced by deforestation of tropical forests, "desertification" caused by excessive wood cutting in dry forest environments, and catastrophic utilitarian effects resulting from the loss of biological species. These concerns are different in detail from Egleston's forest "dikes," but they articulate the same sense of impending doom, of a world unable to support humanity.

Moist Mountains and Protected Nature

Water in western mountains has played a major role not only in utilitarian uses of landscape, as suggested by the early forest reserves, but also in the development of the institutions for nature protection in American society. A conventional wisdom, developed by Alfred Runte but earlier articulated by Hans Huth, is that spectacular and monumental scenery in the West has been the dominant focus for national parks in the United States.[35] As a general statement about landscapes protected within the National Park System, this proposition is irrefutable, even though Runte's criticism of such an emphasis naively demeans the importance of scenic spectacles to people.[36] But more specifically, the earliest national parks were not created around just *any* monumental scenery; rather, they were located in western mountains, notably western mountains with an abundance of water. Such landscapes remain the archetype for American national parks today.

Committing CUP development of water on Uintas, eliminated any possibility of national Park status.

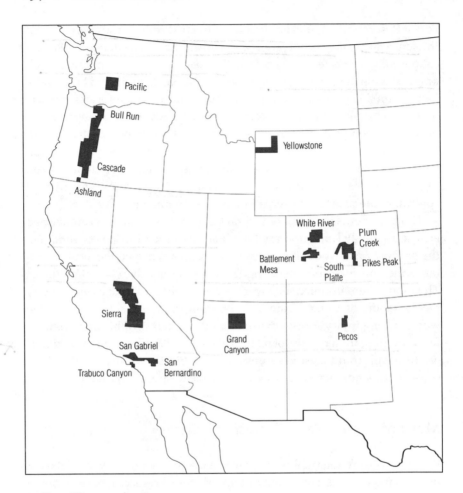

4. *Forest Reserves in 1893.*

The first two landscape reserves epitomize the historical pattern and, for many, the contemporary expression of the ideal "national park." Yosemite Valley, protected as a state grant by Congressional action in 1864, is most photographed for its soaring cliffs and plunging waterfalls. But the flat valley floor, traversed throughout its length by the cool and peaceful Merced River winding through moist meadows and forests of pine and oak, also seems an essential element of the appeal. The vertical cliffs alone, without waterfalls, river, meadows, or forests, would hardly have generated, it seems, as much early attention. Similarly, the scenic oddities which led to the establishment of Yellowstone National Park in 1872, geysers and hot springs, the Yellowstone River and its Grand Canyon, are features of moving water in a high-elevation environment. Although not the generally rugged and dissected landscape of Yosemite, the Yellowstone Plateau is flanked by mountain ranges, gouged by numerous rivers, and clothed in the distinctively western vegetation of coniferous forest. It is hard to imagine that the thermal features would have attracted so much early attention, or would continue to be so appealing, if they occurred in an arid plain of creosote bush desert.

Subsequent to the Yosemite Grant and Yellowstone National Park, Congress established additional national parks in comparably moist mountain environments. In 1890, three parks were created on the west slope of the Sierra Nevada in California: Yosemite (surrounding the initial state grant), Sequoia, and General Grant (which was expanded to become Kings Canyon in 1940). Mount Rainier in Washington (1899) and Crater Lake in Oregon (1902) protected areas in the Cascades of the Northwest, followed by Glacier in Montana (1910) and Rocky Mountain in Colorado (1913), both in the Rocky Mountain system. The other national park that governmental promoter Robert Sterling Yard identified as "of the first order" was Mesa Verde (1906), a reserve protecting prehistoric cliff dwellings on a dissected but forested plateau in southwestern Colorado. ("Second order" national parks at the time included Platt, Sully's Hill, Wind Cave, and Casa Grande.)[37]

The reasons for this early emphasis on landscapes in moist western mountains are varied but likely involve trails of thought that extend far back in time. The more immediate origins lie in the perception of the American West as a "Promised Land," a region "somewhat like the Garden of Eden, with boundless riches in pasture lands and untouched forests."[38] Some observers have stressed deeper roots, noting the importance of western European ideals about landscapes as the basis for American attitudes toward wilderness:

> This was the visual surprise of the Western wilderness: truly wild places that resembled civilization's most ornamental achievement— the estate park—which was, in turn, linked with an image of paradise. . . . [Yellowstone] was the sort of landscape that Constable had painted at Vivenhoe Park, a grassy retreat insulated from the outer world by distant groves, a solitude where cattle or deer munched the turf and gracefully composed themselves into groups.[39]

Still others have seen an older tradition of mountain worship, including Yi-fu Tuan's suggestion that mountains have been long viewed with awe as places "impregnated with sacred power where the human spirit could pass from one cosmic level to another"; the sense of awe, moreover, was not necessarily "sympathetic," but, rather "at once wonderful and terrible."[40] Similarly, Marjorie Hope Nicolson traces the transformation of the older "mountain doom" into the modern "mountain glory" as a reflection of changes in theological notions of perfection and scientific ideas about landforms, linked to each other through the development of aesthetics.[41]

Perhaps related to the increased sensitivity toward mountains, and toward the natural world more generally, outdoor recreation emerged and grew increasingly important in late-nineteenth- and early-twentieth-century America. Peter Schmitt sees this trend as an expression of a larger mood toward "Arcadian" tendencies, the conviction of an urban population that "country life and city culture offered more in conjunction than as opposites" and that "nature's spiritual impact [was greater than] its economic importance." Recreation in the national parks, moreover, conformed to the Arcadian values because the parks "offered the precise blend of luxury and nature that tourists thought appropriate to Western life."[42] Growing numbers of visitors, seemingly expecting the developments necessary for the desired "blend of luxury and nature," brought with them unending controversy over how much and what kind of recreation is appropriate for the parks. Promoted by the first Park Service director, Stephen Mather, as a means of generating support for the new system, recreation eventually became a favorite whipping boy for the lash-holding critics of the national parks: David Lowenthal proclaims it dishonest; John Jakle dismisses it as superficial; Roderick Nash condemns it as destroying nature; Alfred Runte criticizes it for failing to generate support for biologically based reserves.[43] Coming full circle, Stephen Fox faults Mather for his "weakness for plush accommodations and city comforts."[44]

Little argument, however, can be generated about the success of Mather's strategy. Nowhere, moreover, could that strategy work better than in western mountains with an abundance of water. Arid slickrock slopes, desert ranges, dry canyons, no matter how spectacular their scenery, could not match the ease and comfort of travel possible in moist mountainous terrain. Thus, the growing intellectual appreciation of mountains and the emerging energies for outdoor recreation combined to make western mountains, with roaring rivers or cascading streams, an ideal landscape, a restorative sanctuary.

For those who see moist mountains as such an ideal, aesthetics and recreation are appropriate companions. When Roderick Nash, then, declares that John Muir's strong advocacy of recreation in the parks was simply politically "pragmatic," a "camouflage" of his true and biocentric views, Nash not only misrepresents Muir but also simplifies complex human responses to the natural world.[45] Nothing in reality requires that a person be purely "biocentric" or completely "anthropocentric." Muir could honestly urge visitors to "climb the mountains" and see the restorative qualities of mountain sanctuaries, while he recognized the rights of "rattlesnakes." Human reactions to nature may be as variable, and as rich, within an individual as within a society.

Western Mountains and Environmental Diversity

By embracing both biocentric and anthropocentric perspectives, Muir seems too catholic to be a modern environmentalist. Among those active in nature protection today, the rhetoric is dominated by biological matters, concern for nature's rights, worry about "biodiversity" and "complete ecosystems."[46] Given this modern focus, the richness of biological species in western mountains and the relative "natural wholeness" of these mountain ranges, made seemingly discrete entities by their surrounding seas of arid lowlands, receive surprisingly little attention.

Western mountains create steep climatic gradients because they rise from dry environments into humid high elevations, and they separate cool and moist coasts from hot and dry interiors; the rapidly changing climates induce equally rapid changes in biologies in short horizontal distances. Species densities of both birds and mammals, accordingly, are higher in mountainous areas of the Southwest than elsewhere in the country. Similarly, the vegetation complexity is much greater in the West than in the East.[47] Nature reserves which best protect this environmental diversity are several units of the National Park System; wilderness areas on other federal lands encompass only high mountain or desert landscapes, and national wildlife refuges similarly lack great environmental variety. The steepest environmental gradients and their associated biotas within the National Park System include Arizona's new Saguaro National Park (whose environments extend from stands of columnar cactus into dense coniferous forests), Nevada's Great Basin National Park (from sagebrush desert into alpine environments well above timberline), California's Death Valley National Monument (from the sparsest of arid brush at two hundred feet below sea level into pine forests, albeit modest, at elevations 11,000 feet above sea level), and, also in California, the Sierra Nevada's Sequoia National Park (from chaparral and oak woodlands into alpine zones).

This characterization of biological variety within units of the National Park System is not commonly articulated, and modern environmentalists, in spite of their preoccupation with biological diversity, hardly celebrate these examples of successful protection. Rather, their cause celebre is the rare or endangered species, the local lousewort or freshwater clam, an endemic minnow or the grizzly bear. Their concern is not so much for beta diversity, the rates of change in species along environmental gradients, or perhaps even in alpha diversity, the species encountered in particular community samples, as it is in species richness, the number of species collectively existent.[48] So expressed, the contemporary focus in nature protection efforts, that is, rare biological species, is not new, but has a century-long history extending back to the beginnings of institutionalized nature protection.[49]

What may make the contemporary concern for species protection innovative is the heightened recognition that species exist in "communities," and that the protection of species requires protection of a larger whole.[50] The attempt to define biological communities, distinctive regions of plants and animals, is centuries old, but one scheme that influenced professional and popular interpretations of nature for half a century was that of C. Hart Merriam, who sought to organize the biological diversity along environmental gradients in the Mountainous West.[51] Merriam, a scientist with the federal government and the Smithsonian Institution from 1885 until about 1940, assumed that certain temperature characteristics set distributional limits for biological species, and he identified "life zones" within which groups of species coexisted. He stressed the similarities between changes in both temperature and species along the north-south latitudinal gradient across the continent and the elevational gradient upward in high western mountains; the San Francisco Peaks in northern Arizona was his case study for such zonation (figure 5). Merriam's life zones became the common means of organizing biota in the American West, persisting long after the scientific foundation for his scheme was undermined.[52]

Merriam's legacy continues in the variety of systems by which species continue to be organized spatially. Even though the reality of discrete communities in the biological world has long been refuted in the professional ecological literature, the imagery of "complete ecosystems" (implying that boundaries separating one ecosystem from another do, in fact, exist) re-

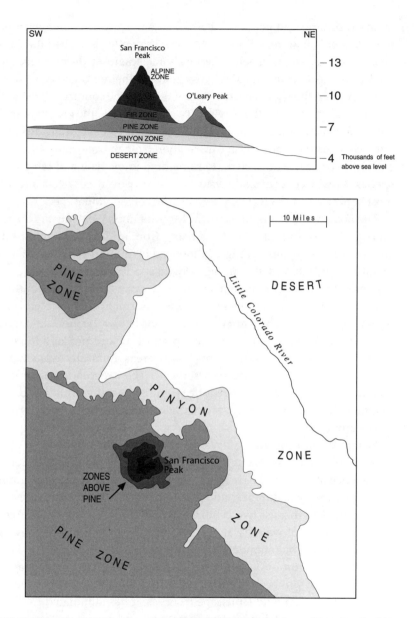

5. *Life Zones of C. H. Merriam. Modified after C. H. Merriam, "Results of a Biological Survey of the San Francisco Mountain Region and Desert of the Little Colorado, Arizona," in North American Fauna No. 3 (Washington, D.C.: Government Printing Office, 1890).*

mains appealing and popular.[53] Perhaps the most well-known example is the "Greater Yellowstone Ecosystem" (more recently also called the Greater Yellowstone "Area," probably reflecting some scientists' desire to recognize the lack of "real" boundaries for ecosystems). Whether called ecosystem or area, however, the regionalization for the Yellowstone country is largely what is believed necessary for the survival of a single species, the grizzly bear. This species focus for the abstraction of an "ecosystem" is biologically defensible, but it changes the emphasis in conservation biology from some amorphous entity, the complete ecosystem, to something immediate and tangible, the species. As with concern for diversity, then, worry over ecosystem integrity is most honestly and productively seen in terms of individual species.

The present species richness in the Mountainous West mirrors the natural condition of humid mountains rising from arid lowlands, but future species richness will be strongly influenced by human activities. Whether or not actually realized, the survival of wild species is nowhere in the world greater than in the Mountainous West. A major reason for this outlook is the historical context of the region: the transformation of wild landscapes by agriculture is largely restricted to lowlands below the mountain ranges; forested lands are in public ownership and thus are unlikely to be converted to dense human settlements; many areas are protected as national parks and other wild landscape reserves.[54] The sanctuaries necessary to maintain species richness will require strengthened governmental controls to protect the concentration of biological resources which characterize the Mountainous West.

When Wallace Stegner proclaims that "[a]ridity, and aridity alone, makes the various Wests one," he articulates the popular convention that the essence of the West lies in its dryness.[55] But this wisdom is incomplete: if the West were a featureless, arid plain, so much of what has happened in the region over the last two centuries would not have occurred. It is the teasing promise of water, water in western mountains rising above arid lowlands, which has stimulated the various themes of people and land in the West. That promise has permitted a spatially restricted western agriculture, prompted protection of mountainous watersheds, and encouraged creation of singular wild landscape reserves; it has stimulated the federal role in farming expansion, water production, and nature protection; it has inspired concern to create sanctuaries for noble human societies, utilitarian resources, and wild nature. Aridity in the lowlands, moisture in the mountains—the two have resonated, and continue to reverberate, in the human involvement with western landscapes.

Notes

1. All numbers used in this section on western water are from U.S. Water Resources Council, *The Nation's Water Resources*, vol. 3, Appendix I (Washington, D.C.: Government Printing Office, 1979).

2. These calculations produce, at best, a general portrayal. In the southern half of the West, "woodland" includes woody plant cover in dry environments, whether or not mountainous, which likely contribute little runoff; here, the vegetation surrogate undoubtedly underestimates the importance of mountains to runoff. In the Pacific Northwest, on the other hand, nonforested vegetation, including farmland, probably contributes to surface runoff, and thus the surrogate could overestimate the importance of mountains.

3. Tom Wolf's review, "The Western Soul has a Watery Grave," was published in *High Country News* (Paonia, Calif.), 3 December 1990, 14–15. The four books that he evaluated were M. Reisner and S. Bates. *Overtapped Oasis: Reform or Revolution for Western Water* (Washington, D.C.: Island Press, 1989); R. Martin, *A Story That Stands like a Dam: Glen Canyon and the Struggle for the Soul of the West* (New York: Henry Holt, 1989); R. Gottlieb, *A Life of Its Own: The Politics and Power of Water* (San Diego: Harcourt Brace Jovanovich, 1988); R. Wahl, *Markets for Federal Water: Subsidies, Property Rights, and the Bureau of Reclamation* (Baltimore: Johns Hopkins University Press, 1989).

4. H. N. Smith, *Virgin Land: The American West as Symbol and Myth* (New York: Vintage Books, 1961), 138–39.

5. B. DeVoto, *The Year of Decision, 1846* (Boston: Houghton Mifflin, 1943), 49.

6. W. E. Smythe, *The Conquest of Arid America* (New York: Harper and Brothers, 1900), verse in foreword.

7. P. N. Limerick, *The Legacy of Conquest: The Unbroken Past of the American West* (New York: Norton, 1987); Limerick, *Desert Passages: Encounters with the American Deserts* (Albuquerque: University of New Mexico Press, 1985), 175.

8. D. Worster, *Rivers of Empire: Water, Aridity, and the Growth of the American West* (New York: Pantheon, 1985), 7.

9. Worster, *Rivers of Empire*, 82.

10. J. W. Powell, *Report on the Lands of the Arid Region of the United States, with a More Detailed Account of the Lands of Utah* (reprint, ed. W. Stegner, Cambridge, Mass.: Belknap Press of Harvard University Press, 1962), 40, 43.

11. Powell, *Report on the Lands*, 36.

12. Powell, in his *Report on the Lands*, 18, thought that a water flow of one cubic foot per second would be adequate for about one hundred acres of irrigated farmland. One cubic foot per second equals seven and one-half gallons per second, or

about 650,000 gallons per day. On an annual basis, this flow is equivalent to about six and one-half acre-feet per year.

13. Powell, *Report on the Lands*, 23, 57.

14. The fundamental importance of the conflicting faiths of ecological optimism and pessimism is a theme in the writings of Daniel B. Luten. See especially "The Limits to Growth Controversy" and "Ecological Optimism in the Social Sciences" in *Progress against Growth: Daniel B. Luten on the American Landscape*, ed. T. Vale (New York: Guilford Press, 1986), 293–335.

15. Wolf, "Western Soul Has a Watery Grave," 15.

16. M. Williams, *Americans and Their Forests* (Cambridge: Cambridge University Press, 1989), 411.

17. J. Ise, *United States Forest Policy* (New York: Arno Press, 1972), 114.

18. William Graf identifies periodic efforts by the federal government to extend its influence over management of public lands in the West, each time focused on a different issue (irrigation land, forest land, grazing land, and wilderness) and each met with opposition by "sagebrush rebels." See W. Graf, *Wilderness Preservation and the Sagebrush Rebellions* (Savage, Md.: Rowman and Littlefield, 1990).

19. For examples, see Ise, *United States Forest Policy*; H. Steen, *The U.S. Forest Service: A History* (Seattle: University of Washington Press, 1976); J. M. Petulla, *American Environmental History: The Exploitation and Conservation of Natural Resources* (San Francisco: Boyd and Fraser, 1977); W. G. Robbins, *American Forestry: A History of National, State, and Private Cooperation* (Lincoln: University of Nebraska Press, 1957).

20. Williams, *Americans and Their Forests*, 398, 415.

21. Williams, *Americans and Their Forests*, 398.

22. For example, F. B. Hough included essays such as the "Influence of Woodlands upon Springs, Rivers, and Streams, and in Causing Droughts" in *Report upon Forestry*, vol. 1 (Washington, D.C.: Government Printing Office, 1878).

23. Petulla, *American Environmental History*, 222.

24. Hough, *Report upon Forestry*, vol. 3 (Washington, D.C.: Government Printing Office, 1882), 8.

25. N. H. Egleston, "Report of the Chief of the Forestry Division, 1884," in *Annual Report of the U.S. Department of Agriculture, 1884* (Washington, D.C.: Government Printing Office, 1884), 160–62; Egleston, "Report of the Chief of the Forestry Division, 1885," in *Annual Report of the U.S. Department of Agriculture, 1885* (Washington, D.C.: Government Printing Office, 1885), 192–96.

26. Egleston, "Report of the Chief, 1885," 204.

27. B. E. Fernow, "Report of the Chief of the Forestry Division, 1888," in *Annual Report of the U.S. Department of Agriculture, 1888* (Washington, D.C.: Government Printing Office, 1888), 607.

28. Fernow, "Report of the Chief, 1888," 613.

29. B. E. Fernow, "Report on the Forest Conditions of the Rocky Mountains and Other Papers," Department of Agriculture, Forestry Bulletin no. 2 (Washington, D.C.: Government Printing Office, 1888), 84.

30. B. E. Fernow, "Report of the Chief of the Forestry Division, 1892," in *Annual Report of the U.S. Department of Agriculture, 1892* (Washington, D.C.: Government Printing Office, 1892), 319.

31. B. E. Fernow, "Report of the Chief of the Forestry Division, 1889," in *Annual Report of the U.S. Department of Agriculture, 1889* (Washington, D.C.: Government Printing Office, 1889), 270, 290.

32. Fernow, "Report on the Forest Conditions," 211.

33. An essay in Fernow, "Report on the Forest Conditions," includes a chapter written by Abbot Kinney titled "The Forests of Los Angeles, San Diego, and San Bernardino Counties, California."

34. A government report by E. A. Bowers is often cited as the draft for the Forest Reserve Act. Bowers's report includes frequent mention of the importance of forests to the maintenance of streamflow. See Bowers, *Plan for the Management and Disposition of the Public Timber Lands*, 50th Cong., 1st sess., 1890, H. Doc. 242.

35. Alfred Runte is usually considered a fundamental critic of national parks in the United States. Earlier, Hans Huth offered a broader assessment of relations between nature and society in the United States, anticipating Runte's identification of "scenery" as important to nature protection. See Runte, *National Parks: The American Experience*, 2d ed. (Lincoln: University of Nebraska Press, 1987); H. Huth, *Nature and the American* (Berkeley: University of California Press, 1957).

36. The logical extension of the criticism of national parks as protecting only scenic spectacles is to imagine a park system that does not include Yosemite, Yellowstone, Mount Rainier, the Grand Canyon, and other singular landscapes. Would anyone really prefer such a system? See T. Vale, "No Romantic Landscapes for Our National Parks?" *Natural Areas Journal* 8 (1988): 115–17.

37. R. S. Yard, *Glimpses of Our National Parks* (Washington, D.C.: Government Printing Office, 1916), 4.

38. Huth, *Nature and the American*, 130.

39. P. Shepard, *Man in the Landscape: A Historic View of the Esthetics of Nature* (New York: Alfred A. Knopf, 1967), 256.

40. Yi-fu Tuan, *Topophilia: A Study of Environmental Perception, Attitudes, and Values* (Englewood Cliffs, N.J.: Prentice-Hall, 1974), 70–72.

41. A key discourse in the transformation of ideas about mountains was Thomas Burnet's "Sacred Theory of the Earth." See M. H. Nicolson, *Mountain Doom and Mountain Glory* (Ithaca, N.Y.: Cornell University Press, 1959), 195–224.

42. P. J. Schmitt, *Back to Nature: The Arcadian Myth in Urban America* (Baltimore: Johns Hopkins University Press, 1969), xvii, 165, 189.

43. J. Ise, *National Park Policy: A Critical History* (Baltimore: Johns Hopkins University Press, 1961), 195–98. Critics of the manifestation of nature protection sentiment make odd bedfellows; they clearly do not agree on the desirability of that sentiment. See D. Lowenthal, "Not Every Prospect Pleases," *Landscape* 12, no. 2 (1962): 19–23; J. Jakle, *The Tourist: Travel in Twentieth-Century North America* (Lincoln: University of Nebraska Press, 1985); R. Nash, *Wilderness and the American Mind*, 3d ed. (New Haven: Yale University Press, 1982); Runte, *National Parks*.

44. S. Fox, *The American Conservation Movement: John Muir and His Legacy* (Madison: University of Wisconsin Press, 1981), 204.

45. R. Nash, *The Rights of Nature: A History of Environmental Ethics* (Madison: University of Wisconsin Press, 1989), 40–41.

46. The natural world in a complete sense includes climates, landforms, soils, and hydrologic characteristics, in addition to biological species, but so strong are concerns for species diversity that the very nature of Nature is usually assumed to be solely biological.

47. R. E. Cook, "Variation in Species Density of North American Birds," *Systematic Zoology* 18 (1969): 63–84; G. G. Simpson, "Species Density of North American Recent Mammals," *Systematic Zoology* 13 (1964): 57–73. High environmental diversity is as characteristic of the West as a geographic region as is aridity or mountains. See T. Vale and G. Vale, *Western Images, Western Landscapes* (Tucson: University of Arizona Press, 1989).

48. R. H. Whittaker, *Communities and Ecosystems*, 2d ed. (New York: Macmillan, 1975).

49. The contemporary interest in species survival is exemplified by a series of articles in *Science* 253, no. 5021 (16 August 1991). Historical treatments of concern for biological species are legion; a good example is R. Doughty, *Feather Fashions and Bird Preservation: A Study in Nature Protection* (Berkeley: University of California Press, 1975).

50. A recent history traces a change in nature protection from concern for biological objects to concern for functional systems. See L. Dilsaver, and W. Tweed, *Challenge of the Big Trees: A Resource History of Sequoia and Kings Canyon National Parks* (Three Rivers, Calif.: Sequoia Natural History Association, 1990).

51. C. H. Merriam, "Results of a Biological Survey of the San Francisco Mountain Region and Desert of the Little Colorado, Arizona," in *North American Fauna no. 3* (Washington, D.C.: Government Printing Office, 1890).

52. M. D. F. Udvardy, *Dynamic Zoogeography* (New York: Van Nostrand Reinhold, 1969).

53. Belief in the reality of "entire ecosystems" may lead to policies which threaten biological species. See A. Chase, *Playing God in Yellowstone* (Boston: Atlantic Monthly Press, 1986).

54. These conditions do not guarantee survival of all existent species, but I suggest that they offer greater likelihood of a persistence of biological diversity in the Mountainous West than in any area of comparable size in the world.

55. W. Stegner, *The American West as Living Space* (Ann Arbor: University of Michigan Press, 1987), 8.

Zones of Concentrated Resources

The special resource base of the Mountainous West includes more than just a surplus of water. Geoecology has focused concentrations of minerals, forage, and timber in these highland environments. Several of our authors assess each of these resources in greater detail. Randall Rohe's contribution examines the local interplay of mountain mineral resources and settlers who converged upon the western highlands in the second half of the nineteenth century. After describing some of the diverse tectonic conditions that lead to mineral formation in mountain settings, Rohe then suggests how local geology often influenced the type of mining activity undertaken and the technology utilized to extract and refine ores. He also notes how mountain isolation and alpine climates affected mining operations in the high country. In the second half of his essay, Rohe reflects on how mining activities changed mountain landscapes. The dramatic depletion of local vegetation, the fouling of air and water, and the alteration of mountain landforms are all vivid and often enduring signatures signaling the consequences of concentrated human exploitation in a fragile highland environment.

Victor Konrad changes the focus to mountain-grazing resources and the often close relationship between mountain-ranching activities and the role of the federal government. Southern Montana's Pryor Mountains are the setting for his detailed look at how the Forest Homestead Act of 1906 opened new western mountain lands to potential settlement. Konrad carefully shows how the diverse environmental niches of the Pryors offered different opportunities for development. Using both field and archival data, he also reconstructs the forest homestead landscape by describing typical mountain settlement patterns, the look of local farmsteads, and the material culture of farmhouses, stables, and barns. Finally, Konrad focuses on the grazing economy which came to dominate much of the Pryors, and he explores the often tense, but always intimate, interrelationship between local ranchers and the Forest Service.

A third essay examines the role of the Mountainous West as a lumber frontier. Michael Williams points out that the western forests differed from their eastern and southern counterparts because they were concentrated in public lands and were often integral parts of environments increasingly valued for their aesthetic and recreational qualities. After sketching early perceptions of western forests and the evolution of their local uses to pioneers and miners, he then details how changing spatial systems of transportation, patterns of growing national demand, and new technologies contributed to the birth of a large commercial lumbering industry, concentrated in the Coast Ranges of the Pacific Northwest. As with Konrad's case study, Williams articulates the close relationship between private users and public bureaucrats in the evolution of the West's forest resources. Weaving in the restorative sanctuary theme, Williams concludes his overview with a discussion of how concentrated western forests inevitably led to sharp disagreements in how best to manage these resources: one person's vision of board feet is another's sacred outdoor cathedral. He ponders how such conflicts, epitomized historically by the different philosophies of Chief Forester Gifford Pinchot and preservationist John Muir, continue today, making the Mountainous West a land of contested, as well as concentrated, resources.

6 / Environment and Mining in the Mountainous West

RANDALL ROHE

The exploitation of many resources shaped the regional character of the West, but probably none wielded greater influence than gold and silver mining. It caused large and rapid movements of population; it established numerous settlements in the West, many of which were permanent; it developed new transportation routes and modified existing ones; and it produced a distinctive cultural landscape. Moreover, gold and silver mining remains an integral part of the popular image of the region. The prospector and his burro vie with the cowboy and his horse as symbols of the West. Many of the characteristics that define the Mountainous West as a regional entity strongly influenced the development of mining. As areas of concentrated resources and islands of moisture, the mountainous areas had the ore deposits, timber reserves, and water supplies critical to mining (see figures 4–6 in chapter 1). At the same time, the mountains acted as barriers to transport and often isolated the mining districts from their supply centers and markets as well as from the rest of the mining West. Critical to understanding mining's role in the evolution and development of the regional character of the Mountainous West is an appreciation of the interaction between mining and these environmental factors. How did the concentration of resources and water as well as the variable isolation of the Mountainous West influence mining? How did mining in turn impact settlement and the fragile western environment?

Environmental Influences on Mining

Most gold occurs in the form of lode or placer deposits. The term *placer* probably originated from the Spanish *plaza de oro*, a place of gold, and simply meant a surface working. Most placers consist of gold-bearing gravels which have been freed from the rock by weathering and then moved and concentrated by processes of erosion and deposition. Lode deposits consist of gold and silver still contained within the rock. Gold, which is chemically inert, retains its original form while being eroded, transported, and deposited, and therefore readily forms placers. Silver, on the other hand, which combines readily with most acids and forms soluble compounds, is not ordinarily found in placer deposits.[1]

In the American West both placer and lode gold occur primarily in areas that have been subjected to tectonic activity (figures 1 and 2). Most of the gold deposits are associated with and are perhaps genetically related to small batholiths, stocks, and similar intrusive bodies of quartz monzonite of Jurasaic to Tertiary age. In areas where no geological disturbance has taken place, so that the rocks still lie horizontal, such mineral deposits are rare or inferior in value. Reflecting this, maps of gold-mining districts show that most follow the mountain ranges, while few districts came into being in the Columbia and Snake River Plateau and the Colorado Plateau.[2]

Like gold, silver occurs in the mountainous rather than the level parts of the West because the deposits originated during periods of earth movement, when ascending hot liquids flowed into fissures and cracks in the earth's crust and formed "veins" that wind and twist through the older rock as veins do through the human body. Sometimes the hot ore-bearing solutions rising from below actually penetrated solid rock, perhaps aided by minute cracks, dissolved it, and substituted new minerals for the original matter forming "replacement deposits."[3]

After 1848, the western states contributed the bulk of the gold mined in the United States. From 1848 to 1854, gold production in the United States multiplied seventy-three times, an increase almost entirely due to the discovery of placer gold and the subsequent development of placer mining in California. From California, the mining frontier eventually moved eastward to envelop much of the Mountainous West.[4]

While lode mining began in California during 1849–50, it contributed relatively little of the total gold output until 1860. A notable expansion of lode production began about the middle 1860s that resulted primarily from development of the Mother Lode in California and the Comstock Lode in Nevada. The search for gold in the West also led to the discovery and development of many silver, lead, zinc, and copper deposits from which gold was extracted as a by-product. With improvements in mining and metallurgical techniques and the development of large low-grade base metal deposits, by-product gold became a significant fraction of the annual domes-

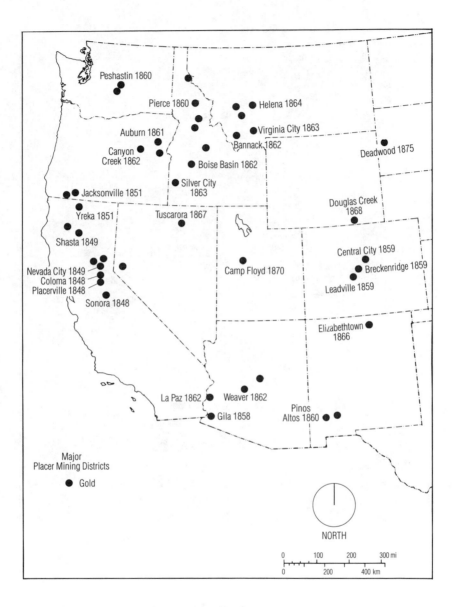

Peshastin 1860

Pierce 1860

Helena 1864

Auburn 1861

Virginia City 1863

Canyon
Creek 1862

Bannack 1862

Deadwood 1875

Boise Basin 1862

Silver City
1863

Jacksonville 1851

Tuscarora 1867

Douglas Creek
1868

Yreka 1851

Shasta 1849

Central City 1859

Nevada City 1849

Camp Floyd 1870

Breckenridge 1859

Coloma 1848
Placerville 1848

Leadville 1859

Sonora 1848

Elizabethtown
1866

La Paz 1862

Weaver 1862

Gila 1858

Pinos
Altos 1860

Major
Placer Mining Districts

● Gold

NORTH

| 0 | 100 | 200 | 300 mi |

| 0 | 200 | 400 km |

1. *Major Placer Mining Districts and Dates of Discovery.*

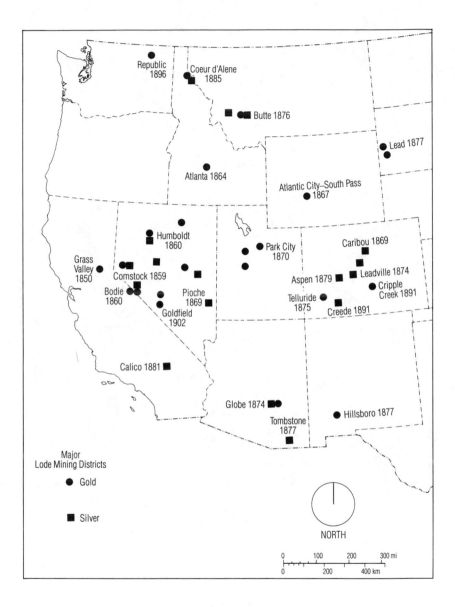

2. *Major Lode Mining Districts and Dates of Discovery.*

tic gold output. The four leading states, in order of total gold output, are California, Colorado, South Dakota, and Nevada.[5]

The Comstock of Nevada, discovered in 1859, was the first major silver district in the United States. During 1859–61, the production of gold exceeded that of silver on the Comstock, but for the period 1860–80 silver accounted for 57 percent of the yield. Following the development of silver mining on the Comstock, important silver discoveries continued until after the turn of the century (figure 2). Historically, Montana ranks first in silver production, followed by Utah, Colorado, Idaho, Nevada, and Arizona.[6]

While geology restricted most occurrences of gold and silver to the mountainous areas of the West, the mountain environment varied greatly. Each setting had its own set of limitations and opportunities and affected the development of mining somewhat differently. George Hubbard summarized the interrelationship:

> In each locality a method of extraction and reduction capable of handling the ore in its mineral associations, and also adapted to the conditions of water, fuel, and transportation, must be devised. Because of the relation of mining and reduction processes to the vicinal geographic conditions, the latter may seem in cases to control the output; and so they do.[7]

Geology and geomorphic history, which varied from area to area, greatly influenced the type of mining that occurred and its likelihood of success. For example, in Montana the great boom and the great bust in silver mining shared the same cause: geological factors that determined the nature of its silver deposits, and government monetary policies that determined what silver was worth. Geologic conditions produced ore deposits of very limited vertical extent but of great richness, enriched deposits that ran as high as a thousand ounces of silver per ton of ore. Their mining brought a boom. When mining reached the primary ores, the grade dropped to twenty to thirty ounces per ton. In many districts this coincided with a precipitous decline in the price of silver and a bust. Mines that continued to prosper despite the price decline did so because of their high-grade ore.[8]

Variations in geology and geomorphic history likewise help explain differences in the development of mining between California and Colorado. Erosion of the Cretaceous rocks of the Sierra with their free-milling ores produced rich and extensive placers of nearly pure gold—deposits that could be worked with relatively elementary methods. Its lode deposits, likewise, proved workable with rather uncomplicated processes. The geology and geomorphic history of the Rockies did not result in the formation of extensive placers. Further, at depths of only about a hundred feet, the rich, weathered, and oxidized ores often gave way to pyritic ores. These "refractory" or "rebellious" ores were not amenable to amalgamation or simple devices of concentration; many mines closed and mining stagnated. So despite the widespread use of standardized technologies, the milling process that emerged in most mining districts had idiosyncracies reflecting the local environment and the use of available materials and power sources to reduce costs.[9]

Geologic conditions often acted as a stimulus in the development of new technology or the modification of existing processes. The early mining operations of California, for example, concentrated on the rich, easily worked placers associated with present-day streams. Small-scale, elementary mining methods such as panning, rocking, toming, and sluicing sufficed. As these deposits became exhausted, miners moved to the gravel hills above the streams and discovered the deep or buried gravels (Tertiary), which were covered by as much as 1,500 feet of younger gravels and volcanic material. Such gravels could not be mined with the traditional methods, and their discovery resulted in the development of new mining methods.[10]

At first the miners excavated the auriferous gravel by means of shafts, tunnels, galleries, and gangways (drifting), and extracted the gold by one of the traditional methods, usually sluicing. Drifting proved a laborious, hazardous, highly speculative, and inefficient means of working the deep gravels. A more effective alternative came in 1853 with the introduction of hydraulicking, which utilized a jet of water issuing under high pressure from a nozzle to excavate and wash the gravel through sluices that caught the gold and disposed of the tailings. This method "made possible the exploitation of thousands upon thousands of acres of auriferous gravel which could not have been profitably handled in any other way."[11]

Initially most of the hydraulic mines were quite shallow and the gravel deposits soft; primitive hydraulic technology—wooden/tin nozzles, canvas hose, and light pressures—proved adequate. Many areas, however, contained a resistant, finely compacted type of gravel known as "cement," which resisted disintegration and tended to break off in hard chunks. By 1857, stamp mills were being built specifically to work such deposits, and during the 1860s, "cement mills" became quite common in California. About 1858, it was discovered that driving a small tunnel into the bank and setting off a charge of gunpowder left the gravel in a more workable condition.[12]

In some parts of California, the most easily worked banks of gravel had already been piped by the early 1860s. A powerful stream of water was needed to work the high hills of resistant material that remained, and this required a discharge pipe fashioned entirely of metal, yet as flexible as canvas hose. Therefore hydraulic nozzles "became very soon the objects of inventive speculation, which resulted in the successful production of very ingenious hydraulic machines." And so the changing nature of the Tertiary gravels brought about the development of improved hydraulic nozzles. In rapid succession came the Gooseneck (1864), Monitor (1868), Dictator (1870), Hydraulic Chief (1870), Little Giant (1871), and others which allowed the working of new or abandoned deposits.[13]

Geologic conditions likewise influenced the development of the technology of lode mining. The Comstock Lode of Nevada offers one illustration. The district has two major faults (the Comstock and Silver City) and several minor ones. During the late Miocene the injection of hot fluids mineralized these faults and deposited quartz containing large amounts of gold and silver. Late in the Tertiary period parts of the mineralized zone eroded, and placer deposits were formed. The first attempts at mining in 1850 concentrated on these placers. However, the scarcity of water and the presence of a black sand that clogged the sluices hindered operations; soon most of these deposits were abandoned to the Chinese—a sure sign of anticipated poor returns. Exploitation of the mineralized faults began in 1859. Unfortunately for the stability of Comstock mining, nature did not distribute the ores evenly but placed them in "ore chambers," "shoots," and "branches." Much of the speculative character of Comstock mining had its origin in this very uneven distribution of ores. Even if one found a rich concentration of ore, it was not easy to mine. The soft, friable bedrock made timbering the tunnels difficult. When used as simple pillars, even the strongest timbers broke and caused frequent cave-ins. The problem led to the development of the square set timbering method in which the timbers interlock and support each other to form hollow cubes in an endless series.[14]

Since the deposits of Comstock were geologically recent and still hot from the hydrothermal heat that formed them, the mines had air temperatures as high as 120 to 130 degrees Fahrenheit. Miners had to work the mine face in loincloths. Even though the mining companies provided cooling stations and spent $1,000 per day for ice, the miners seldom worked the face for more than an hour at a time. A description of the Julia mine, "the very hottest mine in the world," penned in 1879 claimed that the men could not work more than five minutes at a time in parts of the mine. Some mines encountered water at a depth of less than fifty feet. It literally rained inside some mines and men worked in nothing but rain slickers. Sometimes their drills hit a vein of scalding hot water, as high as 170 degrees Fahrenheit. The water problem called for pumping machinery, and as the mines reached greater and greater depths, larger and larger pumps were required; the result was "the construction of some of the most powerful and effective steam and hydraulic pumping apparatus to be found in any part of the world."[15]

Even after extracting the ore, problems remained. The United States had no previous experience in treating silver ores. One effective refining technique known as the patio process had been developed in Mexico. The crushed ore was spread in large circles and teams of mules, burros, or horses were driven through it to further crush it and mix it with quicksilver, salt, and copper sulfate for amalgamation. It was tried on the Comstock but proved generally unsuccessful there. Almarin Paul found the answer by combining the essentials of several Mexican techniques in mechanized form in the Washoe Process. Instead of relying upon the sun's heat to speed the amalgamation process, it utilized steam-heated pans. Only the fabulous wealth of the Comstock silver deposits enabled the mining companies to overcome excessive heat, subsurface flooding, lack of timber, scarcity of surface water, little fuel, and peculiar and irregular distribution of ore.[16]

Just as environmental conditions often stimulated the development of new technology, they often played a major role in the diffusion of that technology. As barriers to transport, the mountains often isolated mining areas from new technology. Largely as a result of its ruggedness and remoteness, its sparse population, and its geology, the mining regions of northwestern California proved a backwater in the diffusion and adoption of improved hydraulic methods. The Mining Commissioner's Report of 1873 reported that the miners were able to realize good wages without recourse to more advanced methods. There was no incentive to change their way of mining. Rodman Paul characterizes the region as a "retarded mining frontier occupied by a sparse population of men of little wealth and inferior initiative," a region "rich enough to furnish a living with primitive modes of mining, but not rich enough to attract to it men of substantial capital or outstanding ability."[17]

As late as 1881, a correspondent of the *Mining and Scientific Press* wrote in a description of mining on the Klamath River:

Why this industry [hydraulic mining] has remained so backward here is owing to a variety of causes, such as our remote and isolated position, deterring the introduction of more recent improvements and preventing the investment of capital in our mines. Time and cost of freight and travel considered, this section of country is as distant from San Francisco as Salt Lake City or Tucson, and nearly as far off as Denver, Colorado. Not until the past few years did any railroad come within 350 miles of this camp, the nearest point on any being now 200 miles away. This has been a great detriment to the mines, keeping out the agents of moneyed men as well as the promoters of new ideas, methods and devices.[18]

The isolation and rugged terrain of many mining districts in particular slowed the development of lode mining. Bringing in coal or charcoal, machinery, or fuel wood, or shipping out ore or concentrates, was expensive and difficult. The San Juan Mountains of Colorado illustrate this to a degree. They contain hundreds of peaks over 13,000 feet and nearly a quarter of all the peaks in North America over 14,000 feet. Historian Robert Brown describes the setting: "frequent rock slides, early snows that became deep drifts and remained well into summer, plus the highest general altitude in Colorado, all combined to retard growth and progress in this potentially rich region." Even after numerous discoveries in 1870, no one wintered in the San Juans in either 1870, 1871, or 1872. In many of what later proved to be prime locations, the snow reached depths of twenty-five feet or more, and traces lasted to the following July. The difficulties of transportation in the San Juans encouraged an early experimentation with tramways that stretched down and around mountainsides from mine to mill or to a railroad.[19]

When rail transportation arrived, it invariably invigorated lode mining; mines that had been idle for years reopened, mines once considered worthless became valuable, mills started up, and a new era in quartz mining began. Even after the arrival of the railroad, however, winter snows could still isolate a mining region. In the winter of 1883–84, it snowed twenty days straight in the San Juans and interrupted railroad service to Silverton for seventy-three days.[20]

Invariably reports on new mining districts discussed the pros and cons of the district's climate. Newspapers, geologic reports, and mining company prospectuses all mentioned it. The varied climates of the Mountainous

West both fostered and hindered the development of mining. Although mountains served as islands of moisture, there was great variability in rainfall within and between ranges. The climate of California required the construction of dams and mining ditches to augment the natural water supply in order to extend the mining season. At the same time, that state's climate proved conducive to river mining. Its summer drought resulted in a period of low water that facilitated the working of the stream beds by river mining—the use of dams, ditches, and flumes to divert streams from their natural beds and mining the bed with rockers, toms, or sluices.[21]

While all forms of mining required water, none of them used the quantities that hydraulicking did. The water needs of hydraulic mining brought into existence a vast system of mining ditches, flumes, canals, and reservoirs in California. Yet the day-to-day variations in climate still exerted an influence. Observers of the period often commented upon the frustrating situation: "our mines are now in excellent condition, and were it not for the extreme scarcity of water would this year have made a noble showing. But scarcity of water is what's the matter; under existing circumstances we are at the mercy of the seasons and the past season has been unmerciful."[22] Most attempts at hydraulicking in the Southwest failed because of lack of water. In fact, many of its placer deposits could be worked only by dry washing—concentrating the gold by use of air.

The availability of timber for all purposes and a plentiful supply of water enhanced a region's value as a mining section, "as the scarcity of wood and water has ever been among the most serious obstacles to profitable and extensive mining."[23] Water played an additionally important role in the location of concentration mills and smelters. Transportation costs dictated a location of such facilities as close as possible to the mines. The need for water, however, sometimes caused them to be located a dozen or more miles from the mines in better-watered (usually valley) locations. The mills of Charleston, Arizona, built in the San Pedro River Valley to serve the silver mines at Tombstone, some ten miles away, are but one example.[24]

While the mountainous areas of the West contained most of the region's exploitable stands of timber, their quantity and quality varied greatly according to precipitation and other factors. The availability of timber especially affected the development of lode mining. The lode mines required huge amounts of timber to support the miles of tunnels, shafts, adits, and passageways. Besides lumber for mine props, railroad ties, and mine buildings, lode mining often required large amounts of wood for fuel or cordwood to run the steam engines that powered the mill works, including the stamps, roasting ovens, pans, separators, and agitators. The mines consumed lesser amounts of cordwood to power hoisting works, compressors, and pumps. Smelters used prodigious quantities of wood in the production of charcoal. Nevada, in particular, because of its arid climate, often lacked an adequate supply of wood, which in turn greatly hindered its mining development. When Myron Angel discussed its mining districts in his early history of that state, he often mentioned whether they had a locally available supply of wood and water, sometimes emphasizing their importance as much as that of the ore deposits. In parts of Nevada, the lack of a better alternative forced the mining and milling companies to resort to the use of sagebrush as fuel.[25]

Mining Settlement

The mountain environment strongly affected not only mining but its associated settlement as well. Because most gold deposits occur in the mountainous and semi-mountainous areas of the West, the sites of most mining settlements differed only in detail. Typically, the primary consideration in site selection consisted of proximity to mining operations. Any level or nearly level location near the mines proved sufficient. Characteristically, the towns either paralleled a stream or the line of mineral deposits.[26]

The typically rugged terrain severely limited the width of the main streets, which often traversed the slope dividing the settlement into an upper and lower town. Often narrow canyon walls allowed only enough room for one long main street with rather short cross streets, sometimes roughly graded with mine waste:[27]

The gulch is so narrow that it affords but one street, which wanders along the sides of the muddy stream in an exceedingly tortuous style. Consequently, the town lots [of Blackhawk in the Central City district, Colorado] are to all intents and purposes set up on edge, with their front commencing on the first piece of solid rock off the street, and their back tilted upon the mountainside at almost any angle you may choose. To reach a front door one must climb up a steep pair of stairs, often 10 or 15 feet high, and a fall off a front porch is a matter requiring the immediate assistance of a surgeon. On the other hand, back doors, in a majority of cases, open directly upon a solid face of granite, and it is frequently possible to pass without effort or discomfort directly from the rear of the roof to the ground.[28]

Probably nowhere was a rectilinear plan so ill adapted to a site as at Cripple Creek, Colorado. This was rugged country, and the streets rose and dipped steeply, "like a ship on a stormy sea," as they crossed the broken slopes of the mountainside. Bennett Avenue, the principal thoroughfare, sloped so steeply from one side to the other that it had to be divided into two terraced lanes, one fifteen feet above the other, supported by a retaining wall. The site of Idaho Springs provides an example of the other extreme. Its relatively level site resulted in a more regular plan.[29]

The climate of the mountains likewise had its effect on the mining towns. Caribou, Colorado, at an elevation of some 10,000 feet, was known as the place where the winds begin. Pictures of the town in the 1870s and 1880s show numerous buildings braced on their east side. Besides wind, Caribou received lots of snow, sometimes enough to bury buildings. Once a blizzard ruined even a Fourth of July picnic. Such climatic conditions caused modifications in the various Eastern architectural styles common to most mining towns. According to Thompson, the heavy snow loads in Colorado required increased roof pitches and bracing; and the mountain climates made porches largely ornamental and caused a reduction in their size. The difficulty of constructing basements resulted in their elimination. The often small residential lots resulting from the rugged terrain necessitated the crowding of homes together. Homes were often only two or three feet apart, eliminating the use of side windows.[30]

Geology influenced the type of mining, and the type of mining in turn greatly influenced the nature of the mining town—its size, its relative permanence, its composition, and so forth. Settlements associated with river mining, for example, proved particularly transitory: "Canvas towns, with stores, express offices, and drinking and eating saloons, spring up like magic, and are noisy and populous. But the first winter rain destroys the whole busy picture. . . . The miners pack up their things and hasten to . . . their winter claims."[31] Such settlements stand in sharp contrast to the more permanent and often larger hydraulic mining and lode-mining communities.

In 1859, the local newspaper editor at North San Juan, an important hydraulic mining town in California, reviewed the town's progress to that point. It had a population of about a thousand, with roughly one hundred families. Main Street contained eight brick buildings, and the town had a school, a church, three hotels, two restaurants, about sixty stores, and numerous shops and other buildings.[32] Just a year later, a correspondent of the *Appeal* wrote that North San Juan already presents the appearance of a city, and is growing rapidly. There are quite a number of fire proof brick buildings erected and occupied, and several more under way of construction. . . . I think I can safely assert that there are more pretty cottage houses, surrounded with beautiful gardens, and flowers, and orchards, than in any other town of its size in the State.[33]

The cottage houses reminded another writer of "an Eastern village, where thrift, industry, peace, and quiet predominate."[34]

The mining towns as single function communities were self-contained and self-sufficient, which in time contributed to their decline and sometimes their extinction.[35] After mining ended, often nothing remained to justify a town's continued existence. Population drifted away, and soon places like North San Juan became ghost towns. Today, these ghost towns contribute greatly to the regional character and popular image of the West.

Environmental Impact of Mining

While the physical environment notably affected mining and its towns, the towns and their industry in turn greatly changed the local environment. The construction of streets in some narrow creek bottoms entailed grading the slopes and filling in the creek. The surrounding forest quickly disappeared for lumber and fuel. Typically, early photographs and sketches of mining towns indicate a scarcity of timber. Often, in fact, they show only a few scattered trees with no undergrowth nearby. The demand for charcoal generated by the smelters at Eureka, Nevada, had a tremendous impact on the pinyon pine forests surrounding the town. An acre of woodland yielded 200 to 300 bushels of charcoal. Charcoal consumption at Eureka reportedly reached as high as 1.2 million bushels per year. From four thousand to five thousand acres of woodland had to be cut annually to supply this much charcoal. Wagon trains loaded with charcoal, four immense wagons coupled together, and drawn by teams of twelve to sixteen mules, were a common sight on the streets of Eureka. By 1874, the demand for charcoal had denuded the surrounding mountain slopes for a radius of twenty miles. In 1878, the charcoal operations took place an average distance of thirty-five miles from town and employed eight hundred workers.[36]

The streams on which the towns stood became the gutters for their garbage and sewage. A classic photo of Central City shows outhouses built on

3. *Central City, Colorado, 1864. A surveyor laid out the streets so that they followed the winding floors of Nevada, Gregory, and Eureka Gulches. The main streets followed the creek at the bottom of the steep gulch that led up from the right-hand side of the plat and branched into two forks. Other streets laid out parallel to these roughly followed the contours of the valley walls. Short, steep cross-streets provided access up and down the slopes. This view of Central City shows not only how the physical environment (the terrain) influenced the town's layout but how the town affected the natural environment through destruction of vegetation and pollution of streams. (Courtesy Western History Department, Denver Public Library.)*

silts over Clear Creek (figure 3). Pollution became so bad in Telluride that the city council hired men to remove dead animals, garbage, and other refuse from the San Miguel River.[37]

The mills and smelters of the lode-mining towns filled the air with "sulphurous fumes," "coal dust and darkness," "cough-compelling" odors, and "villainous vapors" (figure 4). The mountain environment with its narrow canyons, thin air, and temperature inversions exacerbated such air pollution.[38] Eureka, Nevada, gained a well-deserved reputation for the poor quality of its air:

> We could smell Eureka before we got here. Anybody can smell it a couple of miles off, unless anybody has a defect in his olfactory perceptions or has his nostrils plugged up with sasfoetida. The scent

4. *Boston and Colorado Smelting Works. The smelter filled the air with smoke that contained deadly compounds of minerals and gases and that helped Black Hawk, Colorado, acquire a reputation for "cough-compelling" odors. (Courtesy Western History Department, Denver Public Library.)*

arises from the fumes from the smelting furnaces and the decomposition of organic matter in

THE BIG DITCH

But the big ditch is the worst. The big ditch is a small creek that runs through the canyon in which Eureka lies, and into which all the sewerage of the town empties and all the refuse is dumped. There is not enough water running through the course to carry off the solids deposited in it, and for the entire length of the town there is a reservoir of solid and liquid nastiness which smells to heaven. The stink arising from it is frightful and pervades the entire canyon.[39]

"Black clouds of dense smoke from the furnaces, heavily laden and heavily scented with the fumes of lead, arsenic and other volatile elements of the ores" constantly filled the air and covered the town with soot, scale, and black dust, so that it resembled a manufacturing town in the Pennsylvania coal regions. The problem became so bad that elongated stacks were run up the canyon walls and then vertically to vent the fumes.[40]

While the mining towns and mills had a notable impact on their surroundings, it was the mining itself which really devastated the land. The mountain environment in which most gold and silver mining occurred was a fragile one. While the size and particular species of trees varied with latitude, elevation, annual precipitation, and other factors, the slopes were almost always steep and the soils thin. Any disturbance that removed vegetation invariably produced accelerated erosion on the affected hillsides. Above timberline the tundra proved especially delicate; the slightest disturbance left scars that will probably last for hundreds of years. Even with simple machinery and primitive methods, the thousands upon thousands of miners collectively affected a large area and had a noticeable impact on the land. Numerous period writers left vivid descriptions of the effects of the early mining operations,[41] including this comment on a trip to Pikes Peak: "In traversing through the mining country, we cannot fail to notice the many holes and trenches that have been dug in the mountainsides, the gulches, ravines, and in the bars and shoals of the streams."[42] Clear Creek, Colorado, received its name because it was "as pure and bright as distilled water." By 1864, a writer, however, compared the once limpid stream to the Thames at Blackfriars. Ten years later, a visitor remarked to a resident of Colorado, "if that is a specimen of your clear creeks, I'd like to see one of the muddy ones."[43]

The history of mining in the West is one of changing technology, with each successive improvement bringing a greater destruction of the land, but nothing compared to hydraulicking (figure 5). Both the amount of land affected and the degree of alteration changed dramatically with its introduction. It was mass production applied to mining. Hydraulicking enabled four or five men to do the work of fifty men using traditional methods. The result was devastation that must be seen to be appreciated. William Brewer, a member of the California State Geological Survey in the early 1860s, observed, "I have seen works and effects that one would imagine it would take centuries to produce, instead of the dozen years that have elapsed since the work began."[44]

Even early hydraulicking removed upwards of fifty to one hundred cubic yards of material daily. Contemporary observers used such phrases as "literally forbidding," "extreme desolation and ruin," and "remediless and appalling" to describe its impact. The hydraulic mines commonly consisted of "an open cut of huge dimensions." In the mid-1880s, an observer described the North Bloomfield mine as a "barren amphitheater, so vast that it could contain a whole settlement and so deep that a high church steeple could hardly reach to the ledge." The North Bloomfield mine utilized three nozzles and 30.5 million gallons of water, twice as much as used by the en-

5. *Hydraulicking at Elizabethtown, New Mexico, circa 1880. Few areas of the Southwest contained the requisite natural conditions to enable hydraulic mining. The aridity of much of the region particularly inhibited this form of mining. This photo indicates that where hydraulicking did occur, it had an impact comparable to other parts of the West. (Courtesy Museum of New Mexico, neg. 5232.)*

tire city of San Francisco. Dozens of similar mines operated in California during the height of hydraulic mining. The total amount of material excavated in the Sierra Nevada by hydraulic mining was eight times that removed in the construction of the Panama Canal.[45]

The newspapers of the 1860s, 1870s, and 1880s are filled with graphic accounts of hydraulic mining and its impact on the land. The following note appeared in the *Marysville Appeal*:

Astronomers tell us that there are pits in the moon, seventeen thousand feet deep; they say also, that any object on the moon, two hundred and fifty feet high, may be detected by the most powerful glasses now in use. If there are astronomers on the moon with equally potent instruments, they will soon be able to detect changes in the surface of California, through the agency of hydraulic mining. . . . It is fast changing mountains on the face of the State into pits. It is, too, an invention which, to the end of time, will defy all competition for tearing all beauty out of a landscape, and setting up the "abomination of desolation" in its place.[46]

The spoilation that hydraulic mining invoked on the Sierra, the Sacramento Valley, and elsewhere in the West provides a particularly poignant example of American rapacity. It not only carried off the timber and grass cover, but cut away entire hillsides, leaving behind small canyons and gravel and rock wastelands. Its tailings filled nearby streams, which became yellow with mud and decimated fishlife. The accumulation of tailings raised streambeds, changed channel configurations, and increased the periodicity and destructiveness of floods. The rivers transported increased quantities of debris into the estuarial bays of San Francisco, initiated extensive shoaling, diminished the tidal prism, and caused a decline in the bays' aquatic life.[47]

In many cases the interrelationship between mining and the environment was a complex, multifaceted one. The geology, vegetation, and climate of the Sierra Nevada foothills produced conditions conducive to landslides—landslides that sometimes covered mining claims, that destroyed dwellings, ditches, and equipment, and that occasionally caused loss of life. In turn, by undercutting slopes, removing timber, and increasing soil moisture through ditch seepage, hydraulic mining exacerbated this mass wasting.[48]

The peak of gold and silver mining in the West is long past. Yet it is difficult to travel through most parts of the region without seeing evidence of the mining era. From abandoned mines to deserted towns, the West is full of reminders of this period. Among the most prominent of these remnants are the various landscapes created by mining. They range from the subtle and faint landscapes produced by traditional placer mining to the obvious and dramatic ones that resulted from hydraulicking and dredging.

Characteristically, the traditional methods produced landscapes with a shallow, hummocky appearance. Small, round, somewhat evenly spaced, and more or less symmetrical piles of rock and gravel often dot such areas, and small, shallow trenches or cuts mark the adjacent hillsides. Typically, these cuts average only one or two feet deep and less than five yards wide. The small-scale nature of the traditional methods and their widely scattered locations often make recognition of their landscapes difficult.[49]

In contrast, dredging produced a striking and distinct landscape (figure 6). It completely destroyed the original stream courses and caused the channel to shift and often divide into multiple channels. It completely overturned and rearranged the existing soil. Once broad, flat valleys be-

6. *Tonopah No. 2 Dredge, on the Swan River near Breckenridge, Colorado. In the 1890s a new method, dredging, was developed that allowed the mining of the beds of the larger streams that traversed the goldfields. This early-twentieth-century photo graphically shows the tremendous impact that dredging had on the land. It converted the once gentle floors of mountain valleys into a rugged terrain of alternating ridges and valleys. (Courtesy American Heritage Center, University of Wyoming.)*

came a series of nearly parallel ridges and valleys. After saving the gold, the dredge redeposited the coarse gravel in the form of large orderly rows ten, twenty, or thirty feet high over the finer gravel, clay, and sand. Many of the lakes and ponds that resulted from dredging remain part of the landscape.[50]

The patterns of the various tailings produced by placer mining show a strong geological influence. Factors such as topography, nature of the substrata, the position of the ore vein, and depth of overburden, in fact, largely determined the patterns of these tailings. Their persistence, too, reflects natural conditions—the differential rates of weathering under different climates. Their longevity in desert regions is notable. Long after the mills, headframes, tipples, buildings, and similar structures disappear, the man-made topography will remain. The excavations, tailings, waste dumps, slag piles, and other cultural landforms are therefore among the more important, if not most important, indexes of human activity in any mining district. Because of their powerful visual impact, large size, relative permanence, time-specific technological origin, Richard Francaviglia makes a convincing case for such features as the "ultimate artifact."[51]

Conclusion

Perhaps the lingering stigma of environmental determinism accounts for relatively few studies by geographers that examine the role that physical geographic factors played in the development of mining. Yet physical geography greatly influenced mining. The presence of profitable deposits as a concentrated resource, of course, represented the bottom line. Geology largely determined that such deposits occurred in the mountainous regions of the West. Within these regions, the availability of timber, the adequacy of water, the ruggedness of the terrain, the extremes of climate, and the degree of isolation all played important roles in the development and success of mining. Low-grade deposits located in remote, rugged, inaccessible areas characteristically resulted in a retarded development, if that, of mining. Physical factors largely explain the technological development of mining region by region; technological development largely dominated economic growth; and economic growth, or lack of it, largely explains the history of mining.

While environmental conditions greatly influenced the development of mining, mining in turn greatly affected the environment. Even the relatively simple mining methods of the early years had a notable impact on the land. Later, hydraulicking, dredging, lode mining, and its related methods of ore processing brought increasing devastation to the land—destruction of vegetation, alteration of terrain and drainage conditions, pollution of air and water, and the formation of new landforms.

Each distinct type of mining exhibited that distinctiveness in its alteration of the natural landscape, and each method produced its own unique landscape. The inherent characteristics of each method limited the landscape that it produced to certain localities and resulted in a highly uneven spatial impact. The simple methods displayed a rather broad geographic range, while the large-scale, more complex forms proved rather restrictive. The latter, however, exerted a greater and more permanent impact on the land. Through these various forms of mining, humans left a vivid imprint on the Mountainous West.

Notes

1. Rodman Wilson Paul, *Mining Frontiers of the Far West, 1848–1880* (New York: Holt, Rinehart and Winston, 1963), 3–7; James M. Hill, "The Mining Districts of the Western United States," U.S. Geological Survey Bulletin no. 507 (Washington, D.C., 1912), 6–9; A. H. Koschmann and M. H. Bergendahl, "Principal Gold-Producing Districts of the United States," U.S. Geological Survey Professional Paper no. 610 (Washington, D.C., 1968), 3–6; Alan M. Bateman, *Economic Mineral Deposits* (New York: John Wiley and Sons), 421–23, 455–57; Charles W. Henderson, "The History and Influence of Mining in the Western United States," in *Ore Deposits of the Western States*, vol. 1 (New York: American Institute of Mining and Metallurgical Engineers, 1933), 751–57.

2. Paul, *Mining Frontiers*, 3–7; Hill, "Mining Districts," 6–9; Koschmann and Bergendahl, "Principal Gold-Producing Districts," 3–6; Bateman, *Economic Mineral Deposits*, 421–23, 455–57.

3. Paul, *Mining Frontiers*, 3–7; Hill, "Mining Districts," 6–9; Koschmann and Bergendahl, "Principal Gold-Producing Districts," 3–6; Bateman, *Economic Mineral Deposits*, 421–23, 455–57.

4. Robert H. Ridgeway et al., "Summarized Data of Gold Production," U.S. Bureau of Mines Economic Paper no. 6 (Washington, D.C., 1929), 14, 61; E. D. Gardner and C. H. Johnson, "Placer Mining in the Western United States," U.S. Bureau of Mines Information Circular no. 6786 (Washington, D.C., 1934).

5. Koschmann and Bergendahl, "Principal Gold-Producing Districts," 5–6.

6. Paul, *Mining Frontiers*, 65, 87, 103, 105, 127, 132, 146, 148, 159.

7. George D. Hubbard, "Gold and Silver Mining and Reduction Processes as Responses to Geographic Conditions," *Scottish Geographical Magazine* 27 (August–September 1911): 424–25.

8. Robert A. Chadwick, "Montana's Silver Mining Era: Great Boom and Great Bust," *Montana Magazine of Western History* 32 (Spring 1982): 18, 23–29, 31.

9. Rodman W. Paul, "Colorado as a Pioneer of Science in the Mining West," *Mississippi Valley Historical Review* 47 (June 1960): 38–42; Hubbard, "Gold and Silver Mining," 422; Donald Hardesty, "Industrial Archaeology on the American Mining Frontier: Suggestions for a Research Agenda," *Journal of New World Archaeology* 6 (1986): 50.

10. Philip Ross May, *Origins of Hydraulic Mining in California* (Oakland: Holmes Book Co., 1970), 33–36; Randall Rohe, "Hydraulicking in the American West: The Development and Diffusion of a Mining Technique," *Montana Magazine of Western History* 35 (Spring 1985): 19–20; Robert L. Kelley, "Forgotten Giant: The Hydraulic Gold Mining Industry in California," *Pacific Historical Review* 23 (November 1954):

343–46; Rodman W. Paul, *California Gold: The Beginning of Mining in the Far West* (Lincoln: University of Nebraska Press, 1967), 147–53.

11. Randall Rohe, "Origins and Diffusion of Traditional Placer Mining in the West," *Material Culture* 18 (Fall 1986): 146–49; May, *Origins of Hydraulic Mining*, 40–47; Rohe, "Hydraulicking in the American West," 19; S. F. Emmons and G. F. Becker, "Statistics and Technology of the Precious Metals," *The Tenth Census of the United States, 1880* (Washington, D.C., 1885), vii; Rossiter W. Raymond, "Statistics of Mines and Mining in the States and Territories West of the Rocky Mountains," 44th Cong., 1st Sess., 1877, H. Doc. 159, serial 1691, 365.

12. Rohe, "Hydraulicking in the American West," 22; Paul, *California Gold*, 157–58.

13. Rohe, "Hydraulicking in the American West," 23–24; Rossiter W. Raymond, "Statistics of Mines and Mining in the States and Territories West of the Rocky Mountains," 42nd. Cong., 3d Sess., 1873, H. Doc. 210, serial 1567, 416; *Nevada City Daily Transcript*, 22 April 1868, 26 July 1868, 24 June 1868, 24 June 1870, 25 March 1869, 24 June 1870, and 27 April 1872; *Calaveras (Calif.) Chronicle*, 4 October 1873.

14. Grant H. Smith, "The History of the Comstock Lode, 1850–1920," University of Nevada Bulletin no. 37 (July 1943): 2–4, 20, 24, 71–73; Hardesty, "Industrial Archaeology," 50–51; Paul, *Mining Frontiers*, 58, 61, 65, 100.

15. *Virginia Evening Chronicle* (Virginia City, Nev.), 24 October 1877, 1 July 1879, 8 August 1879, 2 September 1879, 9 September 1879, 15 October 1879, and 3 November 1879; Dan De Quille, *A History of the Comstock Silver Lode and Mines* (Virginia City, Nev.: F. Boegle, 1889), 43; Smith, "History of the Comstock," 41–45, 244–45, 278–81; *Nevada City Herald*, 27 August 1878.

16. Ernest Oberbillig, "Development of Washoe and Reese River Silver Processes," *Nevada Historical Society Quarterly* 10 (1967): 10–11, 14–25; Paul, *Mining Frontiers*, 65–67; Paul, *California Gold*, 188–89.

17. *Mining and Scientific Press*, 11 January 1868; H. C. Burchard, *Report of the Director of the Mint upon the Statistics of the Production of the Precious Metals in the United States* (Washington, D.C., 1881): 86, 380, (1882): 27; Raymond, "Statistics of Mines and Mining" (Washington, D.C., 1873), 97; Raymond, "Statistics of Mines and Mining in the States and Territories West of Rocky Mountains," 43d Cong., 1st Sess., 1874, H. Doc. 141, serial 1608, 150; Paul, *California Gold*, 96–98.

18. *Mining and Scientific Press*, 15 October 1881.

19. Robert L. Brown, *An Empire of Silver* (Caldwell, Idaho: Caxton Printers, 1968), 27, 56, 61, 209.

20. *Deer Lodge (Mont.) Weekly Independent*, 15 June 1872; De Quille, *History of the Comstock Silver Lode*, 27; Chadwick, "Montana's Silver Mining Era," 20–21; Brown, *Empire of Silver*, 172.

21. Randall Rohe, "Origins and Diffusion," 140–45; *Shasta (Calif.) Courier*, 16 November 1861; *Eureka (Calif.) Sentinel*, 19 October 1871; *San Francisco Evening Bulletin*, 21 January 1863; H. C. Burchard, *Report of the Director of the Mint upon the Statistics of the Production of the Precious Metals in the United States* (Washington, D.C., 1882), 250. On the importance of weather and climate, see *Georgetown (Colo.) News*, 24 January 1856; *Nevada Journal*, 19 April 1863; *San Joaquin (Calif.) Republican*, 13 September 1859 and 14 September 1859.

22. *Weaverville (Calif.) Trinity Journal*, 17 April 1875. See also: *Sacramento Union*, 28 January 1857; *Helena (Mont.) Daily Herald*, 7 April 1874; *Trinity Journal*, 6 December 1873 and 28 May 1874; *Weekly Independent*, 22 May 1869.

23. Burchard, *Report of the Director* (1882), 272.

24. Richard V. Francaviglia, "The Ultimate Artifact: Interpreting and Evaluating the Man-Made Topography of Historic Mining Districts" (paper presented at the annual meeting of the Society for Historical Archaeology, Reno, Nev., 1988), 18; *San Francisco Evening Bulletin*, 8 December 1871; Myron Angel, *History of Nevada, with Illustrations and Biographical Sketches of Its Prominent Men and Pioneers* (Oakland: Thompson and West, 1881), 430, 453, 489, 502, 539–41, 562.

25. Randall Rohe, "Man and the Land: Mining's Impact in the Far West," *Arizona and the West* 28 (Winter 1986): 305–8; *Mississippi Valley Lumberman*, 3 April 1885; *San Francisco Evening Bulletin*, June 1871; *Auburn (Calif.) Placer Herald*, 26 November 1864; *Marysville (Calif.) Appeal*, December 1865; "History of Lumbering in Western Nevada," *The Timberman* (June 1941): 11–14, 50, 52, 54, 56, 58, 60, 62; *Virginia Evening Chronicle*, 12 October 1874, 30 October 1874, and 24 September 1879; *Shasta Courier*, 16 November 1861; Angel, *History of Nevada*, see 364, 388, 392–96, 414, 416, 419 for examples; Stanley Paher, *Nevada Ghost Towns and Mining Camps* (Berkeley: Howell-North Books, 1970), 183, 200; *Eureka Sentinel*, 19 October 1877 and 29 November 1877; *Humboldt (Calif.) Register*, 18 August 1866; *Winnemucca (Nev.) Silver State*, 17 February 1872.

26. "A Year in Montana," *Atlantic Monthly*, August 1866, 240; *Rocky Mountain News* (Denver), 16 October 1860.

27. James Biggins, "Historical Geography of the Georgetown, Colorado, Silver Mining Area (Ph.D. diss., University of Colorado, 1972), 21–22, 29–31; *San Francisco Evening Bulletin*, 8 June 1878; Brown, *Empire in Silver*, 241; Ralph Mann, *After the Gold Rush: Society in Grass Valley and Nevada City, California, 1849–1870* (Stanford: Stanford University Press, 1982), 10–11, 14–15.

28. *Engineering and Mining Journal*, 29 September 1877.

29. John W. Reps, "Bonanza Towns: Urban Planning on the Western Mining Frontier," in *Pattern and Process: Research in Historical Geography*, ed. Ralph E. Ehrenberg (Washington, D.C.: Howard University Press, 1975), 280, 283; *Cities of the American West: A History of Urban Planning* (Princeton: Princeton University Press, 1979), 472–73.

30. Duane A. Smith, *Silver Saga* (Boulder: Pruett, 1974), 110, 155–56, 189, 199; Thomas Gray Thompson, "The Cultural History of Colorado Mining Towns, 1859–1920" (Ph.D. diss., University of Missouri, 1966), 303.

31. *San Francisco Evening Bulletin*, 4 January 1859.

32. *North San Juan (Colo.) Hydraulic Press*, 2 April 1859.

33. *Marysville Appeal*, 21 April 1860. See also *San Francisco Evening Bulletin*, 11 March 1861.

34. *Nevada City Daily Transcript*, 29 October 1870.

35. Mining did supply the urban centers, markets, and capital necessary for the development and expansion of transportation to and within the mining regions; and mining resulted in the development of outfitting and supply towns and attendant transportation routes. See, for instance, Randall Rohe, "Feeding the Mines: the Development of Supply Centers for the Goldfields," *Annals of Wyoming* 57 (Spring 1985): 40–56.

36. De Quille, *History of the Comstock Silver Lode*, 99; Mann, *After the Gold Rush*, 16, 137; Biggins, "Historical Geography," 187; Randall Rohe, "The Geography and Material Culture of the Western Mining Town," *Material Culture* 6 (Fall 1984): 100–103; *San Francisco Evening Bulletin*, 8 November 1878 and 31 January 1878; *Humboldt Register*, 10 November 1866; *Eureka (Nev.) Daily Sentinel*, 15 September 1877 and 17 January 1878; Eugene M. Hattori, Marna Ares Thompson, and Alvin R. McLane, "Historic Pinyon Pine Utilization in the Cortez Mining District in Central Nevada," University of Nevada System, Desert Research Institute Technical Report no. 39 (July 1984), 5–6, 25–27; Charles D. Zeier, "Historic Charcoal Production near Eureka, Nevada: An Archaeological Perspective," *Historical Archaeology* 21 (1987): 83, 86; Rohe, "Man and the Land," 307.

37. Duane E. Smith, "My Profit, Your Land: Colorado Mining and the Environment, 1858–1900," in *A Taste of the West*, ed. Duane A. Smith (Boulder: Pruett, 1983), 102.

38. Rohe, "Man and the Land," 336–37; Smith, "My Profit, Your Land," 96.

39. *Eureka (Nev.) Daily Leader*, 19 July 1878.

40. *Biennial Report of the State Mineralogist of the State of Nevada for the Years 1871 and 1872* (Carson City, 1873), 68; Angel, *History of Nevada*, 430.

41. Rohe, "Man and the Land," 301–2, 314, 315, 325, 327; Duane A. Smith, *Mining America: The Industry and the Environment, 1800–1980* (Lawrence: University of Kansas Press, 1987), 5, 14–15, 61; J. D. Borthwick, *Three Years in California* (Edinburgh: William Blackford and Sons, 1857), 92.

42. C. M. Clark, *A Trip to Pikes Peak and Notes by the Way*, ed. Robert Greenwood (San Jose, Calif.: Talisman Press, 1958), 85.

43. Maurice Morris, *Rambles in the Rocky Mountains: With a Visit to the Goldfields of*

Colorado (London: Smith, Elder, 1864), 108–9; *Rocky Mountain News*, 14 October 1874; *Oshkosh (Wisc.) Northwestern*, 16 August 1877.

44. William H. Brewer, *Up and Down California in 1860–1864: The Journal of William H. Brewer*, ed. Frances P. Farquhar (New Haven: Yale University Press, 1930), 328.

45. Randall Rohe, "Man as a Geomorphic Agent: Hydraulic Mining in the American West," *Pacific Historian* 27 (Spring 1983): 6–7; Rohe, "Man and the Land," 316–19; *Marysville Herald*, 9 February 1856; *Alta California*, 10 January 1856; *Mining and Scientific Press*, 7 July 1877; *Nevada City Daily Transcript*, 10 December 1879; *Sacramento Union*, 10 October 1859; *Marysville Appeal*, 15 January 1861 and 17 July 1872.

46. *Marysville Appeal*, 6 January 1861.

47. Rohe, "Man as a Geomorphic Agent," 10–14; "Man and the Land," 302, 325–26, 328–36.

48. *San Francisco Evening Bulletin*, 20 December 1877; *Nevada City Daily Transcript*, 23 January 1866; *Trinity Journal*, 8 April 1876 and 15 April 1876.

49. Randall Rohe, "Gold Mining Landscapes of the West," *California Geology* 37 (October 1964): 224–28.

50. Rohe, "Gold Mining Landscapes," 228.

51. Neville Ritchie, "Archaeological Interpretation of Alluvial Gold Tailing Sites, Central Otago, New Zealand," *New Zealand Journal of Archaeology* 3 (1981): 66; Francaviglia, "Ultimate Artifact," 28, 34.

7 / Homesteading the Pryor Mountains of Montana

VICTOR KONRAD

Mountains in the American West are at once islands of concentrated resources and ranges of marginal lands. The spatial concentration of stored moisture, exposed minerals, terraced timber, and regenerative forage is especially apparent in mountains set in arid regions where lower slopes and valleys are barren. Here, rather than on mountains located in humid, mid-latitude regions, the fundamental factors affecting settlement and land use—vertical distribution of different environments and the different seasonal conditions at each level[1]—seem more emphatic and more distinct from the lands below. Amid dry and less productive lands, the stratification of mountain resources appears more etched in the alpine profile, and the schedule for the exploitation of these resources is more aligned with seasonal changes. These properties of resource concentration and differentiation have attracted humans since North America was first occupied, and the attraction has persisted for settlers into the twentieth century.

This essay deals with the exploitation of concentrated resources at the close of the frontier in the Pryor Mountains of Montana. Homesteading national forests is worthy of attention and study for several reasons. It comprises one of the last homesteading efforts, an effort which extends to the limits of the settlement frontier in the continental United States. Second, forest homesteading is extremely well documented by several government agencies and to some extent by the homesteaders themselves. Finally, it represents the culmination of an approach to the land, a set of attitudes which pervaded the aggressive settlement of much of the United States west of the Mississippi. The following discussion is focused on home-steading in the Pryor section of the Beartooth (later Custer) National Forest. Only a small area of national forest, the Pryor Division nevertheless contains distinct and well-preserved examples of national forest home-steads and stock-grazing homesteads and is adjacent to homesteads acquired through the General Land Office by conventional means. This allows comparison of Montana homesteading experiences in one locale; it also provides comprehensive documentation of a homesteading process and landscape found elsewhere in Montana and in the other states of the Mountainous West.

The Forest Homestead Act engendered a limited but distinct forest homestead movement.[2] Examination of this movement in the Pryor Mountains reveals the characteristics of this final surge of homesteading, for it tells us who was involved, under what conditions they settled, and why they left. Also, the study reveals the impact of settlement on the mountain environment; the experience in the Pryors helps us to understand the complex nature and variation of homesteading and dispels the notion of a consistent and stereotyped homestead experience.

Set in the basin and canyon lands of the Montana-Wyoming boundary country, the Pryor Mountains are a block-fault range that, along with the northern portion of the Big Horn Mountains, form the northeastern margin of the Big Horn Basin (figure 1). Whereas the western to southern flank of the Pryors is a gentle slope with regularly spaced and deeply dissected narrow canyons, the eastern slope is an abrupt scarp with fewer and relatively less eroded canyons. Elevations above sea level range from 4,000 feet to 8,900 feet, considerably lower than that attained by the adjacent Big Horn Mountains to the east or the Beartooth and Absaroka Ranges west of the Big Horn Basin.[3] Because of their lower elevation and drier climate, the Pryor Mountains never were glaciated during the Wisconsin stage of glaciation.[4] In the Pryors, zonation of vegetation is well correlated with elevation, although a mosaic pattern is created by differences in exposure, slope, and moisture availability. Lower western and southern flanks of the mountains are an arid land with xerophytic flora. Riparian areas occur along the eastern flank adjacent to the Bighorn River and in larger canyons. Foothills and lower canyons contain an open, Rocky Mountain juniper woodland, whereas upper canyons grade into forests of limber pine, Douglas fir, and common juniper, and then into high-altitude forests of spruce and fir. The highest elevations and exposed slopes are a mosaic of spruce-fir patches surrounded by low herbs and dwarf shrubs.[5] Natural lakes do not occur, and running water is elusive due to the wide exposure of karst terrain. Yet wildlife prevails everywhere and is concentrated in the canyons where running water is found.

During the nineteenth and early twentieth centuries, these mountains were visited occasionally by explorers and fur traders before settlers began arriving on these marginal lands after the turn of the century. Throughout

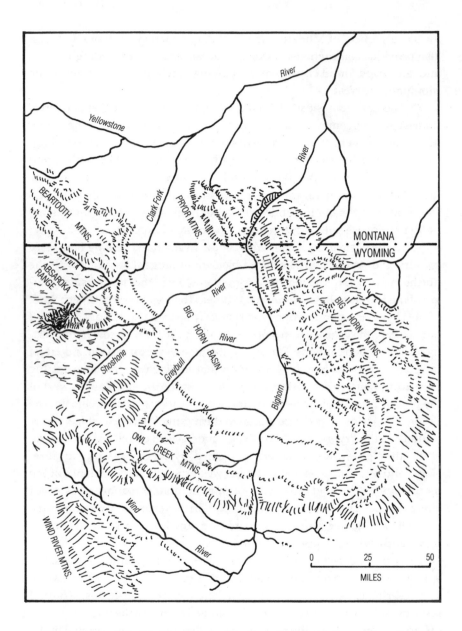

1. Physiography of the Big Horn Basin. The figure has been redrawn from air photos and previous renderings.

this time of discovery, and for a considerable time before, native activity prevailed in the Pryors and culminated in Crow Indian use of the area for hunting, acquisition of lodgepole pine, and ceremonial purposes.[6] For the Crow, and apparently for their predecessors during more than ten thousand years of occupation, the Pryor Mountains offered islands of moisture and coolness, as well as reservoirs of concentrated resources within the arid Big Horn Basin and the valley of the Yellowstone River.[7] In these highlands the native peoples also sought restorative sanctuary, engaged in rites of passage at Dry Head Vista, and explored the unknown in Big Ice Cave (figure 2). The mountains gave sanctuary as well from the earlier white settlers who viewed the Pryors as barriers in the path of agricultural expansion across the upper high plains. However, in the late nineteenth century, the Pryors, like most of the Mountainous West, were claimed by the federal government and placed under the direct control of the National Forest Service, the National Park Service, and the Bureau of Land Management. A natural sanctuary for one people became a legislated sanctuary from another, but the rules of land and resource use would evolve very slowly in a complex of interests and competing policies. The Pryor Mountains were declared public lands, but they remained essentially open to private uses aimed at exploiting the diverse and concentrated resources prevailing in this isolated and fragile enclave.

The Forest Homestead Act

It is generally acknowledged that by the end of the nineteenth century the frontier had passed in the coterminous United States. Ownership and use of most good agricultural land was established, settlement patterns were set, and the excess of population moved off the land to the city. In Montana, and throughout the Mountainous West, the turn of the century saw rapid and extensive redefinition of land and its uses, for between 1890 and 1920 the vast public domain was alternately reserved, homesteaded, preserved, reduced, leased, and reclaimed.[8] Indian lands were reduced by sale or were transferred to other federal agencies; with the repeal of the Timber Culture Act in 1891, the president established forest reserves within the jurisdiction of the U.S. Department of the Interior (USDI). In 1898 a Forest Division was created in the U.S. Department of Agriculture (USDA); the recreational use of forest reserves was legislated in 1899. In 1905 all forest

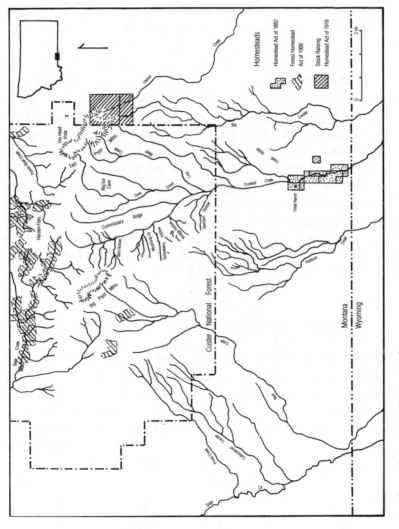

2. *Pryor Mountain Homesteads.*

reserves were transferred from the General Land Office (GLO) in USDI to USDA; two years later forest reserves were elevated to national forest status; and from 1906 to 1920 a series of new laws expanded opportunities for homestead entry in national forests.

The significance of the Forest Homestead Act of 1906 has not been fully evaluated because the law came into effect at a time of considerable homesteading activity in adjacent GLO lands.[9] Notwithstanding late-nineteenth-century claims that arable land was virtually exhausted, land disposed of under the Homestead Act (1862) amounted to 138 million acres between 1898 and 1922, as opposed to 70 million acres between 1868 (first year of patents) and 1897.[10] Although large amounts of land patented after 1897 were subsequently withdrawn from entry, the intensity of early-twentieth-century homestead activity remains so impressive as to overshadow any component of this activity.

One component, homestead entry into national forests, resulted from criticism of President Roosevelt's policies of setting aside the public domain and, according to critics, removing potential agricultural land from settlement. On 11 June 1906, the Forest Homestead Act permitted agricultural entry of suitable land in forest reserves; immediately "June 11 Homesteaders" explored a new settlement frontier where elevation, forests, and additional government regulation joined the uncertainties of frost, drought, and market conditions to establish a marginal environment for homesteading.[11] The marginal nature of this homesteading was further assured when the Enlarged Homestead Act of 1909 excluded national forests.[12] Reclassification of national forest lands in 1910 eliminated almost one million acres of potential agricultural land from these reserves and further limited the potential for homesteading. Realizing the mounting difficulties and constraints on national forest and other marginal land homesteaders, Congress passed laws reducing the time needed to perfect an entry from five to three years and allowing absence by "homestead settlers and entrymen" where difficult environments allowed only seasonal occupancy.[13] The 1916 act "to provide for stock-raising homesteads" of 640 acres saw a rapid move by livestock producers to encroach on public lands where formerly they had been excluded.[14] This legislation heralded the decline of national forest homesteads. Already, homesteaders in the reserves were finding it more advantageous to raise stock than to sustain farming in a marginal environment, and by 1940 national forest homesteads were either abandoned or amalgamated to form ranches in the national forests.

Extending the Settlement Frontier into the Pryors

Virtually coincident with the Forest Homestead Act, the Pryor Mountain Forest Reserve was proclaimed in 1906 and was transferred by executive order to the jurisdiction of the newly formed Beartooth National Forest in 1908. Originally opened to timber use from both Montana and Wyoming with the Pryor Mountain Act of 1901, this vulnerable mountain island was first reserved and then immediately opened to homesteaders while livestock producers jealously eyed the new competition for resources on the reserve.[15] This looming competition for scarce resources in a marginal environment, warned E. S. Gosney in a presentation to the American Foresters' Congress of 1905, would soon undermine the viability of forest reserves.[16] At the outset, positions of confrontation were established among homesteader, rancher, and resource manager. The story of this strained relationship is essentially the story of the Pryor Mountain homesteading experience and of homesteading in other national forests.

In Montana, homesteading national forest lands coincided with the land rush which brought new settlers to many parts of the state.[17] Railways, among them the Chicago, Burlington and Quincy, the Northern Pacific, the Great Northern, and the Chicago, Milwaukee, and St. Paul, expanded their land advertisements to include pamphlets on how to secure national forest homesteads in the "land of fortune," the "treasure state." The lure of government land, mountain land, and land in three years instead of five were all cited as incentives to homestead in scenic Montana.[18] The cardinal rule of homestead selection was to choose the best land and to avoid the marginal land surrounding it. As better agricultural lands were taken, as middlemen became involved in the allocation process, and as unfamiliar environments were encountered, more homesteading of marginal land took place. Responses to marginal land were either abandonment or adjustment. Adjustment to marginal environments for agriculture has been studied extensively, and three responses are emphasized in the literature: using more land as practiced in dryland farming throughout the high plains of the North American West; using ethnic or religious group cooperation to pool labor and capital and to minimize the impact of loss in bad years; and making the land produce more through a "technological fix" such as irrigation as practiced by Mormon settlers.[19]

All three adjustments were evident in agricultural lands adjacent to the Pryors: irrigation in the Shoshone Basin south of the Pryors, cooperative farming among the Crow in the Big Horn Valley to the northeast, and dryland farming in the Yellowstone Valley to the northwest. In the Pryors, adjustment to marginal land was accomplished through integrated resource use. To sustain a homestead in the Sage Creek Valley, settlers combined subsistence agriculture with the growing of fodder crops such as oats and alfalfa, animal husbandry, timber cutting, and hunting. In essence, like the Crow before them, Pryor Mountain homesteaders learned the environment, came to appreciate its constraints, and exploited different facets at different seasons in order to survive.

Three distinct homesteading responses characterized adjustment to the low, mid-elevation, and mountain-top environments in the Pryor region. Outside the national forest, on lower Crooked Creek to the south, nine families established homesteads below 4,500 feet on the only watered land between the Pryors and the Wyoming border. The Sage Creek settlement occupied virtually all the arable land at mid-elevation (5,600–6,600 feet) in the national forest. Above 7,500 feet were the Bainbridge and Greathouse homesteads on Big Pryor and two stock-raising homesteads adjacent to the national forest on East Pryor (figure 2).

Settlers in the Sage Creek Valley found a topography of bench land incised by waterways and springs to form narrow bottom lands along the creek and steep-sided gulches of adjoining intermittent streams. Irregular homesteads of approximately 160 acres were surveyed to include as much bottom and bench land as possible and to avoid steep slopes and gulches. Surveyed by metes and bounds within an unsurveyed township and range grid, forest homestead entry surveys produced an adjustment to terrain and reflected a settlement pattern in stark contrast to the consistent rectangular survey outside the national forest. Homestead boundaries were fenced, trails were extended from farmsteads to roads paralleling Sage Creek and it tributaries, cultivation was initiated, and the first log structures were raised. A landscape emerged with farmsteads located adjacent to springs or the creek, small acreages of cereal and fodder crops confined on nearby bottom land and raised bench land, and stock grazing extended throughout the remainder of holdings (figure 3).

The Settlement Landscape

The Sage Creek homestead landscape may be reconstructed from the detailed descriptions in the homestead entry surveys completed by the For-

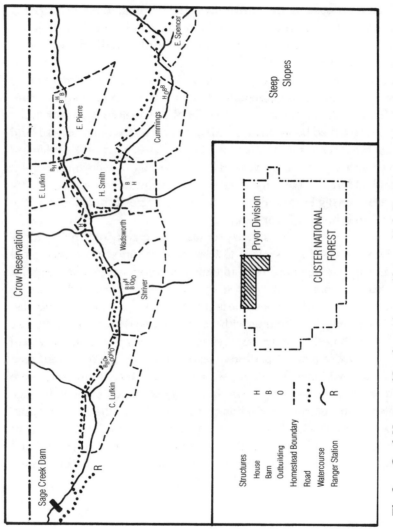

Structures

House	H
Barn	B
Outbuilding	O

Homestead Boundary — —

Road • • •

Watercourse ∿

Ranger Station R

2. *The Sage Creek Homestead Landscape in 1915 (Source: U.S. Department of Agriculture, Forest Service, Field Notes and Plats, H.E.S., Beartooth National Forest, 1913–16).*

est Service; individual homestead files compiled by both the Forest Service and the General Land Office; Carbon County tax, school, deed, and land records; maps drawn for the Forest Service, General Land Office, and the county; and census data for the years 1900 to 1940. These data, and information recounted by informants, help to establish the changing pattern of population, acreage, farmsteads, cultivation, improvements, and structures in the Sage Creek settlement episode.

During its first twenty years, the Sage Creek community grew from a few families to a population just shy of eighty persons (figure 4). By 1915, 20 percent of the population provided service activities, worked in sawmills, or furnished labor for the Forest Service. Blacksmithing was the foremost service activity, and the six or seven part-time blacksmiths found customers among homesteaders, livestock producers, lumberers, and forest rangers. The post office on the Cummings homestead, with Blanche Cummings as postmistress, lasted for a year from 1910 to 1911. In 1915, it was reinstituted on the Shriver property, with Nettie Z. Shriver as postmistress, and it continued there until 1932.[20] The schoolhouse operated in peak settlement years from 1911 to 1926. In 1920 the Beartooth National Forest was excluded from further homesteading. The years of decline were marked by loss of services, slightly more gradual outmigration after homestead losses and replacements in the wake of the 1919–23 droughts, aging population, and amalgamation of properties.[21] During the 1920s, the tendency was to sell the homestead or lose it to the bank, which then sold the property. During the 1930s, combined properties owned by newcomers accounted for most of the holdings. Subsequently, the Schwend Ranch and several smaller stock concerns amalgamated properties.

Original holdings were surveyed with care to conform to the 160-acre standard in size. The paradox of this substantial effort soon became apparent, for only a fraction of each homestead was fenced and cultivated. Although combined acreage of homesteads exceeded 3,000 acres by 1920, fenced acreage was only 1,000 and cultivated acreage a mere 500 (figure 4). Consistent with the increased emphasis on stock raising after 1920, cultivated acreage fell and fenced acreage continued to rise.

Comparison of cultivated acreage and soil characteristics for homesteads surveyed between 1913 and 1916 shows no correlation of better soils, such as clay and black loams, with greater acreage cultivated. Soils characterized as rocky and sandy by surveyors were cultivated to the same extent as more fertile clay and black loams. If homestead entry surveys 244, 115, and 246, which were surveyed soon after entry, are set aside, it is apparent

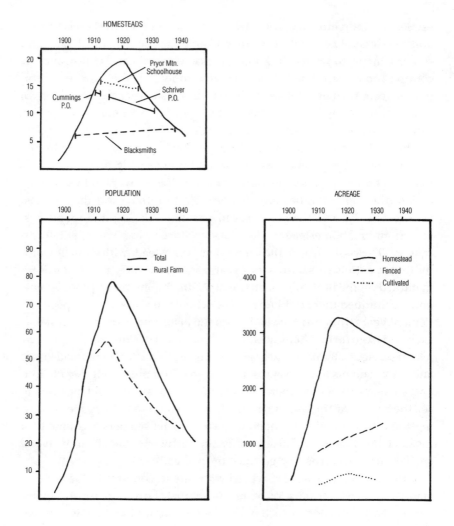

4. Sage Creek Homesteads: Population and Acreage (For Homesteads Surveyed by U.S. Department of Agriculture, Forest Service, 1913–16) (Sources: USDA, Forest Service, Field Notes and Plats, H.E.S., Beartooth National Forest, 1913–16; Bureau of Land Management, GLO Records, Billings; Bureau of the Census, Census of U.S., 1910, 1920, 1930, 1940; Carbon County, Report of County Supt. Schools, 1893–, Tax Levies, 1896–, Landbook, 1880–, Deed Record, 1888–; C. A. Gibson, Map of Carbon County, 1912; USDA, Forest Service, Map of Custer National Forest, Beartooth Div., Montana, 1933, 1938).

that almost all homesteaders raised only the minimum twenty to thirty acres considered necessary to satisfy Forest Service examiners that cropping requirements for patent were being met. With sixty acres in barley, winter wheat, and oats, George Perkins (H.E.S. 168) placed considerably more emphasis on grain farming than his neighbors. He raised no stock, hired his teaming, and sold crops to fellow homesteaders.[22] Other Sage Creek homesteaders brought with them the prevailing determination to adapt the land to wheat, but in the Pryors only George Perkins was briefly successful. By 1915 and 1916, when most of the surveys were completed, settlers were growing alfalfa and other fodder crops.

Distinctions among Sage Creek homesteads extended to the farmstead, which varied considerably in size, value, function, complexity, and appearance. The homestead landscape in 1915 reveals that farmstead structures were clustered, but beyond this common characteristic they assumed many configurations, ranging from a linear arrangement along stream and road (C. Lufkin) to the segregation of house and farmyard (Cummings) (figure 3). Most farmsteads in 1915 consisted of a simple log or frame cabin with one or more log barns nearby. Rarely did the houses exceed two hundred dollars in value, and few barns or outbuildings such as chicken houses, stables, or root houses matched house valuations. Homesteaders with sizable numbers of horses and cattle—Charles Lufkin, William Shriver, and Henry Spencer—built more substantial houses as well as a larger collection of outbuildings. These incipient ranches usually included a blacksmith's shop and semisubterranean cold storage. In addition to keeping stock, homesteaders cut timber and worked for the railroad to obtain cash and develop their properties. This further supports the lack of correlation between value of structures and cultivated acreage. Only a newcomer, such as Henry Wadsworth, or a dependent, such as the widow Elizabeth Spencer, conformed to this expected correlation for a farming homestead.

Houses and barnyard structures were either of log or frame construction. Douglas fir and lodgepole pine were both plentiful and readily available on nearby national forest land. Permits were required for cutting logs and sawing lumber for initial construction, for improvements, and for sale. For example, in 1923 Charles Lufkin obtained a special-use permit to establish a portable sawmill near the Dryhead Ranger Station to saw logs for Chester Fenner, Ira Hilker, and himself.[23] Recorded more often are examples of timber trespass by homesteaders like Lufkin, who cut and sold 2,154 railroad ties to the Yellowstone Park Railway Company, or O. W. Ly-

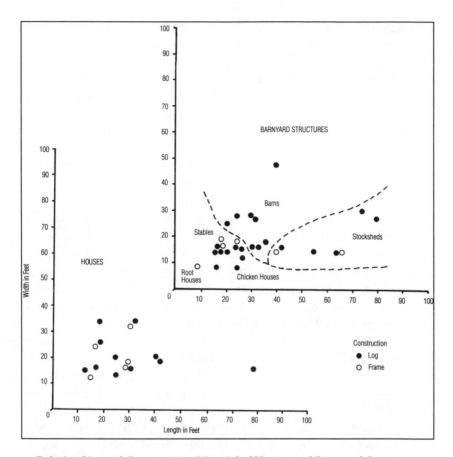

5. *Relative Size and Construction Material of Houses and Barnyard Structures on Sage Creek Homesteads (For Homesteads Surveyed by U.S. Department of Agriculture, Forest Service, 1913–16) (Source:* USDA, *Forest Service, Fieldnotes H.E.S., Beartooth National Forest, 1913–16; see also Department of the Interior, Bureau of Land Management,* GLO *Records, Billings.)*

man of Cowley, Wyoming, who removed twenty-two house logs from the vicinity of the saddle between Sage and Crooked Creeks.[24]

There was no relationship between structure size and building material (figure 5). Some large houses were built of logs, and some small homes were constructed with boards. Chester Fenner's house featured sawed and notched corners, lime chinking between logs, framed doors and windows, and a board and batten roof. The Shriver house, although of contemporary pyramid roof design and characterized by other twentieth-century features, was built of rot-resistant Douglas fir logs, as was every structure on the homestead, including the privy (figure 6). The large barn was constructed of simply notched fir logs forming two matched cribs. Each was raftered with lodgepole pine and roofed with sawed Douglas fir. These barns, in one or two crib configurations, were characteristic of Sage Creek homesteads. The three single-crib structures can be differentiated from the four double-crib forms and the one large log barn with dimensions of fifty feet by forty feet (figure 5). Stables, of both frame and log construction, were between fifteen and twenty feet long and approximately fifteen feet wide. Chicken houses and detached cold cellars were smaller, and stock sheds were characterized by their extreme length. The size and number of stock sheds attests to considerable emphasis on animal husbandry soon after homesteads were established.

On the mountain, beginning a farming homestead was a pretense for other activities. Both George Bainbridge and R. A. Greathouse established a presence on Big Pryor by 1912 and immediately used their homesteads as stockholding locations. Bainbridge became acquainted with Big Pryor through seasons of sheepherding on the mountains.[25] Although Greathouse later relinquished his claim, Bainbridge proceded to clear a section of Douglas fir and lodgepole pine, improve several springs, and build a farmstead on the forest edge at 7,700 feet. Homestead remains at the site include a log structure that alternately served as a house, sheep shed and game-hanging enclosure, a cold cellar, and log cabin.[26] Stove fragments, wagon parts, and other debris attest to homesteading activity, and the land near the cabin appears to have been cultivated as a garden. His claim was finally patented 11 October 1919. Then Bainbridge moved his farmstead southeast to the other end of the property, built another cabin and a larger barn, and enlarged a more substantial spring to form a stock pond.[27] Huddled next to a Douglas fir stand at 7,900 feet and situated just below the lip of mountain-top meadows, the location often holds snow into July. On a level area several hundred feet below, Bainbridge tried to raise feed for eighty-seven cattle and forty horses, but he was repeatedly unsuccessful and was obliged to rely on his grazing permit.[28] In 1924, he did not use his permit privilege but farmed in Warren, Montana, instead.[29] The Bainbridge family retained their land and used their national forest grazing permit successively in later years.

Sage Creek's homestead landscape was also not consistent. In less than a decade almost twenty farms were established by homesteaders who varied in background, experience, and commitment to the land. For each,

6. The William Shriver Homestead, Sage Creek, Montana. (Photo by the author.)

their forest homesteads, the adjacent grazing land, the forested slopes of the Pryors, the upland meadows, and even the Crow Reservation Range meant something different. For George Perkins, the land provided a livelihood and took most of his time. Alternatively, for Charles Lufkin, who maintained grazing permits in all seasons beginning in 1912, the homestead was merely a ranch headquarters; even before the drought of 1919, the move to stock raising was well established.[30] For some homesteaders, homesteading was indeed the original intent. The national forest homestead, uniquely situated in a regulated and protected government grazing preserve, made stock raising not only easy but also profitable. In 1910, Ranger Abbot commented on the Sage Creek settlement for the *Beartooth Forester* newsletter: "Some of the claims applied for are where it would be impossible for anybody to maintain a winter residence although to hear some of the applicants talk, one would think that Pryor Mountain contained the biggest part of the Banana Belt and pineapple grew wild."[31] For most Sage Creek homesteaders, such intimations served only to placate the Forest Service. As Abbot observes in the same report, stock routinely drifted onto the Crow Reservation or south onto national forest lands. In addition, homesteaders were utilizing timber resources, and nearby ranchers and herders were bringing sheep, cattle, and horses to Pryor grasslands. Change was imminent, and from the beginning the forest homestead developed as a base for mountain grazing.

The Grazing Residual

Even if you somehow outlasted the weather, then, no foothills homestead you built for yourself could head off a future of national forest boundaries and powerful livestock companies. Like much else in the wresting of this continent, the homestead laws were working to a result, right enough, but not to the one professed for them. The homestead sites my father could point out to me by the dozen—place upon place, and our family soil among them—in almost all cases turned out to be not the seed acres for yeoman farms amid the sage, nor the first pastures of tidy family ranches. Not that at all. They turned out to be landing sites, quarters to hold people until they were able to scramble away to somewhere else.[32]

Ivan Doig's reminiscence expresses the frustration of homesteaders and perhaps the recognition as well that they had participated in a frontier experience relevant for generations before, but an experience that had little validity and provided few rewards in a modern world. In the Pryor Mountains, stock raising gave the only certain income, and those who had not come to the Pryors with a stock-raising way of life in mind soon found themselves immersed in it.

Stock-raising homesteads were designated by the secretary of the interior.[33] Although none of these 640-acre "homesteads" were assigned to the Pryor Division because it was in the jurisdiction of the USDA, the General Land Office did make designations on East Pryor immediately adjacent to the national forest. Entries began in 1919 with Joseph M. Parsons's application for all of Section 8, Township 8S, Range 28E. After his relinquishment and two other attempts at settlement, the claim was entered in 1934 by Otto F. Krueger of Garland, Wyoming. During the next five years he achieved the minimum residence of five months each year to gain the patent.[34] Krueger's cabin is situated on the east slope of upper Layout Creek valley and faces a prominent trail leading to summit meadows on east Pryor above a spring at the head of Layout Creek. The cabin, built of substantial fir logs on a limestone foundation, is sturdy and remains well preserved. In the immediate vicinity of the old cabin are found numerous remnants of pipe and galvanized metal from conduits and holding tanks for water because in the summer the spring flow is negligible and may cease. Krueger maintains that obtaining water for his stock on East Pryor was a greater problem than facing the inclement weather at the beginning and end of every grazing season.[35] The Stock-Raising or Section Homestead Act brought a minimal impact to the Pryors where Forest Service personnel, Sage Creek homesteaders, and Crooked Creek ranchers effectively utilized or controlled all available grazing land. The few entrymen taking advantage of this last of the homestead acts found considerable opposition and competition for a grazing resource which was deteriorating by the 1930s.

Between the boundary of the national forest and the Wyoming border, Crooked Creek provided a limited and sinewy portion of arable land (figure 2). From 1912 to 1937, ten patents were issued for one-quarter and one-sixteenth sections under the original Homestead Act of 1862.[36] Among the first to patent homesteads were James H. Kelsey, Bessie Strong, Cecil Huntington, Harvey King, and Samuel Legg. Most of these early homesteaders on Crooked Creek attained ownership of their small holdings in advance of Sage Creek settlers on the other side of the mountain. Kelsey and Strong in particular were well acquainted with the Pryors and the timber and grass resources, and as early land owners in the area, they quickly asserted their presence throughout the mountains.

Livestock was their immediate and major concern. The Pryor meadows were absolutely necessary for the livelihood of Crooked Creek homesteaders; accordingly, the settlers utilized mountain resources to the utmost. In a sense, the Pryor Mountains, and particularly the national forest lands, were considered Crooked Creek domain. Under the ranchers' code, and despite Forest Service permit restrictions, these users felt that they were in the best position to manage the grass resource. The Forest Service was tolerated at best by the local ranchers and confronted when others gained access to the water, grass, and timber of the Pryors. They agreed with President Theodore Roosevelt's directive to Secretary James Wilson:

> In granting grazing permits you give preference first to the small near-by owners; after that, to all regular occupants of the Reserve range; and finally to the owners of transient stock. . . . The small nearby owners are the homesteaders, the men who are making homes for themselves by the labor of the land and to bring up their children thereon. . . . If after these have been admitted, there still remains an ample pasturage, then the owners of transient stock . . . should be admitted. These men have no permanent abode, do very little to build up the land, and are not to be favored at the expense of the regular occupants, large or small.[37]

The Pryors barely provided for their needs, felt these homesteaders, and consequently Forest Service provision of grazing rights to livestock producers from nearby communities in the Montana and Wyoming border country caused concern, then conflict. Crooked Creek residents, who raised mainly cattle and horses, were most concerned about the entry of large sheep flocks to the national forest during summer grazing season.

In the 1910s and 1920s, the mountains were often fully stocked, and large grazing operations like the Davis Sheep Company found annual grazing permits disapproved.[38] Many instances of overstocking were due to unpermitted stock from homesteads entering the national forest range. In 1923, Mrs. Edna Hetland was cited for stock trespass when 134 cattle and 31 horses drifted onto the range.[39] Without effective fences, which the homesteaders opposed and often neglected to maintain, such trespass was a common occurrence. Initiatives by the homesteaders to restrain stock were immediately supported by the Forest Service. In 1923, Sullivan, Strong, Tillett, and Hetland were granted a special-use permit to corral and pasture horses on national forest land.[40] In the same Forest Service permit file is a map outlining the land use on the Strong and Sullivan holdings along lower Crooked Creek. Illustrated are patchwork fields of alfalfa, crested wheat, and clover as well as garden and orchard plots. Only 2.6 acres of arable land remained idle, and a mere 5.2 acres were used for pasture. Stock was held in the sixteen enclosures evident on the map, but the animals were pastured on the public domain. The Forest Service demanded the restraint of stock, and the homesteaders complied, but only when it suited their advantage.

Regulating Livestock Use

By the 1920s, with only drought to experience and poor yields to show for their first decade at Sage Creek, most homesteaders sold their property and moved. Those who stayed either had come with the intention of raising stock or had adjusted to animal husbandry as they came to know the Pryors. The survivors were to learn that raising stock in these mountains was fraught with difficulties as well.

Homesteaders were obliged to conform to laws and management policies that they had only a minor role in forging. It was the end of the homestead era, and the disposition of remaining public lands was under considerable scrutiny.[41] After several decades of enabling legislation, public land law was becoming exclusive, and laws were leading to the "closing of the public domain."[42] Management policies were attempting to integrate conservation and utilization of public lands in a climate of ever-increasing conflict of interests.[43] The concentrated resources of the Mountainous West were often at the center of such disputes. Critical among these were conflicts between sheepherders and cattle raisers who competed for the same public range land. Enthusiastic development of the sheep industry coincided with the development of national forest grazing allotments.[44] In Montana and adjacent Wyoming, the industry became the mainstay of many local economies during the first quarter of the twentieth century and usually competed with cattle- and horse-raising enterprises in adjacent communities.[45] Some viewed increased access to the high country as the answer, a safety valve for the heightening competition for grazing lands. They found advocates among those resource managers who felt that national forests should be self-supporting, but adversaries among other managers who saw the forest reserves vanishing.[46]

The use of national forest ranges became a major issue throughout the West as resource managers debated the use of these public lands. In 1902, the General Land Office distributed a circular advocating temporary grazing in forest reserves.[47] As grazing on federal lands became more of an issue, advocates like Will C. Barnes wrote numerous articles for sheep and cattle industry journals, urging use of forest ranges and cooperation with the Forest Service.[48] In 1926, Barnes testified before Congress on this matter. The national forest range was considered important to maximize production goals in the stock industry, but opponents of increased use of these lands cited mounting instances of land and water abuse resulting from overgrazing of marginal lands.[49] In addition to resource abuse, cattle raisers and sheepherders encroached on public lands without authorization.[50]

This alarmed all federal land managers, particularly many foresters who had always eyed grazing as a menace in national forests. Due to encroachment and resource abuse problems which occurred soon after forest reserves were formed, Gifford Pinchot outlined instructions to his Forest Service personnel regarding grazing trespass.[51] These instructions formed the basis of an ever more complex permit and fine system for controlling use of national forest lands by the public. The problems and politics of grazing regulation heightened as competition for permits increased and practices of preference emerged. Some individuals were establishing what amounted to perpetual rights to national forest grazing lands.[52] In any event, this notion prevailed because the Forest Service granted permits according to directives which favored adjacent small-herd owners over large-scale ranchers and transient herders.[53] As long as grazing privileges were not abused, these permit holders could expect to retain their permits. They were valuable and eventually were traded and sold.

In the Pryor Mountains, a microcosm of grazing competition and conflict, of regulation and trespass, and of attempts by the Forest Service to establish a meaningful policy for managing the interrelation of agriculture, forestry, and grazing reflected the national forest homesteading experience throughout much of the Mountainous West. Documentation of conflict is rare in homesteaders' files but does arise occasionally in the lore of the Pryors to provide the opinion and detail that color information established in the records. Forest Service trespass and permit documentation confirms the early and long-established stock-grazing privileges of charter Sage Creek homesteaders Charles Lufkin and W. A. Shriver. In addition to summer grazing permits, they obtained special-use permits to winter stock on national forest lands or keep stock on specified allotments anytime during the year. These were reissued for Lufkin from 1912 and for Shriver from 1914 at an annual cost of between $24 and $28 each. Both pastures were allotted immediately west of the Sage Creek settlement and the Sage Creek Ranger Station. Here, in the shelter of Big Pryor, Shriver was allotted 242.2 acres "for permitted stock (no bulls) and stock exempt from permit (draft animals and milch cows)."[54] During this period, Charles Lufkin and William Shriver not only sustained significant grazing privileges throughout the Pryors but also were granted rights to cut damaged and dead timber. Their monopoly on all of these resources began to decline as other homesteaders established themselves on Sage Creek and as outsiders were granted permits as well. Characteristically, new permits were given to graze bands of sheep on high-elevation meadows from June to October and sometimes longer if reduced snow conditions allowed. Snow drifts furnished water early in the season, and early morning grazing with the dew provided moisture in the dry summer season. Bands would often rotate on and off the mountain to ensure proper watering of sheep and also to maintain full use of grazing resources. Late spring storms were devastating, and on occasion trapped flocks could be saved only by cutting trails through massive drifts on the mountainside.

With increased emphasis on stock in the 1920s, more permits were issued. A rising number of trespass violations encouraged regulation as well. Virtually every Sage Creek and Crooked Creek homesteader recorded trespass violations. Permits to residents from all quarters in the Pryors, among them the Spencers, Thomas Lazar, Anton Garcia, Ellen Strong, and Gracian Murdi, were temporary and for specified numbers of cattle, horses, and sheep.[55] Permit holders would either graze too many animals, exceed time limits, or both. For example, a 1921 report of trespass against Thomas Lazar was for premature grazing of his fifty head of cattle as well as running hogs at will in the national forest. The hogs were rooting forest and range, Shriver's pasture allotment, neighbors' properties, and the Sage Creek Ranger Station meadow.[56]

In an attempt to regulate trespass and urge homesteader responsibility for conservation of the meadows, Ranger Gary O'Neil called a meeting of Sage Creek permittees in June 1920. The Sage Creek Livestock Association was formed to work with the Forest Service in controlling allotments and assessing fees to support salt provision and fence maintenance.[57] Charter members present were A. E. Brown, E. Lufkin, H. Ray, R. G. Spencer, J. R. Stevens, J. E. Cothran and W. C. Moody. Among those absent were principal stockmen Charles Lufkin, Thomas Lazar, and Chester Fenner. Since

Lufkin and Lazar were among the most frequent permit violators as well, the association began without full support and never fully achieved the objectives sought by the Forest Service. In fact, the organization assumed the characteristics of a coalition against the Forest Service and violations continued as before.

Statistics on stock allotments and assessments tabulated annually by the association and the Forest Service enable detailed analysis of grazing in the Sage Creek vicinity of the national forest (table 1). Charter members such as the Bostic and Raish and the Van Loon and Long cattle companies each grazed an average of fifty animals annually for the years during which they held allotments. By 1921, stock companies were established in the Pryors; by 1928, they and several large ranches took most of the allotment. Sage Creek homesteaders whose mainstay was stock raising (C. A. Fenner, H. L. Ray, T. Lazar, and W. C. Moody) increased their allotments through the period, but their stock characteristically was of poor quality. Other homesteaders, such as Hilker, Spencer, and Shriver, renewed permits after letting them lapse for some time. However, the dominant trend saw homesteaders sell or relinquish their allotments as they left Sage Creek. In the case of Charles Lufkin, his large allotment was sold to nearby rancher J. W. Chapman when Lufkin retired from the land in his seventies. The Sage Creek Livestock Association was more of an advantage to new member ranchers and stock companies because it handled their permit affairs and assured provision of salt for stock and maintenance of fences. For the Forest Service, the association offered a simplified approach to permit and trespass regulation. This involved an annual meeting at which allotments were adjusted and fees assessed for salt and fencing based on allotment size and a per-head assessment predicated on anticipated costs. Everyone in the association paid the same per-head assessment multiplied by their allotment. When the association was new, costs were higher for badly needed supplies and fencing; then assessments per head fluctuated on a biennial resupply basis; finally, they dropped as the association fell into decline (figure 7). Per-head assessments proved higher for homesteaders who were charter members, but lower rates prevailed in later years for larger-herd owners who took over allotments. Like other stock associations, this one eventually worked into the hands of more powerful ranchers and was manipulated to their advantage.[58]

In the 1930s, the decline of the Sage Creek Stock Association, the increasing demand for range-use permits from outsiders, deteriorating range conditions, and the impact of the Taylor Grazing Act led Custer (for-

TABLE 1.

Stock Allotments Approved for the Sage Creek Livestock Association, Pryor Division, Custer National Forest, 1921–1928 (Source: National Archives, Seattle, record group 95, Custer National Forest closed files 63-B602, Sage Creek Livestock Association, box 67409, Cooperation, 1920–28).

Association Member	Annual Stock Allotment								Total	Avg
	1921	1922	1923	1924	1925	1926	1927	1928		
C. A. Fenner	25	39	37	45	50	60	73	67	396	50
A. G. Peaplow	10	7	8	12	15	15			67	11
H. L. Ray	28	36	37	13	26	32	60	40	272	34
S. Schroyer	8	10	10	7	10	10			55	9
R. G. Spencer	12	10	11	6	12	12			63	11
J. R. Stevens	23	28	33	21				10	115	23
E. Lufkin	28								28	28
A. E. Brown	50	50	46	49					195	49
T. Lazar	50	45	50	50	54	70	101	107	527	66
C. Lufkin	175	175	140						490	163
M. Wrote	55	55	40	50					200	50
W. C. Moody	25	21	23	26	38	58	67	69	327	41
Bostic & Raish	50	50	50	50	75	50	30		355	51
VanLoon & Long	50	50	50						150	50
W. W. Roberts		15	15						30	15
I. Hilker				10	10	65	18	16	119	24
G. B. Teeples				15	40	60	40	60	215	43
J. W. Chapman				126	240		113		479	160
A. Garcia					14	14	14	20	62	16
J. A. Dowdle					45				45	45
E. E. Godfrey					20	20	25		65	21
L. D. Spencer est.						25			25	25
W. A. Shriver							12	12	24	12
L. E. Tindel							16		16	16
Cummings Bros.								33	33	33
J. Kuchinski								100	100	100
H. Lane								30	30	30
C. L. Hammond								60	60	60
Annual totals	589	591	550	480	584	536	564	649	4543	511

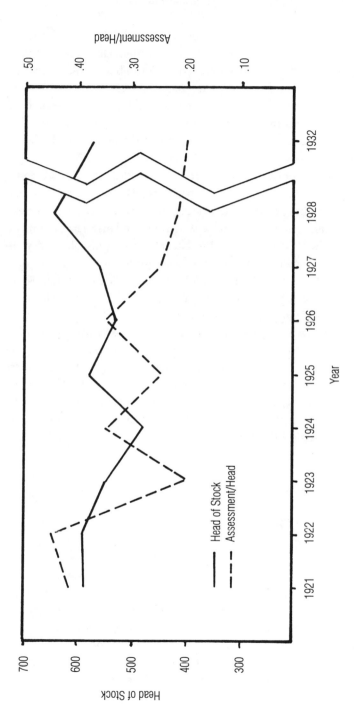

7. *Stock Allotments and Assessments for the Sage Creek Livestock Association, Pryor Division, Custer National Forest, 1921–1932* (*Source: National Archives, Seattle, record group 95, Custer National Forest closed files 63-B602, Sage Creek Livestock Association, box 67409, Cooperation, 1920–32*).

merly Beartooth) National Forest officials to establish more elaborate "Range Management Plans."[59] For the Pryor Mountain Division, cattle and horse management units were established, and the Sage Creek and Dryhead units together comprised the former Sage Creek Stock Association allotment. Sheep allotments continued to command high meadows and included four parallel north to south units on Big Pryor and one on East Pryor. Game management units were defined for canyons of the south slope, for the desert edge, and in Bear Canyon on Big Pryor.[60]

Within this regulatory structure the remnants of the homestead era remained boldly outlined on the map. The homestead boundaries which persist on Smith's map of 1933 retained little significance in that year, for most of the homesteaders had left. For those who remained on Sage Creek, and their neighbors on Crooked Creek, life became more difficult, and year-round residence in the Pryors became more and more a practice of the past. In 1941, A. M. Bainbridge, who for decades had lived near Warren, Montana, rather than at her family homestead on Big Pryor, was cited for noncompliance in sustaining her sheep and cattle on Big Pryor. Apparently, the homestead land was not used to cultivate fodder for her increased allotment as indicated in her permit applications. Between 1934 and 1940, annual cultivation was claimed on between 16 and 40 acres of the 160-acre homestead. Yet only two tons of alfalfa and thirty-five bushels of seed were harvested, all in 1934. No feed was produced in other years due to drought, early frost, or grasshopper epidemic. In 1945, the permit was finally sold to John D. Zmemer, a local sheep raiser.[61]

Conclusions

The Forest Homestead Act opened the high country of the Mountainous West to a wave of late settlement. Islands of concentrated resources, once the refuges of early human inhabitants of North America, the Pryors and other isolated archipelagos in the arid West also attracted settlers pursuing the final frontiers of agricultural expansion. Like the natives before them, some sought the restorative sanctuary of the high country, but most desired the resources now more apparent as wild land was converted to public domain. Drawn closer to the mountains, they could discern the concentration of grasslands, woods, and water resources clearly stratified and available for exploitation. The Forest Homestead Act laid public land open to private and inevitably competing uses.

This essay records the pattern and the process of homesteading the Pryors. Homesteads at Sage Creek, East Pryor, Big Pryor, and Crooked Creek represent alternative strategies to high-elevation settlement and resource use. Their remnants and the ample documentation left by homesteaders and government stewards of the land reveal a detailed account of hardship and persistence, success and failure, at the margins of the settlement frontier.

By the 1930s, the Pryor Mountains were again a part of the grazing residual of the Mountainous West. Here, too, as Ivan Doig has recalled for other mountain areas, powerful livestock companies moved up the mountain in a relentless search for available fodder, and national forest authorities attempted to enforce their boundaries against trespass and resource abuse. Resulting conflicts caught homesteaders in between. Living within national forest boundaries, they were obliged to abide by the special regulations established for homestead use of the reserved land. Nevertheless, they were forced to compete for the grazing residual with livestock producers who gained access to the land through arrangements made with regional head offices of the Forest Service. Homesteaders in the Pryors viewed the competition from stockmen and the regulation enforcement by national forest rangers as unbearable burdens when added to the already oppressive constraints of the marginal land and the mountain climate. They decided that this was no longer a place for them, and that they were obliged to leave.

Was there a place for the homesteader in the Pryor Mountains, or in other national forests throughout the Mountainous West? One assessment suggests that homesteading within reserved land boundaries was ill-conceived from the beginning, that permanent settlement was entirely incompatible with the philosophy and the environment of national forests. Another view suggests that homesteading in the continental United States needed to run its course, and that homesteaders could commit human ingenuity and adaptation to even the most marginal land and make it flourish. Although in the end the Pryor Mountain homesteads did not flourish, the homesteaders had established a place for themselves in the mountains. They were obliged to leave it due to external pressures, but while they could afford to stay, Pryor residents used resources from the forest and the meadow to complement the meager return from the soil. A new homesteading experience was originated and sustained until the pressures for excessive resource extraction became too great. Then the homesteaders participated in the depletion of their own sustaining environment. In the end, we are left with a lingering question. Did the Pryor Mountain homesteaders and their cohorts elsewhere in national forests extend the frontier or merely facilitate its final passage?

Notes

1. Larry W. Price, *Mountains and Man: A Study of Process and Environment* (Berkeley and Los Angeles: University of California Press, 1981), 393.

2. Thomas M. Kerlie, "Some Chapters on the Forest Homestead Act with Emphasis on Western Montana," (master's thesis, University of Montana, 1962).

3. D. L. Blackstone, "Structure of the Pryor Mountains, Montana," *Journal of Geology* 48 (1940): 590–618.

4. R. F. Flint, *Glacial and Quaternary Geology* (New York: John Wiley and Sons, 1976).

5. C. L. Porter, *A Flora of Wyoming*, University of Wyoming Agricultural Experiment Station Bulletin no. 402 (Laramie, 1962).

6. Edwin T. Denig, *Five Indian Tribes of the Upper Missouri: Sioux, Arickara, Assiniboines, Crees, Crows* (Norman: University of Oklahoma Press, 1961); Denig, "Of the Crow Nations," Bureau of American Ethnology Bulletin no. 151 (Washington, D.C., 1953); Robert H. Lowie, *The Crow Indians* (New York: Farrar and Rinehart, 1935).

7. Robson Bonnichsen et al., "False Cougar and Shield Trap Caves, Pryor Mountains, Montana," *National Geographic Research* 2 (Summer 1986): 276–90.

8. Vernon Carstensen, ed., *The Public Lands: Studies in the History of the Public Domain* (Madison: University of Wisconsin Press, 1963).

9. *U.S. Statutes at Large* 34 (1906): 233–34.

10. Louise Poffer, *The Closing of the Public Domain: Disposal and Reservation Policies, 1900–1950* (Stanford: Stanford University Press, 1951), 134–35.

11. Poffer, *The Closing of the Public Domain*, 138.

12. Entrymen could claim 320 acres. *U.S. Statutes at Large* 35, 639.

13. *U.S. Statutes at Large* 36, 288.

14. *U.S. Statutes at Large* 39, 862.

15. *U.S. Statutes at Large* 31, 862.

16. E. S. Gosney, "The Protection of Home Builders in the Regulations of Grazing on Forest Reserves," *Proceedings*, American Foresters' Congress, 1905, 218–27.

17. Lloyd P. Jorgensen, "Agricultural Expansion into the Semi-Arid Lands of the West North Central States during the First World War," *Agricultural History* 23 (1949): 30–40.

18. Great Northern Railway Company, *Montana: The Treasure State* (St. Paul: Great Northern Railway, 1913).

19. Marion Clawson et al., *Farm Adjustments in Montana*, Montana Agricultural Experiment Station Bulletin no. 377, 1940; Frederick C. Luebke, "Ethnic Group Settlement on the Great Plains," *Western Historical Quarterly* 8 (October 1977): 405–30; Lowry Nelson, *The Mormon Village: A Pattern and Technique of Land Settlement* (Salt Lake City: University of Utah Press, 1952).

20. David W. Harvey, "A General Historical Survey of the Pryor Mountains" (master's thesis, Western Washington University, Bellingham, 1975), 45.

21. James H. Shideler, *Farm Crisis, 1919–1923* (Berkeley: University of California Press, 1957).

22. Armitage to Ferguson, "Report on Homestead Claim," 8 October 1915, Beartooth National Forest—Claims, H.E. 06521, Billings Land District, U.S. Forest Service.

23. National Archives and Records Service, Seattle, Record Group 95, Custer National Forest closed files 60-A157, box 31288, Lufkin, 1 August 1923.

24. National Archives, Seattle, file 60-A43, box 1194, Trespass, 24 September 1907.

25. In 1911, Bainbridge's sheep and lambing operations were discussed in the U.S. Forest Service publication *Beartooth Forester* (April 1911): 12.

26. Victor Konrad, Pryor Mountain Historic Resource Inventory, field notes of the 1982 Survey and Survey Form 82–2–24, Bainbridge I, Montana Historic Preservation Office, Montana Historical Society, Helena.

27. Konrad, no. 82–2–32, Bainbridge II.

28. National Archives, Seattle, file 60-A43, box 31281, O'Neil to Supt. F. S., 14 April 1923.

29. National Archives, Seattle, file 60-A43, box 31281, Bainbridge to Supt. F. S., 1 January 1924.

30. National Archives, Seattle, file 60-A157, box 31288, Lufkin, 14 June 1912.

31. *Beartooth Forester* (November 1910): 11–12.

32. Ivan Doig, *This House of Sky: Landscapes of the Western Mind* (New York: Harcourt Brace Jovanovich, 1978), 29.

33. *U.S. Statutes at Large* 39, 862.

34. U.S. Department of the Interior, General Land Office, Billings, serial files, 034971; USDI, Bureau of Land Management, *Montana Controlled Document Index* (Billings: BLM), patent 1108780.

35. Otto Krueger, interview with author, East Pryor Mountain, 5 July 1981.

36. *U.S. Statutes at Large* 12, 392.

37. Theodore Roosevelt to James Wilson, 26 December 1905.

38. National Archives, Seattle, file 60-A157, box 31296, Annual Grazing Permits, Davis Sheep Co., 2 March 1925.

39. National Archives, Seattle, file 60-A43, box 1194, Trespass—Hetland, 10 May 1923.

40. National Archives, Seattle, file 60-A157, box 31293, Cattle and Horse Permits—Strong, 3 August 1923.

41. H. H. Chapman, "The Future Disposition of Our Remaining Public Lands," *Journal of Forestry* 24 (May 1926): 439–99.

42. Paul W. Gates, "Public Land Issues in the United States," *Western Historical Quarterly* 2 (October 1971): 363–76; see also Poffer, *Closing of the Public Domain*.

43. Marion Clawson and B. Held, *The Federal Lands: Their Uses and Management* (Baltimore: Johns Hopkins University Press, 1957).

44. Harold E. Briggs, "The Early Development of Sheep Ranching in the Northwest," *Agricultural History* 11 (July 1937): 161–80.

45. Glen Barrett, "Stock Raising in the Shirley Basin, Wyoming," *Journal of the West* 14 (July 1975): 18–24.

46. T. S. Woolsey, "Can National Forests Be Made Self-Supporting?" *American Lumberman* 2141 (1916): 59; K. D. Swan, *What the National Forests Mean to Montana*, U.S. Department of Agriculture, misc. circular 48 (Washington, D.C., 1926).

47. B. Herman, *Temporary Grazing in Forest Reserves*, U.S. General Land Office circular (Washington, D.C.: 1902).

48. Will C. Barnes, *Western Grazing Grounds and Forest Ranges* (Chicago: Breeder's Gazette, 1913); "Adaptation of National Forests to the Grazing of Sheep," *American Sheep Breeder and Wool Grower* 36 (1916): 73–75; "The Forest Service and the Stockman," *Producer* 1 (1919): 5–9; "Stockman and Forest Ranges," *Breeder's Gazette* 83 (1923): 394–95; "Livestock on Ranges of National Forests," *Angora Journal* 14 (1925): 23.

49. T. Gallegos, "National Forest Grazing and Maximum Mean Production," *Producer* 3 (1921): 9–11.

50. J. O. Oliphant, "Encroachments of Cattlemen on Indian Reservations in the Pacific Northwest, 1870–1890," *Agricultural History* 24 (1950): 42–58.

51. Gifford Pinchot, "Instructions Regarding Grazing Trespass," U.S. Department of Agriculture, Forest Service (Washington, D.C., 1908).

52. P. L. Buttrick, "Politics and Perpetual Rights—Some Aspects of Grazing on the National Forests," *Journal of Forest History* 26 (1928): 34–56.

53. Paul H. Roberts, *Hoof Prints on Forest Ranges: The Early Years of National Forest Range Administration* (San Antonio: Naylor Company, 1963), 42–54.

54. National Archives, Seattle, file 60-A157, boxes 31288 and 31293.

55. National Archives, Seattle, file 60-A157, boxes 31285, 31288, 31293, 31296, and 31297.

56. National Archives, Seattle, file 60-A43, box 1194.

57. National Archives, Seattle, file 63-B602, box 67409.

58. F. P. Johnson, "Advantages of Cooperation between the Government and Livestock Associations in the Regulation and Control of Grazing on Forest Reserves," *Proceedings*, American Forestry Congress, 1905, 228–31; A. F. Furman and E. P. Ball, "Operating a Grazing Association," *Journal of Land and Public Utility Economics* 19 (1943): 94–98.

59. *U.S. Statutes at Large* 48, 1269.

60. K. E. Chriswell, *Range Management Plans, Custer National Forest, Beartooth Division, Pryor Mountain District* (Billings: U.S. Department of Agriculture, Forest Service, 1936); National Archives, Seattle, file 62-A486.

61. National Archives, Seattle, file 60-A43, box 31281.

8 / The Last Lumber Frontier?

MICHAEL WILLIAMS

The obvious is frequently overlooked, in history as in life. The forests that clothed the mountains of the American West are largely ignored as historians concentrate on mining communities, mountain men, cowboys, and irrigation when writing about the region. Yet, the abundant stands of Douglas fir, redwood, spruce, cedar, pine, and other trees that clothed these ranges were the basis of the economic life of many of the western states. Arguably, their preeminence as a resource was not challenged until questions of the consumption and allocation of the water that flowed off the mountains came to the fore during the mid-twentieth century.

Besides their abundance, the forests of the Mountainous West were physically the last lumber frontier in the United States. The ever-expanding and generally westward-moving wave of lumber exploitation spread from New England, through New York and Pennsylvania during the mid-nineteenth century, carried on to the Great Lake states during the 1880s, and then swept down through the Southern states during the 1890s; by the beginning of this century it had leaped the Great Plains and reached the Mountainous West.[1] The story of lumber exploitation in the West, the last region, was different from those of the other regions. In the words of one commentator: "the lumbermen's westward migration now ended. The blue Pacific Ocean, not another ridge of green forests, now met their gaze. Thoughts shifted to permanence."[2] But while some things were subtly different, the conditions of exploitation did not change with locality. If anything, they intensified since the region was a dependent periphery to a powerful and dynamic urban core that had grown up in the Midwest during the later nineteenth century. As before, lumbermen were "operating in a political environment that invited graft and corruption" and were a part of the "expansive and turbulent dynamics of late nineteenth- and twentieth-century capitalism."[3] The alternate booms and troughs of production resulted from the destructively competitive economic environment, and while here and there efforts were made to achieve permanence and stability, forests were destroyed and many communities disappeared.

What was significantly different about the forests of the West was the fact that they were concentrated on mountains in the last of the public lands, lands that were spectacular in their scenic beauty and a treasure house of natural wonders that captured the imagination and concern of the increasingly environmentally conscious society emerging in the United States. Foremost among these wonders were the trees themselves, the giant redwoods and sequoias of the forests. Inevitably, therefore, there would be attempts at conservation.[4]

The story of human interaction with the forests of the Mountainous West began with efforts to identify the trees and delineate the extent of tree cover. Once the picture of the lushness of nature's bounty was clarified, the process of turning it to market advantage could follow.

Where and What Forests?

Folk knowledge of individual species of American trees and their particular utilitarian qualities had accumulated from the beginning of settlement. Knowledge was put on a scientific basis after the mid-eighteenth century with the detailed and acute observations of Kalm, the Bartrams, and the Michaux. But these observations were eastern in their content, and it was not until Thomas Nuttall compiled his supplement to François André Michaux's North American Sylva between 1842 and 1849 that the fruits of exploration and "botanizing" in the West, especially by David Douglas, were included in the American picture.[5]

But it was literally a case of the forests not being seen for the trees, and even as late as the mid-nineteenth century there was little idea of the composition or extent of the tree cover, particularly in the interior of the western third of the continent. Indeed, the forests on the mountain spines were not the prime object of early exploration and settlement. Furthermore, the physical isolation of mountain zones from the main centers of settlement added to ignorance about the Mountainous West.

This lack of knowledge was displayed on the map compiled by Professor Joseph Henry, secretary of the Smithsonian Institution, in 1858.[6] It crudely distinguished two types of prairie and three types of forest, and was considered the most accurate map of its time (figure 1A). After the early 1860s, more utilitarian considerations dominated. The destruction of the eastern forests shifted the debate away from the character of trees and their relation to agricultural potential, to the stock of timber which was such an essential commodity in everyday American life.

On behalf of the Bureau of Census, in 1873 William H. Brewer brought together the individual Land Office plats and other surveys and attempted to compile a map of both distribution and *density* of woodlands by six categories of acres per square mile. It was, he said, "a compromise in which I have tried to show as far as possible what is known of the woodlands" (figure 1B). The montane nature of the forests was shown for the first time, and the nearly total cover of the magnificent Pacific coast forest was delineated clearly. Ten years later, in 1884, Charles Sargent produced his massive *Report on the Forests of North America* together with a *Folio Atlas of Forest Trees of North America* as a part of the Tenth Census. Like Brewer before him, but working on a much surer basis, Sargent attempted to summarize "the present productive capacity of the forest" by providing a map of "average forest density" in nine geometrically graded categories (simplified as six in Figure 1C) of cords per acre. Never before had the western forests been displayed in such detail.[7]

While others such as Edgar Ensign and Henry Gannett added more of the extent and commercial potential of the forests, the emerging school of professional ecologists was investigating ideas connected with plant formation, association, succession, and climax.[8] Slowly the idea was emerging that broad forest types were in some sort of dynamic relationship with their environment. By 1924 foresters had accepted the concept of dynamic equilibrium and had incorporated it into their maps of "natural vegetation" (figure 1D).

Using the Forests: The Early Stages

Every settler who wound his way west hacked at the available trees on the lower slopes for fuel, fences, and house construction. But commercial exploitation of forests had to await a number of conditions, the most important of which was accessibility to a market. Eastern markets were out of the question on account of distance (over two thousand miles) and cost of transporting this bulky, low-unit-value-for-weight commodity. Despite an apparent insatiable demand for lumber in the prairies, none went east until after 1880, and then only a little because of the high freight rates.

The California gold rush of 1849 provided just such a local production stimulus and market, but exploitation of the forests was fragmented be-

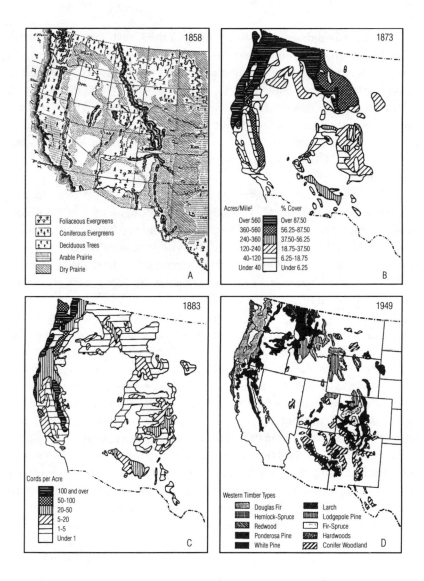

1. *Representations of the Forests of the Mountainous West, 1858–1948. (1A) 1858,*
"The forest and prairie lands of the United States." (Joseph Henry.) (1B) 1873, The
density of woodland in the United States. (Simplified from William H. Brewer.)
(1C) 1883, The density of existing forests. (Simplified from Charles S. Sargent.)
(1D) 1956, Major forest types. (Source: Stephen Haden-Guest, John K. Wright, and
Eileen M. Teclaff, A World Geography of Forest Resources, New York: Ronald
Press, 1956, 151.)

cause of the ruggedness and steep slopes of the Coast Ranges and Sierra Nevada. Inland communication was minimal, and egress was limited to a few points along the stormy, surf-ridden, and fog-bound coast—such as Santa Cruz, Monterey, Santa Barbara, San Francisco Bay, and Puget Sound, where safe anchorages could be developed. Consequently, after the initial burst of demand from the forty-niners was over, timbermen cast their gaze to the countries around the Pacific rim, such as Australia, New Zealand, Hawaii, China, Chile, and Peru, which were far more accessible than the East Coast.[9]

In the development of this international trade, any rock, promontory, or inlet which provided shelter was utilized. The "dogholes," as the sailors called them, were of two kinds. On the Californian redwood coast, timber was sent thundering into the holds of ships down chutes constructed over the cliff edges. On the Oregon and Washington coasts, many streams ended in shallow estuaries which ships could enter or leave only if hauled in or out by steam tugs.

The short and fast-flowing streams that plunged to the coast off the mountain ranges offered little access to the inland forest stands, unlike those on the eastern side of the Cascade Range. The turbulent streams were of limited use for driving logs, and often the canyon-like nature of the valleys (particularly in the Sierra) inhibited access by road or rail, so ox-teams had to be used to get the timber out. The lack of large natural drainage networks meant that exploitation proceeded in a series of isolated river basins, each separated from the other, and each being operated at a scale of production that was less than economical compared to anywhere else in the nation at that time. Only the areas of Puget Sound and San Francisco Bay offered favorable combinations of safe harbor, nearby timber, and access inland. Thus, both locations, but San Francisco in particular, became the focus for the sawed timber from the numerous other submarginal mills elsewhere along the coast, receiving up to 96 percent of the cargoes coming out of ports like Humboldt Bay, San Jose, Bodega Head, and Santa Cruz.

Much of the capital, technical know-how, and personnel for the lumber industry came from the Old Northeast. These operators realized that survival depended on access to a variety of timber types and a variety of markets, and that ownership of sailing fleets ensured security and flexibility. These were the essential ingredients of such successful regional firms such as those controlled by Pope and Talbot and by Asa Mead Simpson.

Some idea of the regional pattern of lumbering can be reconstructed for the Coast Ranges and the Sierra/Cascades that shows the value of sawed lumber by county for the census years 1860, 1870, and 1880 (figure 2). In 1860, production was concentrated in the redwood forests in the counties around San Francisco Bay. Other local concentrations were evident in the goldfield areas of the western slopes of the Sierra Nevada. In Puget Sound only Kitsap County was prominent at this time. By 1870, the value of production had quadrupled along the California coast, and lumbering activity was pushing north into Del Norte County, again emphasizing the importance of seaborne communication. But the situation in Washington is a blank since the data are missing. By 1880, production had intensified and spread everywhere, but particularly into the Douglas-fir region of Oregon and along the margins of the Willamette Valley, where agricultural settlement was pushing onto the lower slopes of the ranges. Around Puget Sound the pattern of activity was a forerunner of the intensive lumbering that was to come.

The patterns established by the 1880s changed little despite the completion of three northern transcontinental railroads between 1883 and 1887. The Northern Pacific ran to Tacoma, and the Union Pacific and Southern Pacific connected with Portland. Instead of immediately opening the westernmost forests to eastern markets, however, the new lines opened up the nearer forests of the intermontane states of Montana and Idaho to the "treeless" plains. Nor did railroad tariffs help. They were still heavily loaded in favor of "core" states like Michigan and Illinois, which continued to dominate trade as far west as Idaho until the late 1890s. It was not until James J. Hill cut freights on his newly completed Northern Pacific to forty cents per hundredweight to St. Paul and fifty cents to Chicago that the logs began to roll eastward.[10]

Besides generally opening up trade and joining the western periphery to the Midwest "core," the railroads had another far-reaching impact. Federal inducements to build lines in the form of land grants gave the railroad companies huge parcels of timberland that could be either used for logging or sold off to lumber companies with offers of advantageous mill sites and even special freight rates. Thus, huge spatial monopolies were created that were important in the exploitive boom that came after 1900.

With the railroads came a new inflow of capital, technology, and personnel from the Great Lakes region, which was fast being depleted of easily available timber. Later, when the southern stands also appeared close to depletion, there was a similar migration, the notorious example of this shift being the movement of the three thousand people and the machinery from old McNary, Louisiana, to new McNary, in eastern Arizona's White Mountains.[11]

The newcomers ignored the Pacific cargo trade, with its scattered and un-

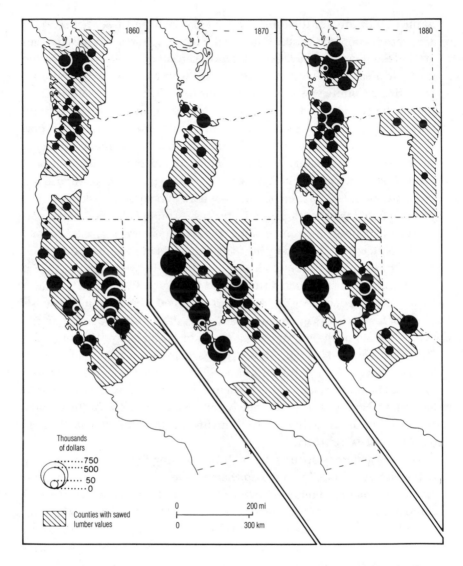

2. *Lumber Production by Value, 1860, 1870, and 1880 along the Pacific Coast (Source: U.S. Census).*

certain foreign markets, and concentrated instead on what they knew best, integrated production from stump to market for a discriminating domestic market that required a high-quality, standardized product. Their operations were aggressive and well financed, whereas the coastal traders were disorganized and underfinanced. The certainties of the railroad replaced the vagaries of the sailing craft. Fairly rapidly the coastal traders were eliminated (with the notable exception of Pope and Talbot), and eastern capital and industrial technology, Great Lakes lumbermen, and a national American market laid the foundation for a great boom in lumber production.

Technology Transfer and Adaptation

In every lumbering region the technology of cutting, extraction, and production had adapted subtly to local environmental conditions, and the Mountainous West was no exception. Owing to the difficulties of transport through and around the region's mountain barriers, anything that reduced the cost of movement was pursued aggressively. River transport, which had been developed to a fine art in New England, the Great Lakes states, and, to a lesser extent, the South and Appalachia, was not possible in the short, fast-flowing, but sometimes intermittent, streams of the West. With the exception of some rafting on the Columbia and the quiet waters of Puget Sound, most logs were yarded or skidded out of the forest by ox teams. But the lack of frozen ground made this difficult until local producers hit on the simple idea of the skid road (figure 3). In an effort to increase production further, loggers extended the roads for up to two miles into the forests and substituted horses for oxen because of their greater agility and speed. In time, incredibly engineered logging railroads penetrated the canyons and ranges, and logs from inaccessible high ground were transported many thousands of feet downslope in equally cleverly engineered flumes.[12]

However, methods of extraction were still expensive and not geared to the large-scale, mechanized, industrial exploitation aimed at mass markets which promised economic success in lumbering. Nothing changed until John Dolbeer tried out his invention of a stationary steam-powered hauling engine in Eureka in 1881. With the later addition of steel cables, the Dolbeer donkey engine revolutionized logging in the difficult terrain of the West. Bigger logs than ever before could be hauled out of the forests on skid roads, and costs were halved. Draught animals quickly disappeared, and production rose phenomenally. The total amount of lumber cut in the

3. B. F. Brock Logging Camp, circa 1892. The camp is located in Washington's Coast Ranges (Cowlitz Country). The bullock team in the foreground is hauling over a skid road. (Courtesy Forest History Society, Durham, N.C.).

states of California, Washington, and Oregon rose fourfold during the boom of the 1880s, from 0.6 billion board feet in 1879 to 2.6 billion in 1889 (particularly in Washington) and 2.9 billion in 1899. Lumbering evolved from simple, small-scale, and scattered ventures to operations that were increasingly complex, large, and concentrated. The forests of the mountains of the other states in the region were inherently less productive and yielded only 0.5 billion board feet by 1899, of which 44 percent came from Montana and 27 percent from Colorado.

Agriculture and Grazing

In emphasizing the moutain forests one should not forget that the mountains were also the scene of some agricultural activity and more often grazing activity. Steep slopes, poor soils, heavy timber, and heavy rainfall made land clearing difficult, and the usual progression from forest to farmland that had come to be expected in the East was not repeated in the West. In addition, heavy buying of potential homestead plots by speculators and lumber companies militated against farm creation. In Washington alone, just under three million acres were alienated between 1860 and 1870 without restriction. Most went not to small holders but to Puget Sound lumber companies and the Northern Pacific Railroad. The two million acres alienated under the Timber and Stone Act of 1879 also went the same way.[13]

Probably no more than 250,000 acres were cultivated in Washington by 1915, exemplifying the region's departure from the forest-to-farmland progression that characterized the East. The result was a dilemma for the timber companies because they were left with a tax burden on the already logged lands that could not be passed on to would-be farmers. Many companies let the cutover land revert to the states rather than pay taxes.

Although the agricultural impact on the mountains remained minimal, that of grazing was extensive. From the time of the earliest settlement in the West, sheep and cattle had been driven up from the dry, hot lowlands to the summer pastures in the lightly timbered and open uplands of the Sierra Nevada, Cascades, and Coast Ranges. But overgrazing and damage to vegetation by fire as pastoralists attempted to "green up" the pastures brought them into conflict with other interest groups, such as those concerned with water supply and quality for urban areas (and later hydroelectric projects, particularly in the Sierra Nevada), townsfolk, and recreationalists.

After 1897, the federal government gradually introduced regulations into its new forest reserves which excluded grazing from scenic areas, controlled stock numbers, and led to the issuing of five-year licenses. These, and later controls, were established through accommodation and compromise based in turn on a concept of acceptable carrying capacities. Significantly, their implementation firmly established the Forest Service as the overriding manager of the national forests and hence the mountainous watersheds.[14]

Using the Forests: After 1900

When Frederick Weyerhaeuser and others purchased 900,000 acres of prime timberland around the southern end of Puget Sound from the Northern Pacific Railroad at $6.00 an acre in 1900, it signaled the clear end of the old

coastal trade and the beginning of the inland trade. It underlined the co-
alescing of new capital, new attitudes, and new scales of operation and
production that were the hallmarks of twentieth-century capitalism, and
that endeavored to create a vertically integrated monopoly from stump to
plank. Weyerhaeuser's move was obvious. His Great Lakes states' stocks
were running down, and also he may well have struck a favorable deal concerning freight rates with James J. Hill, the owner of the Northern Pacific.
Weyerhaeuser set about consolidating his patchwork of alternate odd-
numbered sections into compact blocks by buying 100,000 acres from
small-scale owners and a further 221,000 acres from the Northern Pacific.
Northern Pacific sold an additional 200,000 acres of prime Douglas fir to
him for $5 an acre, with the company calculating that lines without loads
were useless (figure 4).

In all, Weyerhaeuser's purchases totaled 1.9 million acres, but they were
dwarfed by the controlling interest of the Southern Pacific and Northern
Pacific Railroads through land grants of 4.5 and nearly 3.2 million acres respectively. Vast as these areas were, the real significance of the holdings
was revealed in the estimates of the stumpage, or timber, growing on
them. The Weyerhaeuser company, together with direct subsidiaries, held
95.6 billion board feet of standing timber, which ranked second in the
country after Southern Pacific, with 105.6 billion board feet. However,
when all the interlocking interests of the Weyerhaeuser family throughout
the country were grouped, the total stumpage was a staggering 291.1 billion board feet. In addition to these giants was a group of sixty-one owners
in the Pacific Northwest that held a combined 334.4 billion board feet, or 33
percent of all the regional stumpage.[15]

There is some evidence that Weyerhaeuser did not exercise its monopoly unwisely. Land was sold to small-scale operators to keep them in
business, and the company did not enter into milling operations in competition with them until 1912, when it established the massive Mill B at
Everett. However, it immediately dominated the business from then on.
Its size, stumpage, and solvency allowed the firm not only to withstand
the onslaught of depression between 1900 and 1905, but even to buy
more mills, land, and cutover, to start fire-control and sustained-yield
programs on some of its lands, and to encourage others to do the same.
Smaller firms, however, cut frantically during the uncertain early years of
the century just to stay in business, and the forests suffered from rapacious
clearing.[16]

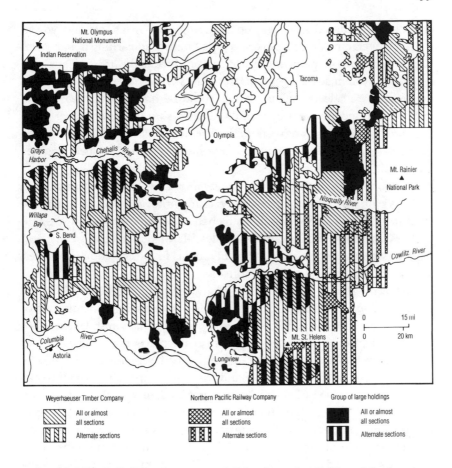

Legend:

Weyerhaeuser Timber Company
- All or almost all sections
- Alternate sections

Northern Pacific Railway Company
- All or almost all sections
- Alternate sections

Group of large holdings
- All or almost all sections
- Alternate sections

4. Land held by F. K. Weyerhaeuser, and Other Large Landholders, Northwestern Washington, circa 1913. (Simplified from U.S. Bureau of Corporations, The Lumber Industry, vol. 2, pt. 1.)

More New Technology

The steep and rugged slopes of the region were, as ever, impediments to production, but technological and management changes were under way that would not only boost production in the West but diffuse back into the older lumber production regions of the East.

The Dolbeer donkey engine had helped enormously, but rocks, stumps, and debris hindered hauling, and dragging tore up shoots and young trees. To overcome this, loggers developed high-lead yarding in 1906 from earlier experiments pioneered in Michigan during the 1880s. They perfected the system some ten years later with skyline logging in which two tall trees were selected whereby logs could be hauled well clear of the ground. Production went up tenfold, and by 1919 there were over three thousand cable yarders at work in the Pacific Northwest, many powered by diesel engines. The difficult-to-move steam-powered Dolbeer engines were rapidly abandoned.[17]

Undoubtedly the introduction of crawler or caterpillar-tread tractors as early as 1905 was to be the most far-reaching innovation of all. When the steel arc or A-frame hoist was first attached to its rear during the 1920s, the tractor was transformed into a versatile lead-line skidder, cable yarder, and loader. Even the largest redwood and Douglas fir logs could now be lifted at one end and snaked out of the forest.

Just as the tractor opened up the logging areas of rugged terrain in the Cascades and Coast Ranges, so the complementary invention/adoption of the logging truck allowed the logs to be taken out of the forest. While only 6 percent of logs were moved by truck in 1930, the percentage climbed to over half in a decade, and the days of the logging railroad were numbered (figure 5).

In the cases of both the tractor and the truck, expensive capital works were avoided, steep inclines could be negotiated, and small and scattered stands could be reached. All these technical innovations increased the grip of the large companies on the forests, but it was paradoxical that when these innovations were linked with the development of the portable chain saw, they spawned a new phenomenon, the "gyppo" loggers. These were small-scale, independent, individual operators who scoured the forests for remnants that the large companies either did not or could not cut. In the end the gyppos led to even greater forest clearing.[18]

In the mills, electric engines replaced steam engines, reducing fire risks and allowing individual prime movers to power parts of the manufacturing process, rather than having it centralized around the steam engine. Every process was improved and mechanized, and mobility, flexibility, and productivity rose. The new technology was in response to the increasing difficulty of getting accessible, good-quality timber, which drove up costs in a region already remote from its main market but growing at a time of decreasing national demand and economic stress.[19]

It is difficult to say whether the innovations and changes in land purchases, technology, and organization were the cause of or the response to

5. Twentieth-Century Logging in the Mountainous West: Trucks, Tractors, and Hoists. (Courtesy Forest History Society, Durham, N.C.)

the long boom in production that occurred from 1900 to about the beginning of the second World War. It was more likely an interactive process, as cause and effect fed off each other in an ever-upward spiral of production. Lumber production in the three West Coast states increased over sevenfold to reach 14.1 billion board feet by 1929, more than the total output of the country in 1869. There was then a dropback during the depression years to 10.6 billion board feet in 1939. All other parts of the western mountain states showed the same trends, although at much lower levels of output. The Rocky Mountain North Division, which consisted of Montana and Idaho, rose to 1.4 billion board feet in 1929 and then dropped back to .94 billion in 1939. The Rocky Mountain South Division produced 0.486 billion board feet in 1929 before declining to 0.431 billion in 1939.

Forest Conservation: Public and Private

The acquisition of timber on the public lands of the West through blatant corruption and fraud and through the rapacious felling of trees led to cries from many quarters to preserve for all America part of the rich bounty of the last forests on public lands. Particularly blameworthy had been the Free Timber Act of 1878, which had been introduced by western representatives to give residents of the eight Rocky Mountain states of Colorado, Nevada, New Mexico, Arizona, Utah, Wyoming, Idaho, and Montana the right to cut timber on "mineral lands, for building, agriculture, mining or other domestic purposes." It was, of course, impossible to police; first "mineral lands" had to be defined and then legitimate needs designated. The Timber and Stone Act of the same year, which applied to the three western coastal states and Nevada, was "even more vicious in its provisions" by allowing any miner or farmer to take timber by clearing land in order to make a claim or start a farm—"taking the timber necessary to support his improvements." Congress passed yet another act in 1879 which further liberalized timber getting by retrospectively excusing those who had stolen timber from the public lands on payment of $1.25 an acre. It was, stated Congressman Bragg, "an act to license timber thieves on the public domain."

The already bad situation worsened in 1882 when Secretary of the Interior Henry Teller broadened the scope of the Free Timber Act to allow "lumber dealers, mill owners, and railroad contractors to cut timber even for commercial purposes, and for sale as well as use." Everywhere, individuals and companies stripped the timber without making payment to the government and with no regard for the consequence to the environment. For example, around the Comstock mines in Nevada, thousands of acres were felled between 1870 and 1893, and here, as in all other cases, the government was incapable of finding the culprits. With only fifteen agents throughout the West (later the number increased to fifty-five), abuses could not be detected, and in any case, those agents received little cooperation from western territories sympathetic to residents within their boundaries and antagonistic to federal "interference." So strong did the demand for access to resources become that eventually in 1891 the Permit Act, which allowed the free use of timber for *any* domestic purpose, was passed with barely a ripple in the House.

Possibly even worse abuse came through the railroad land grants, alluded to already. Permission to cut timber for constructional purposes along the right-of-way went well beyond the railroad, and the phrase "adjacent to" was reinterpreted by Teller in 1880 as "within fifty miles of the track and even beyond the terminus." In Washington, some railroads were built in thickly timbered areas with no pretense of carrying passengers but merely to strip the trees. In 1887, the Northern Pacific actually made its own surveys designating the land that it could claim. Needless to say, it maximized its timber yields.[20]

But attitudes were slowly changing. While these specifically western maneuvers were going on, events in the East were to have an effect on all forest lands. It was a complex story, too long to be told here, but suffice it to say that various pressures and influences were all working toward forest conservation. Also, during the 1880s even the lumbermen themselves became so concerned at the chaotic conditions of their industry, with its overproduction, gluts, low prices, and close-downs, that they were willing to tacitly agree with their enemy's demands and capitalize on public appeals for conservation and regulation. Of course, they insisted that the remedial measures be geared to the industry's needs and the specific requirement of stabilizing the market, and although collusion cannot be proved, the larger lumber operations and the federal bureaucracy were certainly moving in the same direction.[21]

Forest Preservation

In 1890, all these pressures and concerns came together to produce what was arguably the biggest change to the forests of the Mountainous West, and even to the region as a whole, since the advent of European settlers. When the change occurred, it was not by design but by chance and without fanfare. The success of forest preservation bills in Congress had not been great; there were too many vested interests. Between 1870 and the end of the century, well over two hundred bills relating to forestry and tree planting had been introduced, and none had succeeded in regulating cutting or creating reserves.

What happened is not absolutely clear, but in 1890 the long-awaited bill to amend the land laws was introduced entitled "a Bill to Repeal the Timber Culture Laws," which everyone realized were ineffectual and a vehicle for abuse. The bill passed and ended up in the Senate, which then passed it on to a conference committee. There an obscure rider (section 24, subsequently known as the Forest Reserve Act) was attached, probably illegally, which stipulated that the president "may from time to time set apart and reserve [land] in any State or territory having public land bearing forests . . . wholly or in part covered with timber or undergrowth . . . as public reservations." The bill was hurried through Congress, and the rider was not noticed. A close reading of the *Congressional Record* suggests that Representative Peyson, who was in charge of the bill, had steamrolled it through a distracted and inattentive House, as repeated calls for it to be read, printed, and seen were denied, sidestepped, and evaded.[22]

At last the president had the power to remove land from the public domain, thereby enabling forests to be reserved. Almost immediately after the passage of the act, President Benjamin Harrison created 13 million acres of reserves, and his successor, Grover Cleveland, added another 4.5 million acres about a year later (figure 6). In ten years a total of 47 million acres was set aside, and within another ten years it was nearly 200 million acres, almost all but a few million acres in the Mountainous West. In one blow the resource geography of the West was redrawn. It would never be the same again.

Forest Management

The Forest Reserve Act of 1891 had proved that the forests were worth preserving, but the real question now was how they should be managed. It was both a practical and a philosophical question. Broadly speaking, the conflict was between those who saw the forests as restorative sanctuaries for recreation and wilderness, rather like extensions of national parks, and those who saw the forests as concentrated resource zones to be used wisely for national benefit.

Two outstanding personalities, John Muir and Gifford Pinchot, personified the conflict. Muir, an immigrant Scottish farmer, had absorbed the transcendentalist thoughts of Thoreau and Emerson, but he had popularized and articulated them to a far wider audience "with an intensity and enthusiasm that commanded widespread attention." His books became minor bestsellers. In his almost phenomenological approach to nature, the total immersion of self in one's surroundings produced a mystical experience and an awareness of the rest of Creation. "The clearest way into the universe," wrote Muir, "is through a forest wilderness." By the time the forest-use debate was getting under way, he had two outstanding achievements behind him: the creation of an enlarged Yosemite National Park in 1890 and the formation of the Sierra Club in 1892 (of which he was president for twenty-two years). Pinchot, on the other hand, was a well-heeled, hardheaded, ambitious, and talented young-man-in-a-hurry who had re-

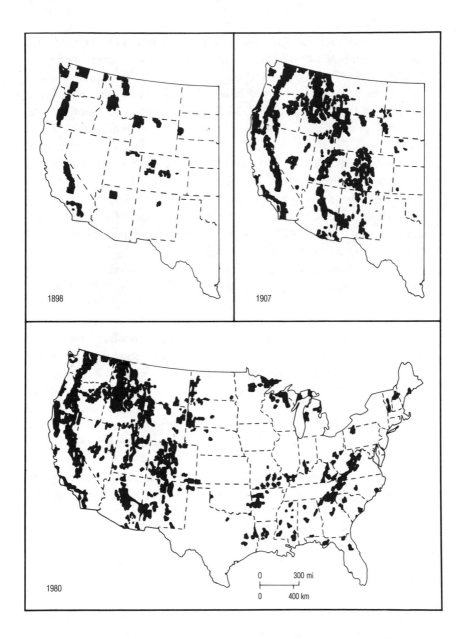

6. *National Forests of the United States, 1898, 1907, and 1980. (National Archives, GRG 95, container 108, and official maps.)*

turned to the United States in 1891 from forestry school in Germany and France, determined to make his mark on the American forest scene. He held firmly to the "wise-use" concept, so well outlined by Samuel Hays in his *Conservation and the Gospel of Efficiency*. By various steps Pinchot moved other players to one side, players like Bernhard Fernow (chief of the Forestry Division of the Department of Agriculture) and eventually Charles Sprague Sargent of the Arnold Arboretum. Cashing in on his influential connections, particularly to Theodore Roosevelt, but also capitalizing on his undoubted abilities, he rose in influence to succeed Fernow as chief of the Forestry Division in 1898.[23] Although Muir and Pinchot got on well initially, perhaps because both had an all-consuming love of forests, in the ultimate analysis Muir's loyalty was to wilderness and preservation, and Pinchot's was to civilization and forestry.[24]

In 1896, the National Academy of Sciences appointed an advisory committee to look into the practicality and necessity of preserving timberland; into the effect of forests on climate, soils, and water runoff; and into legislation to prevent current malpractice. It was chaired by Sargent and included General Henry L. Abbot, army engineer; Professor William Brewer, the noted Harvard botanist; Arnold Hague, U.S. Geological Society; Alexander Agassiz; and Pinchot as secretary. Sargent wanted more reserves; Pinchot wanted a management strategy. Eventually, Sargent's view prevailed, and President Grover Cleveland created another thirteen reserves of 21.2 million acres in Montana, Wyoming, Idaho, Washington, Oregon, Utah, and California with no mention as to how they were to be administered, managed, or used.

The outcry from the western states was unanimous, and their representatives put such pressure on Congress that the Forest Management Act was pushed through the House rapidly and enacted on 4 June 1897. Battles over the wording and provisions of the bill were complex, but given the uproar in the West, the emphasis was distinctly utilitarian, an emphasis probably lobbied for by the lumberers. Basically, the secretary of the interior was given power to regulate "the occupancy and use" of the reserves, which could not be established except to "improve and protect the forests" or, significantly, to "secure favourable conditions and water flow" or to "furnish a continuous supply of timber for the use and necessities of the citizens of the United States." Therefore, although the bill did not specifically grant full commercial use, it did not deny it or exclude it, a factor of significance in future years. For example, although grazing was not recognized as a legitimate use of the forests, it was not forbidden but ultimately was regulated. Nor was lumbering or the generation of hydroelectric power forbidden; the latter rapidly became a major consideration in the western watersheds. In addition, the bill allowed mining and agriculture in lands considered "more valuable than forest lands."[25]

The great flaw of the bill was the forest-lieu provision won by the West at the last minute in order to allow settlers and owners to exchange land within the newly reserved areas for equivalent land outside. As we have seen, lumber companies and railroads used this provision in order to fell timber rapidly in reserved lands and then trade in the cutover for timbered land elsewhere. Over three million acres were affected in this manner. Needless to say, the lumber companies supported these provisions, as they did the reserve system generally, because, almost paradoxically, it eliminated competing ownership from public timberland and boosted the prices of existing privately held land and its timber. It was yet another example of the climate of corruption.[26]

Whatever the immediate disadvantages, however, there is no doubt that the 1891 Forest Reserve Act and the 1897 Forest Management Act had laid the foundations for all subsequent action in the western forests by establishing the principles of land withdrawal and management.

The Forests Today

There have been numerous twists and turns in the development of production and policy in the western forests throughout the present century. Books have been written about it; suffice it to say that the application of the all-new technologies of extraction and the wartime demand for wood, followed by an extended boom in homebuilding, pushed production beyond the 1929 peak of 14.1 billion board feet per annum. From the 1950s to the present, production has been running at 15–18 billion board feet in the Western Division and 2–4 billion board feet in the Rocky Mountain Division. Without a vast program of replanting, such levels of extraction cannot be maintained without the diminution of forest stock. Although the evidence is not altogether clear, the general view is that destruction has ensued to the detriment of the last lumber frontier.

As early as 1920, Chief of Forestry William Greeley noted that even in "the magnificent softwoods" of the West, there was "local evidence of destruction, warnings that the conclusion of the story will be the same as that of other regions and in far less time than has been estimated," something which later Forest Service surveys seemed to substantiate. The competition, so prevalent in the later nineteenth century, intensified during the first third of the twentieth, as lumbermen cared only to get the best logs out of the woods at the lowest possible cost. Henry Graves, Greeley's predecessor, noted the "feverish haste" to cut out and get out, and so it went on.

The destruction was most marked in the areas around Puget Sound, Grays Harbor, and Willapa Bay in Washington, where locational and terrain factors had encouraged early exploitation (figure 7). By 1947, half of Washington's capacity had disappeared. Production had shifted south to the Columbia River and North Bend in Oregon, where the new technology of tractors, trucks, and bulldozers made it possible to tackle timber stands on the steepest slopes. The cutovers, the abandonment of plant and infrastructure, and the declining towns everywhere were telling pointers to what Ferdinand Silcox, then chief of forestry, in 1934 called "quick liquidation instead of sustained yield." After the 1940s, "image-conscious lumbermen, sales-minded National Forest Service personnel, researchers seeking novel explanations and progress-oriented political agencies had managed to 'de-emphasize the factor of timber exhaustion,' considered to be too 'old hack' or too simple to properly explain town failure." But it was present all the same.[27]

The simple idea that replanting should just about keep pace with consumption was attractive, but with harvest running at roughly twice the rate of growth, it rarely became a reality. Government and producers paid lip service to the idea; few did anything practical. The concept of sustained yield went through many emphases, first as a means of limiting excessive production and achieving industry stability, then as a method of achieving community stability, and finally as a means of sustaining the natural productive capacity of the forests. But the idea was all but dead by the mid-1930s, rejected by an industry that saw it as a method of control, thus creating a federal monopoly, and because it smacked of "socialism." When the Multiple Use–Sustained Yield Act was passed in 1960, there was no mention of community stability.[28]

By the mid-1950s, stocks on private lands were diminishing, and lumbermen looked increasingly to the public timberlands of the states, the Bureau of Land Management, and the national forests, where, indeed, there have been increased levels of cutting. The giant Weyerhaeuser firm was paralleled after 1956 by Georgia-Pacific, which bought up the last remaining areas of old-growth forest in Oregon. Increasingly, there was a concentra-

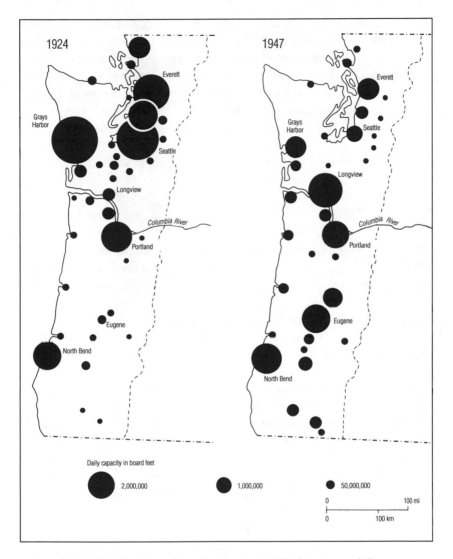

7. Installed Daily Capacity of Lumber Centers in Washington and Oregon, 1924 and 1947. (Based on Woodrow R. Clevinger, "Locational Change in the Douglas Fir Lumber Industry," Yearbook of the Association of Pacific Coast Geographers 15 (1953): 23–31.)

tion of stumpage in the hands of the few. Both firms embarked on a policy of vigorous cutting, Georgia-Pacific to finance the buyout and Weyerhaeuser to keep up with the trade, while also engaging in log exports to Japan. By the 1980s, mill closures were happening everywhere. Georgia-Pacific had virtually cut out its purchases of twenty-five years before and closed mills in the Coos Bay district and elsewhere. Even the massive Weyerhaeuser mills at Everett and Raymond, Washington, and Klamath Falls, Oregon, closed.[29]

Conclusion

Rudyard Kipling's stricture of 1889 to Americans that the "grabbing" from "Nature's shelves" and "moving on" had to stop has been forgotten. Lumber firms are looking increasingly at the timber stands of the South, where a warmer climate is producing massive regrowth. The Forest Service's 1982 analysis of future timber stocks suggests that the inventory of softwood stocks in the South will rise from 341 billion board feet in 1976 to 638 billion in 2030, while those of the Pacific Coast will fall from 1,176 billion board feet to 805.[30]

There is no doubt, too, that two other factors have had a major influence on the perception of lumber firms in the region. First, an increasingly environmentally conscious society in the West, aptly epitomized in the case of the spotted brown owl that nests in the old-growth stands of forests on public lands and that now has been declared an endangered species, has made the old liquidation policies difficult, if not impossible. An earlier example was the "Save the Redwoods" campaign.[31] Second, because so many of the forests of the West are in mountainous locations, they are scenically attractive and prone to being removed from commercial use and placed in reserves, such as national parks or wilderness, thus diminishing the supply of potential timber.

Until the lumber companies cease to behave like rapacious multinationals in their own country, the forests of the Mountainous West will be under pressure, as they have been since Europeans first saw them some 150 years ago. Sadly, "thoughts of permanence" have not predominated, and the Mountainous West may not be the last lumber frontier, but merely one more stage in the restless movement of the industry across the continent in search of supplies.

Notes

1. For example, Michael Williams, *Americans and Their Forests: An Historical Geography* (Cambridge: Cambridge University Press, 1989); Thomas R. Cox, Robert S. Maxwell, Phillip D. Thomas, and Joseph J. Malone, *This Well-Wooded Land: Americans and Their Forests from Colonial Times to the Present* (Lincoln: University of Nebraska Press, 1985); Evelyn M. Dinsdale, "The Lumber Industry of Northern New York: A Geographical Examination of Its History and Technology" (Ph.D. diss., Syracuse University, 1963).

2. Harold K. Steen, *The U.S. Forest Service: A History* (Seattle: University of Washington Press, 1977), 174.

3. William G. Robbins, "Western History: A Dialectic on the Modern Condition," *Western Historical Quarterly* 20 (November 1989): 429–49, particularly 433; Robbins, "The Social Context of Forestry: The Pacific Northwest in the Twentieth Century," *Western Historical Quarterly* 16 (1985): 413–14; Donald W. Meinig, "American Wests: Preface to a Geographical Interpretation," *Annals of the Association of American Geographers* 62 (1972): 160, 170, 173–75, 179, 181.

4. Williams, *Americans and Their Forests*, 289–90; Thomas R. Cox, "Trade, Development, and Environmental Change: The Utilization of North America's Pacific Coast Forests to 1914 and Its Consequences," in *Global Deforestation and the Nineteenth Century World Economy*, ed. Richard P. Tucker and John F. Richards (Durham, N.C.: Duke University Press, 1983), 14–29.

5. François André Michaux and Thomas Nuttall, *The North American Sylva; or, A Description of the Forest Trees of the United States, Canada, and Nova Scotia* (Paris: C. D'Hautel, 1819), translated from the French, 3 vols; Francis W. Pennell, "Travels and Scientific Collections of Thomas Nuttall," *Bartonia* 18 (1936): 1–51; Robert Elman, *First in the Field: America's Pioneering Naturalists* (New York: Mason-Charter, 1977).

6. Joseph Henry, "Meteorology and Its Connection with Agriculture," in *House Report of the Commissioner of Patents for 1858*, 35th Cong., 1st sess., 1858, H. Doc. 32, serial 954, 429–93 and frontispiece.

7. Williams H. Brewer, "The Woodland and Forest Systems of the United States," plates I, III, and V, together with commentary, in *A Statistical Atlas of the United States, Based on the Results of the Ninth Census*, ed. Francis A. Walker (Washington, D.C.: Government Printing Office, 1874); Charles S. Sargent, "Report on the Forests of North America (Exclusive of Mexico)" in *The Tenth Census of the United States*, vol. 9 (Washington, D.C.: Government Printing Office, 1884).

8. Edgar T. Ensign, *Report on the Forest Conditions of the Rocky Mountains and Other Papers*, U.S. Department of Agriculture, Forestry Division, bulletin no. 2 (Washington, D.C.: Government Printing Office, 1889); Henry Gannett, *Forests of the United*

States (Washington, D.C.: Government Printing Office, 1899; also printed in U.S. Geological Survey, *19th Annual Report*, 1897–98, pt. 5).

9. For the Pacific trade, see Thomas R. Cox, *Mills and Markets: A History of the Pacific Coast Lumber Industry to 1900* (Seattle: University of Washington Press, 1974). Other accounts of the early lumber industry are in Cox, "The Passage to India Revisited: Asian Trade and the Development of the Far West," in *Reflections of Western Historians*, ed. John A. Carroll (Tucson: University of Arizona Press, 1969), 85–103; Edwin T. Coman and Helen M. Gibbs, *Time, Tide and Timber: A Century of Pope and Talbot*, Stanford Business Series no. 7 (Stanford: Stanford University Press, 1949); Edmond S. Meany, "A History of the Lumber Industry in the Pacific Northwest to 1917" (Ph.D. diss., Harvard University, 1935); Robert E. Ficken, *Lumber and Politics: The Career of Mark E. Reed* (Seattle: University of Washington Press, 1979).

10. Robert W. Vinnedge, "The Genesis of the Pacific Northwest Lumber Industry," *Lumber World Review* 45 (25 December 1923): 30–31; John H. Cox, "Organizations of the Lumber Industry in the Pacific Northwest, 1889–1914" (Ph.D. diss., University of California, Berkeley, 1937), 6–70, 137–65; Ralph W. Hidy, Frank E. Hill, and Allan Nevins, *Timber and Men: The Weyerhaeuser Story* (New York: Macmillan, 1963), 212–13.

11. For the movement from the Great Lakes states, see James E. Defebaugh, *History of the Lumber Industry in America* (Chicago: American Lumberman, 1906–7), 1:452–53; Hidy, Hill, and Nevins, *Timber and Men*, 207–27; Howard B. Melendy, "One Hundred Years in the Redwood Lumber Industry, 1850–1950" (Ph.D. diss., Stanford University, 1953), 23–24; Herman H. Chapman, "Why the Town of McNary Moved: A Tragedy of the Southern Pines and a Parallel Which Carries Its Own Lesson," *American Forests and Forest Life* 30 (1924): 589–92, 615–16, 626.

12. For traditional methods of moving logs, see Melendy, "One Hundred Years," 231–32, 245–46. For the newer methods, see Meany, "History of the Lumber Industry," 246–48; Alfred J. Van Tassel and David M. Bluestone, *Mechanization in the Lumber Industry: A Study of Technology in Relation to Resources and Employment Opportunity*, National Research Project Rep. no. M-5 (Philadelphia: Philadelphia Work Projects Administration, 1940), 10–11; Peter J. Rutledge and Richard H. Tooker, "Steam Power for Loggers: Two Views of the Dolbeer Donkey," *Forest History* 14 (1970): 19–29.

13. For the disposal of the public lands, see Frederick J. Yonce, "Lumbering and the Public Timberlands in Washington: The Era of Disposal," *Journal of Forest History* 22 (1978): 4–17; Stephen A. D. Puter and H. Stevens, *Looters of the Public Domain by S. A. Puter, King of the Oregon Land Fraud Ring* (Portland, Ore.: Portland Printing House, 1908), 22–35, passim.

14. Harold K. Steen, "Grazing and the Environment: A History of Forest Service

Stock-Reduction Policy," *Agricultural History,* 49 (1975): 238–42; William Voigt Jr., *Public Grazing Lands: Use and Misuse by Industry and Government* (New Brunswick, N.J.: Rutgers University Press, 1976), 43–203; Ronald F. Lockmann, *Guarding the Forests of Southern California: Evolving Attitudes toward Conservation of Watersheds, Woodlands and Wilderness* (Glendale, Calif.: Arthur H. Clarke, 1981), 91–112, 135–41; Lawrence Rakestraw, "Sheep Grazing in the Cascade Range: John Minto vs. John Muir," *Pacific Historical Review* 27 (1958): 371–82; Frederick V. Coville, *Forest Growth and Sheep Grazing in the Cascade Mountains of Oregon,* U.S. Department of Agriculture, Forestry Division, bulletin no. 15 (Washington, D.C.: Government Printing Office, 1898).

15. Hidy, Hill, and Nevins, *Timber and Men,* 211–15, 222–24, 277; Roy E. Appleman, "Timber Empire from the Public Domain," *Mississippi Valley Historical Review* 26 (1939): 193–208; Ross R. Cotroneo, "Western Land Marketing by the Pacific Northern Railway," *Pacific Historical Review* 27 (1968): 299–320; U. S Bureau of Corporations, *The Lumber Industry,* vol. 1, pt. 1: 20–29, 208; vol. 3, pt. 3: 173–76.

16. Hidy, Hill, and Nevins, *Timber and Men,* 231–32, 274–76, 305–9; Robert E. Ficken, "Weyerhaeuser and the Pacific Northwest Timber Industry, 1899–1903," *Pacific Northwest Quarterly* 70 (1979): 146–54.

17. Based on Nelson C. Brown, *Logging: The Principles and General Methods of Harvesting Timber in the United States and Canada* (New York: John Wiley, 1949), 73–78, 84–85, 124–28; Van Tassel and Bluestone, *Mechanization in the Lumber Industry,* 12–16; L. Wright Newell, "Logging the Pacific Slopes," in U.S. Department of Agriculture, *Trees: Handbook of Agriculture, 1949* (Washington, D.C.: Government Printing Office, 1949), 82–83.

18. Van Tassel and Bluestone, *Mechanization in the Lumber Industry,* 17–18, 37–39, 42–45; Nelson C. Brown, *Logging Transportation: The Principles and Methods of Log Transportation in the United States and Canada* (New York: John Wiley, 1936), 33–59, 70–77, 176–80, 186–93, 211–12.

19. Van Tassel and Bluestone, *Mechanization in the Lumber Industry,* 26–27; Ralph C. Bryant, *Logging: The Principles and General Methods of Operation in the United States* (New York: John Wiley, 1926), 161–62.

20. John Ise, *The United States Forest Policy* (New Haven: Yale University Press, 1920), 62–75, 83–89; U.S. Department of the Interior, *Annual Report* (Washington, D.C.), 1878: xiii–iv, 1885: 22, 1887: 566–67; Edward A. Bowers, "The Present Condition of the Forests on the Public Lands," *Publications of the American Economic Association* 6 (May 1891): 67–70.

21. See Williams, *Americans and Their Forests,* 399–404; William G. Robbins, *Lumberjacks and Legislators: Political Economy of the U.S. Lumber Industry, 1890–1941* (College Station: Texas A & M Press, 1982), 17–19, 110–12, passim.

22. For the passage of the bill, see Williams, *Americans and Their Forests,* 409–11;

Roy M. Robbins, *Our Landed Heritage: The Public Domain, 1776–1936* (Princeton: Princeton University Press, 1942), 304.

23. For Muir, see Linnie M. Wolfe, *John of the Mountains: The Unpublished Journals of John Muir* (Boston: Houghton Mifflin, 1938), 313–15; Roderick Nash, *Wilderness and the American Mind* (New Haven: Yale University Press, 1967), 123–33. For Pinchot, see Martin N. McGeary, *Gifford Pinchot: Forester Politician* (Princeton: Princeton University Press, 1960); Harold J. Pinkett, *Gifford Pinchot: Private and Public Forester* (Urbana: University of Illinois Press, 1970). See also Samuel P. Hays, *Conservation and the Gospel of Efficiency: The Progressive Conservation Movement, 1890–1920* (Cambridge, Mass.: Harvard University Press), 22–48.

24. Nash, *Wilderness*, 414.

25. Robbins, *Our Landed Heritage*, 311–24.

26. U.S. Bureau of Corporations, *The Lumber Industry*, vol. 1, pt.1, 230–31; Robbins, *Lumberjacks and Legislators*, 24.

27. William B. Greeley, in U.S. Forest Service, *Timber Depletion, Lumber Prices, Lumber Exports, and the Concentration of Timber Ownership* (Capper Report), 66th Cong., 2d sess., 1920, S. rept. on Res. 311, 13–14; Henry Graves, "Federal and State Responsibilities in Forestry," *American Forests* 31 (1925): 677; Robbins, "Social Context of Forestry," 416–18; Kenneth A. Erickson, "The Morphology of Lumber Settlements in Western Oregon and Washington" (Ph.D. diss., University of California, Berkeley, 1965), 405–14; William G. Robbins, "Timber Town; Market Economics in Coos Bay, Oregon, 1850–1980," *Pacific Northwest Quarterly* 75 (1984): 146–55. For a classic case study of the depletion and decline of settlements, see Washington State Planning Council, *The Elma Survey* (Olympia: 1941).

28. David A. Clary, "What Price Sustained Yield? The Forest Service, Community Stability, and Timber Monopoly under the 1944 Sustained-Yield Act," *Journal of Forest History* 31 (1987): 4–18; William G. Robbins, "Lumber Production and Community Stability," *Journal of Forest History* 31 (1987): 164–72.

29. See Dennis C. Le Master, *Mergers among the Largest Forest Products Firms, 1950–1970*, Washington State University, College of Agricultural Research Center bulletin no. 854 (Pullman: 1977); Walter J. Mead, *Competition and Oligopoly in the Douglas-Fir Lumber Industry* (Berkeley: University of California Press); Robbins, "Social Context of Forestry," 424–25.

30. Rudyard Kipling, *From Sea to Sea* (New York: Doubleday, 1889), 2:155; U.S. Forest Service, *An Analysis of the Timber Situation in the United States, 1952–2030*, Forest Resources Report no. 23 (Washington, D.C.: Government Printing Office, 1982), 148–99.

31. Susan R. Schrepfer, *The Fight to Save the Redwoods: A History of Environmental Reform, 1917–1978* (Madison: University of Wisconsin Press, 1983).

Areas of Government Control

Given the nature of western land disposal and ownership patterns, it is hardly surprising that discussions of concentrated resources in the Mountainous West involve the actions and policies of the federal government. As the chapters by Vale, Konrad, and Williams vividly demonstrate, a convergence of historical circumstances put control of much of the Mountainous West into the hands of Washington. Richard Jackson's overview of the federal presence in the West traces the dynamic nature of this historical interrelationship. Jackson begins by reconstructing traditional nineteenth-century practices of federal land disposal that put sizable portions of the public domain into private hands. He then recounts the significance of two legislative acts passed in 1872 that represent both a major shift and an enduring schism in federal attitudes toward western lands: on the one hand, Yellowstone National Park is established, suggesting a new public role in preserving and managing federal holdings; on the other hand, the Mining Act of 1872 confirms the rights of private individuals to claim and develop the Mountainous West. Jackson shows how the tension inherent in these evolving philosophies continued to be a lightning rod of debate and conflict as the Forest Service was created and as western ranchers resisted the growing government presence in the grazing economy. He brings his overview up to the present by tracing the post-1930s shift in government management in the Mountainous West from policies designed to benefit local residents to policies which reflect changing national needs, interests, and values. This inevitably has led to greater calls for preservation and conservation of western lands, and Jackson concludes his essay with a sampling of modern resource management issues in the Mountainous West that reflect these persisting tensions.

9 / Federal Lands in the Mountainous West

RICHARD H. JACKSON

The eleven states comprising the mountainous region of the American West exhibit a complex mosaic of property ownership. Within this mosaic the dominance of the federal government is evident to even a casual observer (figure 1). The federal government as western landlord is overwhelming in states such as Nevada, 80 percent of which is federally owned, a figure that easily exceeds the regional average of nearly 54 percent. Federal ownership in even the lowest state (Montana) stands at nearly 30 percent (table 1).[1] The dominant role of the federal government as land owner ensures controversy over land management and disposal. Changing issues, goals, and values of western and nonwestern residents and land users result in conflicts and confrontations that are constantly reviewed in local and regional newspapers of the West.[2]

The ongoing controversies involving the federally owned land represent the culmination of nearly two centuries of federal involvement in the region. The public and private debate over the federally owned land is but one manifestation of a fundamental philosophic change regarding the federal role in American land, a change that began in the late nineteenth and early twentieth centuries. Historically America has been dominated by an ethic of private land ownership, an ethic antedating nationhood. With the advent of the new nation, the federal government began a century and a half of transferring federally controlled land into private ownership. Based on the rural ethic that espoused the ideal of the yeoman farmer as the basis of American values, this process of land transferral allowed the cash-poor but land-rich government to establish hundreds of thousands of owner-occupied farms in the nineteenth century.

The changing economy and geography of late-nineteenth- and early-twentieth-century America brought important alterations in the historic role of the federal government as land agent. As the growing nation expanded its control to the Pacific, it acquired the vast area of the Mountain-

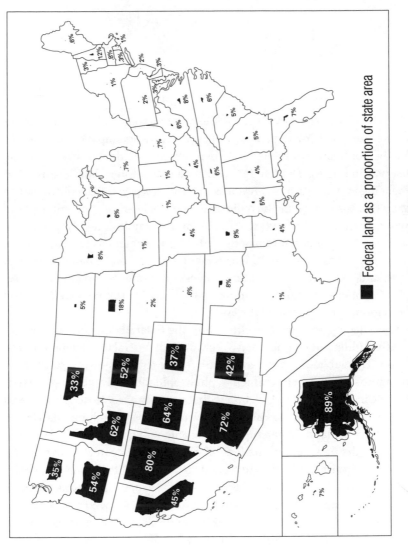

■ Federal land as a proportion of state area

1. *Federal Land (Including Indian Trust Lands) as a Proportion of State Land Area.*

TABLE 2.

Federal lands (including Indian lands) as a percentage of total land in the Mountainous West, 1990.

	Bureau of Land Management	Forest Service	Total Federal Lands	Indian Trust Lands	Federal and Indian Lands
Arizona	16.9	15.5	44.5	27.4	71.9
California	17.1	20.4	44.5	0.5	45.0
Colorado	12.6	21.7	35.5	1.2	36.7
Idaho	22.5	38.6	60.6	1.5	62.1
Montana	8.7	18.0	29.4	3.4	32.8
Nevada	68.4	7.3	78.9	0.1	80.0
New Mexico	16.3	12.0	33.1	9.1	42.2
Oregon	25.5	25.4	52.2	1.2	53.6
Utah	42.1	15.3	60.0	4.2	64.2
Washington	.7	21.2	29.6	5.7	35.3
Wyoming	29.5	14.8	48.6	3.0	51.6

Source: *Federal Land Statistics: 1990.*

ous West. Less suited for the traditional yeoman farmer, these mountainous lands stimulated changes in the disposition of federal lands, changes that have continued to evolve until the present. The land disposal system that worked effectively in areas that were level and abundantly watered was ineffective for lands where verticality exceeded horizontality, or where drought was the norm rather than the exception. The geography of the region dictated a new federal role in land disposal, a system which came to emphasize continued federal ownership but private use of the mountains, high plains, and valley regions of the states of the Mountainous West.

Private use of the federal domain reflects the traditional importance of the federal lands as zones of concentrated resources for local communities who relied on its water, timber, mining, and grazing resources. In practice, the federal lands of the Mountainous West have become a vast tributary area controlled by the federal government for the well-being of the communities located in the inhabitable portions of the region. Fortunately or unfortunately, social changes in the twentieth century have caused the traditional federal land management practices underlying the private use of the federal lands of the Mountainous West to be challenged. The growing urban population of the region and surrounding areas, with ever-greater leisure and affluence, questions the longstanding tradition of private interests utilizing the federal lands for mainly local benefits. This conflict of interest is not one that demands transferal of federal lands to private ownership, but rather one of a clash of private interests: the clash between timber producers, miners, farmers, and ranchers who have based their economic well-being and survival on free or cheap use of the federal lands versus the growing numbers of environmentally and recreationally oriented users who demand that the federal lands be managed to benefit the entire nation, rather than being restricted for the benefit of local interests. Conflicts over the federal lands are not new, however; only the actors and interests have changed. The historical geography of the Mountainous West illustrates both the dominant role of the federal government in the region and the constantly changing set of issues behind the ever-shifting alliances and conflicts between miners, timber producers, cattle producers, environmentalists, recreational users, and private-interest groups such as hunters, resort owners, and river runners.

The Federal Government as Landlord

Colonization and settlement of North America by Europeans was associated with a profound and fundamental change in property ownership and philosophy, a change central to the conflicts over land in the Mountainous West. The tremendous geographic size, diversity, and wealth of the new continent made it impossible to restrict colonizers to the traditional feudal land ownership system of Europe, which created a new societal norm of individual land ownership (freehold tenure). Widespread private ownership represented a remarkable break from the European experience of the settlers, which emphasized the feudal relationship of tenants to the wealthy land-ruling classes. As the basis of power, wealth, and prestige, European lands were held by relatively few land owners in a system that prevented the general upward mobility of the peasantry and restricted their movement from employer to employer.[3]

Emergence of freehold tenure in the American colonies was associated with individual farmers who wrested their farms from a primeval forest, shedding their European cultural baggage and acquiring independence and individualism in the process.[4] Self-reliant and self-motivated, the

American yeoman farmers were independent because of the land that they owned. Emergence of the private ownership ethic was important to the framers of the Constitution of the new nation in the late eighteenth century, as they incorporated these ideals into the Constitution. The U.S. Constitution states that "The Congress shall have power to dispose of and make all needful rules and regulations respecting the territory or other property belonging to the United States."[5]

The federal government's role as land regulator of the new nation incorporated earlier decisions made by the Constitutional Congress and has shaped a policy of land management and disposal that persisted for one hundred and fifty years (from 1780 to the 1930s). The basic principles associated with this constitutional declaration were as follows:

- that the lands ceded to the new nation were for the benefit of all the states
- that federal lands were to be granted and settled under regulations defined by the U.S. Congress
- that new states would have the same rights as old states

These principles reflected the desire of the old states (the thirteen colonies) to ensure that by giving up their territory to the new nation they would not lose the benefit thereby.[6] Legislation and regulations developed over the next century to dispose of the federal lands represented an ongoing clash of interests between the old and new states as the old states attempted to ensure that disposition of the federal lands benefited the entire nation rather than only the new territory or state.[7]

The land distribution program of the nineteenth century represented compromises between the old states' attitudes and those of the new, based on the Ordinance of 1785. The Ordinance of 1785 divided the land into six square-mile townships that were subdivided into thirty-six sections of 640 acres each. The land was to be sold at public auction, but with a minimum reserved price of a dollar per acre. Conflict between the eastern states' desire to raise funds to defray the Revolutionary War debt and soldiers' pensions versus the new territories' desire to attract yeoman farmers was resolved by auctioning alternate townships whole and as 640-acre sections.

Over time, the conflict between the old states and the new states and territories led to modification of the Ordinance of 1785 either to raise more money or to provide cheaper land, depending on whose interests were in the ascendancy. In 1796, the price was raised to two dollars an acre, but half the price could be deferred for one year, reflecting a compromise between the old and new states' views. Four years later, Congress amended the land law so that one-half of a section could be purchased, with half of the price deferred for two to four years. Between 1804 and 1820, the minimum was lowered to 160 acres and then to 80 as the minimum price dropped to $1.25 per acre with the repeal of credit in 1820. By 1832, minimum acreage had declined to 40 acres, and by 1841, the Pre-emption Act allowed anyone who had settled on unsurveyed land to purchase the 160 acres that they occupied at the minimum price without competition. The federal role in land disposition thus continued to become more magnanimous as new states and congressmen of the new territories became numerically more powerful, culminating in the Homestead Act of 1862, which allowed any head of family or anyone over twenty-one years to receive a free 160 acres by living on the land and cultivating it for five years.[8]

The growing liberalness of the federal government in disposing of the land included direct or indirect cash payments to the new territories or states. Ohio, the first of the new western states formed from the public domain, joined the Union in 1803 and was recipient of federal largesse in the form of a revenue-sharing program. The state was granted 5 percent of the proceeds of the public land sales within its borders in return for agreeing not to tax these newly sold lands for five years and to spend the 5 percent grant on schools and transportation improvements. As other states entered the Union, they waived their future interests in the federal lands (including taxation), but in return they gained portions of the public domain for the states themselves. Initially one section of each township was granted as "school land sites," but over time this increased to four sections per township.[9] Individual states were also granted other portions of the federal estate on an individual basis to provide for transportation, state hospitals, land grant universities, and other public uses as part of nearly five thousand individual congressional acts dealing with land disposal.[10]

While Congress was primarily concerned with transferring the federal domain to private or state ownership, it also passed acts that maintained federal ownership of specified lands. Acquisition of the Louisiana Purchase in 1803 nearly doubled the size of the nation, and Congress passed two laws in 1807 reserving ownership of the known lead deposits on the public lands in today's states of Illinois and Missouri and authorizing the government to lease them for cash.[11] Conflict with state interests over continued federal ownership of lands and resources culminated in the Supreme Court decision of 1840 that Congress retained the right to manage public lands even after states were established, providing the basis for permanent federal ownership of much of the land in the Mountainous West nearly a century later. The immediate effect of the Court's ruling, however, was the opposite, prompting Congress to authorize the sale of the federally owned lead lands in Illinois, Arkansas, and the territories of Wisconsin and Iowa.[12] Growing interest in disposal of the lands west of the Mississippi led to adoption of the Homestead Act's free land policies in 1862 and congressional authorization in 1864 to sell at public auction coal lands which had formerly been retained by the federal government.

The growing privatization of the federal lands in response to new states' demands for autonomy and economic growth were the dominant theme in the latter half of the nineteenth century as the American frontier moved west. A countercurrent of concern for the environment emerged at the same time, however, epitomized by the publication of *Man and Nature: Of Physical Geography as Modified by Human Action* by George Perkins Marsh in 1864. Recognition by Marsh that unbridled exploitation of the earth resulted in environmental degradation stimulated the beginnings of a fundamental change in attitude toward the public land in the 1870s, resulting in the government hesitatingly beginning an era of land reservation in contrast to its earlier century of land disposal.

Nineteenth-Century Conflicts and Compromise

The conservation principles incorporated in *Man and Nature* were important to the emerging philosophy of environmentalists such as John Muir, Gifford Pinchot, and Theodore Roosevelt. Growing recognition that the wholesale disposal of the federal estate was associated with fraud, waste, and environmental degradation prompted the emergence of policies to reserve areas of the West that were unsuited for traditional homesteading. The increasing environmental concern of a few individuals was instrumental in beginning the change from an era of disposal to an era of reservation, but it probably would have failed were it not for the growing opposition in Congress to what was perceived in the East as a government giveaway to the new western states. This perception was an outgrowth of the vast land grants that Congress used in stimulating construction of railroads across the West. Grants in 1862 and 1864 resulted in millions of acres being directly transferred to the railroads as a subsidy and tied up an area of even greater size for decades as the railroads delayed their selection of specific townships for their ownership.[13]

The increasingly marginal lands encountered in the Mountainous West prompted the new western territories and states to lobby Congress to increase the size of land grants to individuals. Bills such as the Timber Culture Act, the Desert Entry Act, and similar measures doubled or tripled the amount of land that an individual homesteader could receive for private ownership. Such growing generosity with the public lands renewed the competition between eastern and western interests over the purposes of the federal lands. Eastern interests maintained that the intent of Congress was for the entire nation to benefit equally from the federal lands, while the western states maintained that since these lands were within their boundaries, they should be the primary beneficiaries. By the 1870s, it was clear that not only was much of the land in the Mountainous West unsuited for the yeoman farmer for whom the land disposal legislation presumably had been written, but land was being obtained fraudulently in order that the more valuable timber and minerals thereon could be exploited for private gain.[14] By the 1870s the commissioner of the land office publicly stated that there was little land in the Mountainous West which could be homesteaded and testified about the fraudulent nature of many such entries.[15]

In 1872, the growing conflicts between the eastern and western states led to the uneasy alliance of eastern states and environmentalists versus western states and miners as two important laws were passed which have directly affected the Mountainous West's land in subsequent years. The first of these laws recognized that the natural features of today's Yellowstone Park were unique and needed to be protected by remaining in federal control. Yellowstone National Park was withdrawn to create a "public pleasuring ground" in perpetuity in 1872.[16] At the same time, to gain support of western states, the 1872 Mining Act was also passed, continuing the tradition of private use of the federal domain.

The Mining Act attempted to bring some order to the disposal of mineral rights associated with the federal lands, order that had been completely missing in the years since the Supreme Court's ruling of 1840. During this time the development of resources on the lands of the Mountainous West had contributed to the economic and population boom of the entire American West. Mining "rushes" to California, Nevada, Idaho, Montana, and Colorado were associated with exploitation of minerals on the federal lands in the mountainous regions. The 1872 Mining Act simply validated the general procedures which had developed over the previous three decades in the absence of federal controls. The law granted miners an unconditional right to mine on federal lands for all minerals except coal. Individual miners could stake a claim and mine free of charge, or could purchase the land for $2.50 to $5.00 an acre, depending on the type of claim, if they preferred the security of private ownership. Claims could not exceed 160 acres, but there was no limit on the number of claims that each person or corporation could hold on an indefinite basis as long as one hundred dollars per year in work was done on each claim. The 1872 Mining Act was defended as a type of homestead act allowing miners access to minerals on federal land, an action deemed necessary for the speedy development of the West.[17]

Like the policy change implied by federal ownership of Yellowstone, the 1872 Mining Act had a long-lasting effect on the federal lands of the Mountainous West. Miners had previously enjoyed the privilege of exploring for minerals on federal lands, but the 1872 act granted them an apparent right to file claim on any federal land for minerals and to exploit the minerals for free. As long as the miners did not care about permanent ownership of the land there were no requirements to prevent them from exploiting all minerals except coal for their own use. Not until 1976 were prospectors even required to report their claims to a federal agency, the Bureau of Land Management. The bill has had two long-lasting impacts on the federally owned land of the Mountainous West: first, directly governing the exploitation of many minerals found on federal land and, second, establishing the principle of private dominion over public minerals, a principle that remains until the present. While subsequent amendments have added natural gas and oil to coal as minerals to be leased, the metallic minerals on federal land are still governed by the 1872 law and its subsequent amendments.[18]

The effects of the 1872 congressional legislation reverberated through the Mountainous West in the subsequent century. The incipient reservation of federal land ultimately led to the present pattern of land ownership in the West in which large portions of the region are directly owned by the federal government, but they also have led to conflict and confrontation as the use of federal lands for mining has prompted conflict between locals, environmentalists, miners, and federal agencies. This conflict was and is centered on the ownership and use of the public domain in the region.

The Federal Government as Permanent Landowner

Federal reservation of land in Yellowstone represented the first act to authorize permanent federal control of part of the Mountainous West (the Yosemite area was designated as a reserve by President Lincoln in 1864, but it was subsequently transferred to state control). Between 1891 and 1893, sixteen forest reserves totaling 17,005,000 acres were added to permanent federal ownership, almost exclusively in the Mountainous West. Congressional action in 1897 provided for the establishment and funding of a service to manage these forest lands and allowed withdrawal of other lands, creating a total of twenty reserves with 38,897,840 acres. Administration of the forest reserves was transferred from the general land office to the Department of Agriculture and the Forest Service in 1905. This transfer was accompanied by additional withdrawal of forest land from the public domain, so that by the end of 1906 the new Forest Service administered 106,999,138 acres of formerly public lands. By the end of 1909 this had swelled to 141,267,530 acres.[19] Essentially all of these lands were in the Mountainous West, and they continue to constitute the overwhelming majority of national forest lands, with the eleven intermountain states comprising 83 percent of all Forest Service land.[20]

While the withdrawal of forest land provided the beginning of permanent federal ownership of much of the Mountainous West, the 1872 Mining Act continued to allow private use of federally owned or controlled lands. One of the unforeseen side effects of the 1872 Mining Act was the proliferation of fraudulent mining claims by individuals who were trying to obtain a portion of the federal domain. Such claims were made on national forest lands by individuals who wanted the timber or the land for other uses and who could obtain it by simply filing a claim for unspecified and unproven mineral resources.

The conditions of the Mining Act are in curious contrast to the development of the management program for the national forest land. The acts which initiated the reservation of forest land in the Mountainous West provided that a fee be charged for logging and grazing uses. Congress recognized that federal ownership would impact the states of the Mountainous West, so it determined in 1906 that 10 percent of net proceeds from timber sales would be returned to counties with federal forest land. The stated purpose of this revenue sharing was to assist the states in developing roads and schools in the county or counties where national forest lands were located.[21] Passage of a new revenue-sharing act in 1908 increased the share of revenues to 25 percent, representing a victory for the states in the Mountainous West as it implicitly acknowledged the duty of the federal government to reimburse them for continued federal ownership of land within their boundaries.

Growing concern over the mineral resources on the public lands of the Mountainous West led to passage of the 1920 Mineral Leasing Act, which extended the authority of the secretary of the interior to leasing not only coal but also petroleum and natural gas on federally owned lands. This act required that lands believed to contain such resources be leased by competitive bid under the direction of the secretary of the interior. Over time these competitive bids were expanded and amended, but they basically still remain today, requiring payment of royalties to the federal government for extraction of coal, petroleum, natural gas, or oil shale on federal lands. In practice, the revenues from such leasing programs or sales by the secretary of the interior have accrued to the states in which the resources are located, thus providing an important element in the economy of the states of the Mountainous West. Revenues generated under provisions of the Mineral Leasing Act were allocated by a fifty-forty-ten formula: 50 percent to the state where the revenue was generated, 40 percent to a "reclamation fund" to support water projects in the western states, and 10 percent to the general fund of the U.S. treasury.[22] In reality, no separate reclamation fund has been maintained or dispersed, and this 40 percent has gone directly to the general fund of the federal government. But since the cost of water-related reclamation projects in the Mountainous West has been far greater than the value of the 40 percent of leasing generated in the past, this has not created a problem. In the twentieth century, more than the total value of all mineral leasing revenue has been returned to the states either directly as their 50 percent share, or indirectly through federal spending for reclamation, highway, and other projects. While widely criticized by environmental and other groups as an inefficient and a fraudulent program for disposing of the nation's wealth, the 1920 Mineral Leasing Act is important because it signaled the end of simply granting the resources on federal lands to private users and it required direct payment for resource exploitation. This change in fundamental philosophy vis-à-vis the federal domain became ever more important in the decades after 1920.

The End of the Disposal of Federal Land

Charging for use of fossil fuels on federal lands was followed shortly by legislation that effectively ended disposal of the remaining federal domain.

Stretching across much of the Mountainous West are rugged plateaus and arid hills and mountains unsuited for the dream of the conventional yeoman farmer, but important in the ranch operations that had come to occupy much of the region in the latter half of the nineteenth century. These lands include scattered forests at higher, moister elevations, but in general are characterized by mixed grass and shrub vegetation cover. Various congressional acts designed to assist the reclamation and settlement of this land were passed between the 1880s and 1930s. By 1930, most of this western non–Forest Service land remained in federal ownership, but was effectively controlled by the private interests of the ranching industry.

The federal lands of the Mountainous West subject to grazing pressure were vast in area but of limited productivity. Unfortunately, since the land was owned by the federal government and not by individual ranchers, there was little or no incentive to maintain the proper number of livestock to prevent overgrazing. In terms of simple profit, the individual graziers would best protect their own interests by continuously increasing the number of cattle placed on the range, since in the absence of private ownership any forage not consumed by one individual's livestock would be consumed by someone else's. The earliest recognition of this phenomenon was associated with attempts in the late nineteenth and early twentieth centuries by ranchers in Montana and Wyoming to discriminate between outside ranchers who brought cattle or sheep into a region for grazing upon the federal lands and permanent settlers using the same grazing lands. The argument of the permanent ranchers centered on the tendency for migrant ranching interests (especially sheep interests) to simply move through an area and "eat out" the pastures on federal lands that were essential to the economic success of the permanent settlers.[23]

Overgrazing combined with recurrent drought in the Mountainous West in the 1920s and 1930s to cause serious losses to the ranching industry of much of the region. Several congressional bills were proposed in the late 1920s and 1930s that would limit the use of the public domain by animals. Finally, the continuing drought caused President Roosevelt to use his executive power in 1934 to withdraw all of the balance of the federal land in the Mountainous West area from homesteading or other disposal. Passage of the Taylor Grazing Act proposed by Democratic Representative Edward Taylor of Colorado the same year provided that these lands would be reserved for a final disposition until after it had been determined which were suitable for homesteading under the various laws then on the books.[24] Ranchers supported the bill as they assumed the government would invest in fencing and other improvements to the rangeland while preventing further diminishment in its size.

Developing Federal Lands for Broad Public Use

The combination of protecting unique natural features by establishing national parks such as Yellowstone, mineral lands leasing, and withdrawal of lands through the Taylor Grazing Act made the federal government the largest landholder in the West (figure 2). Management of the federal lands after 1934 evolved from a policy designed to provide primary benefit for the permanent residents of the states of the Mountainous West—especially private interests such as mining, timber harvesting, and ranching—to one that recognizes the importance of the region's federal lands to the well-being of not only the local residents but the entire nation as well. This transition has been primarily a phenomenon of the last quarter of the twentieth century. Prior to that time, management of the Forest Service lands largely represented attempts to maintain timber yield, administer mining leases, and control grazing activities in the hands of local ranching interests.

After passage of the Taylor Grazing Act, the Grazing Service was established to regulate grazing on the newly withdrawn land. As originally envisioned, the director of the Grazing Service was to work with local ranchers to establish grazing districts which would be administered by the local ranchers' representatives. It was anticipated that these representatives might set reasonable fees according to the Taylor Grazing Act, but that the act would not require creation of a new government bureaucracy, relying rather on one government agent for advice concerning the federal regulations.[25] The ranchers' committees had to determine whether a fee for grazing on lands covered under the Taylor Grazing Act should be charged, and if so, the amount to be required. Under pressure from eastern interests who felt that the lands were being used by the western ranchers at the expense of the rest of the country, the committees finally agreed in 1936 to charge a minimal fee (five cents per animal per month for cows or horses or one cent per month for sheep).[26] The significance of this tiny amount was not in the revenues raised or in reduction of grazing pressure; it was important because it was the beginning of the transition to active federal regulation and management of all federal lands by the late twentieth century. Tensions and value conflicts between different groups today reflect the wrenching impact of this change from free local use and abuse of the

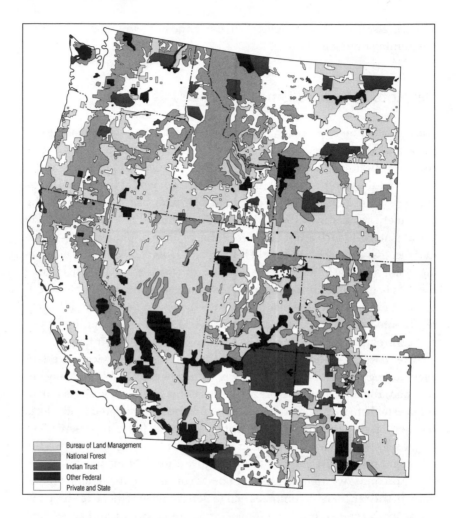

2. *Land Ownership in the Mountainous West. State-owned school sections and small parcels of private land are included in federal lands as scale of map makes it impossible to show them.*

Mountainous West's federal lands to government management and fee-based broad public use.

The processes by which the federal lands of the Mountainous West were brought into permanent public ownership represented decades of compromise between the conflicting interests of local residents and those Easterners who viewed the federal lands as a national heritage. While changes since the Taylor Grazing Act appear to give nonlocal interests a greater role in management divisions and use of western federal lands, the local interests still receive the primary benefit. Direct revenues from leases on the federally owned land provided the eleven states of the Mountainous West with nearly one billion dollars a year in revenues in the 1980s.[27] This represents income from nearly fifteen thousand grazing permits on Bureau of Land Management lands, more than one hundred thousand mineral leases (primarily oil and gas leases), and thousands of timber sales.[28] Beyond the actual cash income of the federal lands, they are the site of hundreds of millions of acres used for recreation, the majority of the national forests, parks, and recreation areas of the United States, and the home for wildlife that contribute to the recreational experience of users of the federal land and that ensure the continued preservation of species. As islands of moisture in an arid region, the mountains of the West and their federal lands are the source for most of the water which provides irrigation and domestic water for the communities within the borders of the Mountainous West. The headwaters of many of the great rivers of the United States, as well as smaller western rivers and streams, begin in the federal lands of the region.

In spite of western arguments that federal ownership of large areas of their states is unfair, the continued concentration of the private benefits from federal lands in the economies of the region belie western concerns. Management of the federal lands of the West has been debated since the Taylor Grazing Act, but ultimate jurisdiction lies with individual agencies whose decisions are based on federal legislation. The largest agency within the eleven western states is the National Forest Service, controlling 167,768,000 acres within the region.[29] The second largest agency in the mountainous region is the Bureau of Land Management, created in 1946. Its lands are technically still the public domain, since there has never been a formal determination that they would never be transferred to private ownership.[30] The BLM manages 166,857,000 acres of land in the region, which constitutes 95 percent of all BLM land in the forty-eight adjacent states.[31] Other agencies that control millions of acres individually in the Mountainous West include the U.S. Department of Defense, approximately 30 million acres; the Fish and Wildlife Service, approximately 30 million acres; the National Park Service, 25 million acres; and the Water and Power Resources Service (formerly the Bureau of Reclamation), 7.5 million acres.[32]

Management and use of the vast holdings of the federal government in the Mountainous West represents an ongoing series of compromises between the various parties affected. Following the successful adoption of the Taylor Grazing Act, the concept that fees would be charged for use of the federal lands increased in importance. Since these revenues were essentially returned to the local economy, they directly benefited western states through jobs, taxes, and expenditures of those involved in the exploitation of coal, oil, natural gas, or timber. Lease payments to western states were augmented by "payments in lieu of taxes" on small areas of land acquired by the federal government for defense-related activity. Over time the western states maintained that they should also be given such payments for all federal land, even if they were also benefiting from recreation, mineral leasing, grazing fees, or timber sales. In 1976, Congress acquiesced, agreeing to pay up to seventy-five cents per acre in lieu of taxes to every county in which specified federal lands were located.[33]

While the federal lands of the Mountainous West continued to increase in financial importance to the western states, legislation affecting their administration and use was being removed from the direct or indirect use and control of the residents of the region. The first and most important act of Congress affecting management of the federal lands of the Mountainous West was the Forest Service's Multiple Use–Sustained Yield Act of 1960. This act officially directed that the Forest Service was to be engaged in more than simply managing the forests to maximize sustained timber yield. The act required the Forest Service to include recreation, wildlife, watershed management, and scenic and other nontimber-producing uses in its management plans.

In the absence of a direct congressional mandate to emphasize multiple use, the BLM continued to emphasize grazing. Two acts that passed in 1964, the Wilderness Act and the related Classification and Multiple Use (CMU) Act, did provide the beginnings of planning for multiple use on BLM lands, however. The CMU Act was particularly important to the Bureau of Land Management, for it authorized the agency to inventory the land remaining in the public domain and to determine which should be disposed of and which should be retained and managed under multiple-use concepts, providing implicit recognition that at least some BLM land would remain permanently in federal ownership. The Wilderness Act required the Forest Service and the Bureau of Land Management to determine which areas should be permanently preserved as wilderness areas and protected from other activities. The growing congressional recognition that the federal land of the Mountainous West should be used for more than commodity extraction for the benefit of local interests has prompted conflict between ranchers, loggers, miners, and the growing numbers of recreational users of the federal lands in the Mountainous West.

Recreational Use of the Mountainous West

The post–World War II years have seen tremendous changes in America. Increasing affluence, mobility, and leisure time have affected the conflict between local interests in the federal lands of the Mountainous West and the broader American public's views and interests. Growing numbers of individuals and groups within and outside of the region now recognize the Mountainous West as a restorative sanctuary for recreation or simple escape from their urban and suburban lifestyles. Increasing recreation pressure on federal lands, accompanied by a growing concern for the environment, has raised questions among users about the traditional management of federal lands in the region. Environmental concerns prompted passage of the National Environmental Protection Act of 1969 (NEPA) and establishment of the Environmental Protection Agency (EPA) the following year. The EPA effectively included all sectors of the public in management decisions relating to the federal lands of the region since EPA regulations required preparation of an environmental impact statement (EIS) for any action of a federal agency whose actions significantly affected the quality of the human environment. Although initially directed at federal agencies, this mandate has been expanded not only to include action undertaken directly by the agencies but also "Federal decisions to approve, fund, or license activities which will be carried out by others."[34] The impact of NEPA and the EPA on the federal lands of the Mountainous West is diverse, including EIS documents for timber harvest in the Forest Service lands and leasing in grazing districts by the BLM. As part of the EIS process, interested individuals and groups are given the opportunity to express their views and to raise concerns over the proposed action.

Growing public interest and environmental concern also led to passage of the Federal Land Policy and Management Act (FLPMA) of 1976, in which Congress formally recognized the diverse public purposes which should be considered in management of the public lands.[35] The effective impact of FLPMA was to change the single-purpose focus of the Bureau of Land Management from grazing to the multipurpose standards previously required of the Forest Service by the Multiple Use–Sustained Yield Act of 1960. The act reflected changing public priorities that had culminated in the environmental movement of the late 1960s and early 1970s. By the end of 1976, it was clear that management of the public lands could no longer exclusively emphasize single purposes such as timber, mining, or grazing, but must include a wide range of activities for the benefit of both the residents of the Mountainous West and those visitors who came to the region to enjoy the federal lands. This change in use of the federal lands was accompanied by a significant change in the revenue sharing associated with the income from the federal lands in the Mountainous West. The basis for calculating the return to counties of the revenue from timber sales was increased from 25 percent of net receipts to 25 percent of gross receipts, the states' share of coal-leasing revenues was changed from 37.5 to 50 percent of gross revenues, and payment in lieu of taxes went from ten to seventy-five cents per acre.[36] The combination of changes in revenue sharing was designed partially to offset the perception by western legislators that the Mountainous West was subsidizing the balance of the country by providing recreational or other public opportunities on federal lands in contrast to eastern states which had been given essentially all of the federal lands within their borders for transferral to private uses. The congressional actions of 1976 represent a fundamental philosophic recognition that the federal lands of the Mountainous West would remain in federal control, and that for the western states the revenue transfers would be a substitute for the free land which had been given to eastern states.

Ongoing Debate over Use of Federal Lands

The expanded revenue sharing which implicitly recognized both the role of the federal lands in the economies of the western states and their importance as a national heritage for use by locals and nonlocals alike did not end the ongoing conflicts that have colored the use of the federal lands of the region. In the years since the passage of the 1976 acts, there have been repeated conflicts between the traditional local users who have relied on the federal lands for their livelihood and the growing numbers of users representing urban recreationists and environmentalists. The number and nature of these conflicts is nearly as diverse as the number of communities in the Mountainous West itself, but several broad categories of conflicts can be recognized that illustrate the future issues that will affect the choices governing the use of the federal lands in the region.

The first of these is illustrated by the dramatically entitled "sagebrush rebellion" of the late 1970s and early 1980s. The "rebellion" is the most recent attempt by western states to gain control of the federal lands within their boundaries in spite of the 1976 compromises granting them greater revenue from the federal government. It began with Nevada claiming that the federal ownership of land in the state effectively stifled growth of urban centers such as Las Vegas and raised threats to the continued success of ranching and mining. The Nevada state legislature passed a bill in 1979 (AB415) in response, claiming all land within the state administered by the BLM as state property. By the end of 1980, Utah, Wyoming, New Mexico, and Arizona had enacted bills similar to that of Nevada, with Wyoming extending its claims to Forest Service land as well. Idaho, Colorado, Washington, California, Alaska, and Hawaii passed similar sagebrush rebellion legislation proposing various investigations to determine what should be done about the federal land within their borders. The media designation of sagebrush rebellion seemed an accurate description of a phenomenon that in one year had swept across the Mountainous West, but the actual spark that ignited the rebellion in Nevada represented the end of years of effort on the part of the state to obtain state or private ownership of part or all of the federal domain within its boundaries.[37]

The causes of the rebellion were complex, reflecting both the high proportion of federal ownership in the western states and growing concern on the part of the traditional triad of miners, ranchers, and loggers concerning their use of the federal lands. The livestock operators feared that changes in federal management of the Bureau of Land Management and other federally owned lands would negatively affect their economy. They were particularly incensed by requirements for preparation of environmental impact statements assessing the impact of grazing on the public lands. By the late 1970s, the draft proposals of these EIS documents were being circulated, calling for reduced numbers of animals on much of the western land because of overgrazing. For the first time, widespread adoption of the goals in FLPMA incorporated recreational and environmental values in the management of much of the federal land, including representation of nontraditional user groups such as environmentalists, hunters, and hikers in advisory roles while decreasing representation from the traditional user groups of ranchers, miners, and loggers.

The fears of the traditional user groups that spawned the sagebrush rebellion illustrate the changing concerns for the western public lands. The actions of the five states that actually passed legislation claiming ownership of federal lands within their borders was clearly unconstitutional in light of all previous litigation that had firmly established the right of the federal government to control and dispose of the public domain; it indicates a last-gasp attempt to wrest the federal lands from the public for the benefit of private interests in individual states. The rebellion itself faded out after 1981 in the face of growing organized opposition from conservation and other user groups and the growing dispute within the ranks of advocates of seizing federal lands between those favoring state control and those favoring privatization.[38] The outgrowth of the rebellion was to greatly politicize the attitudes of the various groups in the Mountainous West relative to the federal lands. The support for measures to gain control of the federal lands revealed a general urban/rural division. Rural residents and state legislators were generally overwhelming in their support for the rebellion, but urban residents tended to be less supportive, indicating the differing values of each group in reference to the federal lands. The end result of the rebellion was not to transfer the majority of federal lands to private ownership but to encourage cooperation and compromise in their management. For the states in the Mountainous West, the most immediate effect of the rebellion was speeding up the process of transferring the reserved school-lands sections in the federal lands to state ownership. Since these school sections are distributed within the federally owned land, however, they create a checkerboard pattern of land ownership, making it difficult for the states to effectively administer them or to lease them for revenue for the state.

A second category of conflicts over the federal lands emerged in the 1980s as states wrestled with use of these school lands. Sale or lease of state-owned school sections to private owners produced private enclaves surrounded by federal lands, and these enclaves created a setting for activities that were inimical to the avowed goals of federal land management planning. The result has been an effort to exchange federal and state lands in order to give the state ownership of a block of land on the margins of the federal property. Then the sale or lease of the state property would not interfere with federal management goals.

Issues relating to the use of these state lands have again revealed the rift between rural and urban residents in the Mountainous West. Residents of urban centers such as Salt Lake City prefer to maintain the state lands in public ownership so that they can be used for recreational or environmental uses, while residents of rural areas continue with their plea for relief from what they perceive as bondage to federal and state land ownership limiting their economic growth and well-being. Tensions related to how the state-owned land surrounded by federal lands is to be used have led to such confrontations as Utah's 1989 threat to sell state school lands in scenic areas such as Zion National Park or Arches National Park to private entrepreneurs for gas stations, motels, or other commercial activities, thereby destroying the integrity of the park experience. It is doubtful that the state could actually do so because of the great division among the public and the legislators as to the appropriate use of the land, but the existence of such threats represents the ongoing tradition of demands by the western states for greater ownership of the federal land within their boundaries.

Another category of conflict is related to the impact of federally owned property on adjacent private lands. This has taken many forms, from the development of management plans that regulate the materials and manner of construction of fences and buildings in the Sawtooth Valley and Stanley Basin of Idaho surrounded by the Sawtooth National Recreation Area, to attempts by the National Park Service to affect the location of a movie theater in Springdale, Utah, in 1991.[39] In the former case the management plan for the Sawtooth National Recreation Area requires the communities and counties involved to prepare comprehensive plans and appropriate zoning ordinances to ensure compliance with the plan for the National Recreation Area. In the Zion National Park case, a firm proposed building a multiple-screen movie theater immediately outside the entrance to Zion National Park. Since the tiny community of Springdale, which lies adjacent to the park, has long felt that it gained little direct economic benefit from the park, community leaders accepted the proposal to build the complex in spite of objections from the National Park Service and a variety of environmental groups who pointed out that it would obscure the magnificent panoramas that visitors experience approaching the park entrance.

Similar conflicts have been experienced elsewhere, as in Wyoming and Montana where buffalo from Yellowstone National Park invade private ranch lands and compete with the livestock, consume valuable hay reserves, and create tension between the ranchers and the Park Service. The issue extends beyond these private lands themselves, where the private interests historically utilized the federal lands for grazing, lumbering, or other activities. In Utah a major conflict has developed between ranchers and the Forest Service over growing elk herds which consume much of the same vegetation as livestock. The resulting confrontation pits traditional ranchers against hunters and environmentalists and the National Forest Service. In other communities, decisions to limit the number of animals allowed on traditional grazing lands or to limit or prevent logging because of environmental damage or endangered species, as well as a host of other use-related issues, pit the traditional commodity users of the federal lands against the modern urban recreationists and environmentalists.

A final category of modern conflict involving federal lands relates to concerns over the ability of the federal government to manage the lands for the best interests of the residents of the region. In 1991, the government acknowledged that nuclear testing in Nevada in the 1950s occurred even though scientists suggested that the best location would be along the Carolina coast, where radioactive fallout would be carried out to sea. The recommendations were ignored in favor of the federal lands which already were owned and controlled, thus raising important questions about the ability of the federal government to make choices that will be equitable to all users of federal lands. The tendency to use the federal lands for activities such as disposal of nuclear waste, weapons testing, or other undesirable activities causes many in the Mountainous West to question whether the federal government actually considers the needs of the region.

Conclusion

The ongoing confrontations over the use of federal lands in the Mountainous West represent the tensions associated with the de facto change from an implied federal domain that would ultimately be given to the states, to a permanent federal heritage which will remain in public control. The present conflicts are but the latest in the ongoing saga between the residents of the region and the federal government. Recognition that the Mountainous West was distinctly different from the balance of the nation in which the federal land was largely transferred to private interests has been slow to develop among the residents of the Mountainous West. Desires to have individuals profit from federal lands have fueled the relationship between the federal government, the state governments, and private interests in the region. The historical geography of the Mountainous West both illustrates the process by which the federal lands were preserved, and indicates that confrontation will continue in the future. The cycle of exploitive activities associated with miners, ranchers, farmers, and loggers that characterized the first century of use of the federal lands in the West established a strong bias toward privatization. In combination with the American ethic of the yeoman farmer and private land ownership, this has created a powerful tradition in the West that mitigates against continued federal ownership.

The profound changes in American society in the last half-century have created new attitudes and forces that ensure continued conflict over the federal lands. Where exploitation of federal lands has been the historic trend, preservation and management related to environmental concerns are the modern norm. The change from a rural society to an urban society has created a division between the traditional rural users of the federal lands and today's dominant urban populations. The net effect is to create conflict and changing coalitions of interest groups to address these conflicts. Sportsman groups may side with federal agencies in issues regarding numbers of wildlife, thus opposing ranchers who see wildlife as a threat to grazing. The same sportsman groups may side with ranchers who oppose the federal agencies concerning the "hunting" of buffalo to minimize their threat to ranchers around Yellowstone Park.

The ongoing conflicts within the individual states of the Mountainous West over the use of federal lands reflect the changing role and value of the various resources contributed by the federal lands. From 1850 to 1950, the use of the federal lands for exploitive activities proceeded with relatively little conflict because the values of the majority of the population were congruent with the existing use of federal lands. The growth in recreational and environmental concerns combined with federal legislation in the 1970s to change the relationship between uses and users in the region, fomenting controversy and strife. This situation will continue for the foreseeable future as the region comes to grips with the recognition that the unique nature of the Mountainous West precludes privatization of the majority of the federal lands, a conclusion reinforced by the permanent withdrawal of federal lands as new national parks are created or wilderness areas established. The traditional triad of users (miners, ranchers, loggers) resists these changes and the growing influence of environmental, recreational, and other interest groups in managing the federal lands of the region. As the dichotomy between these groups and their values lessens over time, we can expect the conflicts to decline as well, but the process of accommodation will apparently extend well into the next century.

Notes

1. John G. Francis and Richard Ganzel, eds., *Western Public Lands: The Management of Natural Resources in a Time of Declining Federalism* (Totowa, N.J.: Rowman and

Allanheld, 1984), 38; Bureau of Land Management, *Public Land Statistics, 1989* (U.S. Department of the Interior, Washington, D.C. 1990), 5.

2. Ray Grass, "Cattle versus Elk for Home on the Range," *Deseret News* (Salt Lake City), 28 May 1991, is but one example of numerous articles appearing in newspapers in the West.

3. Richard H. Jackson, *Land Use in America* (London: Edward Arnold, 1981), 14.

4. Henry Nash Smith, *Virgin Land: The American West as Symbol and Myth* (Cambridge, Mass.: Harvard University Press, 1950), 153–56.

5. U.S. Constitution, art. 4, sec. 3.

6. Phillip O. Foss, ed., *Federal Lands Policy* (Westport, Conn.: Greenwood Press, 1987), 80.

7. Foss, *Federal Lands Policy,* 81.

8. Jackson, *Land Use in America,* 19–20.

9. Sally E. Fairfax and Carolyn E. Yale, *Federal Lands: A Guide to Planning, Management and State Revenues* (Washington, D.C.: Island Press, 1987), 76.

10. Jackson, *Land Use in America,* 19.

11. Carl J. Mayer and George A. Riley, *Public Domain, Private Dominion: A History of Public Mineral Policy in America,* (San Francisco: Sierra Club Books, 1985), 25.

12. Mayer and Riley, *Public Domain, Private Dominion,* 37.

13. Jackson, *Land Use in America,* 20.

14. Jackson, *Land Use in America,* 22.

15. Louise E. Poffer, *The Closing of the Public Domain: Disposal and Reservation Policies, 1900–1950* (Stanford: Stanford University Press, 1951), 9.

16. Poffer, *Closing of the Public Domain,* 15.

17. Mayer and Riley, *Public Domain, Private Dominion,* 43–44.

18. Mayer and Riley, *Public Domain, Private Dominion,* 44–46.

19. Poffer, *Closing of the Public Domain,* 220–24.

20. BLM, *Public Land Statistics, 1989,* table 11.

21. Foss, *Federal Lands Policy,* 84.

22. Fairfax and Yale, *Federal Lands,* 18.

23. Marvin Klemme, *Home Rule on the Range* (New York: Vantage Press, 1984), 5.

24. Jackson, *Land Use in America,* 22.

25. Klemme, *Home Rule on the Range,* 8.

26. Klemme, *Home Rule on the Range,* 23.

27. Fairfax and Yale, *Federal Lands,* 78; BLM, *Public Land Statistics, 1989,* tables 11 and 12.

28. Francis and Ganzel, *Western Public Lands,* 155.

29. BLM, *Public Land Statistics, 1989,* table 11.

30. Jackson, *Land Use in America,* 22.

31. BLM, *Public Land Statistics, 1989*, table 10.

32. Jackson, *Land Use in America*, 49.

33. Fairfax and Yale, *Federal Lands*, 18.

34. Elaine Moss, ed., *Land Use Controls in the United States* (New York, Dial Press for Natural Resources Defense Council, 1977), 225.

35. Francis and Ganzel, *Western Public Lands*, 153.

36. Fairfax and Yale, *Federal Lands*, 154–57.

37. Francis and Ganzel, *Western Public Lands*, 31–32.

38. Francis and Ganzel, *Western Public Lands*, 33.

39. Jackson, *Land Use in America*, 52.

Restorative Sanctuary

It should be clear by now that the five themes we have used to define the Mountainous West are inextricably bound together. The following essay by Lary Dilsaver recognizes this interplay and highlights the role of the restorative-sanctuary theme in understanding the resource conflicts of the Sierra Nevada. Dilsaver shows that it is not enough to conceive of a single preservationist impulse that has shaped the landscape of the Mountainous West. Rather, a more penetrating view reveals that there have been many shades of preservation arguing for different degrees of sanctuary and resource protection. The setting for Dilsaver's case study is the southern Sierra Nevada and the region which evolved into Sequoia and Kings Canyon National Parks. He describes the changing ranks of the preservationists as different issues presented themselves. The chief initial targets of all concerned were the lumbermen and livestock grazers who threatened to radically alter the mountain environment. A diverse collection of conservationists, preservationists, nearby valley farmers, and others combined to thwart these initial nemeses. Once the Sierra Forest Preserve was created, however, Dilsaver demonstrates how the fundamental split between those advocating multiple use and preservation affected the Sierra Nevada. Government agencies further contributed to the conflict as Forest Service and National Park interests vied for control of Sierra lands. Even after the national parks were created, preservationist forces could not agree on using the parks as recreational playgrounds or as wilderness sanctuaries. Dilsaver concludes his overview by noting that today even the hardcore wilderness advocates are at odds with one another: biocentric purists now wish to prevent even stock access into much of the back country. Overall, his essay is a vivid illustration of how all of the themes of the Mountainous West combine to shape the evolution of particular places and landscapes.

10 / Resource Conflict in the High Sierra

LARY M. DILSAVER

The Mountainous West is an area of inevitable conflict. As areas of concentrated resources, as islands of adequate moisture, and as areas specifically prized for recreation, mountains stand as targets for many interest groups. Irrigation farmers, power companies, loggers, miners, shepherds, hikers, campers, and resort-goers covet these qualities. And they invariably seek to exclude each other's antithetical activities. Because the West also was the last major settlement region in America's lower forty-eight states, it gave the government time to ponder prior misuse of the nation's resources and to take a role in shaping future use in this region. Hence, the historical geography of the Mountainous West reflects a political struggle pitting lobby groups, special interests, and philosophically opposed agencies against one another.

The southern Sierra Nevada provide a classic case study of the sequence and variety of conflicts that have affected the Mountainous West. The purpose of this chapter is to show how one section of that region, the Sequoia–Kings Canyon Wilderness Area, is the end result of five political conflicts. These battles first withdrew the land from the alienation process, then created and expanded two national parks, prevented road building, and established ecological management and wilderness legislative protection. A fifth struggle, presently under way, results from efforts to exclude horses and other recreational stock from the area. In each of these conflicts, an increasingly preservation-oriented group has shed allies from previous fights, sacrificed terrain in order to win sufficient support, and sought ever more exclusive biological management. The specific methods have run the gamut from compromise, through trade-offs and inducements, to outright intimidation and character assassination.

Exploitation vs. Conservation, 1885–93

The high country of the southern Sierra Nevada forms one of the most familiar and formidable mountainous zones of North America. Peaks tower over 14,000 feet near the steeply descending fault scarp of their eastern margin. The western profile is gentler, yet deep glacial canyons of the Kaweah, Kern, Kings, and San Joaquin Rivers create a rugged and majestic landscape. The region has long been recognized as an area of important and spatially concentrated resources. Between the elevations of 3,500 and 8,000 feet a rich mixed conifer forest of pine, cedar, and fir is further distinguished by the presence of most of the remaining groves of giant sequoia (*Sequoiadendron giganteum*). These enormous trees, ranging up to three hundred feet in height and forty feet in diameter, seemed both a bonanza and a challenge to the first loggers to encounter them (figure 1). Interspersed with the sequoia–mixed conifer forest and scattered in the rocky alpine areas above are numerous meadows providing forage for both wildlife and domestic stock. Of greatest value, however, is the water resource of the Sierra snowpack and streams. Westerly winds drop up to forty-five inches of precipitation within the confines of Sequoia and Kings Canyon National Parks. Below and to the west, the richest agricultural counties in the United States receive barely ten inches. While these tangible resources have excited practical attention for decades, it is the space, open forests, and mild climate that recreationalists of every stripe have sought.

The first European invasion of the Sierra Nevada came after James Marshall's discovery of gold in 1848. Prospectors and their followers explored the entire range within a few years. They found little mineral wealth in the southern Sierra save for a minor silver strike in the Mineral King Valley during the 1870s. However, their exploration opened the country and its resources to more appropriate exploitation. Cattle ranchers quickly moved into the Sequoia–Kings Canyon region seeking cool summer pastures. In 1856, rancher Hale Tharp discovered the most spectacular sequoia grove, appropriately named Giant Forest, and began a common practice by patenting claims to several of its meadows. The predominance of cattle, however, was short-lived as flocks of sheep from the San Joaquin Valley were introduced to the region by the 1860s. Their impact profoundly changed the high country. John Muir later wrote, "Not only do the shepherds, at the driest time of the year, set fire to everything that will burn (in order to encourage pasture regrowth), but the sheep consume every green leaf, not sparing even the young conifers . . . and they rake and dibble the loose soil

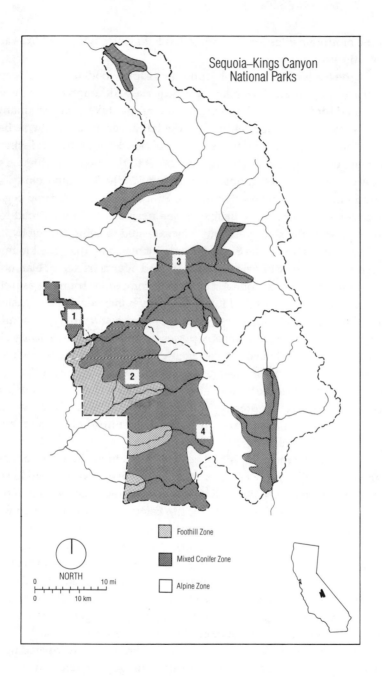

1. Location and Vegetation Zone Map (1—Grant Grove; 2—Giant Forest; 3—Kings Canyon; 4—Mineral King).

of the mountainsides for the spring floods to wash away, and thus at last leave the ground barren."[1]

On the heels of cattle and sheepherders came woodcutters and loggers, their eyes popping as they beheld the sequoias. Although the brittle wood was good for little more than shingles and grape stakes, they cut many sequoias after 1880, including those of the largest grove at Converse Basin. Many other species, including sugar pine, ponderosa pine, and white fir, further attracted loggers. In 1885, the threat to the forest heightened with the arrival of a group of utopian socialists called the Kaweah Colony. They filed for most of Giant Forest under the Timber and Stone Act and began to organize a lumber-cutting business. The necessity to build a road to the grove delayed their progress, but they expected to begin cutting by 1890.[2]

The exploitation of the Sierra Nevada increasingly disturbed many observers for a variety of reasons. Federal land agents balked at blatant misuse of the Timber and Stone Act by lumber companies trying to gain cheap title to thousands of acres of forest. With such inexpensive and easily obtained trees, these companies often employed disturbingly wasteful cutting practices. After one company successfully gained title to nearly all the forest of the Kings River drainage, agents pressed their bosses to withdraw what remained before it was too late. Others, including respected Visalia newspaperman George Stewart and preservationist John Muir, pushed for withdrawal in order to preserve the magnificent trees for their own sakes. As monuments of American nature, they were fit to match and surpass anything in Europe.[3]

However, the most important voice of concern in the 1880s came from San Joaquin Valley farmers. Their survival and livelihoods depended on irrigation, which in turn depended on the snow, rains, and runoff of the Sierra Nevada. As the farmers saw it, the key to retention of Sierran waters was the vegetation cover of the mountain slopes. Hence the actions of loggers, cattle ranchers, and especially sheepherders directly threatened them. In addition, there was a related belief that the presence of vegetation encouraged rainfall. Removal of the trees, farmers argued, would both accelerate the loss of water from the mountains as well as decrease its supply from precipitation. Many scientists and agricultural agents echoed this belief and the farmers' alarm at mounting watershed destruction.[4]

In 1884, a landmark court decision in San Francisco anticipated the outcome of this first resource controversy. Judge Lorenzo Sawyer ruled against the mining industry and its practice of dumping hydraulic mine tailings into streams. The winners in the case were farmers who used water from those streams in the Sacramento Valley. Aside from destroying a large component of the state's founding industry, the decision placed the interests of agriculture ahead of a very lucrative but exploitative business. From that time forward, few decisions or laws have challenged the preeminence of California agriculture with its obvious sustainability.[5]

During the late 1880s, the sides were drawn in the southern Sierra. On one side, a few itinerant shepherds, cattle producers, and local lumber companies had little but cultural tradition and free-market capitalism to support their position. On the other side, a powerful group of conservationists, preservationists, recreation enthusiasts, farmers, urban dwellers from the coast, scientists, land agents, and even the Southern Pacific Railroad and its lumber subsidiaries, based further north and vying for the same market, applied pressure to Congress to overcome that obstacle of tradition.

In September 1890, the conservation forces achieved their first victory with the establishment of Sequoia and General Grant National Parks, the second and third oldest in the system. Small as they were, some 163,816 acres, the withdrawal of these two parks derailed many of the lumber operations, including that of the Kaweah Colony. In disbelief that traditional practice and free enterprise could be so summarily suspended, colonists refused to abandon their cutting. When forced to halt by the army, they even tried to have the troops arrested. Even many farmers in the San Joaquin Valley, while rejoicing at the conservation of the forest, were troubled by the implications of this summary withdrawal of public land already under application for alienation.[6]

However, the two parks were but a spectacular fraction of the southern Sierra resource area. Men like John Muir, George Stewart, and Gifford Pinchot sought ways to reserve a much larger portion. The answer came in 1891 when President Benjamin Harrison signed a bill allowing the president to withdraw forested lands for conservation purposes. Immediately, the General Land Office moved to identify for withdrawal a huge tract in the southern Sierra Nevada. On 14 February 1893, as his lame-duck term drew to a close, Harrison proclaimed the Sierra Forest Reserve. This immense parcel of land contained more than four million acres and subsequently was subdivided into four national forests.[7]

The creation of the forest reserve did not stop all the activities which the diverse conservation allies feared. It did stop sheep grazing and deliberate burning, but it established only theoretical control over logging, cattle grazing, and many other exploitative activities. However, it was a huge victory for conservationists, farmers, and preservationists as well as a major shift in the approach of American culture to resources and the land. In addition, it established the federal government as the permanently controlling force and assured that all future conflicts would occur in the political arena.

Multiple Use vs. Recreation and Preservation, 1916–40

The uneasy grouping of allies that led to withdrawal of the Sierra Forest Reserve was, of course, unlikely to persist. After two decades of relative calm, a serious philosophical split developed between those who would preserve resources unchanged for recreation and inspiration and those who would see them conserved but still used. This split, personified by John Muir and Gifford Pinchot, led to the creation of two government agencies emotionally charged with promoting the two philosophies. The first and larger agency was the U.S. Forest Service, established in 1905. Its personnel espoused a policy of multiple use of resources for the greatest national good. They argued that lumbering, mining, cattle grazing, hunting, recreation development, reclamation, and water development all had a place in the Forest Service scheme. Given control of the Sierra Forest Reserve and later the national forests that derived from it, forest rangers firmly believed that theirs was the fairest and most democratic policy.[8]

Eleven years later, Congress created the National Park Service. Its first director, Stephen Mather, was an unabashed promoter of preservation and recreation. He also carried out a vigorous acquisitive campaign aimed at wresting lands of scenic beauty away from the Forest Service. One of the first targets Mather identified was the mountainscape of the southern Sierra.

The philosophical split between government agencies served to focus the division between various interest groups. The Park Service came to rely on such organizations as the Sierra Club and the Emergency Conservation Committee as well as carefully cultivated backers from distant urban areas. Those aligning with the Forest Service included local irrigation associations, chambers of commerce, most local politicians, and the majority of the people already using the region. The latter formed a particularly weighty opposition group in debates before Congress.[9]

In the quarter century from 1916 to 1940, these two forces of preservation and conservation and the government agencies that represented them jockeyed for public support and control of the southern Sierra Nevada. Despite deep and occasionally vicious antagonism, the two sides twice compromised to allow a fivefold expansion of the national parks. Although this was but a fifth of the original forest reserve, it removed from use and development enormous areas of timber and forage as well as critical sites for irrigation and power structures.

Preservation forces had begun agitating for park expansion in the early years of the twentieth century. However, it was not until the creation of the National Park Service in 1916 and the Federal Power Commission in 1920 that the campaign became serious. During the summer of 1920, the Los Angeles Bureau of Power and Light infuriated locals by applying to develop the water and power resources of the Kings River. The San Joaquin Light and Power Corporation scrambled to counterfile on the same or nearby sites, while park backers and preservationists explored immediate and drastic ways to block all water developments and expand the two parks.[10]

Stephen Mather huddled with Forest Service officials in order to gain support for a park of some 900,000 acres encompassing an area similar to the boundaries of the parks today. The majority of the area that he proposed consisted of the rocky alpine reaches of the Kings and Kaweah drainages. However, he also sought the forested land along the lower Kings River, the Mineral King Valley, and most of the damsites proposed by power developers. Chief foresters Henry Graves and William Greeley had an agenda as well. They favored park status for the commercially useless country above treeline, but demanded exclusion of the western, forested edges of the proposed park as well as a transfer of the southern 43 percent of existing Sequoia National Park to the Forest Service. This latter area contained both excellent grazing areas and important forest reserves, including several large sequoia groves.[11]

As the details of the proposed compromise reached the public, an outcry arose from many camps. All proponents of water development forced the government to abandon park status for the Kings River drainage basin. In addition, recreation cabin owners, aware of tighter restrictions on use and development by the Park Service, succeeded in getting Mineral King omitted from the bill. Finally, preservationists roasted both government agencies, charging complicity, dereliction of duty, and betrayal of the public for even contemplating transfer of southern Sequoia National Park to the Forest Service. That portion of the compromise also quickly disappeared. In 1926, a publicly shaped compromise bill expanded Sequoia National Park eastward to the crest of the Sierra (figure 2).[12]

For some nine years the compromise seemed to satisfy preservationists

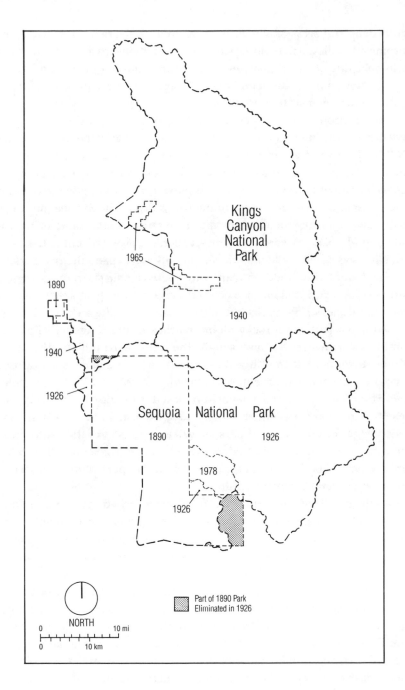

Kings
Canyon
National
Park

1965

1890

1940

1926

Sequoia │ National   Park

1890   1926

1940

1978

1926

Part of 1890 Park
Eliminated in 1926

NORTH

0   10 mi

0   10 km

2. *Expansion of Sequoia–Kings Canyon National Parks, 1890–1978.*

and allowed reclamation advocates to continue their competition for the Kings River. With the election of Franklin Roosevelt as president, however, the campaign to expand the parklands resumed. At the center of the conflict was irascible Secretary of the Interior Harold Ickes, an avowed enthusiast of wilderness preservation. Only the inability of Congress to solve the counterclaims of Los Angeles, the San Joaquin water and power interests, and tourism developers, who planned a huge resort complex in Kings Canyon, allowed the Kings River country to remain as a potential wilderness. Ickes aimed to seize the region by playing off the various development factions against each other.[13]

After an abortive attempt in 1935 to have the Kings River area declared a national park, Ickes and the Park Service began negotiations with various local factions. They convinced the San Joaquin power and water group that the best way to serve their needs and overcome the imperialism of Los Angeles was to sponsor two Ickes-designed bills. One would create a huge alpine Kings Canyon National Park but exclude the two major damsites. A second would order the Bureau of Reclamation to build a large dam and power facility on the lower Kings River, west of the park. Meanwhile, Ickes convinced resort developers to back a wilderness park with promises to develop a tourist complex that would serve up to four thousand people in Kings Canyon. And he convinced the preservation lobby to accept a park without its two Yosemite-like valleys, Kings Canyon and Tehipite, where dams were proposed.

The political campaign that ensued in 1939 was remarkable for its ferocity and malice. Still opposed to a Kings Canyon National Park were some reclamation interests, many businesses, and resource users who preferred the less restrictive controls of the Forest Service. The Forest Service itself took the lead in the anti-park campaign, actively speaking against the park, Harold Ickes, and the Park Service. Charges and countercharges of wiretapping, burglary, intimidation, slander, and bribery inflamed locals and eventually spilled onto the floor of the House of Representatives. There the congressman who sponsored the park bill charged an anti-park colleague with a flagrant attempt to frame him for bribery. This last episode destroyed the credibility of anti-park forces and led to the creation of Kings Canyon National Park, incorporating tiny General Grant Park, in March 1940.[14]

Although the later stages witnessed a level of viciousness rarely seen in a conservation battle, it was compromise that ultimately allowed the enormous expansion of Sequoia and Kings Canyon National Parks to some

830,000 acres. With the later additions of Kings Canyon and Tehipite Valley in 1965, as well as an equally cantankerous acquisition of Mineral King in 1978, the two parks now contain nearly 20 percent of the old Sierra Forest Reserve (figure 2).[15] By exploiting a split within the federal government, playing on regional fears of Los Angeles, and engaging in clever diplomacy when necessary, the forces of preservation and recreation defeated those favoring conservative use. In so doing, they blocked all grazing, timber cutting, mining, hunting, and water development from a very large piece of the Mountainous West.

Recreation vs. Wilderness Sanctuary, 1927–47

During the National Park Service's first decade, while its staff campaigned for more and larger parks, they also vigorously encouraged road building and recreation in existing units. Their reasons included justification of the parks' existence to a skeptical and practical public, preservation of the agency itself, threatened with absorption by the Forest Service, and personal belief by early Park Service personnel that most forms of recreation were prudent and proper uses of scenic areas.[16] In the southern Sierra parks, recreational development consisting of auto roads, cabins, camping areas, and various services was concentrated at Giant Forest and General Grant Park. The later addition of the Kings River country focused plans on Kings Canyon as a third major tourist zone.

However, the bulk of the areas added in 1926 and 1940 lay inaccessible at the time of transfer to park status. Three proposals to change that roadless status and bring development pitted the uneasy park allies against each other even as they continued to struggle against resource users. The Middle Fork Road, the Sierra Way, and the Kings Canyon–Independence Road all promised new and easy access to magnificent scenery, or threatened to drive asphalt wedges and the clamor and chaos of crowds into the wilderness, depending on one's point of view (figure 3).

The earliest proposal, the Middle Fork Road, was a simple plan to extend Sequoia's new southern approach road eastward along the Middle Fork of the Kaweah River in a gradual, carefully engineered ascent and then return it along the northward plateau to Giant Forest. There it would continue on to General Grant. Park engineers had already completed a steeper, more winding road which Director Horace Albright sneeringly dismissed as a "rathole."[17] However, Park Superintendent John White and

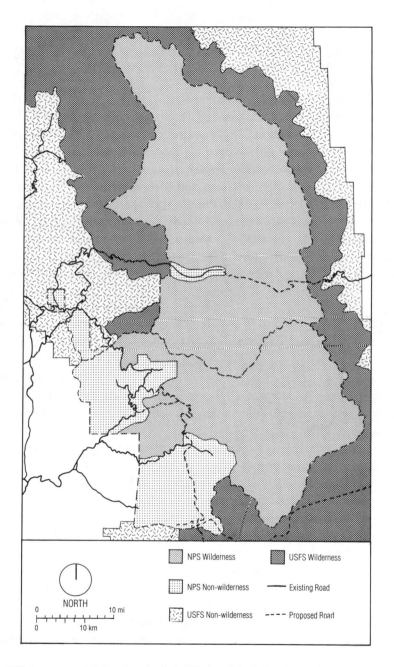

3. Wilderness and Other Lands of the National Park Service and U.S. Forest Service, plus Existing and Once Proposed Roads.

preservationists feared destruction of the park's major scenic vista as well as the serenity and solitude of the backcountry. After a few tenuous years of sidestepping the issue, White succeeded in getting the Middle Fork Road plans dropped in 1931.[18]

Much more serious was an ambitious project known as the Sierra Way. Seven counties, dozens of towns and chambers of commerce, the California Automobile Association, and hundreds of tourism and service businesses promoted this park-to-park highway during the early 1930s. As originally planned, the road was to begin south of Sequoia National Park and provide Sequoia, General Grant, and Yosemite with a moderate speed link maintaining elevations higher than 7,000 feet. Later, plans expanded to include portions linking Lassen Volcanic National Park and the Oregon border country. Campgrounds and occasional development areas were to be built along the western side of the road.[19]

Preservation groups such as the Sierra Club as well as the Park Service itself vigorously opposed the Sierra Way. According to park officials, this opposition rested on a growing belief that inspiration and exercise were the proper activities for park visitors to enjoy. White in particular decried auto-bound visitors and the disruption they brought to the natural scene. But with such potent backing, it seemed during the early days of the Civilian Conservation Corps that the Sierra Way was sure to be built. However, White again prevailed by initially refusing appropriations for the road and then outlasting the availability of funds for such an expensive engineering project.[20]

The final of the three projects owed part of its origin to yet another characteristic of the mountains, the barrier that they present to regional transport. For several decades residents of the Owens Valley had sought a transalpine road in the southern Sierra. In 1940, as the creation of Kings Canyon National Park approached, they intensified their campaign to have the highway into Kings Canyon extended over the mountains to the town of Independence. This link would have provided the only crossing of a 160-mile mountain wall separating them from the coast and its cities. Unfortunately for the Owens Valley people, the preservation lobby had grown far too strong. The lobby succeeded in getting Kings Canyon National Park established as a wilderness park. Bowing to their continued pressure, Congress in 1947 passed an additional law specifically banning roads and structures from the new park.[21]

The effort to link the Owens and San Joaquin Valleys simply came too late onto a scene where wilderness preservation was steadily becoming the principal government mandate. The failure of these projects to expand auto access and its concomitant recreation development seriously thwarted a large segment of the public attempting to use the area. Enforcement of the roadless character of the backcountry left nearly 98 percent of the two parks undeveloped, useful only to those who could hike or ride horses. Even as a restorative sanctuary, the mountains continued to suffer vigorous dispute and polemic opinion.

Wilderness Democracy vs. Preservation, 1963–84

One of the most successful means of generating support for a roadless backcountry was the almost evangelical encouragement of the "wilderness experience." This experience was initially and incessantly promoted by the Sierra Club and similar organizations; after 1930, it became a primary part of the Park Service plan to educate and entertain visitors.[22] Park personnel built highly publicized trails and exhorted the casual visitor to leave the car and learn from the wilderness. After 1960, the American public seemed to accept the message. Backcountry use skyrocketed as an environmental and experiential culture became the dominant vocal component of the parks' clientele. During the 1960s the number of hikers entering the backcountry rose more than 600 percent.[23] Along with this precipitous increase came a rising awareness of the need to protect wilderness resources both legally and scientifically.

The possibility of further legal protection came with the passage of the 1964 Wilderness Act.[24] Immediately, park planners set about determining what areas in the two parks merited such designation. As they planned their proposal, two points became obvious. First, only areas without any development could be included. Zones around the existing backcountry camps and picnic areas should be excluded. Second, whatever became designated as wilderness also became inviolate to any future Park Service plans, no matter how appropriate they might later seem.

In 1966, with these thoughts in mind, the Park Service proposed an area encompassing 87 percent of the two parks. The Sierra Club countered with a proposal of 98 percent. A few desultory protests came from recreation interests favoring no wilderness and more development, but theirs was a fading and feeble voice. Preservation and backcountry enthusiasts had succeeded in infiltrating the ranks of the Park Service itself and in becoming the loudest and most persistent voice in the public planning procedure.

After a good deal of argument which strained the Park Service–preservationist alliance, the agency took a narrower view of the Wilderness Act and proposed only 85 percent of the two parks for such status in a 1971 master plan. Conspicuously absent were a number of "donut-holes" around weather stations and other human features (figure 4). Preservationists and the park planners traded further angry charges, and the confusion served to bog down the proposal for more than a decade.[25]

The final successful proposal was somewhat anticlimactic and represented another compromise. In 1984, a sweeping California Wilderness Bill designated 736,980 acres of Sequoia and Kings Canyon as the state's largest wilderness area.[26] Gone were the "donut-holes" despised by the Sierra Club as islands of potential development. However, the bill also omitted the southernmost portion of Sequoia and included only 85 percent of the two parks. Preservationists accepted this diminished wilderness because it was part of a much larger bill affecting many areas. Once again sacrifice of part of the terrain assured fervently sought protection for the remainder.

While the legal squabble over wilderness status dragged on through two decades, another more serious issue—that of scientific resource protection—entered the spotlight. Over the years, Park Service understanding of resource protection had evolved but not kept pace with advances in ecology and scientific sophistication. Initial efforts concentrating on protection of individual objects of scenic wonder gave way to an immature policy of "atmosphere preservation."[27] The latter coincided with the increased importance of a park "experience" for the visitor. But by the late 1950s, scientists from outside the Park Service, as well as preservation organizations armed with their findings, began criticizing the agency for scientifically immature and negligent management.[28]

Then, in 1963, an advisory board chaired by A. Starker Leopold released a report seriously faulting the entire focus of Park Service resource management and charging them to make ecological preservation the highest priority. Both the Sierra Club and the Wilderness Society printed the report in their respective journals, and Secretary of the Interior Stewart Udall ordered that its findings be adopted as policy.[29] Overnight the Park Service shifted money, personnel, and philosophy into scientific management for resource preservation. This dogmatic shift further sealed the backcountry from any future development despite the delays in full legal wilderness designation.[30]

The combination of vastly increased backcountry use and a zealous pursuit of ecological purity led inevitably to management problems. For de-

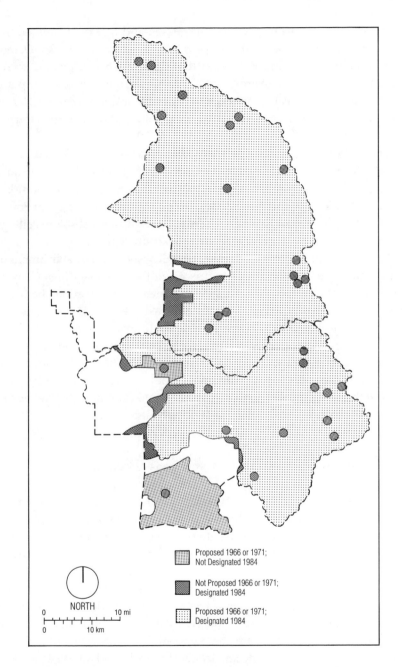

4. Areas Proposed for Wilderness Status in 1966 and/or 1971 and Those so Designated in 1984.

cades, park personnel had covertly discussed and quickly dismissed the concept of limits on the number of people allowed into the parks. Democratic tradition and a lingering sense that Congress had stipulated recreation as a purpose equal to preservation forestalled any serious attempts at front-country limits. Park planners also believed that auto access and large-scale development had already levied the greatest possible human impact on the ecosystem.

The backcountry, however, presented an area much less affected by humanity. Moreover, it was used by a preservation-oriented clientele willing to accept and even promote tighter controls for resource protection. Between 1972 and 1974, the Park Service, in cooperation with adjacent Forest Service districts, began issuing wilderness permits with absolute ceilings on the number of people entering each backcountry trail.[31]

Implementation of this wilderness permit system and establishment of equivalent legal designation further isolated the Sequoia–Kings Canyon backcountry as a management region of unusual preservation character. Ironically, the Forest Service also established wilderness areas around three sides of the parks. They were able to do this because these alpine areas had long been ignored by resource users intent on lower elevations and recreationists drawn to the parks (figure 3). But the level of protection provided in the national park wilderness, both in 1984 and in decades past, made it the closest approximation to the Leopold Committee's "vignette of primitive America" available in the southern Sierra Nevada.

Tradition vs. Pedestrian Purists, 1985–Present

Proper definition of "primitive America" has indirectly brought about the most recent battle over the Sequoia–Kings Canyon high country. From the assortment of users vying for the alpine resources, the final two groups, one on horseback, the other on foot, now face each other in a campaign no less vehement and hysterical than those which have preceded it. Hikers, who now comprise 95 percent of the backcountry users, wish to exclude stock entirely from the wilderness. Their reasons include the preservation of the meadows, which were damaged by sheep a century ago and kept from recovery by subsequent horse and mule use, the maintenance of trails, which are severely affected by saddle stock, and a fervent wish to avoid horse droppings on the trails.[32]

Although this conflict has been a vocal one for less than a decade, it has roots as old as the parks. Park biologists studied the state of the meadows as early as 1935 and began a regular series of observations during the 1940s. Park rangers ruled some meadows off limits for grazing as early as 1941. Heavy use and continued foraging by cattle during the Forest Service years left much of Kings Canyon National Park in particularly bad condition.[33]

The program to withdraw meadows from recreational stock use accelerated with the adoption of ecological management after 1963. Still, serious conflict did not materialize until preparation of a backcountry stock-use plan in 1984. During the public planning process mandated by the National Environmental Policy Act, hiking enthusiasts and the preservation organizations that they dominated called for extremely stringent controls on stock use, leading eventually to its exclusion. The Park Service devised a draft plan that seemed, at least to horsemen, to fit this extreme position. It called for much more study of the effects of stock use on meadows.

To the surprise of park officials, the stock users proved to be a considerably more powerful lobby than their numbers would indicate. Letters, phone calls, and pressure on local congresspeople came from many wealthy and powerful people coordinated by a group calling itself the High Sierra Stock Users Association. Their crescendo of opposition forced the Park Service to abandon most of its plan save only some further withdrawals of heavily stressed individual meadows.[34]

The issue at stake is essentially the same as in all the previous conflicts. One group seeks to preserve a portion of the mountains in a condition approximating that of no human contact. Recognition that Native Americans had already altered much of the region so far has not been an issue. On the other side, another group wants to engage in an activity which they claim is theirs by birthright and cultural tradition. Horse camping in the mountains predates the parks and recalls the glory of exploration and colonization of the American West, an episode removed by only a few generations from our collective experience.

In the early 1990s, the Park Service is engaged in trying to draft a new stock-use management plan. Two lobby groups are at work both in the southern Sierra Nevada and in the halls of Congress. The Backcountry Horsemen of California demand their rights and vilify those who would exclude them as selfish elitists. The High Sierra Hikers Association demands adherence to ecological policy and calls for the outright elimination of horses and mules in the wilderness backcountry. Short of that, they insist that riders pack in all their animal feed, not allow any off-trail travel, and place canvas diapers on their horses. During spring 1991, letters coming to the Park Service seeking to influence the stock-use planning procedure were ninety-nine to one in favor of the hikers' position. Experience has shown, however, that victory for one side will not come without cost. The likeliest outcomes of this latest controversy are, first, a stipulation that virtually all feed must be packed in, a condition already met by most horsemen; second, a reduction in the number of trails to be used by horses while hikers remain free to use any; and third, the near elimination of off-trail stock travel (figure 5). Once again, the most preservation-oriented side of the conflict will achieve most of its objectives over most of the terrain. The portions of the backcountry ruled inviolate to stock use will become an even more anachronistic landscape from a pre-European era.[35]

Conclusion

The Sequoia–Kings Canyon Wilderness Area lies today a region apart from its surroundings, a zone of historic conflict shaped by successive victories of the preservation lobby. In each battle, those who favored the minimal form of human-environment interaction have shed former allies, sacrificed some portion of their territory, and cajoled or coerced the government into ever more stringent protection policies.

From a four-million-acre forest reserve held for conservation, pieces now totaling 864,384 acres have been further withdrawn for recreation and preservation. Of those, some 85 percent have been designated wilderness, thus eliminating construction of highways and cabins. And within the wilderness, further controls challenge democratic traditions of unlimited access and the use of horses. This tightly controlled, limited-access backcountry consists in large measure of sparse meadows and gleaming rockfaces above treeline. Much had to be sacrificed to hold an area in such complete withdrawal.

The long and continuing conflict, erupting into five distinct battles, illustrates the competition that the themes of the Mountainous West generate among the public both in the region and nationally. The concentrated resources of trees, meadows, and minerals repeatedly draw those for whom pragmatic use of the land is the only sensible course. The vast significance of the water resources of these moisture islands deeply affects millions in the valleys and cities around them. The recreation resources of space, beauty, solitude, and adventure cluster like magnets for those same millions as well as countless others around the world; but the question of

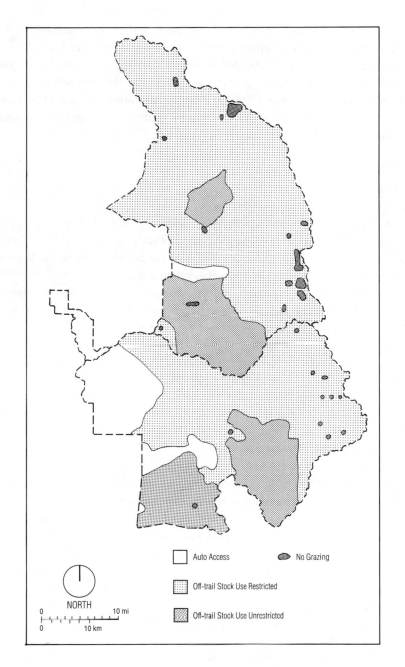

	Auto Access		No Grazing
	Off-trail Stock Use Restricted	
	Off-trail Stock Use Unrestricted	

NORTH

| 0 | | | | | | | | | | 10 mi |
| 0 | | | | | 10 km | | |

5. Backcountry Stock Use Areas Showing Off-Trail Stock Restriction Zones and Meadows Restricted from Grazing.

what type of recreation remains unresolved. And all the competitors for these prizes of the Mountainous West scheme and maneuver for influence over a government itself divided into goal-oriented agencies. In the last analysis, the resource management decisions made in the southern Sierra Nevada, as well as those affecting most of the Mountainous West, have been political ones. They can be undone tomorrow should the balance among competing forces shift or the operative philosophy change.

Notes

1. John Muir, "The American Forests," *Atlantic Monthly* 80 (August 1897): 153; Walter Fry, "The Discovery of Sequoia National Park . . .," Sequoia Nature Guide Service, Bulletin no. 1 (22 November 1924); Douglas Strong, "A History of Sequoia National Park" (Ph.D. diss., Syracuse University, 1964), 54–59.

2. Strong, "History of Sequoia," 61–62; William C. Tweed, *Kaweah Remembered: The Story of the Kaweah Colony and the Founding of Sequoia National Park* (Three Rivers, Calif.: Sequoia Natural History Association, 1986), 1–6.

3. Strong, "History of Sequoia," 89–94.

4. William R. Dudley, "Forest Reservations; with a Report on the Sierra Reservation, California," *Sierra Club Bulletin* 1 (1896): 264–65.

5. Robert L. Kelley, *Gold vs. Grain: The Hydraulic Mining Controversy in California's Sacramento Valley; A Chapter in the Decline of the Concept of Laissez-Faire* (Glendale, Calif.: Arthur H. Clark, 1959).

6. Tweed, *Kaweah Remembered*, 12–15.

7. Strong, "History of Sequoia," 139–44.

8. Still the best history of the Forest Service is found in Harold K. Steen, *The U.S. Forest Service: A History* (Seattle: University of Washington Press, 1976).

9. Alfred Runte, *National Parks: The American Experience*, 2d ed. (Lincoln: University of Nebraska Press, 1987); an excellent discussion of the split between agencies is found in Hal Rothman, " 'A Regular Ding-Dong Fight': Agency Culture and Evolution in the NPS-USFS Dispute, 1916–1937," *Western Historical Quarterly* 20, no. 2 (May 1989): 141–61; and in Douglas Strong, *Dreamers and Defenders* (Lincoln: University of Nebraska Press, 1988), 61–133.

10. Lary Dilsaver, "Land-Use Conflict in the Kings River Canyons," *California Geographer* 26 (1986): 59–80.

11. Strong, "History of Sequoia," 193–292.

12. Strong, "History of Sequoia," 193–292; Daniel J. Tobin, "A Brief History of Se-

quoia National Park," unpublished manuscript in Sequoia National Park Library [1941?]; Willard Van Name, "A Menace to the National Parks," *Science* 56 (22 December 1922): 705–7.

13. Dilsaver, "Land-Use Conflict."

14. Lary Dilsaver, "Conservation Conflict and the Founding of Kings Canyon National Park," *California History* 69 (Summer 1990): 196–205.

15. For the stories of the later Kings Canyon and Mineral King additions, see, respectively, Lary Dilsaver and William Tweed, *Challenge of the Big Trees: A Resource History of Sequoia and Kings Canyon National Parks* (Three Rivers, Calif.: Sequoia Natural History Association, 1990), 237–40; and John L. Harper, *Mineral King: Public Concern with Government Policy* (Arcata, Calif.: Pacifica, 1982).

16. Runte, *National Parks*, 82–105; Allen Chamberlain, "Scenery as a National Asset," *Outlook* 95 (28 May 1910): 169.

17. John White to Howard Hays, 1 December 1933, Sequoia National Park Archives, filed chronologically under "Roads and Trails."

18. Dilsaver and Tweed, *Challenge of the Big Trees*, 128–32.

19. Dilsaver and Tweed, *Challenge of the Big Trees*, 182–85.

20. Rick Hydrick, "The Genesis of National Park Management: John Roberts White and Sequoia National Park, 1920–1947," *Journal of Forest History* 28 (April 1984): 75.

21. "Proposed Road over Kearsarge Pass Opposed by Sierra Club," *Sierra Club Bulletin* 29 (June 1944): 2; Dilsaver and Tweed, *Challenge of the Big Trees*, 218–19.

22. John White, "Atmosphere in the National Parks" (address at the Special Superintendent's Meeting, Washington, D.C., 10 February 1936), transcript in Sequoia National Park Library.

23. See "Annual Backcountry Report," Sequoia and Kings Canyon National Park (1971), 9–10.

24. Public Law 88-577, 88th Cong. (3 September 1964).

25. Dilsaver and Tweed, *Challenge of the Big Trees*, 275–78.

26. Public Law 98-425, 98th Cong. (28 September 1984).

27. White, "Atmosphere in the National Parks."

28. Lowell Sumner, "Biological Research and Management in the National Park Service: A History," *George Wright Forum* 10 (Autumn 1983): 3–27.

29. Stanley Cain et al., "A Vignette of Primitive America," *Sierra Club Bulletin* 48 (March 1963): 2–11. A letter from Secretary of the Interior Stewart Udall is also printed with the report.

30. Sumner, "Biological Research and Management."

31. Sequoia–Kings Canyon National Parks (SNP hereafter), "Backcountry Management Plan" (1973).

32. Paul Fodor, Sierra District Ranger, SNP, interview with author, Sequoia National Park, Calif., 10 December 1990.

33. John Rutter and Bruce Black, "Backcountry Use Report, Sequoia and Kings Canyon National Parks," SNP (February 1953); Carl Sharsmith, "A Report on the Status, Changes and Ecology of Back Country Meadows in Sequoia and Kings Canyon National Parks" (San Francisco: National Park Service Western Region, 1959).

34. William Tweed, Management Assistant, SNP, interview with author, Sequoia National Park, 23 June 1990; SNP, "Stock Use Management Plan" (February 1986).

35. Paul Fodor, Sierra District Ranger, SNP, telephone interview with author, 4 March 1991.

The Mountain-Valley Interface

Clearly, the Mountainous West is a special kind of place, sharing a unique set of physical, economic, and political attributes. Ultimately, however, we are not well served by isolating this subregion of the West or by denying its interplay with the nearby lowlands. Indeed, many western pioneers in the past century settled in valley locales and established strong ties to nearby mountain environments. The final four essays sample disparate valley settings across the West and explore the ways in which the historical geographies of these places are linked to the resources of the nearby mountains.

The Sierra Nevada serve as the setting for two assessments of the mountain-valley interface. Robert Sauder skillfully integrates the themes of the Mountainous West with the evolution of the Owens Valley, just east of the Sierra crest. He shows how the water, minerals, and isolation associated with the presence of surrounding mountains fundamentally shaped the human landscape and evolving spatial systems of the Owens Valley region. Combining an intimate knowledge of land records and local landscapes, Sauder traces the evolution of Owens Valley settlement, including the tensions which grew between local residents and thirsty Los Angelenos to the south. Ultimately, Sauder recounts how nature and the isolation of the small population of the valley conspired to deprive local residents of the resources or the political clout necessary to establish a prospering agricultural economy.

To the north, the Tahoe Basin serves as the focus for John James's overview of the Sierra Nevada region. After an initial survey of how the themes of the Mountainous West aid in understanding the Sierra, James focuses on the settlement and development of the pivotal Tahoe Basin region. Although the basin itself escaped the worst of the mining rushes, its nearby slopes were tapped for huge supplies of lumber to sustain nearby mining towns, both to the east and the west. He then chronicles the consequences of the basin's accessibility to the growing millions of Californians in search of a mountain playground. This theme emerged as a dominant issue after World War II as all-season use of the basin and its resources expanded. James completes his review with an assessment of the challenges of managing and planning in a highland basin that includes two separate state bureaucracies as well as a multiplicity of local government agencies. Growing problems of pollution, traffic congestion, and persisting drought are among the challenges facing modern-day residents of the region.

John Dietz and Albert Larson offer another look at an interior mountain-ringed basin in their review of southern Colorado's San Luis Valley. Calling the region a microcosm of the Mountainous West, Dietz and Larson reconstruct the varied sequence of settlement and utilization of the region, illustrating how valley residents have always been intimately tied to the San Juan and Sangre de Cristo Ranges on the west and east. Early Hispanic residents harnessed mountain streams for their irrigation ditches and grazed their livestock on nearby mountain slopes. Anglos flocked to the region in search of concentrated precious metals in the high country as well as lowland farm acreage, and their supply lines and migration routes etched enduring spatial patterns across the valley. Finally, the authors note the increasing role of the region as a restorative sanctuary: a heritage of isolated Mormon settlements has been augmented by a growing flow of tourists, retirees, and New Age colonists intent on finding the good life among the Rockies. As we have seen elsewhere, the values of these newcomers often clash sharply with the more traditional resource users of the valley environment.

Mormon colonization moves to center stage in Jeanne Kay's interpretation of Utah's settlement geography. Kay reviews each of the five themes of the Mountainous West and demonstrates how the Mormons constantly integrated their valley settlements with the nearby mountains. Kay emphasizes female views of the settlement process, and her humanistic approach offers fresh insights on the significance of western mountains in the daily lives of those who lived in their midst as well as on their margins. In a similar vein, she concludes her essay with a broad consideration of the theological, metaphorical, and psychological roles that mountains played for Mormon men and women.

11 / Mountains and Lowlands: Human Adaptation in the Owens Valley

ROBERT A. SAUDER

The fragmented topography of the Mountainous West underscores a dualism between mountains and lowlands, and the utilization of these contrasting landscapes resulted from the development of a symbiotic relationship between the two. Located in the ranges of the West were precious minerals, the exploitation of which required settlement of adjacent lowland districts. The successful colonization of the arid lowlands, in turn, depended upon an adequate water supply to support agriculture, and it was the snow-fed streams of nearby mountains that made settlement of the lowlands possible.

Because of this reciprocal relationship between mountains and lowlands, the West's fragmented landscape led to the evolution of a patchwork of detached frontiers that were isolated from each other, as well as from larger centers of population on the region's periphery, thus hindering their sustained development. The ranges of the West, therefore, were areas of *concentrated resources* to be exploited, as well as *islands of moisture* upon which lowland settlement would depend, but they also were *barriers to interaction* among the emerging centers of population in the region. One frontier illustrating these three themes was Owens Valley, located in east-central California in the shadow of the Sierra Nevada. Owens Valley represents one of the oldest frontier communities to develop outside the communal Mormon realm in the arid West, and many of the processes and patterns of human adjustment that evolved in this valley were repeated throughout much of the Mountainous West. This chapter examines the frontier experience in Owens Valley in order to illuminate the significant role that mountains played in shaping settlement in adjacent lowland districts of the Mountainous West.

Owens Valley:
The Intermountain Setting

Owens Valley, situated between the glaciated peaks of the Sierra Nevada and the drier landscape of the Inyo-White Mountains, lies on the western margin of the Great Basin (figure 1). It is a region of outstanding natural beauty. Bounded on the west by the Sierra escarpment, with a crest averaging 12,500 feet and culminating in Mt. Whitney at 14,495 feet, and on the east by the Inyo-White Range, averaging 10,000 feet, the valley's topographic relief is matched by few other places in the Mountainous West.

As the adjacent mountain blocks rose, and as the valley floor subsided, volcanic vents and fissures poured out large amounts of lava and pyroclastic debris, much of which now lies buried beneath thousands of feet of valley fill. Volcanic eruptions have continued until recent time in areas north of Bishop and south of Big Pine. Approximately one million years ago a series of ash flows filled the north end of Owens Valley, forming a rhyolitic volcanic tableland (figure 1). More recent volcanic activity has occurred along the margins of Owens Valley south of Big Pine, where a conspicuous volcanic field of cinder cones and basalt has formed. With the exception of these recent volcanic deposits, the flatness of the valley floor is interrupted only by three groups of hills—Tungsten, Poverty, and Alabama Hills—each projecting as a knob of bedrock above the valley fill.

The west face of the Inyo-White Range is striking in its nearly linear trend, while northwest of Bishop the Sierra front is offset about eight miles to the west, forming Round Valley, a branch of the main valley. Owens Valley reaches its greatest width and highest elevation in the Round Valley–Bishop region. From the margin of the volcanic tableland in Round Valley, to the dry bed of Owens Lake, the elevation of the valley floor descends from 4,800 feet to 3,600 feet along a distance of approximately seventy-five miles. The Owens River drains the entire Owens Valley depression. Rising in the Sierra Nevada in Mono County to the north, the river emerges from a gorge that it has carved into the volcanic tableland and, following the general tilt of the land, flows eastward along the southern edge of lava. Northwest of Laws, the Owens River bends to the south and hugs the east side of the valley for most of its distance, originally emptying into the Owens Lake depression. Later, the Los Angeles Aqueduct was constructed to divert the surplus flow of the river to the growing metropolis to the south. Numerous

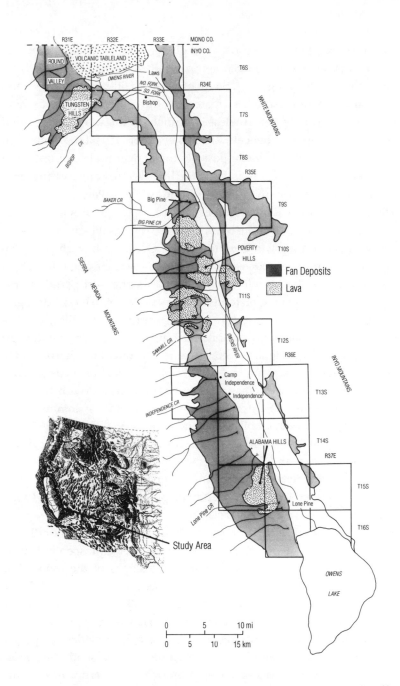

1. The Intermountain Setting of Owens Valley (Source: Erwin Raisz, "Landforms of the United States," inset map, reprinted with permission).

perennial creeks, fed by the snows and glaciers of the Sierra, flow out of their canyons, across the alluvial apron which they have deposited, toward the Owens River (figure 1). South of Poverty Hills, many of the Sierra streams sink into the loose detrital material of the valley fill before reaching the Owens River; they nevertheless contribute to the vast underground water reservoir housed beneath the valley floor. It is these snow-fed streams of the Sierra that made possible the agricultural colonization of Owens Valley, for the streams draining the Inyo-White Range are intermittent and convey little runoff from the east side of the valley.

The Sierra Nevada Range, however, also casts a rain shadow over Owens Valley, and much of the Mountainous West, as it captures and depletes moisture-bearing winds off the Pacific Ocean. Although precipitation is variable from year to year, Owens Valley averages only five to six inches annually and is therefore deserving of its title—"the land of little rain."[1] The aridity of the region tends to limit vegetation to hardy, drought-resistant plants, but subterranean conditions in Owens Valley, as elsewhere in the Mountainous West, influence surface biotic communities. At the base of the alluvial slopes where streams flow out of the Sierra, and in the Owens Valley floodplain, the water table is forced near the surface, causing marshes and wet grasslands to be interspersed with the more ubiquitous drought-resistant desert scrub communities dominated by sagebrush, grease wood, rabbit brush, and bunch grass. The Owens Valley Paiute, the region's native inhabitants, subsisted off a variety of desert scrub and grass seeds and the roots of tubers found in the marshes and wet grasslands.[2] At higher elevations on the mountain slopes facing Owens Valley, woodland predominates; the pinyon pines of the Inyo-White Range provided an additional aboriginal staple.

Soils in Owens Valley are the result of the decomposition of the adjacent mountains; those on the Sierra side have been derived almost entirely from granitic material, while those adjacent to the slopes of the Inyo-White Range have resulted from the weathering of sedimentary material. Much of the Round Valley–Bishop region is characterized by recent, relatively fertile, alluvial deposits where the water-laden Sierra streams spread out over the valley floor. Streams draining the Sierra are more widely dispersed south of Poverty Hills, and soils therefore tend to be sandy and more poorly watered, as well as more alkali prone. The northern valley's abundant stream flow, lush green meadows, and fertile, alkali-free soils were features quickly identified by the valley's pioneer settlers.

Zones of Concentrated Resources

Although the mountains adjacent to Owens Valley supplied an important resource which was harvested by its aboriginal population during their seasonal round of activities, it was precious metals, gold and silver embedded in the nearby mountain slopes, that stimulated white settlement of the valley. Because of Owens Valley's distance from major overland immigrant routes into California, the region was largely unaffected by the California gold rush of 1849. But a decade later, when the mines of the Mother Lode began to play out, prospectors searching for new veins of ore abandoned the Sierra Nevada for the ranges of the western Great Basin. Gold and silver discoveries at Monoville in 1859 and Aurora in 1860, both located north of Owens Valley, quickly transformed the valley into a "thoroughfare" to the new mining settlements of the eastern Sierra.[3] Cattle ranchers from the southern San Joaquin Valley and the Tejon country of Southern California, responding to the demand for food in these mining centers, launched cattle drives over Walker Pass and into Owens Valley on their trek to the booming markets. After discovering the fine grazing possibilities in Owens Valley, some stockmen decided to avoid the long drives by locating stock ranches in the valley. In August 1861, Samuel Bishop, with a herd of five hundred to six hundred head of cattle, established the first stock ranch in Owens Valley.[4] Bishop's ranch was located about three miles southwest of the town that today bears his name.

By the fall of 1861, nearly a dozen ranches were operating in the valley.[5] Cattle grazing on the natural meadows destroyed seeds and roots of native plants that were the staples of aboriginal subsistence. The increased lumbering in the adjacent mountains, to supply the nearby mines, also depleted the pinyon forests upon which the Owens Valley Paiute depended as a source of winter food. Faced with no other choice for survival, the Indians began to prey on the cattle of pioneer settlers. Early in 1862, Colonel George Evans of the First Infantry of California Volunteers was sent to Owens Valley to study the Indian situation. He reported that the Indians were determined to carry out their threat that no whites should live in the valley, but it was his belief that "The mining interests [of the region] are too great for the whites to give . . . up lamely."[6] Evans noted that the Indians would agree to allow whites to pass through the valley to and from Aurora, and that whites could locate in the mountains and work the mines, but that they could not settle permanently in the valley. Yet Evans insisted that "the mines will be of small value unless the valley can be settled and grain and vegetables grown and beef raised to feed the miners with."[7] Evans was persuasive, for his report led to the establishment of a military garrison, Camp Independence, in Owens Valley in July 1862, and within a year the Indian population was largely subdued.

Clashes between whites and Indians caused mining activity in the immediate vicinity of Owens Valley to progress slowly. With the cessation of Indian hostilities, several mining centers appeared on the east side of the valley near the mines of the Inyo-White Range. All were short-lived centers of activity, however, quickly abandoned in favor of the more permanent agricultural settlements that subsequently emerged on the valley's west side.

It was not until 1865, with the discovery of the rich Cerro Gordo silver mines in the Inyo Mountains east of Owens Lake, that a substantial economic base developed in the immediate vicinity of Owens Valley. Mining activity farther north was now on the wane, and interest began to focus on the Owens Valley region. By this time, a more permanent class of settlers was arriving in the valley, and the pioneers began to push for the initiation of local civil government. The formation of mining districts in the early 1860s had brought rudimentary administration to the region, but the valley's growing population now warranted the establishment of local county government. In March 1866, Inyo County was carved out of what had been the "shadowy jurisdiction" of Tulare County, and the town of Independence was selected to be its county seat.[8] It was therefore the resources contained in the mountain slopes of the western Great Basin and the onset of mining in the Owens Valley region that led to the expropriation of Indian lands, the establishment of an economic motive for the agricultural colonization of this isolated arid valley, and the formation of local civil government. This same process was repeated in many settlement frontiers scattered throughout the Mountainous West.

Islands of Moisture

Although the valuable minerals found in the nearby mountains inspired white settlement of Owens Valley, it was the prolific flow of the snow-fed streams of the Sierra that made permanent settlement possible and that shaped the early patterns of occupance in the valley. Similarly, the higher mountain peaks, representing islands of moisture in a vast sea of aridity, made the development of irrigated agriculture feasible across the Mountainous West, giving rise to its fragmented pattern of irrigation and settlement (figure 2).

The first irrigators in Owens Valley were not its pioneer settlers, but instead were the Owens Valley Paiute. To enhance the natural bounty of the land, the Indians diverted many of the streams flowing off the Sierra to the natural meadows found at the edge of the valley floor. They built temporary dams of boulders, sagebrush, and earth across these streams; then they cut shallow ditches to divert water toward the more prolific wild food species, particularly yellow nut grass. These irrigated plots occurred at ten different sites along the west side of Owens Valley; they were most numerous in the better watered north end of the valley. The Indians did not till, plant, or cultivate the land, "but cleverly watched how nature waters the grasses and bulbs, then followed suit."[9] They intensified by irrigation what nature had already provided, and although the Owens Valley Paiute were probably on the verge of horticulture at the time that white settlement of the valley began, they had not quite achieved it.[10]

The first detailed account of Owens Valley was provided in 1855–56 by A. W. Von Schmidt who, under contract with the federal government, conducted the first public land survey of Owens Valley. Von Schmidt's field notes reveal a close correlation between the prevalence of well-watered areas of "fine grass" and what he classified as first-rate soils.[11] During the course of his survey, Von Schmidt made several references to the fields of nut grass under irrigation by the Indians. In fact, these were the only areas that seemed to impress him as having any agricultural value, for he believed most of Owens Valley to be of little use to white settlers.

Three years later a more glowing account of Owens Valley was provided by Captain J. W. Davidson, who had been sent into the valley to investigate charges that the local Indians were rustling horses from other regions of California. After determining that the Owens Valley Paiute were not responsible for the stolen horses, Davidson turned his attention to a detailed examination of the valley's geography and its native inhabitants. Davidson traversed Owens Valley from south to north and, after completing his mission, described the valley as some of the finest country he had ever seen: "a vast meadow, watered every few miles with clear, cold mountain streams, and the grass (although in August) as green as in the first of spring."[12] A popular version of Davidson's journey appeared in the Los Angeles Star in August 1859, and it was the snow-fed streams of the Sierra upon which the article's attention focused: "Beautiful streams of clear cold water come gushing fresh from the snows of the Sierra, at intervals of from one to ten

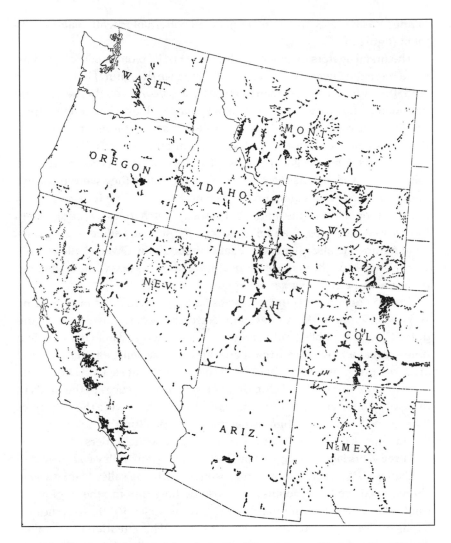

2. *Distribution of Irrigated Lands in the Mountainous West in 1899 (Source: Twelfth Census of the United States Taken in the Year 1900: Agriculture—Part II, Crops and Irrigation, Washington, D.C., 1900, 802).*

miles, irrigating beautiful and fertile portions of the valley."[13] Because of the prolific lateral stream flow, Davidson believed Owens Valley to be "the finest watered portion of the lower half of the state."[14]

Although Davidson's account of the natural conditions of Owens Valley might have been exaggerated somewhat, the abundance of water flowing from the Sierra and the lush green meadows which the streams nourished on the western edge of the valley floor also impressed early settlers. Among the first land locations of record in Owens Valley were its four major townsites—Lone Pine, Independence, Big Pine, and Bishop—all found near important tributary streams descending the east slope of the Sierra and, excepting Lone Pine, all located on old irrigated fields of the Indians. Each of these communities grew in response to the addition of new settlers locating on the fertile land surrounding them. The pattern of patented land entries which emerged by the end of 1876 illustrates the preference of early settlers for isolated locations on the Sierra side of the valley (figure 3). The perennial creeks cascading off the Sierra account for this lopsided settlement pattern, remnants of which are still apparent in the present-day landscape (figure 4).

Adjacent mountains provided the lifeblood for settlement of Owens Valley, and the foremost concern of early pioneers was the ease with which the Sierra streams could be diverted to their newly planted fields. Borrowing from the custom developed by miners in the western mountains regarding the use of water, Owens Valley settlers adopted the doctrine of appropriation, or the right to appropriate water on the public domain. After determining their source of irrigation water, pioneers posted and recorded notices indicating the location of stream diversion, the amount of water claimed, and the place and purpose of intended use. In accordance with this doctrine, the first person to come to a stream and claim its flow had priority to exploit it, making it a form of personal property; over time, a seniority system developed of which the basic principal was "first in time, first in right." Unlike the riparian doctrine adopted by more humid eastern states, where water could legally be used only on land bordering a stream, prior appropriation rights allowed the appropriator to divert water in a stream to any location so long as it was put to beneficial use. Early settlers, after recording their water claims in one of Owens Valley's lateral streams, then ran small diversion ditches out of the stream to their land holdings. The imprint of human activity in the West Bishop region highlights this historical relationship between lateral stream flow and settlement in the valley (figure 5).

By the late 1870s, most of the lateral stream flow in Owens Valley had been appropriated; in an attempt to promote the extension of larger irrigation canals, the *Inyo Independent*, at the time the valley's only newspaper, reported that "all the available water . . . afforded by numerous lateral streams of pure mountain water, is now under claim."[15] There was still

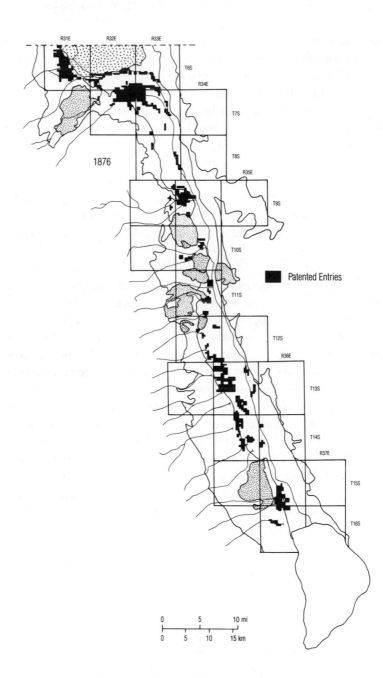

R31E   R32E   R33E

T6S

R34E

T7S

T8S

1876

R35E

T9S

T10S

T11S

■ Patented Entries

T12S

R36E

T13S

T14S

R37E

T15S

T16S

0   5   10 mi
|———|———|———|
0   5   10   15 km

3. Patented Land Entries in Owens Valley through 1876 (Source: Independence District Land Office Tract Books).

4. *An Owens Valley Alfalfa Ranch at the Base of the Sierra Nevada with Sawmill Creek in the Background. (Photo by the author.).*

5. *Aerial Photo of the West Bishop Region Reflecting the Interrelationship between Lateral Stream Flow and Settlement. (Courtesy U.S. Department of the Interior, Bureau of Land Management.)*

abundant land and water available for irrigation in Owens Valley, but to irrigate dry tracts distant from the Sierra streams would require the more difficult diversion of the valley's major stream—the Owens River. The smaller streams flowing off the Sierra could be distributed by individual effort, but to turn out larger streams such as the Owens River required either cooperative labor or aggregated capital.

The timely approval of the Desert Land Act in 1877 resulted in the projection of a number of irrigation canals in Owens Valley, all fed by the Owens River.[16] The Desert Land Act allowed for the entry of one full section (640 acres) of irrigable land with payment of twenty-five cents per acre at the time of entry, and the balance of one dollar per acre due three years later, after showing proof that at least a portion of the parcel had been brought under irrigation. Although the Desert Land Act made no provision for reclamation of arid lands except by individual effort, most of the larger canals in Owens Valley were nevertheless constructed on a cooperative basis. When ditch companies were formed and often incorporated, farmers purchased shares of stock in them, with each share carrying the right for use of a designated amount of water. Farmers themselves constructed the canals during the winter season. Members of the cooperative associations therefore paid their assessments with their own labor.

Most of these partnerships built comparatively small ditches which irrigated only the lowlands, while the higher alluvial slopes remained unwatered. The valley's earliest canals appeared in the Bishop region, and by 1885 seven ditches conducted Owens River water to the arid lands of the valley floor.[17] A slow increase in patented desert land entries followed the gradual extension of irrigation ditches in the valley's north end. Then, in the summer of 1886, there began a genuine rush for Owens Valley's unclaimed public land.[18] Two widely separated irrigation enterprises were largely responsible for influencing this intensified pattern of desert land locations in Owens Valley. In the north, the Owens River Canal served the vacant lands to the west and southwest of Bishop. It was similar to all the others, with its construction involving cooperative effort by local farmers. In the southern townships, construction was begun on the Eastside Canal by Nevada capitalists. It watered the vacant tracts along the east side of the river from the vicinity of Independence southward. The alignment of both canals crossed large tracts of unclaimed desert land, and nonresident entrymen were speculating on the increased values that would result from the extension of irrigation works near their desert land locations.

By 1901, water from the Owens River was diverted through seventeen main ditches and canals, as well as some smaller ones, totaling nearly two hundred miles in length.[19] Most ditches and canals were located in the north end of Owens Valley, and in this region they had a significant influence on the progress of settlement. Here, where a relatively dense pattern of early settlement arose from a natural water supply which could be easily diverted for farming, significant numbers of farmers could join together later to construct cooperative irrigation canals, and settlement could therefore progress.[20] But in the south half of Owens Valley, where population concentrations were initially restricted by less abundant water resources, irrigation developments were much less impressive. Mountains are not uniformly generous as moisture-bearing islands, and the more widely dispersed nature of the valley's southern lateral streams, and their less copious flow, meant that the development of local cooperative irrigation efforts that could tap the flow of the Owens River were hampered. The agricultural colonization of the southern valley lagged far behind that of the north largely because of this important geographical factor.

But the valley's north-end streams, when improperly applied to the land, also brought severe environmental damage in their wake. Ironically, despite the continued expansion of irrigation works and associated increased production in Owens Valley during the 1890s, the amount of irrigated acreage in the valley actually declined by 11 percent during the last decade of the nineteenth century.[21] Apparently as new lands were brought into cultivation, older lands that had been continuously cultivated for many years were simultaneously taken out of production. The principal problem involved the methods used by Owens Valley farmers to irrigate their crops, methods nearly as primitive as those of the earlier Indians. Irrigation in Owens Valley simply involved flowing water downslope from field ditches without control checks or levees. In the early 1900s, one observer noted: "the great majority of farmers in the valley are very lax in their methods. They have taken no special pains to level their land, but irrigate by a system of flooding which over-irrigates in some spots while other spots in the same field may not be touched. In many instances whole fields had been turned into quagmires, and are unfit for anything but grazing purposes."[22] Not only was too much water voluntarily applied to the fields, but the method of distribution was also wasteful, as seepage from the numerous unlined irrigation ditches was substantial.

By the turn of the twentieth century, the north half of Owens Valley was literally drowning in an overabundance of water: thousands of acres once covered by meadow grass and sagebrush and later brought into production through irrigation had now become too wet for use.[23] Owens Valley's naturally poor drainage was aggravated by years of overirrigation from unlined canals constructed across porous soils. And without storage facilities, water for domestic and livestock purposes required a continuous flow throughout the year, preventing the water table from receding during the winter months. But most importantly, the farmers of the valley had not altered their habit of profligate irrigation. As in previous years, an abnormal supply of water for irrigation continued to be used on fields that had never undergone preliminary grading or leveling. According to one survey of agricultural conditions in the valley: "The duty of water is something of which the average farmer in this section knows little—or cares less. Few attempts are made at water measurement or gauging the amount necessary for various soils and crops."[24] The efficiency of agricultural water use among the farmers diverting water from Bishop Creek at the time was estimated to be about 20 percent.[25] That is, less than one quarter of the water applied to the soil sustained crop growth, while the remainder was lost to seepage and evaporation. Hence, although the mountains of the West provided the moisture upon which irrigated agriculture depended, the stream flow had to be properly handled; otherwise, severe environmental problems could result.

Barriers to Interaction

Patterns of settlement that evolved in Owens Valley were influenced by differences in environmental conditions from north to south, as well as by its isolation from the principal nuclei of development in the Far West. The Sierra Nevada represented a formidable barrier between Owens Valley and California's San Joaquin Valley and Pacific Coast settlements, for the mountains could not be easily crossed in the near vicinity of the valley. For those who first settled in Owens Valley, and others who followed, the most immediate obstacle to be overcome was how to transform such an isolated region into a working economy.[26] Essentially, the frontier community that evolved within this narrow trough relied on supplying provisions and services to Cerro Gordo and other mining centers in the western Great Basin. Initially these mining centers created a demand that far exceeded supply. This was the stimulus that encouraged Owens Valley farmers to prevail over the region's harsh arid geography, and that inspired them to carve out permanent communities on the valley floor. But the Sierra Nevada barrier, which severed Owens Valley from much of the rest of California, was a geographical handicap that local residents would never be able to surmount.

In the late 1860s and early 1870s, new mining centers were continually opening in Inyo County, thereby expanding the demand for Owens Valley produce. While most surplus commercial crop and livestock production found its way to nearby booming mining districts, a local market also developed within the valley's emerging agricultural service communities. Provisions from the outside were difficult to secure in this isolated frontier, and residents therefore traded heavily among themselves. Owens Valley's initial prosperity was short-lived, however, for by 1877 a dramatic decline in the price of silver caused a significant downturn in mining activity. The handicap of the valley's isolation had resulted in almost total reliance on nearby markets with boom-or-bust fluctuations. The region's mining bust precipitated an aggravated economic slump in Owens Valley. In May 1877, the *Inyo Independent* reported that "[agriculture] has reached its maximum—seen its best days till a railroad opens a new market."[27] The valley's natural outlet was Southern California, but only products of the mines could withstand teaming across more than one hundred miles of desert to the nearest railhead. Although a number of obstacles to settlement in Owens Valley had been overcome by the 1870s, the major impediment to the valley's sustained economic development, accessibility to Southern California and other expanding West Coast markets, remained unresolved.

Despite the progress of canal construction that had taken place in the north end of the valley by the turn of the twentieth century, the last two decades of the nineteenth century were characterized by a perpetuation of the same economic conditions that emerged in the late 1870s. With the collapse of the only market for the valley's surplus farm products, the nearby mines, Owens Valley languished in its isolation, falling far behind the agricultural districts located opposite the Sierra Nevada barrier. The primary obstacle to recovery was addressed with the initiation of service by the Carson and Colorado Railroad in the summer of 1883. It linked the valley to the outside world for the first time. But the new line was of little use in transporting grain and other products to the more settled regions of the West, and it therefore was met with little local fanfare.

Although the extension of the Carson and Colorado into Owens Valley was inspired by the region's mining activity, by the time it reached the valley the initial period of mining excitement in the region was largely over. The original intention of the builders of the Carson and Colorado was to connect Carson City with the Colorado River by rail, but the widespread economic depression of the 1880s forced the railroad to "dead-end" at Keeler (formerly Hawley) on the east shore of Owens Lake (figure 6). As with other narrow-gauge lines constructed in the Mountainous West, the function of the Carson and Colorado was to transport bulky freight over rugged terrain to the main-line railroads, then on to distant markets. To the north of Owens Valley, its rails were put down across the fragmented topography of the western Great Basin, finally skirting the western flank of

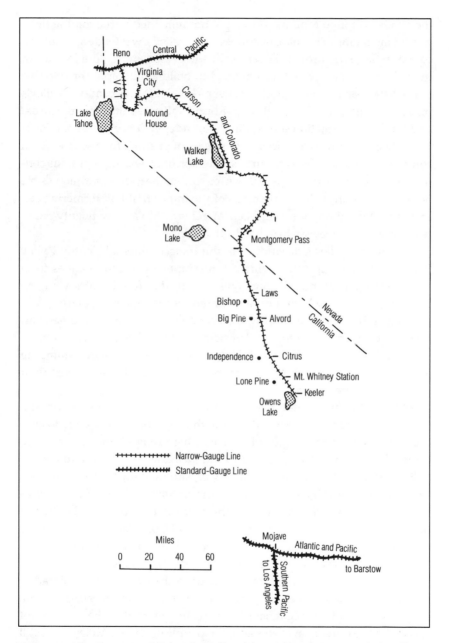

6. *Route of the Carson and Colorado Railroad from Mound House to Keeler, Showing Owens Valley Stations (Source: Adapted from David F. Myrick, Railroads of Nevada and Eastern California, vol. 1, 1962, Berkeley, Howell-North Books, 169).*

the White and Inyo Mountains to tap what remained of the mining business of the region. The route overlooked the valley's west-side agricultural communities, so in order to be served by the Carson and Colorado, each of the valley's permanent settlements had to build a rail depot three to five miles distant on the east side of the Owens River. Laws became the valley's principal station, serving the Bishop–Round Valley region; Alvord, Citrus, and Mt. Whitney Station served Big Pine, Independence, and Lone Pine, respectively (figure 6). Ironically, after years of pushing for a southern rail connection, the first line came in from the north, providing circuitous connections with the San Francisco Bay Area, rather than with more accessible Southern California. Many products of the mines that had formerly been carted to the rail depot serving Los Angeles at Mojave by twenty-mule-team wagons now began to move north by rail.

But Owens Valley's distance from the transcontinental Central Pacific Railroad at Reno, and the required transshipment of commodities from narrow-gauge to standard-gauge rails, meant that freight rates were exceedingly high—too high for the shipment of the majority of farm products out of the valley. The rail line did broaden the beef market somewhat, making it now possible to ship livestock to West Coast markets. Otherwise, the Carson and Colorado did little to stimulate the valley's slumping agricultural economy, as most farmers were still unable to market their crops outside the region.

Without the anticipated mining activity upon which the Carson and Colorado's livelihood depended, and with the inability of farmers to ship their produce out of the valley because of high freight rates, the railroad hoped that improved accessibility would facilitate immigration to Owens Valley. Most westward migrants, however, shunned the long and arduous side trip to Owens Valley. From the transcontinental line at Reno, a prospective settler would have to ride the Virginia and Truckee Railroad to Mound House to connect with the Carson and Colorado, then travel over 200 miles across sparsely populated desert terrain to reach the north end of the valley. From the south, the traveler faced a 120-mile stage trip, operating semiweekly, across the Mojave Desert to the Carson and Colorado's southern terminus at Keeler. The railroad, therefore, not only carried little freight traffic, but few passengers as well. Ten years after the initiation of service by the Carson and Colorado, the people of Owens Valley were still "pining" for a railroad connection with Los Angeles.[28]

Strapped by excessive freight rates to northern markets, Owens Valley farmers began to look to alternate forms of production, that is, to something that could profitably make the long journey out of the valley. Stock raising had always been a major activity, and with consumer demand for beef expanding, it took on increased importance, particularly since livestock was about the only commodity from Owens Valley that could withstand the cost of rail shipment to the West Coast. The inability to market grain and other products of general farming caused an outmigration of many of the valley's pioneer farmers, facilitating the absorption of their relatively small farm units into large cattle ranches. The southern region was better suited to stock raising because of its less abundant water resources and smaller number of irrigation canals compared to the north, and because of the much smaller home market for local produce.

The trend toward large livestock farms was not enthusiastically endorsed by the valley's newspapers, particularly in localities south of Big Pine where the process was most pronounced. The *Inyo Independent* in 1887 stated that "While it is very desirable to have capital invested in the county, yet if that capital is to be used in buying out small farmers in order to make big stock ranches, we would be better without it than with it."[29] Reflecting on the high freight rates for shipping farm products out of the valley, the *Independent* recommended fruit production as an alternative to stock raising.[30] Although fruit, particularly apples and peaches, was of increasing importance, it had not expanded beyond the needs of local demand, and late spring frosts, a common occurrence in the valley, tended to hamper the development of this activity. The *Inyo Register*, the northern valley's newspaper published in Bishop, suggested that dairy farming could counteract the trend toward large stock ranches.[31] Dairying would subsequently become one of the leading enterprises in the north half of Owens Valley.

One Owens Valley farmer summarized the forces operating against the general farmer in the early 1890s: "It is almost impossible to export farm produce from the valley. Freight cost is a complete bar to that. The home market is so limited that but a small amount of produce can be consumed. What I expect for the future is, that as stockmen have lately been increasing their interests in the valley, this will grow till stock raising will be the only interest left of any importance, and the land will be owned mostly by stockmen."[32] This observation would ultimately prove true, at least for the southern half of the valley. Toward the end of the 1890s, little had changed in the region to counter the economic trends which had begun two decades earlier. In 1897, in its annual survey of California counties, the *San Francisco Chronicle* confirmed the ongoing difficulties in the valley: "Owing to its isolated location Inyo County has fallen far behind her sister counties in the marvelous development that has characterized California in the past ten years. [Because of] limited facilities for transportation, little grain is raised beyond that needed for home consumption, and that, indeed, is true of all agricultural products."[33] Again, early in the twentieth century, the *Chronicle* noted that there had been "no special movement in Inyo County . . . to call it directly to the attention of the outside world."[34]

In 1900, the Southern Pacific Railroad purchased the Carson and Colorado, which inspired new hope for a long-awaited southern extension to Mojave providing continuous rail service to Los Angeles. Southern rail service did not come, however, until a few years later and then as a by-product of the construction of the controversial Los Angeles Aqueduct. Instead, in the summer of 1900, a Nevada mining boom at Tonopah and Goldfield set the stage for a period of renewed development in the valley. The discoveries at Tonopah and Goldfield, both little more than one hundred miles distant from Bishop, opened a new and lucrative market for Owens Valley's farm products since the majority of the valley's surplus produce could now supply these two booming mining centers. Yet the valley continued to remain isolated from the rest of California because the long-anticipated extension of the Carson and Colorado Railroad to Mojave did not materialize until 1910. Geographically, the eastern Sierra was more closely tied to Nevada, and Owens Valley's population, although large enough to have played a significant role in Nevada affairs, was little considered in California's legislature.[35] According to the *Inyo Register*, Inyo County did not even have the honor of being a "California point" which a cross-country traveler at the time could reach for only $25.00. An additional fare of $18.95 was required at Reno for travel into the valley.[36] Owens Valley was located in what at the time was referred to as "undiscovered California."[37]

Owens Valley's isolation from the rest of California hampered its development in other ways as well, for without an ongoing infusion of new people and ideas, change was inhibited, and attitudes and methods of farming which originally were implanted in the region were perpetuated. In light of the provincial agricultural procedures used by valley farmers, the *Independent* at the turn of the century commented facetiously that a further advantage of a rail link to the south, besides the ability to market produce in Southern California, would be to "bring people here that in many ways would make the present residents wake-up to more modern ways of ranching."[38] The primitive techniques of irrigation employed by valley farmers are but one example of this backwardness. There are many others. By the early twentieth century, dairying had become the leading activity in the north half of the valley, yet Owens Valley cows produced only 53 percent as much milk as those elsewhere in the state.[39] A significant problem associated with dairying in Owens Valley involved the quality of the dairy herds, as many farmers were trying to develop what was jokingly referred to as an "all round cow" by crossing beef with dairy cattle.[40] Owens Valley dairying therefore remained a small-scale enterprise compared to other parts of the state.

Drainage was another serious problem that hindered the valley's development. By the early 1920s, it was estimated that 60 percent of the land in the Bishop region required drainage.[41] Although some farmers in the valley had attempted to undertake small-scale drainage, their efforts were impeded by the lack of satisfactory outlets for discharge. Only a large-scale coordinated system of drainage involving the entire community of farmers would bring about a general lowering of the water table. In 1917, two engineers from the U.S. Department of Agriculture were sent into Owens Valley to investigate the feasibility of such a system.[42] Their inquiry confirmed that drainage should be undertaken; in fact, it was revealed that Owens Valley had a greater need for drainage than any other region which they had examined to date.[43] The estimated cost for farmers living within the proposed drainage district averaged twenty dollars per acre, but by bonding the district, the cost could be paid back over a twenty-year period. To bear such a burden was difficult for valley farmers to accept, for the cost of originally diverting the water was small in comparison. Discussion of the drainage issue dragged on for months. Finally, early in 1919, the *Inyo Register* reported that there was "no special encouragement for hopes of adoption of a general [drainage] system."[44]

The engineers from the Department of Agriculture had warned that organization would prove to be the most difficult obstacle to the formation of a drainage district: "To accomplish results, it will be absolutely necessary for people to co-operate."[45] Because of the valley's isolation over the years, it had developed into a fortress of rural conservatism, characterized by antiquated methods and nonprogressive attitudes. The pioneer sense of individualism that was spawned at the time of settlement and which became firmly entrenched in the valley worked against such large-scale communal endeavors. Although the upper valley's irrigation canals were monuments to the cooperative efforts of its settlers, the farmers paid for the canals with their own labor, thereby keeping the canal enterprises free from indebtedness. Cooperative action was comparatively easy to arrange for canal construction since all cultivators were in need of a water supply. In contrast, cooperation was significantly more difficult to achieve in connection with drainage because all irrigated land did not become waterlogged simultaneously. The process was a gradual one, where the lower-lying lands suffered first. Since the irrigators in a district did not have equivalent and concurrent needs for drainage, many farmers did not understand, or appreciate, the value of a coordinated system. The formation of a drainage district was, therefore, a much more ambitious, and provident, endeavor—too farsighted to gain a consensus among a majority of farmers, and the idea was subsequently rejected.

A final example of the valley's inertia ultimately led to its downfall. Early in the twentieth century, the City of Los Angeles purchased land and water rights to the southern half of Owens Valley and, after completion of the Los Angeles Aqueduct, tapped the surplus flow of the Owens River. Although Los Angeles's control of surplus Owens River water would effectively foreclose options for future developments in the south half of the valley, the more intensively cultivated north end remained largely unaffected. But in order to avert a future buy-out of northern valley lands by Los Angeles, the *Inyo Register* in 1909 proposed the organization of an irrigation district in accordance with the provisions of the Wright Act of 1887.[46] This was essentially a protective measure which would prevent Los Angeles from acquiring irrigation ditch stock to the detriment of shareholders who would not favor selling. But the irrigation district concept was not taken up at the time because of lack of interest in the valley.

Ten years later, however, when the northern valley's way of life was more imminently threatened by Los Angeles, the irrigation district idea resurfaced. Due to a prolonged drought which plagued the entire southwest during the early 1920s, combined with the phenomenal expansion of Los Angeles, the city began to discuss ways of augmenting the aqueduct's flow. In the northern Owens Valley a growing sense of urgency to seek protection emerged. For three consecutive weeks early in 1920, the *Inyo Register* discussed the importance of organizing an irrigation district for the Bishop region, but the newspaper's advice fell upon deaf ears.[47] Organizing behind a common cause was alien to valley residents, as evidenced by their unwillingness to join together in the formation of a drainage district. A year and a half later the *Register* again broached the subject: "the formation of a[n] [irrigation] district . . . [is] the greatest step that can be taken in self defense."[48] But still no action was taken by valley residents. Finally, in an attempt to shake the valley out of its apathy, the *Register* published a front-page map showing the properties in Owens Valley owned by Los Angeles.[49] The map was used to reinforce the need for action, for it graphically revealed how the city's property extended unbroken from Owens Lake to a point just three sections southeast of Bishop. Yet even this was not enough to overcome the valley's ingrained disposition toward inaction.

Meanwhile, Los Angeles was becoming desperate for water, and in May of 1922, the city began purchasing water-bearing lands in the north end of Owens Valley. It was these land purchases that finally inspired the need for action on the irrigation district plan among valley residents. But by the time the district was formally organized under the laws of the state, Los Angeles had dismantled nearly half of the original area encompassed by the Owens Valley Irrigation District. The irrigation district was now so mutilated as to make its operation impracticable. Although the effort by Owens Valley residents to save their valley was sincere enough, it came too late to reverse the course that Los Angeles seemed determined to follow. The historic aversion of Owens Valley residents toward progressive action to further the region's development ultimately contributed to the demise of agriculture in the valley, for in the wake of the city's purchases, most of the valley's remaining productive farmland was quickly dried out and abandoned. Had Owens Valley been less isolated and more able to interact with other western regions, its residents might have been more responsive to new ideas, and the demise of agriculture and its associated lifestyle might have been prevented.

Conclusion

Patterns of human occupance in Owens Valley, and elsewhere in the dry, rugged West, were influenced by the region's mountainous topography. Gold and silver contained in the mountain ranges stimulated settlement of adjacent lowland districts, and it was the snow-fed streams of the mountains that made colonization of the lowlands possible. Borrowing the doctrine of prior appropriation from the western miners, small streams draining the mountain slopes were first diverted to newly planted fields. In those areas served by abundant lateral stream flow, sizeable settlement clusters developed, and small-scale cooperative irrigation endeavors were subsequently undertaken to divert larger streams into a more extensive network of canals, thereby expanding irrigated agriculture in the lowlands. But the mountain streams, if improperly handled, brought with them an environmental backlash. In time, primitive and profligate irrigation techniques employed by western farmers and seepage from unlined canals waterlogged the soils, creating a desperate need for large-scale co-ordinated drainage systems in the lowlands. Because of the conservative individualism that was spawned in the isolated frontiers of the Mountainous West, cooperative developments of this magnitude were difficult to accomplish.

The ranges of the Mountainous West, therefore, while both stimulating and facilitating permanent settlement in the region, also served as obstacles to interaction between people and places. The isolated nature of the emerging frontiers hampered both the diffusion and acceptance of new ideas and technologies, and their distance from large markets made them almost totally reliant on the boom-or-bust fluctuations of the nearby mines. Because of the mines, some emerging frontiers were eventually linked to the outside world by narrow-gauge railroads, but their distance from the main-line railroads, and the necessity of having to transship commodities from narrow- to standard-gauge lines, made freight rates too high for the shipment of the majority of farm products to larger markets. These factors tended to inhibit the sustained development of the detached frontiers of the Mountainous West. The Owens Valley experience illustrates that mountains as concentrated resources, as islands of moisture, and as barriers to interaction often played conflicting roles in shaping settlement in adjacent lowland districts.

Notes

1. Mary Austin, *The Land of Little Rain* (Boston: Houghton Mifflin, 1903).

2. Robert L. Bettinger, "Aboriginal Human Ecology in Owens Valley: Pre-historic Change in the Great Basin," *American Antiquity* 42 (January 1977): 5.

3. W. A. Chalfant, *The Story of Inyo* (Bishop, Calif.: Chalfant Press, 1933), 127.

4. Chalfant, *Story of Inyo*, 142.

5. Roger D. McGrath, *Gunfighters, Highwaymen and Vigilantes: Violence on the Frontier* (Berkeley: University of California Press, 1984), 17.

6. *Official Records of the Union Confederate Armies in the War of the Rebellion*, part 1, vol. 50 (Washington, D.C.: Government Printing Office, 1897), 49.

7. *Official Records*, 50.

8. Chalfant, *Story of Inyo*, 240.

9. Donald Worster, *Rivers of Empire: Water, Aridity and the Growth of the American West* (New York: Pantheon Books, 1985), 32.

10. Julian Steward, *Ethnography of the Owens Valley Paiute*, University of California Publications in American Archaeology and Ethnography, vol. 33 (Berkeley: University of California Press, 1933), 248.

11. Robert A. Sauder, "Sod Land Versus Sagebrush: Early Land Appraisal and Pioneer Settlement in an Arid Intermountain Frontier," *Journal of Historical Geography* 15 (October 1989): 407.

12. Philip J. Wilke and Harry W. Lawton, eds., *The Expedition of Capt. J. W. Davidson from Fort Tejon to the Owens Valley in 1859* (Socorro, N.M.: Ballena Press, 1976), 20.

13. Quoted in Wilke and Lawton, *Expedition of Capt. J. W. Davidson*, 33.

14. Quoted in Wilke and Lawton, *Expedition of Capt. J. W. Davidson*, 27.

15. "Owens River Valley," *Inyo Independent* (Independence, Calif.), 6 January 1877, 2.

16. Robert A. Sauder, "Patenting an Arid Frontier: Use and Abuse of the Public Land Laws in Owens Valley, California," *Annals of the Association of American Geographers* 79 (December 1989): 557.

17. "About Ditches," *Inyo Register*, (Bishop, Calif.), 14 April 1885, 3.

18. Sauder, "Patenting an Arid Frontier," 557.

19. "Inyo County, California," *Inyo Register*, 18 April 1901, 1.

20. Robert A. Sauder, "Powell's Vision of Arid Land Settlement Reexamined: Owens Valley, California," *Yearbook of the the Association of Pacific Coast Geographers* 52 (1990): 83.

21. U.S. Census Office, *Twelfth Census of the United States Taken in the Year 1900: Agriculture—Part II, Crops and Irrigation*, table IX (Washington, D.C.: Government Printing Office, 1902), 826.

22. J. S. Cotton, "Agricultural Conditions of Inyo County, California" (1905, typewritten), Eastern California Museum, Independence, Calif., 4.

23. J. C. Clausen, "Report of the Owens Valley, California" (November 1904, typewritten), Metropolitan Water District, Los Angeles, 17.

24. California Development Board, "Agricultural and Industrial Survey of Inyo County, Calif." (September 1917, typewritten), Eastern California Museum, Independence, Calif., 2 (Irrigation and Drainage).

25. William L. Kahrl, *Water and Power: The Conflict over Los Angeles' Water Supply in the Owens Valley* (Berkeley: University of California Press, 1982), 256.

26. Robert A. Sauder, "The Agricultural Colonization of a Great Basin Frontier: Economic Organization and Environmental Alteration in Owens Valley, California, 1860–1925," *Agricultural History* 64 (Fall 1990): 78–101.

27. "The Need of a Railroad to Our Farming Interest," *Inyo Independent*, 5 May 1877, 2.

28. "A Visitor's Estimate," *Inyo Register*, 6 June 1893, 3 (reprinted from the *Los Angeles Times*).

29. *Inyo Independent*, 30 July 1887, 2.

30. *Inyo Independent*, 11 July 1890, 2.

31. "As It Appears," *Inyo Register*, 28 January 1892, 2.

32. "What Farmers Say," *Inyo Independent*, 6 March 1891, 3.

33. Quoted in "A Truthful Statement," *Inyo Register*, 6 January 1898, 2.

34. Quoted in "A Review of the County," *Inyo Register*, 3 January 1901, 3.

35. *Inyo Register*, 12 January 1905, 2.

36. *Inyo Register*, 3 July 1902, 2; 31 July 1902, 2.

37. Joseph B. Lippincott, "The Reclamation Service in California," *Forestry and Irrigation* 10 (April 1904): 164.

38. "Railroad," *Inyo Independent*, 16 February 1900, 3.

39. "Make Dairying Pay," *Inyo Independent*, 28 January 1922, 1.

40. "Make Dairying Pay," 1.

41. Harold Conkling, "Report on Owens Valley Project, California" (U.S. Bureau of Reclamation, Department of the Interior, September 1921, typewritten), 26.

42. "Drainage of Lands Urged by Experts," *Inyo Register*, 22 March 1917, 1.

43. "Drainage of Lands," 1.

44. *Inyo Register*, 27 February 1919, 2.

45. "Drainage of Lands," 1.

46. "Irrigation District Proposed," *Inyo Register*, 8 July 1909, 2.

47. "Valley Welfare in Organizing District," *Inyo Register*, 19 February 1920, 1; "District Needed for Good of Valley," *Inyo Register*, 26 February 1920, 1; "District Needed by Irrigation Interests," *Inyo Register*, 4 March 1920, 1.

48. "What Has Become of the Irrigation District?" *Inyo Register*, 18 August 1921, 2.

49. *Inyo Register*, 26 August 1921, 1.

12 / Lake Tahoe and the Sierra Nevada

JOHN W. JAMES

The Sierra Nevada are one of the major mountain regions of western North America, stretching over 250 miles north-south near the eastern border of central California. The region merges on the north with the southern Cascades and with the Transverse Ranges on the south (figure 1). It is, with some variation, about 50 miles wide. Its spectacular landscape, in great contrast to the surrounding lowlands, makes the Sierra Nevada one of the most beautiful areas in the world. The year-round recreational facilities are a magnet to city dwellers from near and far. The region is also extremely important as a source of water and power for the fast-growing surrounding lowlands.

The Sierra Nevada are an excellent example of how the historical characteristics of the Mountainous West have sculpted the landscape. Although landform formation and the modifications made by ice and water have set the stage for the human impacts of the past 150 years, they are by no means the sole factors in today's geographic mountain scene. The pursuit of the region's concentrated mineral and timber resources has had an overwhelming influence on the present flavor of the landscape. In addition, more recent use of the region as a restorative sanctuary has accelerated the impact of tourism. This chapter summarizes the importance of the Sierra Nevada (1) as a barrier in the historical geography of the region, (2) as a traditional supplier of water (for domestic use, hydroelectrical power, and recreation) and of concentrated mining and timber resources, and (3) as an increasingly important sanctuary for modern civilization. Indeed, more than ever before, the Sierra conjures up the imagery of John Muir a century ago: "Climb the mountains and get their good tidings. Nature's peace will flow into you as sunshine flows into a tree. The winds will blow their own freshness into you, and the storms their energy, while cares will drop off like Autumn leaves."[1]

After a brief description of the overall Sierra Nevada, the unique Lake

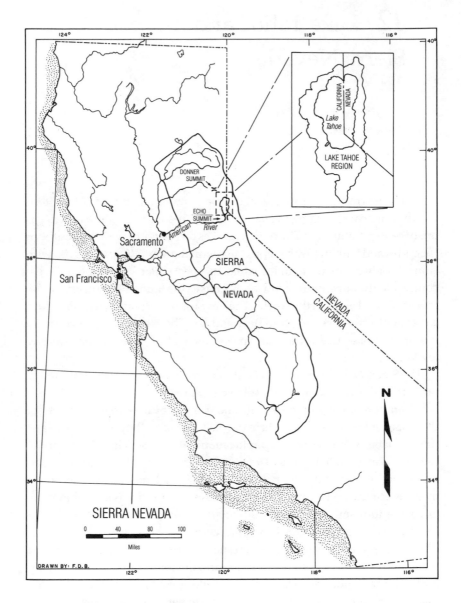

1. Map of California and Nevada Indicating Sierra Nevada, Lake Tahoe, and Other Prominent Points.

Tahoe Basin is examined to illustrate these major themes in greater detail. Tahoe is the largest and deepest alpine lake in North America, and it serves as a focus of tremendous population and recreational pressures that threaten the future of the entire region. Is it still a restorative sanctuary? Has development gone too far? Have water, air, and land resources been stretched to the limit? Can government planning cope with these issues? These and other concerns demonstrate the continuing reality of these mountain themes.

Physical Setting

Typical of the Mountainous West, it is the complex physical geography of the Sierra Nevada that forms a unique setting for subsequent human occupance and development. The range is a tilted fault block. A major fault zone bounds the block on the east, and it was along this zone that the range was uplifted and tilted westward so that its crest and high peaks are mostly located on the eastern edge of the mass. As the block was uplifted, the steep, east-facing escarpment was cut into by the erosive action of temperature, precipitation, wind, frost, and ice, and a series of steep-gradient canyons developed. Though the uplift started many millions of years ago, much of it occurred in the last two million years. A present-day relief of 10,000 to 11,000 feet along the eastern slopes in the southern portion of the range dramatizes the extent of the tremendous uplift.[2] The highest peaks in the Sierra are mostly in this southern portion of the range and vary in elevation from about 11, 000 to 14,000 feet above sea level, with Mt. Whitney (14,495 feet) the highest peak in the coterminous United States. Summits in the northern portion are much lower and average only 7,000 to 9,000 feet north of the Lake Tahoe Basin.

The more gentle west-facing slope has been dissected by several streams, much longer than those of the eastern slope. Such rivers as the Yuba, American, Mokelumne, Stanislaus, Merced, Kings, and Kern have carved deep valleys into the predominant granite and some volcanics. All but the Kern drain either into the Sacramento River in the north or into the San Joaquin River in the south, and ultimately into the combined delta of those two rivers and into the San Francisco Bay and the Pacific Ocean. The Kern River has internal drainage into Buena Vista Lake Basin, south of the San Joaquin River.

The Sierra also share the glacial history of the Mountainous West. During the Pleistocene ice ages, which started around 1 to 1.5 million years ago and ended in North America only about 10,000 years ago, the river-eroded valleys were covered several times by large alpine glaciers. Glacial climates became dominant at least four times, and each glacial period was characterized by deepening and advancing glaciers. The ice carved U-shaped valleys down to about the 5,000-foot level on the western slopes. So much ice existed in the high cirque areas near the Sierra crest that an ice cap was formed by the glaciers. This cap extended almost two hundred miles from Lake Tahoe to the southern high Sierra near Mt. Whitney.[3]

Finger-like valley glaciers extended from the cap. They were long on the more gentle western slopes, but shorter on the sharply uplifted eastern face. The glacial erosion that took place is spectacular, with large cirques and moraines and thousands of glacial lakes dotting the alpine and subalpine landscape. Such striking and beautiful landforms are the focus of Yosemite National Park and the Lake Tahoe Basin. The latter is a structural depression (graben) located between the main Sierra vertical fault block and the Carson Range "splinter" to the east. It filled with water from glacial meltdown and stream flow, reaching a depth of over 1,600 feet in its northwest corner. Due to its setting and elevation (from 6,200 feet at lake level up to 10,000 to 11,000 feet atop the higher peaks surrounding it), the basin has unique climatological and ecological features.

The climate of the Sierra Nevada is a creation of three interacting characteristics.[4] First, the circulation around and the subsidence and stability within the eastern Pacific Ocean anticyclone, which is strong in the summer and overlapping the West Coast, and weak in the winter and pulled away from the area, causes drought during the summer season, with precipitation confined mainly to the wintertime. Periods of several years of drought result when this eastern Pacific high-pressure area does not loosen its grip on the region during the winter half-year and when the mid-latitude jet stream storm track is weakened, split, or pushed to the north. Examples of these drought periods are the early to mid-1930s, the mid-1970s, and the mid-1980s to early 1990s.

Second, the latitudinal location of the Sierra (between 36 degrees and 40 degrees north latitude) and the location near the moderating waters of the Pacific Ocean make the range's climate unusually mild. Although below-zero readings are common in valley locations each winter, they are rare on mountain slopes. Also, daytime readings below freezing are not common, in contrast to the Rocky Mountains.[5]

The third interacting climate control is the northwest-southeast trend of the range, which puts it at nearly a right angle to the wintertime storm track. Accentuating the role of the range as an island of moisture in the region, this orientation makes for copious precipitation during the wet season (November–April) on the windward western slopes, but it has a sharp rain-shadow effect on the more sheltered leeward eastern face.[6] Precipitation averages from 30 inches in the foothill area to 70–80 inches at the 4,500- to 6,500-foot elevation in the northern half of the range, which is closest to the storm track. However, the leeward slopes are usually blocked from the heaviest precipitation, with 20–40 inches most common. Higher elevations receive the heaviest snowfall, with an average of 400–450 inches per year in the northern half of the Sierra Nevada. As much as 67 inches has fallen in one day at Echo Summit (5 January 1982), and 800 inches was measured at the 7,000-foot Donner Summit during the winter of 1982–83, with heavier amounts higher up.[7] Snowpacks of 10–15 feet are not uncommon above the 7,000-foot elevation.

As is the case across the Mountainous West, vegetation in the Sierra Nevada is a reflection of climate, slope, elevation, and aspect. Generally speaking, there are five rather distinct zones on the western slopes. From the lower elevations upward they include the lower foothills, upper foothills, montane forests, subalpine forests, and alpine tundra. On the steep and short eastern slopes, four less distinct zones exist: sagebrush/bitterbrush, sagebrush/forest transition, subalpine, and alpine zones are typical of the region.[8] Chaparral, a shrub-like assemblage of broadleaf evergreen shrubs, dominated by chamise, scrub oak, manzanita, and ceonothus, grows in all but the alpine zones on both sides of the range. Chaparral is best developed, however, in the foothill and lower-montane zones as a result of natural and human-caused fires in which the plants involved thrive at the expense of larger woody vegetation. Timber operations, mining, grazing, and vacation/tourism developments have also materially changed the natural vegetation in many locations.

Sierra Overview: Settlement and Use

Several aboriginal tribes lived in the Sierra Nevada before the first European contact with the region. They had little permanent effect on the landscape other than locally through fires set to catch game. The 1700s brought explorers and Spanish missionaries to Alta California. However, their impact on the Sierra was also negligible. In the early 1800s, fur trappers made their way through the region, with such familiar western names as Jedediah Smith and Joseph Walker seeking the game resources concentrated in the mountain range, again with little impact and little record of what they did.

The mid-1800s suddenly brought an end to the pristine serenity of the Sierra Nevada as miners permanently changed the landscape and stamped their imprint on the Sierra. The discovery of gold nuggets in January 1848 at Coloma (near present-day Placerville) began a gold rush from all over the world that was to have great significance in the historical evolution of not only California but the United States as well. It was a classic example of how the development of concentrated resources in the Mountainous West produced sudden and unprecedented changes. By 1850 there were about 50,000 miners in the range. This boom contributed to rapid regional economic development, as banks, retail stores, transport facilities, lumbering, farming, and industry all began in response to the needs of the ever-growing population. This, plus the money generated by mining activity, also hastened statehood for both Nevada and California and spurred the growth of the first urban centers, such as San Francisco, Sacramento, and Virginia City. By the 1880s, the mining era had peaked but not completely ceased, since gold, silver, and other minerals are still being produced in small amounts to this day.[9]

During the early mining period, transportation routes were built across the mountains, but they consisted only of poor and unreliable roads. Indeed, the Sierra barrier became a legendary part of western folklore, beginning with the Donner Party in the mid-1840s and continuing through the gold rush era of subsequent years. Gradually the crude early thoroughfares were replaced by regional and transcontinental railroads during the 1860s, 1870s, and 1880s. Never again could the range prove quite so impenetrable. Later, the first paved highways were built in the 1920s and 1930s. However, the rugged two-hundred-mile central Sierra from Carson Pass to Walker Pass still has no year-round road or rail crossing due to the high elevation and winter weather conditions. Indeed, the area from Tioga Pass to Walker Pass has no road crossing at all, dooming the region eastward of the high peaks to isolation (see chapter 11).

Along with further development of the area and improved transportation facilities came tourists, followed by developers and second-home-owners, who have focused on several dozen major resorts and hundreds of second-home and retirement-home "villages." These developments have had both positive effects (economic growth) and negative effects (environmental problems) on the mountain landscape. For example, the Lake

Tahoe Basin, one of the most beautiful settings in any mountain region, now has periodic air pollution as well as problems with water quality, sewage, and traffic, not to mention the degradation of aesthetics. (This is caused by a year-round population of over 50,000, triple that number on any good ski holiday, and as many as 250,000 during a summer day.)[10] New portions of the mountain region are continuing to be "discovered" by the nearly 30 million residents of California and Nevada as well as persons from other regions of the United States. As environmental impacts increase each year, wilderness enthusiasts strive for legal checks to this rampant growth.

The need for water, power, and recreational facilities has particularly impacted the Sierra Nevada in the present century. Approximately three quarters of the streams that drain the long western slopes are controlled by dams and spillways. The first large water project, in the early 1900s, flooded Hetch Hetchy Valley in Yosemite National Park for water use in San Francisco, covering natural beauty that rivaled nearby Yosemite Valley.[11] The most recent and largest of all the water developments, the Feather River Project (part of the California State Water Project) began in the 1950s and is still not completed in the early 1990s. It conveys water from the Feather River in the northern Sierra to Southern California, with many uses in between. The giant Oroville Reservoir and power facility are the mainstays of this project. Both the California State Water Project and the Federal Central Valley Project link the survival of the state's huge agribusiness to the moisture of the Sierra.

Lake Tahoe Basin: A Sierra Case Study

Lake Tahoe, a recreation region of international fame and beauty, provides a compelling case study of the effect of humans striving for the concentrated wealth of the mountains. The lake, twenty-two miles long and twelve miles wide, covering about 191 square miles, lies in a watershed basin totaling 315 square miles. About one-third of the lake lies in Nevada at a 6,225-foot elevation, with the remainder in California (figure 2). Because of its great depth (much of it is over a thousand feet deep), Lake Tahoe contains 122 million acre feet of water (40 trillion gallons), four times more water than Lake Mead, one of the largest human-made lakes in the world.[12]

Only two lakes in North America are deeper than Tahoe's measured 1,645-foot depth—Crater Lake, Oregon, is 1,930 feet deep, and Great Slave

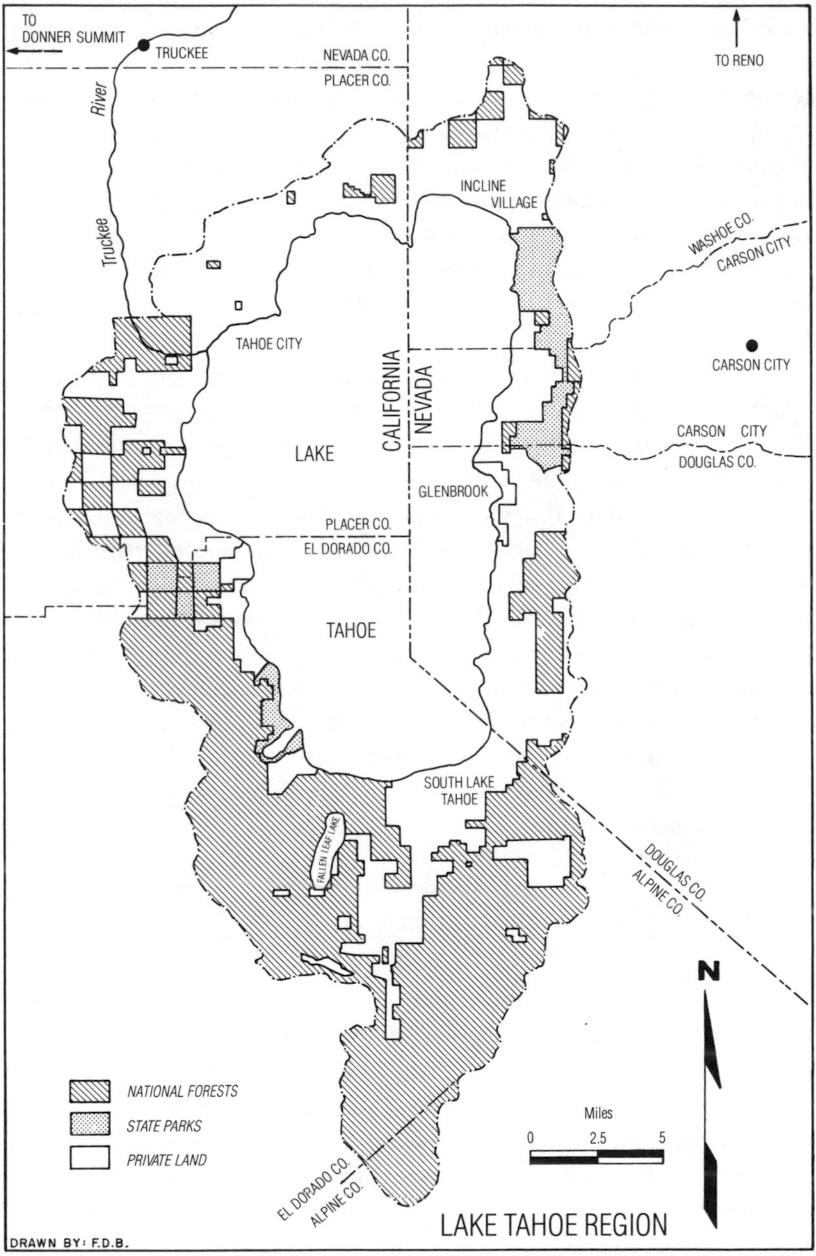

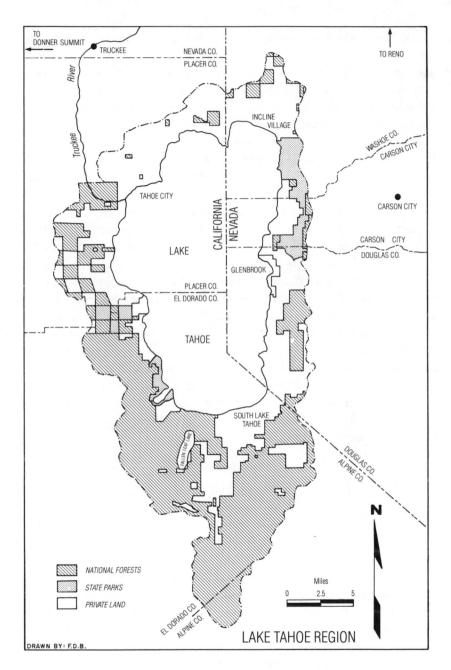

TO
DONNER SUMMIT
TRUCKEE
NEVADA CO.
PLACER CO.
TO RENO
River
Truckee
INCLINE
VILLAGE
WASHOE CO.
CARSON CITY
TAHOE CITY
CALIFORNIA
NEVADA
CARSON CITY
LAKE
CARSON CITY
DOUGLAS CO.
GLENBROOK
PLACER CO.
EL DORADO CO.
TAHOE
SOUTH LAKE
TAHOE
FALLEN LEAF LAKE
DOUGLAS CO.
ALPINE CO.
N
NATIONAL FORESTS
STATE PARKS
PRIVATE LAND
Miles
0
2.5
5
EL DORADO CO.
ALPINE CO.
LAKE TAHOE REGION
DRAWN BY: F.D.B.

2. *Map of Lake Tahoe Region Showing Prominent Sites and Land Ownership.*

Lake in the Northwest Territories of Canada has a depth of 2,000 feet. The great volume and depth of Lake Tahoe and the relatively mild winters in the area do not allow the lake to freeze over. Ice may form in shallow shore areas, but it is normally thin and short-lived. Surface water temperatures normally vary from the forties in winter to the sixties in the late summer. About 50 tons of sediment are deposited in the lake each year, which reduces the average depth by one foot in about 3,000 years.[13] The clarity and purity of Tahoe's waters are outstanding, and visibility in the water is unusually fine.

The first known inhabitants of the Lake Tahoe area were members of the nomadic Washoe tribe. They lived in the area mainly during the summer, spending winters in the milder lower elevations east of the basin in the Carson and Eagle Valleys and in Truckee Meadows. The Washoes' name for the lake was "Tahoe," which meant "big water in a high place." The Washoes were few in number and had little effect on the landscape. Apparently they had been longtime residents of the Sierra, driven into higher country by later-arriving tribes.[14]

Rather than letting the Sierra Nevada serve as a barrier to their culture, the Washoe tribe used it as a place for summer hunting and gathering and as a refuge, indeed a restorative sanctuary, from the heat of the lower elevations to the east. In winter the Sierra Nevada barrier gave lowland areas protection from storms and replenished the east-flowing rivers that made life possible.

The first fur trappers, explorers, and pioneers came into the Sierra Nevada and the Tahoe Basin in the 1820s through the 1840s. Although trappers like Jedediah Smith and Joseph Walker left little written data about their visits, John Frémont's expeditions of 1843–45 provided much information for future generations. One of the goals of Frémont's visit was to find the best locations for emigrants to cross the mountain barrier. Later important passes immediately north (Donner) and south (Carson) of Tahoe were explored by Frémont, while Tahoe itself was cited but not visited. Following the Frémont expedition, groups of pioneers began crossing the region in increasing numbers. These early explorers, trappers, and pioneers saw the Sierra as a barrier that impeded their access to the West Coast. Contrary to the Washoe culture, the Anglos had no interest in the Sierra per se. The mountains were part of the difficult passage to better lands on the western side of the range. These early itinerants, however, must at least have recognized the importance of the water that flowed from the mountains to the lowlands on both sides of the Sierra.

Thus, the pre–gold rush 1840s were comparatively tranquil in the northern Sierra Nevada, with the Lake Tahoe region near but still out of the main flow of pioneers, as they traveled through passes either north or south of the lake in their journeys to California and Oregon. The discovery of gold by James Marshall in the American River, immediately westward and downslope of Tahoe, suddenly brought people from all over the United States who were mainly concerned with only one thing—striking it rich! They had no real interest in the Sierra and no concern about the environment, which they proceeded to ruin. Stream channels were dammed and diverted, and finally hydrologic mining silted up many streams and rivers, causing crop and water loss in the valleys below. Damming and water diversion for hydraulic mining reached far upslope, approaching the Tahoe region by 1880. Throughout the central Sierra, trees were wantonly cut, and the ensuing runoff choked with debris caused floods and water quality problems. Animals were hunted year round, and some species such as the grizzly bear were finally eliminated.

Because mineral resources were not available in the immediate vicinity of Lake Tahoe, however, it was initially spared most of the chaos. This changed with the advent of widespread logging in the 1860s and 1870s. The market for Sierra timber expanded from local mines to burgeoning coastal cities, as well as to the Comstock Lode mining region near Virginia City, Nevada. Over a period of about thirty years, most of the accessible timber was removed from Tahoe and sent by boat, railroad, and water flume to Carson City for use in the Comstock cities and mines. This caused much runoff from bared slopes, sending silt into the lake.

The concentrated resources of gold and silver thus drew thousands to the western slopes, but it was the associated demand for timber that focused on the principal forest belts, including the Tahoe Basin. The resultant damage to Tahoe landscapes brought about by this logging era cannot be minimized. Log chutes and flumes covered the area. Just one logging camp near Tahoe City averaged more than 21,000 feet of saw logs per day, with 645,000 feet cut in the month of July 1882. Tahoe City also had the largest log boom ever assembled up to that time, when 380,000 feet of logs were cabled together and rafted across the lake to Glenbrook, where mills processed them for rail shipment to Spooner Summit and flume travel to Carson City (figure 2).[15] Limited logging still continues, but only on the extreme western fringe of the basin.

The logging era at Tahoe also witnessed the beginning of tourism as several outstanding resorts, such as the Tahoe Tavern at Tahoe City, were built

3. Dam on the Truckee River at Tahoe City. The view is to the north, and Lake Tahoe is to the right about four hundred yards away. The photo was taken in October 1988 in the midst of a five-year (1986–91) drought. Tahoe water is normally several feet deep in the foreground.

around the lake in the late 1800s to serve the well-to-do from San Francisco, Sacramento, and other cities. Entrepreneurs built roads and even a railroad from Truckee to Tahoe City to serve this clientele. Initially, the impacts of logging on the area were minimal. The number of people involved was small and their use generally confined to summertime, since roads remained closed in the winter. Also, Lake Tahoe was close to but not astride the main Sierra Nevada pass at Donner Summit.

Another series of events also began to unfold at Tahoe during the 1860s and 1870s, reflecting an increasing recognition that the basin and its surrounding slopes served as a critical island of moisture for the adjacent regions. Downstream interests on the Truckee River in Nevada decided that a dam at the outlet at Tahoe City would better control the flow to their farms and towns. An old wooden dam built in 1870 was replaced by the present cement facility with seventeen gates in 1910. The dam controls the lake to a little over six feet above the natural rim elevation of 6,223 feet. Occasionally, periods of drought during the twentieth century have stopped the flow of water from Tahoe to the Truckee River, causing great problems

4. *High and Dry Piers at Lake Tahoe's North Shore. The photo was taken in October 1988 at the end of the second year of the 1986–91 drought.*

for downstream locations such as Reno, which receives 80 percent of its water supply from the river. The most noteworthy droughts were during the 1930s, the mid-1970s, and from the mid-1980s to the early 1990s (figures 3 and 4). Evidently, earlier unrecorded droughts were even more severe and long-lasting.[16]

Despite all these developments, the human impact on the Tahoe Basin through the early twentieth century, with the exception of that from logging, remained generally slight. Sheep and cattle were in the vicinity, but their numbers were not great enough to cause environmental problems, unlike elsewhere in the Sierra. Rather than being a physical barrier, the Sierra Nevada functioned as a climate block, and both grazing and recreational use generally matched the "good-weather" season from May through September. The lack of year-round transportation facilities detracted from more permanent settlement and development.

All this was to end after World War II as roads were improved and as the gambling industry became a major factor in the area. Gambling had always been allowed at Tahoe during the "resort era." However, gaming experienced rapid growth in the prosperous 1950s. As the American population became more affluent, as leisure time increased, and as highways were im-

5. View toward the North over South Lake Tahoe Stateline Casino Complex.

proved and made year-round, visitation to Tahoe increased greatly and expanded from a "Memorial Day to Labor Day season" to the full year. Rapidly increasing populations in Sacramento, the San Francisco Bay Area,
and other nearby locales in California and Nevada have naturally sought
the use of such an accessible, relatively nearby area of beauty. The first
year-round casinos opened at Stateline (South Shore) in the 1950s (figure
5). The year-round population of only a few hundred in 1940 blossomed to
several thousand by 1960 and continued to increase rapidly. What had been
the long-awaited event of winter residents in the spring of 1940, the noise
of rotary snowplows opening the roads, multiplied into the drone of traffic
on U.S. Highway 50 in 1960.

Coping with Growth: Tahoe Basin since 1960

Initial concerns over the deterioration of the Lake Tahoe Basin really began
during the "Tahoe Land Rush" that started in the 1950s with expanded
gaming facilities. This in turn led to adoption of yet another characteristic
of the Mountainous West—government management. The Nevada and
California Tahoe Regional Planning Agencies were formed in the 1960s in

response to environmental concerns. In 1969 Congress went further by approving an interstate compact between Nevada and California and establishing the Tahoe Regional Planning Agency (TRPA). The main purpose of TRPA was to set limits on growth and to control land use in the Tahoe Basin. Also, TRPA was to monitor the environmental impact of new development on Lake Tahoe.[17] Unfortunately, following the stated intent of the compact has proven difficult due to three compact provisions:

1. *Dual Majority:* A majority vote of members present from *each state* is required before any action may be taken.
2. *Sixty-Day Rule:* Any project not approved or denied within sixty days is approved by default.
3. *Permitted and Conforming Uses:* Under this provision Nevada retains sole control over gaming.

Because of these three provisions, as well as pressure from special interests and from private landholders who own 42 percent of Tahoe Basin land (55 percent is national forest land, and the rest is state park acreage [figure 2]), TRPA has had only limited success and has approved most major projects. The agency also must frequently face resistance from state and local government units. Part of the role of TRPA is to harmonize the needs of the whole region with the plans of these local units and with the existing land-use plans of state and federal agencies. Each of the five counties that contain private land in the Tahoe Basin—Washoe, Douglas, and Carson City in Nevada and El Dorado and Placer in California—have environmental and planning restrictions, as do the states of Nevada and California. However, TRPA regulations tend to be more restrictive so they usually take precedence, although they are unpopular at times.

The real effect of the restrictions put on developers, plus pressure from environmental groups such as the League to Save Lake Tahoe, is that development has been slowed and made more difficult and more expensive. The perception of the region as a restorative sanctuary has, in effect, created a new type of "barrier" in the Sierra Nevada, where travel and development are made formidable and expensive not because of topography and climate but because of environmental and preservation interests. So, why is there concern? The sheer number of people in such a restricted space is a cause for concern, due to the traffic they create, their need for housing and services, and the resultant general degradation of the basin's aesthetics. In addition, the Tahoe Basin is especially prone to air pollution, a problem increasingly associated with other similar sites across the Mountainous West.[18] The small bowl shape of the basin, the frequent occurrence of temperature inversions that trap pollutants in the lower layer of the air shed, the frequency of high-pressure subsidence and stagnation that allows the inversion about two hundred days per year (more in a drought year and less in a wet year), and the high-elevation location that increases the intensity of the sun rays to produce photochemical smog are all important factors for air quality. The problem period is mainly the winter half-year, as daily winds during summer are more prominent due to regional heating differentials.

The primary damage from air pollution is a restriction of visibility in an area that "markets" its natural beauty. There is also some concern for localized plant damage in areas of heavy traffic, such as South Lake Tahoe, Tahoe City, and Incline. Major pollutant sources are motor vehicles, wood stoves and fireplaces, and dust from roads and building projects. Contrary to popular local belief, most Tahoe pollution has its source there, not with infrequent cases of invasion by smoggy air from the Sacramento Valley. Air pollution remains a problem at Tahoe, despite local efforts to get people to reduce driving, and despite new restrictions on wood-burning stoves.

Other areas of concern in the environmental degradation at Tahoe include sewage disposal, water quality and quantity, plant kill due to salting roads, and plant damage caused by a five-year drought in the years 1986–91 and by unusual sub-zero temperature readings in 1989 and 1990. Four sewage plants service the Tahoe Basin. The oldest, at South Lake Tahoe, California, was one of the world's first tertiary systems. Other plants are located at Round Hill Village and Incline, Nevada, and at Truckee, California. The latter has tertiary capability and handles sewage from the north and west portions of the basin. All treated sewage as well as solid-waste sewage is removed from the basin. However, water quality is a continuing problem due to fertilizers used on lawns and golf courses, and salt and sand used on highways to melt ice, much of which finds its way into streams and the lake. The salt also has a degrading influence on plant life, as trees near highways are dying, especially in drought years when less rain and snow melt means less dilution.

Periodically, natural conditions also adversely impact the features which have drawn people to this corner of the Mountainous West. Water quantity has never been a great problem because growth has slowed somewhat and groundwater is sufficient. However, the recent five-year drought (1986–91) has taxed the system. Lake Tahoe reached its lowest recorded level in December 1990, after one hundred years of measurement. This level, over one and one-half feet below the Tahoe City Dam, will require many wet years to replenish. The drought also took its toll of trees that supply the beauty and wood resources of the region. Tens of thousands died or are dying due to lack of water. Adding to the environmental stress have been two unusually persistent periods (four to five consecutive days) of sub-zero cold in February 1989 and December 1990. In 1989, temperatures reached –43 degrees at Boca (near Truckee), only two degrees short of the all-time California low of –45 degrees set in an infamously cold month, January 1937.[19] During both cold months minimum temperatures in the Tahoe Basin were in the –10 to –30 degree range, depending on the distance from the lake. Ice even formed on the edges of the deep lake. The cold of December 1990, although not quite so severe as a year earlier, caught the plants at a lower ebb on the drought scale and killed off many.

Conclusion

The Sierra Nevada in general and the Lake Tahoe Basin in particular demonstrate the historic themes of the Mountainous West. The region lay in relative isolation until its concentrated resources of minerals and timber drew thousands of would-be millionaires. Quick exploitation of these resources left in its wake severe environmental damage. Upon reaching the mountains, the pioneers recognized two other fundamental characteristics, the concentrations of water and recreation space. Exploitation of those resources has also wrought environmental change. Has development and use gone too far in some areas of the Sierra Nevada? Can the range still be considered a "restorative sanctuary" that offers rest and recuperation to the "needy masses"? The Lake Tahoe Basin is an example of what can happen in the Mountainous West as people crowd into a small portion of this spectacular region. Lake Tahoe's future now depends in large part on government controls and compromise between government agencies. Other areas that have developed too much too fast and that no longer offer what John Muir found in the last century are the Mammoth Mountain Area, Yosemite National Park, and much of the foothill and Mother Lode regions of the west slope. These latter two areas have become havens for retirees, for residents who work in the great Central Valley but who do not want to live there, and for new industry that recognizes the importance of good living conditions in realizing better returns from their workers.

Will the mountains continue to be able to give peace and tranquility to those who seek it? Will we realize the importance of this peacefulness to our well-being? Will we protect and treasure the ability of the mountains to offer it to us? As John Muir so aptly put it: "Come to the woods, green deep woods. Sleep in forgetfulness of all ill. Of all the upness accessible to mortals, there is no upness comparable to the mountains."[20]

Notes

1. John Muir, quoted in Teale, *The Wilderness World of John Muir* (Boston: Houghton Mifflin, 1954), 311.

2. T. Storer and R. Usinger, *Sierra Nevada Natural History* (Berkeley: University of California Press, 1963), 17–22; C. Wahrhaftig and J. Birman, "The Quaternary of the Pacific Mountain System in California," in *The Quaternary of the U.S.* (Princeton: Princeton University Press, 1965): 299–360.

3. Wahrhaftig and Birman, "Quaternary of the Pacific," 299–360.

4. J. James, "Climate of Nevada," University of Nevada–Reno, Bureau of Business and Economic Research Paper no. 84-12 (Reno, 1984), 1–27.

5. D. Miller, "Snowcover and Climate of the Sierra Nevada," University of California Publications in Geography no. 11 (Berkeley, 1956), 1–49.

6. J. James, "Storm Typing and Seedability in Orographic Snow/Rain in the Sierra Nevada of California," *Journal of Weather Modification* 18 (1986): 14–16.

7. J. James, "A Record Breaking Sierra Nevada Snowfall: Its Meteorological and Topographic Causes," *Third Conference on Mountain Meteorology* (Boston: American Meteorological Society, preprint volume, 1984), 144–46.

8. D. Lantis, R. Steiner, and A. Karinen, *California: The Pacific Connection* (Chico, Calif.: Creekside Press, 1987), 417–18; Storer and Usinger, *Sierra Nevada Natural History*, 23–30.

9. Lantis, Steiner, and Karinen, *California*, 438–40.

10. Tahoe Regional Planning Agency (TRPA), *Climate and Air Quality of the Lake Tahoe Basin: A Guide to Planning* (South Lake Tahoe, Calif.; U.S. Forest Service and TRPA, 1971), 1–30.

11. Teale, *Wilderness World of John Muir*.

12. J. Burnett, "Geology of the Lake Tahoe Basin," *California Geology* 24 (1971): 119–30.

13. Burnett, "Geology of Lake Tahoe."

14. Lantis, Steiner, and Karinen, *California*, 419–21.

15. E. Scott, *The Saga of Lake Tahoe*, vol. 1 (Crystal Bay, Nev.: Sierra Tahoe, 1975), 266, 268, 292, 295, 307, 312.

16. W. Nichols, "Drought Duration and Frequency in the North Central Great

Basin and Implications for Water Supply," in *Proceedings of the Symposium on Water-Use Data for Resource Management,* American Water Resources Association Technical Publication series (Tucson: University of Arizona, Water Resources Research Center, 1988), 479–85; S. Harding, "Changes in Levels in the Great Basin Area," *Civil Engineering* 5. no. 2 (1935): 1–12.

17. J. James, 1980, "Lake Tahoe Field Trip Guide" (Reno: University of Nevada–Reno, Geography Department, 1980), 1–16.

18. J. James, "Air Pollution at Lake Tahoe," *Lake Tahoe South* 1 (1970): 10–13.

19. J. James, *Nevada Monthly Climate Summary,* 7 and 8 February 1989, December 1990 (Reno: Office of the State Climatologist), 1–4.

20. John Muir, quoted in Teale, *Wilderness World,* 314.

13 / Colorado's San Luis Valley

JOHN DIETZ AND ALBERT LARSON

Southern Colorado's San Luis Valley serves as a microcosm of much of the Mountainous West. Akin to California's Owens Valley, its fate has been molded by the location and resource base of nearby mountain ranges. Mountain barriers to the west, north, and east serve to isolate the region and have placed the valley in a persistent rain shadow, making it one of the driest places in the southern Rockies. The valley's evolving economy has also been tied to a multiplicity of concentrated mountain resources. Ironically, the very mountains which take away needed moisture serve as seasonal reservoirs of rain and snow that ultimately make their way to the valley floor. In addition, the presence of mineral resources, timber, and grass in the nearby high country has traditionally shaped settlement in the valley. For example, the locations of valley transportation routes, towns, and agricultural operations have consistently been tied to mountain-based resources.

Adding to the complexity of the valley's historical geography is the cultural mosaic which includes a legacy of Native American, Hispanic, and varied Anglo-American influences. Even though the region's land-use practices and local economy reflect many larger modern American trends, there persist to this day variations that reflect previous cultural and economic systems. Even within the mainstream of current development, there are contrasts, contradictions, and paradoxes which mark the valley's pluralistic American society of the late twentieth century.

Physical Geography

Although the valley is called the San Luis, it is in fact the Rio Grande that flows through the valley (figure 1). The valley name derives from the early settlement focal point, San Luis, in Costilla County, which was organized in 1851 and is the oldest existing town in what is now Colorado. Lying between the granitic Sangre de Cristo Mountains which rise abruptly to the

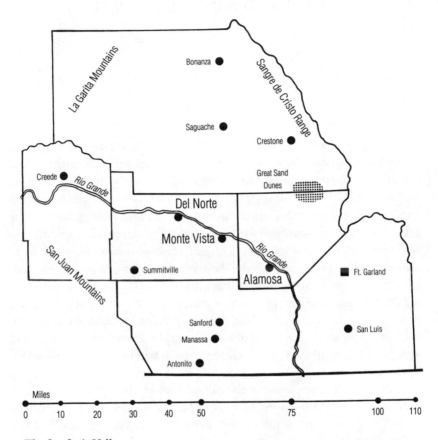

1. The San Luis Valley.

east and northeast and the volcanic San Juan Range to the west and northwest, the valley is partially set off on the south by a smaller range, the volcanic San Luis Hills, through which the Rio Grande flows southward into
New Mexico. While there are peaks at and above 14,000 feet bordering it,
most of the valley itself lies between 7,000 and 8,000 feet above sea level.
Indeed, the valley is a structural basin in the midst of the Mountainous
West. It extends more than one hundred miles north-south with a maximum width of approximately fifty to sixty miles.

As a result of the rain-shadow effect of the mountains, the climate of the
valley floor is mostly desert, with much of the area receiving about six
inches of precipitation per year (figure 2). However, the surrounding

2. *Semiarid Scrublands, Southern San Luis Valley East of Manassa. (Photo by William Wyckoff.)*

ranges are literally "islands of moisture" which give birth to mountain streams (such as the Rio Grande) that provide a critical supply of exotic water for valley irrigation. Streams in the northern half of the valley flow into valley lakes and percolate into underlying aquifers, some of which are quite porous. Artesian wells in the northern valley have been lessened due to irrigation drawdown. Dry lands are given over to grazing or left as wasteland. There is also a large acreage of sand dunes (Great Sand Dunes National Monument) piled up along the eastern side of the valley by the predominant southwesterly winds.

The valley's soils are mostly of a mixture of granitic and volcanic outwash from the surrounding mountains and hills. These soils, which consist of alternating beds of porous sand and impervious clay, permit some seepage of stream and river waters. Beds of sand come to the surface near the edge of the mountains, soaking up the water from mountain streams. The natural vegetation of the valley is a treeless sagebrush and greasewood scrubland, which makes for a stark landscape where water is absent. Although grazing is favored, cropping is possible due to the levelness of the valley and available water for irrigation from both streams and artesian wells. In some places, irrigation has not been successful, with the result that fields have been rendered useless by alkaline salts.

Native American Period

About 1400 A.D., nomadic Ute Indians controlled the San Luis Valley of the Upper Rio Grande. They would claim it as their home for the next five hundred years. That people had inhabited the valley since prehistory is not in doubt. Folsom sites along the valley's eastern side date from approximately 10,000 to 12,000 B.C. Archaeologists have found evidence of at least two other longstanding cultures as well as indications that various tribes periodically mined two turquoise-rich areas.

Of the various Southern Ute bands, it was the Tabeguache group which claimed the San Luis Valley as their domain. From time to time, Apaches, Comanches, Arapahoes, Kiowas, and Cheyennes contested this claim. Hunters and gatherers, the Utes at first established a complementary relationship with the sedentary farmer Pueblos to the south, although eventually the two groups became enemies, due in part to Spanish manipulations. By 1670, the Utes had horses, which allowed them to widen their hunting territory. In that year, the Spanish made their first trading treaty with the Utes, an agreement that lasted into the next century. Despite that treaty, the Utes and Comanches also concluded an alliance that lasted for half a century. During this period, both groups engaged in raids into northern New Mexico, which slowed Spanish settlement. When the alliance broke apart, the Utes allied themselves with the Spanish and Apaches.[1]

In 1694, Governor-General de Vargas attempted to take food from Pueblo Indians at Taos as he had done from others along the trail from El Paso. The Indians refused to trade with him, which thwarted his plan to establish settlements. Fearing attack if he retraced his route to El Paso, de Vargas continued north to the San Luis Valley. There he was attacked by the Utes, who mistook him for their Pueblo enemies. By 1754, other Indians rated the Utes as the "Great Barbarians" of the time. They had become excellent horsemen who hunted the mountains, valleys, and plains. Expanding westward, they forced the Navajos out of their San Juan Mountain homeland and began active trade with the Spanish at Santa Fe.

Through the late eighteenth and early nineteenth centuries, the Utes maintained their firm grip on the valley. In the first year of the American Revolution, a combined Ute-Apache force joined a Spanish army and successfully fought their Comanche enemies. In 1843, when a settlement was begun by Hispanic settlers in the southern part of the valley, harassment by the Utes caused the settlement to be abandoned. However, following the Mexican War and subsequent American control, a gradual demand for Ute removal resulted in two successful military campaigns. The first, in 1855, saw the defeat of the Ute-Apache nations in the San Luis Valley and the Plains; the second resulted in all Utes being removed from the valley in 1879–81. The dispossession of the Utes did not end the conflict, however. They continued poaching game in the San Juan Mountains of Colorado from their Utah reservation home as late as 1914.

The American Explorers

After the Louisiana Purchase in 1803, U.S. interest in the Rocky Mountain area increased. Was there a low-elevation pass to the Pacific? Were there sufficient fur resources for trade? Were there ore bodies large enough to profitably mine? The Lewis and Clark expedition began to provide answers to these questions in the north, and even though the southern Rockies were still part of the Spanish Empire, the Pike expedition of 1805–7 sought these answers in the south. Two years after a brief exploratory crossing by American trapper James Purcell, Zebulon Pike and his men entered the San Luis Valley in early 1807 to explore the Arkansas and Red Rivers. After descending the Rio Grande Valley to the river's junction with the Rio Conejos, they ascended the Conejos a distance of five miles. There they built a stockade. One month later, Spaniards arrived and informed Pike that he was on Spanish territory, "inviting" him to accompany them to Santa Fe.

In 1822, one year after the valley had become part of the northern frontier of newly independent Mexico, American fur trappers and a journalist, Jacob Fowler, crossed the valley on their way to Taos. They returned north into the valley and went west to what is now Creede in present Mineral County before leaving the area. This began a regular pattern of American contact with the valley. By 1840, many trappers, traders, and scouts journeyed through the area along the Taos or "Trapper's" Trail. In 1848, the well-known military leader Colonel John Frémont also explored the valley for the purpose of locating an east-west railroad route to the Pacific Ocean along the thirty-eighth parallel. In December, he and his party became snowbound in the San Juan Mountains just west of the valley. Frémont lost ten men on the harrowing journey and failed to link the valley to a dependable pathway to the Pacific.

Despite the increasing contact and annexation by the United States in 1848, the Utes maintained a presence in the valley for another thirty years. Still, the pace of change increased. Captain John Gunnison traveled through the valley in 1853 as the head of a federally sponsored railroad survey. A year earlier, the American army established its authority in the valley with the construction of Fort Massachusetts. It was designed to protect travelers and potential settlers. After a few years, the army abandoned Fort Massachusetts in favor of a better location six miles south, where they built Fort Garland and named it for the military commander of the Department of New Mexico, John Garland.

Hispanic Settlement

Even as itinerant Americans increased their contact with the valley, more enduring imprints of settlement were being made by Hispanic migrations from the south. Spain had planted permanent colonies in New Mexico by the beginning of the seventeenth century. These settlements eventually extended as far north as the San Luis Valley and Spanish land claims reached even further north. Although the purpose of the settlements was to counter incursions by the French and British, it was the Native Americans who offered the first settlers the most resistance. Eventually, Spain's New Mexican outposts came to be seen not as a buffer but, rather, as an effort to Christianize the Indians.[2] Persistent efforts to settle the San Luis Valley from the south had, by the 1860s, transformed the area into one resembling northern New Mexico.

Although the movement north from Mexico into New Mexico began as early as 1598, evidence indicates only exploration, mining, and trade with Indians in the seventeenth century.[3] The first temporary fort built by the Spanish settlers was in 1768; thereafter, halting steps to take firm control lasted well into the nineteenth century. In 1821, when Mexico declared independence from Spain, the San Luis Valley became the northern frontier of the Mexican state of Nuevo Mejico.

For purposes of colonization, the Mexican government granted land to New Mexicans in 1833. However, Native Americans thwarted this first settlement attempt. Eleven years later, colonists petitioned to try again, but once again Indians forced the abandonment of the Conejos Grant settlement. These failures to gain a foothold would later prove critical to the region, as the U.S. Court of Private Land Claims denied the rights of these claimants due to their lack of settlement.

The first enduring Hispanic settlement in the San Luis Valley occurred in 1851. Two years later, settlers established new communities both east of the Rio Grande on the Sangre de Cristo Grant and west of the river on Conejos Grant land. The latter settlement was given the Sacrament of Confirmation by Archbishop Lamy of Santa Fe. Slowly the infrastructure for full agricultural settlement developed. At the original settlement of San Luis, farmers began irrigation by digging Peoples Ditch #1. It became the first organized irrigation project in the future state of Colorado. Although additional people continued to expand the settled area, farmers were initially obliged to transport their grain to Taos for grinding. Finally, in 1856, they built a local flour mill near the Conejos settlements. Two years later, a similar mill commenced operation near San Luis, where a mercantile store had opened in 1857 (and is still operating in the 1990s). An additional land grant, the Baca Grant #4, was awarded in 1860. Part of an original grant given by the Spanish government in 1821, the Baca Grant expanded the settlement area by 100,000 acres. It was given in lieu of the original land in New Mexico later taken by the U.S. government. Upon passage of the Homestead Act in 1862, the federal government claimed three-fourths of the valley, resulting in petitions for land claims almost immediately.

By the late 1860s, most of the Hispanic settlements had been made, although an 1873 founding on the north bank of the Rio Grande was recorded. There were, at that time, approximately twenty-six communities (*placitas*). Mountain moisture proved to be a critical location factor: each site was situated along the banks of one of the exotic streams issuing from the surrounding high country. These communities contained a population of just under six thousand persons in the Conejos Grant alone.[4]

These early Hispanic nuclei established an enduring Roman Catholic presence in the region. Many towns still support a sizable Catholic community and an active local church organization (figure 3). Local church leaders in the valley have always competed with a Catholic lay brotherhood dating from sixteenth-century Spain. This organization, Los Hermanos Penitentes, was most active from 1850 to 1890 but remains today as an anachronism of the late Middle Ages. The organization became firmly entrenched in northern New Mexico and, with settlement, moved north into the valley. It originally formed in isolation from the mainstream Catholic church and its priests, but it has maintained its strength even after

3. Catholic Church, San Luis, Colorado. (Photo by William Wyckoff.)

churches were located close at hand. The brotherhood's most conspicuous characteristic is their means of expiating sin during Holy Week, including self-flagellation and being bound to wooden crosses. Despite pressures brought to bear on them from both religious and civil authorities, the Penitentes continue practicing their customs today. The San Luis Valley's isolation fostered the continuation of these and other Hispanic cultural practices long after they disappeared in other areas.

Mining Period

Mining is a conspicuous and critical function of the Mountainous West that has left its mark on the San Luis Valley as well as other lowlands of the region. Although early gossip promoting the Pikes Peak gold rush of 1859 told of rich placer mining on the floor of the San Luis Valley near Fort Garland, placer nuggets were never found. Angry mining enthusiasts publicly flogged the rumor's promoter.[5] Despite this disappointment and the fact that the valley was outside Colorado's famed "Mineral Belt," one of the

Mountainous West's best-known zones of concentrated resources, the San Luis Valley was destined to be part of the support infrastructure for mining camps of the San Juan Mountains to the west. Four camps—Summitville, Bonanza, Crestone, and Creede—had the largest impact on the San Luis Valley.

Summitville lay at the 11,000-foot summit of the continental divide at the headwaters of the Rio Alamosa. It boomed in the early 1870s and spawned the emergence and temporary flourishing of other camps in the headwaters area. However, miners could never find strikes of a size to qualify for Leadville or Central City fame. Ironically, in the 1980s and early 1990s, one of the largest gold-mining operations in Colorado systematically dismantled the South Mountain vein at Summitville while sheep grazed on Forest Service lands adjacent to the mountain.

In the early 1880s, miners discovered silver along Kerber Creek at the north end of the San Luis Valley. Among the many camps which instantly blossomed as miners flooded to the area, the Bonanza camp acquired supremacy with "36 saloons and 7 dance halls."[6] Otto Mears, the architect of San Juan toll roads, also built a road to tie Bonanza to the Rio Grande Railroad at Villa Grove, sixteen miles to the east. Mining continued sporadically through the rest of the nineteenth century and even into the twentieth, but the 1893 silver crash effectively ended the boom. To this day, however, signs along Kerber Creek warn "Danger Poison Water" as a result of the hundreds of tailings piles through which the water must seep as it wends its way to the valley floor.

Across the valley a minor gold boom at Crestone developed on lands that were part of the Baca Grant. However, grant owners soon evicted the trespassers. At Orient, near the center of the valley, miners dug iron from limonite ore and shipped it to the Colorado Fuel and Iron mills at Pueblo. These mines operated until 1919, when large Wyoming mines made them obsolete. Further south, turquoise was also mined in the San Luis Hills.

The big mining boom for the San Luis Valley, however, centered on nearby Creede, which flourished in the 1890s. The primary focus was silver, but gold, copper, and zinc were also mined. A branch of the Denver and Rio Grande Railroad from Alamosa to Creede facilitated the flow of supplies in and production out. In this boom area, David Moffat began his fortune, and Soapy Smith honed the skills that later earned him Skagway fame.

Denver-based businessmen controlled the San Juan mining economy and established the need for improved transportation and communication. In particular, the valley town of Del Norte became a flourishing mining supply center and aspired to become the entrepôt for the entire San Juan region. Saguache served as an early mining center as well as a base for Indian agencies, but construction of the Denver and Rio Grande Railroad line over La Veta Pass from Walsenburg in 1878 vaulted Alamosa to the leadership role as the valley's economic center. General William Palmer's Denver and Rio Grande Railroad (D&RG) soon acquired the nickname of "Dangerous and Rough Going." It became the D&RGW after the Western Pacific Railroad acquired it following D&RG bankruptcy in 1918. By 1920, at the height of the region's railroad activity, all lines converged on Alamosa in the center of the valley. At that time, Alamosa was served by daily trains from Pueblo/Denver, Salida, Creede, Durango, and Santa Fe. In addition, the San Luis Southern and San Luis Central Railroads served local towns on the east and west sides of the Rio Grande. Alamosa has remained the center of the valley's economy, a factor that contributed to the creation of Alamosa County in 1913 and to the establishment of Adams State College in 1925.[7]

American Farmers

The tasks of supplying food to miners and, under government contracts, to Indians fell to San Luis Valley farmers. The Spanish settlements generally concentrated on home production and self-sufficiency, although there are records of supplies sent to participants in the Pikes Peak gold rush of 1859. But it was American farmers who led the valley into its role as a food supply region. In 1867, Otto Mears began wheat farming in the Saguache area, and in the same year settlers brought cattle to the valley to begin large-scale commercial ranching operations. Removal of the Utes from the valley the following year freed up more land for agricultural development. The mining boom at Silverton in 1872 further triggered a major expansion of agriculture, while railroad construction enhanced sheep production. Some 500,000 pounds of wool were shipped out during 1878, the railroad's first year.

Sporadic agricultural development continued into the 1880s. In 1882 farmers grew the first commercial potatoes in the Monte Vista area. Ten years later, professional developers incorporated Monte Vista. They were led by Kansan T. C. Henry, who planned extensive irrigation ditches and midwestern-style farms—primarily growing wheat at first. In 1887, an agricultural exhibition at Monte Vista displayed cabbage, potatoes, wheat, fruit, and mushrooms. In the following year, Colorado A&M (Colorado's land grant college) began its San Luis Valley Demonstration Farm just east of Monte Vista, and in the following year a Monte Vista farmer won a national prize for growing the most potatoes per acre (847 1/2 bushels). Much of this burgeoning development relied on irrigation ditches supplemented by artesian wells, some of which provided enough water for 200-acre fields. Wheat also grew on dry land in the north end of the valley.

Into the Twentieth Century

The Silver Panic of 1893 ended the boom days of the San Juan mining camps, and San Luis Valley agriculture fell on hard times. At about the same time, black alkalinity caused by poor drainage in the Hooper/Mosca area began to seriously reduce wheat production. Alternative crops which could be grown at the valley's high elevation had to be found. The first was field peas, which livestock producers initially fed to spring lambs destined for the Chicago market and later to hogs. Eventually sweet clover replaced the field peas in the crop rotation. Sugar beets were tried as early as 1899, but the valley's short growing season proved too hostile for them. Wheat farmers turned instead to alfalfa as winter feed for cattle. In 1920, iceberg lettuce was introduced as a summer cash crop. This led to the first large-scale immigration of migrant labor from Texas and New Mexico into the valley.

As the valley farmers continued to experiment with new crops, the area's ethnic profile grew more diverse. In 1923, Japanese farmers came from California to produce cauliflower, lettuce, and garden peas in the Blanca area. In 1939, Moravian brewing barley (for the Coors Brewery near Denver) was introduced and has continued as a major component of valley agriculture ever since. Recently, the search for alternate commercial systems has continued with the introduction of quinoa (an Andean high-protein grain popular on the health food store circuit), organically produced beef and buffalo, an alligator farm utilizing the hot springs north of Mosca, tilapia farming, and mushroom farming.

Just as much of the Midwest hosted ethnic colonies from all over Europe, the valley also hosted colonies from the Midwest and other places. Swede Lane near Monte Vista attests to the homeland of its early settlers. Dutch settlers claimed the Waverly area just west of Alamosa at the turn of the century, although most withdrew to the Platte Valley in northeastern

Colorado. Mennonites from Kansas homesteaded at Gibson on the Salida-Alamosa line of the D&RG, but retreated when their customary agricultural practices failed. Developers brought colonists to the valley at various times —particularly to Costilla County, where the original land grant made purchase of large acreage possible. Construction of the San Luis Southern facilitated this colonization. The Japanese colonists, originally brought to the valley's east side by the Costilla Development Company, were supplemented in the 1940s by relatives seeking refuge from World War II anti-Japanese sentiment in California. In the New Deal days of the 1930s, a new colony of dust bowl refugees came to the valley as part of a Federal Emergency Relief Administration (FERA) resettlement project in the Waverly area, which had been previously settled and rejected by the Dutch settlers. New drainage ditches improved the quality of agricultural lands, but the project was never considered a lasting success.

The proliferation of agriculture inevitably brought conflict over limited resources. Typically, the federal government became involved. Water wars have always been a part of the San Luis Valley scene. The colonists at San Luis in 1851 secured Colorado Water Right No. 1. Subsequent claims to Rio Grande water led to a demand by New Mexicans and Texans for an embargo on Rio Grande water claims by Coloradans. One was enacted in 1896 and stayed in effect until 1925. By 1900, some 187,500 acres of valley land were under irrigation. Reclamation engineers built reservoirs in both adjacent "islands of moisture"—the San Juans and Sangre de Cristos—to hold water in reserve for late summer flow. Terrace Reservoir on the Rio Alamosa was the largest earthen dam in the world when it was completed in 1912. Later demands on Rio Grande water led to the Closed Basin Project which ensured river flow in the 1980s. Then, in the late 1980s, another battle over San Luis Valley water commenced when current owners of the Baca Grant in the northern end of the valley formed American Water Development Incorporated (AWDI) to market deep artesian water (from aquifers two thousand feet below the valley floor) to thirsty metropolitan areas on Colorado's eastern slope. The proposal instantly aroused fear and opposition from existing valley water users, who assume that any removal of deep water will soon lead to a sinking of surface water. AWDI argues that it owns the water and that Colorado appropriation laws do not apply since the original Baca Grant predates Colorado's absorption into the United States.

In addition to the water resources, forest resources in the valley's fringe have been the close charge of the federal government. President Roosevelt

4. Summer Cattle Grazing, Rio Grande National Forest Northwest of Del Norte. (Photo by William Wyckoff.)

established Cochetopa Forest Reserve in the mountains west of Saguache in 1905. Today the federal government's control of this portion of the Mountainous West is carried on by the San Isabel National Forest and the Rio Grande National Forest, which control both timber resources and seasonal grazing from ranches based on the valley floor (figure 4).

Mormon Settlement

As much of the Mountainous West was a sanctuary for one group or another, the San Luis Valley became a sanctuary within a sanctuary for Latter-day Saints (Mormons) in the 1880s. They needed seclusion for polygamous families recently disallowed by the federal government as a price for Utah statehood. In 1878, Mormon colonists bought federal lands in the Conejos Valley on the west side of the Rio Grande. The towns of Manassa and Sanford became the nuclei of a Mormon (LDS) farming community. Many of the colonists were recent converts from the southern states and from Denmark. In Manassa, a Colorado Stake headquarters building served as the meeting place for summer meetings of church leadership groups. These meetings allowed church leaders to visit with family members who had moved away from Salt Lake City in order to escape the anti-polygamy rules. Such meetings lessened the heartache that the breakup of the multi-wife families caused.[8]

Mormon farmers learned the lessons of agricultural survival in the San Luis Valley just as their gentile neighbors had. They planted grain fields (primarily wheat) and built gristmills to provide flour for bread. Small herds of dairy cows and vegetable gardens contributed to a subsistence living. The boom of mining in the San Juans in the 1880s also provided a market for grain and vegetables on which both LDS and gentile farmers capitalized commercially. In addition, many Saints sought nonagricultural employment outside the colony in the mining camps and on the railroads.

Using the Manassa-Sanford area as a core, LDS colonists spread to other parts of the valley (east of the Rio Grande), to New Mexico, and even to Mexico. Primarily sought as further refuge from anti-polygamy legislation, these colonies were short-lived, and many of their settlers returned to the San Luis Valley or to Utah. In the valley itself, initial holdings were expanded by buying every other quarter-section in the Sanford-Manassa area, thus ensuring eventual control of lands in between.

Today the southwestern portion of the San Luis Valley presents a scene similar to that of Utah's Jordan Valley. Neat fields of alfalfa, potatoes, and barley are interspersed with rows of fruit trees and pastures of dairy cattle. The familiar spires of an LDS church dominate towns consisting of both large houses and modular homes. The diffusion and strengthening of the Mormon presence has diluted the valley's once critical role as a refuge. Now, there are more Mormons in Alamosa than in Manassa or Sanford, and the Colorado LDS Temple originally planned for Manassa was recently built in the larger urban center of Denver.

Tourism Development

Tourism in the San Luis Valley dates from the earliest explorers. However, it has become a major economic activity during the late twentieth century as the relatively unspoiled landscapes of the Mountainous West increasingly have become known as restorative sanctuaries. Ulysses Grant visited Bonanza during its heyday, and numerous other well-known figures have visited the valley to enjoy the hot springs, mountain scenery, hunting, fishing, and historical sites. Current valley development plans focus on drawing ordinary tourists to the valley to spend dollars in an economy where agriculture and forestry products are increasingly difficult to sell for profit.

Ironically, the silver crash in 1893 began the interest in attracting visitors to the valley to compensate for the collapse of the region's principal business. Monte Vista successfully lobbied for the Colorado Soldiers and Sailors' Home to care for indigent Civil War veterans. It now survives as a Colorado Veterans' Home. The D&RG Railroad advertised its lines as scenic. Monte Vista hosted a Good Roads convention as early as 1919. Skiing in nearby mountains dates from the 1930s, and paving the Wolf Creek Pass road (U.S. Highway 160) west of the valley led to the development of a major ski resort there. In addition, federally funded CCC camps in the 1930s constructed trails and campgrounds in the national forests.

Efforts by valley residents led to the creation of Wheeler National Monument (a unique volcanic area) in 1908; it was later demoted to a National Geologic Area because neither the county nor state ever appropriated funds to build access roads. It remains to this day accessible only by horseback or on foot. Efforts to make a national site of the famous sand dunes along the valley's eastern side, where westerly winds drop their sandy load as they depart the valley via the Medano and Mosca Passes in the Sangre de Cristo Mountains, were more successful. Congress established the Great Sand Dunes National Monument in 1932, and it has become one of Colorado's most popular tourist attractions. Efforts to restore Fort Garland as a state historical site and tourist attraction also succeeded. In 1971, local leaders convinced the Colorado and New Mexico state governments to purchase the D&RGW track between Antonito, Colorado, and Chama, New Mexico, when the company abandoned the line. It became the Cumbres and Toltec Scenic Railroad, which draws thousands of tourists each summer. It traverses more varied mountain scenery than the better-known Durango-Silverton route farther west.

Local chambers of commerce throughout the valley boast the area's many attributes. Some eighty-one motels and campgrounds stand ready to serve a population far larger than the present 38,000 residents in the valley. Some communities have made special efforts to attract tourists. Proximity to Taos, New Mexico, prompted leaders in San Luis to develop a "Stations of the Cross" shrine and an artisan center, along with bed and breakfast accommodations to attract tourists.

The Valley as New Age Sanctuary

Throughout much of the modern world, periodic and permanent movements to highland areas for health, freedom, and exhilaration have been especially marked since World War II, although they derive from the Romantic period of the early nineteenth century. The Mountainous West was among the first regions recognized as a sanctuary for recuperation and rejuvenation. Health seekers identified mineral spas and health resorts, as well as the mountains themselves, as landscape features representing the environment's curative powers. They also associated spiritual regeneration with mountain environments, spurred by the blossoming of Romanticism and the increased crowding and congestion of cities. In some Mountainous West areas, there has developed an environmentalist anti-growth sentiment, often espoused loudest by "outsiders." In the case of the San Luis Valley, the anti-growth movement has yet to become strongly organized. If it should, it would run headlong into those who would develop the water resource for outside interests.

Although numerous tourist ventures have developed in the valley, it is the retirees and alternate-lifestyle advocates that are most influencing the valley. Their developments bespeak a desire for a protected, pristine landscape. Due to the valley's size, they present little challenge to other land uses. Some have sought the valley's isolation as a place to build and/or sell hideaways where they or their clients can "escape" the cares of their highly developed and rushed everyday lives. Although second homes are not numerous, there are a number of scattered private retreats of various wealthy American and foreign owners. Large landholding corporations have, on occasion, caused a renewal of culture clashes. Traditional Hispanic activities (hunting and wood gathering) have run afoul of new private ownership policies, resulting in legal action and violence.

There are three corporate/retirement entities in the valley whose developments have been facilitated by acquisition of original Spanish or Mexican land grants. The Forbes Trinchera Ranch, initially developed for wealthy hunters on a private wildlife habitat, has turned to subdivision and sale of "ranchettes." Developers advertised nationally, cut roads, and laid out more than seven thousand plots ranging from five to forty acres. Although they have achieved only marginal success, the Forbes organization has embarked on another similar venture nearby.[9]

A second, similar development, the Los Angeles–based Rio Grande Ranches, has had even less success. It represents the latest scheme on land that has a long history of similar projects. Today, although many lots have been sold, there are perhaps only a dozen houses on the 50,000 acres that are offered in five-acre tracts for $3,000 each.

The Baca Grande Development occupies some 140,000 scenic acres near the north end of the valley. Early developments led to a large cattle-ranching operation and the town of Crestone. In 1979, a think-tank group, formerly based in New York City, leased the old ranch house to be its remote retreat for "thought and contemplation in America." Later, a group of Tibetan monks sought and bought refuge in another part of the ranch. The Aspen Humanistic Institute built a facility for retreats but sold it in 1987 to Colorado College. In January 1988, movie actress Shirley MacLaine and other New Age spokespeople announced that Crestone/Baca Grande represented the center of the universe and that they planned to build a number of facilities there. Meanwhile, the ranch was sold to TOSCO, an oil-shale corporation. The new owners laid out estates and built some expensive homes, but following financial difficulties, they sold the acreage to a group of investors. Some observers speculate that the ranch purchases have been made to avail the owners of the ranch's water rights, later to be sold to thirsty eastern-slope cities and developers.

A new and growing concern for physical and spiritual well-being is currently developing along the western slopes of the Sangre de Cristo Mountains on lands in the original Baca Grant. Health food plantations, including Colorado State University's quinoa grain project, are the result of this unusual development. Other adherents of New Age culture within the area concentrate on religious paths, including Native Americans of several tribes, Carmelite Catholics, Zen Buddhist monks, a Hindu Vedic Temple ashram, and the RedSun Institute, an international educational center for indigenous peoples. Plans to distribute or sell other acreage for like purposes, including an experimental garden and seed bank for high-altitude crops, a world nutritional center, and various healing centers have resulted in a variety of chapels, hermitages, temples, sweat lodges, community buildings, and gardens scattered amid the beautiful foothills of an area believed to possess a mystical harmony for spiritual world togetherness.[10]

Although these developments occupy less than 10 percent of the valley's approximately eight thousand square miles, local reaction is mixed. Laborers welcome the economic opportunities, and all residents are pleased with the tax monies collected, but longtime residents of the valley fear the loss of land and, especially, water resources as well as what they perceive as the idyllic and isolated way of life which they have enjoyed for a century.

Microcosm of the Mountainous West

The San Luis Valley today represents many of the characteristics of the Mountainous West. The region's landscapes include a highland Hispanic agricultural tradition reminiscent of the rural Southwest, a Mormon outlier of Utah, a system of irrigated agriculture with exotic specialized crops, cattle and sheep ranches that run stock between valley bottoms and mountain slopes, a mining presence both in legacy and in practice, and the burgeoning tourist, retirement, and New Age activities that echo the area's changing role as a restorative sanctuary.

Missing is a modern Native American population, though there is a rich heritage of a former presence. Additionally, recent refugees from Nicaragua and Guatemala are finding haven in Alamosa. Also missing today is the military presence which forged the nineteenth-century bonds of the Mountainous West to the rest of the United States. Fort Garland alone remains as a reminder of the distant military past.

The themes of the Mountainous West are exemplified in the San Luis Valley. The surrounding mountains served as barriers to interaction and forced valley residents to become resourceful in fending for themselves. The San Juan and Sangre de Cristo Ranges have served as critical islands of moisture; their watery resources find their way to the valley floor and provide for irrigation of a wide array of crops. The other concentrated resources of the mountains—notably gold and silver, but also including turquoise and timber—have triggered much of the development of the valley. Government involvement has made the decision-making process regarding land-use practices in the region exceedingly complex. State, federal, and even international agencies vie for control. Finally, the function of the valley as a restorative sanctuary is well illustrated, from the Mormon polygamous families of the 1890s to the New Age devotees of the 1990s, not to mention the countless tourists who seek a weekend of quiet reflection camping at the Great Sand Dunes or in one of the nearby national forest campgrounds.

Notes

1. David W. Lantis, "The San Luis Valley, Colorado: Sequent Rural Occupance in an Intermontaine Basin" (Ph.D. diss., Ohio State University, Columbus, 1950).

2. David Hornbeck, "Spanish Legacy in the Borderlands," in *The Making of the American Landscape*, ed. Michael P. Conzen (Boston: Unwin Hyman, 1990), 51–62.

3. "Time-Event Chart of the San Luis Valley," *San Luis Valley Historian* 1, nos. 1–4 (1969).

4. "Time-Event Chart."

5. Virginia McConnell Simmons, *The San Luis Valley: Land of the Six-Armed Cross* (Boulder: Pruett, 1985), 72.

6. Simmons, *San Luis Valley*, 103.

7. Harvey C. Skoglund, "A History of San Luis Valley, Colorado" (master's thesis, Colorado State University, College of Education, Fort Collins, 1941).

8. Judson Harold Flower Jr., "Mormon Colonization of the San Luis Valley, Colorado 1878–1900" (master's thesis, Brigham Young University, Provo, Utah, 1966), 98.

9. Laura Misch, "Forbes Ranch Offers Plenty of Nothing," *Rocky Mountain News* (Denver) (8 November 1987).

10. Maureen Harrington, "A Sacred Space," *Denver Post* (28 July 1991).

14 / Mormons and Mountains

JEANNE KAY

This essay on the early Church of Jesus Christ of Latter-day Saints (Mormons, LDS) in the Mountainous West addresses each of this volume's five themes to show how they operate together within the context of one society: mountains as barriers, as islands of moisture, as locations of natural resources, as government landholdings, and as recreational destinations. Historical geographers tend to think of Mormons as settlers of arid lands of the interior West, yet the deserts of Deseret are everywhere punctuated by mountain ranges, and the Mormon economy and ideology are inextricably connected with the two physiographies.

Just as the Mormon region has varied physical geographies, Mormon society was and is a diverse group, with multiple experiences and interpretations of them. Generalizations about Latter-day Saints and their landscapes can usually be confounded by exceptions. With some caution, therefore, I discuss in this chapter a rural Mormon way of life established in Utah and portions of neighboring states from initial settlement between 1847 and 1869, followed by a period of ingress into the region's distinctive subculture by the federal government and by non-Mormon mining and railroad interests. The Mormon pioneer way of life continued in modified form, particularly in isolated rural communities until about 1920. Parts of this subculture exist today. It is not characteristic of the entire region, however, which includes non-Mormon settlement and a substantial urban corridor along the Wasatch Front.

The empirical sorting of landscape facts is augmented with efforts to understand their subjective meanings to people who lived with them. The humanist's concern with the individual's quest for meaning and significance suggests the value of longitudinal studies of the individual-in-place, whereas the scale at which most geographers work requires horizontal aggregations of individuals as societies. The tension between these two types of studies is not reconcilable: the individual life may be too particular, whereas generalizations about humans in the aggregate may isolate geographers from the motivations of their subjects. Comparing the geographers' generalizations with an individual's experience may help to refine both kinds of perspectives. My informant is Latter-day Saint historian Juanita Brooks. Her autobiography, *Quicksand and Cactus*, describes early-twentieth-century life in the rural Mormon community of Bunkerville, Nevada, an extension of Utah's "Dixie" just a few miles from the Utah and Arizona borders.[1] I conclude with suggestions for additional themes emerging from Brooks's autobiography that were essential to her experience of the Mormon landscapes of the Mountainous West.

A necessary point of clarification concerns my use of the term *mountains*. Mountains are high country, but they are visually defined by the parts of three-dimensional space that are not mountains: the adjacent valleys and canyons. Similarly, the lower-elevation desert valleys derive their character from the mountain rain-shadow effect. A sizable portion of the Mormon high country, the high plateaus, are not mountains to the geomorphologist. Nevertheless, the plateaus' steep perimeters and, for the lands above 8,000 feet, their subalpine climate and vegetation caused the local people to call many of them mountains, and they are so included here. Although much of the Mormon region could thus be termed mountainous, the Mormon cultural landscape was largely restricted to the valleys and canyons. Nevertheless, the transport of mountain resources such as water and timber into the valleys and the transhumance of livestock into summer range in the mountain meadows continually link the physiography and economy of the high country and valleys to the point where it is appropriate to speak of a unified human ecology within a varied terrain. Indeed, mountains have long served as a ubiquitous visual background, if sometimes a distant one, in the daily lives of most residents of the region (figure 1).

The Mormon Experience

What is the religion that motivated the Mormon settlement effort?[2] Mormons claim to be a unique denomination of Christianity within which the biblical Christian church has been restored. They accept the Christian Bible as divinely revealed, as well as several additional scriptures transcribed by founder Joseph Smith, notably the Book of Mormon, from which they take their informal name. Presidents of the church are believed to be real prophets, who may at any time deliver God's word. The faith therefore has an extensive set of its own doctrines, traditions, and scriptures that distinguish it from other denominations. The Mormons' own historiography is a reli-

1. *"West Desert," circa 1908. This photograph shows both the scenic and economic integration of mountains and deserts in the Mormon domain. The sheepherder's outfit in the foreground would move from winter pasture in the valleys to summer pasture in the mountains. (Courtesy Special Collections Department, University of Utah Libraries, no. P0069 #44.)*

giously motivated national epic that follows the lines of the biblical Exodus model, with an emphasis on divine intervention and revelation.

The Church of Jesus Christ of Latter-day Saints originated in upstate New York in the 1820s under the leadership of Joseph Smith, whom Mormons hold to be a true prophet. As he and his congregants immigrated to Ohio, Missouri, and Illinois, they were sometimes attacked or lynched by neighboring settlers, who felt that the Mormons were dangerous fanatics. Mormons thus understood their origins as latter-day Israelites in a climate of persecution, which, as with the biblical Israelites in Egypt, culminated in a long exodus to the promised land, termed *Zion* or *Deseret* by the early Saints.

The indigenous historiography of subsequent Latter-day Saint settlements within the Great Basin and Colorado Plateau emphasizes the visionary yet practical guidance of Joseph Smith's successor, Brigham Young, the
unshakable faith of the pioneers, and the miracles that sustained them despite the enormity of Building the Kingdom within one of America's least
forgiving environments. Indeed, the stories of pioneer Mormon hardships
and heroism are everywhere embedded in contemporary worship and
"faith-promoting" history within the religion. While secular scholars may
deprecate religiously motivated historiography, it gives a fundamental res-
onance within the subculture that secular scholarship cannot aspire to
match. The former instructs the young in their traditions and heritage, it
teaches morals and values through factually based anecdotes and action-
packed epics, and it instills a deep pride in what one's church and its members have become.

An appreciation of the Latter-day Saints' own beliefs about their settlement history is indeed basic to understanding why and how they under-
took to occupy the Great Basin and their persistence as a distinctive subculture. Their belief that establishing their distinctive cultural landscape was
an act of worship was a principal motivation of Mormon settlement. In a re-
versal of the medieval Christian concept of *contemptus mundi*, Mormons accepted a religious obligation to restore their portion of the Earth after the
Fall back toward the Garden of Eden. They believed that developing the
land was as religiously inspired as attending church or praying.[3] Mormon
historian Juanita Brooks recalled:

> Grandpa thought of all his life as a mission. Whether he was . . .
> stampeding cattle or building a dam, he thought he was laboring in
> the Lord's Vineyard. Sometimes it looked like he was trying to estab-
> lish a vineyard where the Lord never intended one to be. He broke
> the ground, cleared off the brush and rocks, struggled with the river,
> killed the rattlesnakes, and left his part of the Lord's Vineyard better
> than he found it.[4]

Religion was the lens through which the early Mormons saw, shaped,
and interpreted their landscape; and everyday landscapes provided the
metaphors with which they expressed their faith on a daily basis. Early
church leaders planned an entire regional settlement pattern and hand-
picked its shock troops of pioneers, who were "called" to develop a new
community, just as they might be called to become an apostle or president
of the Relief Society. Such settlers' feelings toward their new landscape
were thus more than economic or nostalgic: God's own Prophet made

one's labors in a designated place a type of divine guidance regarding one's unique life purpose. As Juanita Brooks explains:

> the Church was everything to us. It was for the Church that we were all here; it was the Church that had drawn our parents from all the far countries. Even the building of the ditch and the dam, the graveling of the sidewalks, the planting of cotton or cane had its inception in the Church, for ours was a temporal gospel as well as a spiritual one.[5]

The Mormon example contradicts idealism's claims that it is possible for the secular geographer to "rethink" peoples' thoughts and truly to enter into others' experiences.[6] Outsiders or gentiles (as non-Mormons are often called in that region) would find it nearly impossible to experience the world-view and traditions that generated Mormon historiography and the cultural landscape, short of religious conversion to the faith. Despite the enormous volume of primary and secondary sources on the Mormon past, traditional Mormon scholars writing their own peoples' history and geography—even when for a general audience—assume an ecclesiastical vocabulary, appreciation for testimonies to the faith, and fondness for heroic narrative that may be difficult for the outsider to assimilate. A more empirically minded generation of Mormon scholars writing for the secular academy have published high-quality, objective scholarly studies, but these may reveal little of the personal Mormon experience of the land. This second type of scholar, admirably exemplified by historian Leonard Arrington and geographer Richard Jackson, nevertheless display a mastery of primary sources and insights into church institutions that would be extremely difficult for a non-Mormon to master.[7] Criticisms of Mormondom, such as by Bernard DeVoto or Fawn Brodie, regardless of their aptness, ultimately reveal little of lived and personal Mormon experience as it made sense to their subjects.[8]

Perhaps the closest melding of lived "insider" experience of the Mormon landscape written for "outsider" levels of comprehension comes from the writings of Wallace Stegner (non-Mormon former Utah resident), geographers Gary Peterson and Lowell Bennion, or from the autobiographical memoirs of Latter-day Saint essayist Edward Geary and historian Juanita Brooks.[9] Her autobiography is a rare hybrid that details the insider's daily life with the scholar's detached view of personal events that point to generalizations about the larger society.

Brooks shows something of the geographer's eye for landscape pattern in her description of the view from the high river terrace behind Bunkerville, Nevada, during a Sunday school hike around 1905:

At the second level we rested . . . ."See the town? Can you find your own home in it? Look at the Meeting House, set off there by itself. Everybody comes to the Meeting House, so we will count from there."

We found the School House in the northwest edge of Bunkerville, the Store and the Post Office together, and the Bishop's house next to them. Every home had its quarter-of-a-block for corrals, garden, fruit trees, or vineyard. . . . There were also three brand new brick houses going up—not adobe, but real, burned brick!

"Now look at the blue mountains far to the east. Behind them is St. George, a big city with a temple and a tabernacle. This is where our young folks go to get married, so some day you may go there, too."

None of us had been as far as that.

"Now look at the fields, up above the town and just behind it, and way down below it. They look like a quilt made of square blocks, with the cottonwood trees the stitching to hold them together."[10]

Brook's chapter concludes with the return home, and the girl's realization that "the place would never be quite the same again since I had seen it in relation to the Wide, Wonderful World." Brooks thus reveals an insider's understanding of this volume's five themes as well as others that will be treated separately in more detail.

Barriers to Interaction

The very presence of Juanita Brooks and her family in an isolated community within one of the most rugged and arid regions of the United States implies much about the role of mountains as barriers. The mountain barriers that the Mormons first encountered in 1847 provided both hardships and advantages. The hazards of ascending and descending sometimes trackless mountain passes with teams and wagons en route to the Salt Lake Valley can scarcely be imagined in this era of interstate highways and four-wheel drive vehicles.

Brooks's childhood memoir reveals that mountains and plateaus continued to be formidable barriers within the Land of Zion long after the American frontier and Gathering of Zion officially ended. Travelers in the Great Basin were on rugged ground as soon as they left a valley. Travel within the Colorado Plateau's terrain of red sandstone slickrock and steep canyons was even more treacherous. The earliest pioneers to new valleys sometimes recorded tying large logs to their wagons to serve as brakes on the steep descents, or even lowering wagons down cliffs by rope. Although dirt roads had been cut to Bunkerville at its establishment fifteen years earlier, it is still small wonder that its citizens in 1905 seldom traveled the distance of forty miles to St. George, Utah, except on that most compelling business, a Temple marriage ceremony.

The transcontinental railroad was completed in northern Utah in 1869, and various spurs and trunk lines followed, particularly to transport minerals. Only the arrival of automobiles and paved roads ended the real isolation of many communities, however. A railroad station thirty miles away could still mean a two-day journey by wagon.

Isolation of valleys tucked between mountain ranges and extensive rock deserts continues as a fact of contemporary life for some Mormon communities that are accessible in winter only by a single dead-end paved road. A 105-mile stretch of Interstate 70 across east-central Utah has no services for motorists, even today. Bunkerville's isolation ended in earnest, however, with the extension of Interstate 15 along the Virgin River and the expansion of neighboring Mesquite's stateline casinos.

Despite some bitter instances to the contrary, Mormons also perceived their mountain ramparts as protecting them and isolating them from a hostile federal government and non-Mormon populace. The advantages of mountain barriers—in addition to putting a thousand miles between themselves and their enemies—were the Mormons' hope of enjoying relative isolation from persecution and the freedom to develop their own faith and the institutions that framed it.

Principal among the institutions sustained by isolation from the rest of the nation was polygamy.[11] It was practiced by a sizable minority of Mormons as a revival of the plural patriarchal family of the Old Testament, until church decree banned it in 1890, after several years of bitter federal prosecution. Brooks recorded having five paternal grandmothers, one of whom was her biological grandmother, but all of whom were considered to be relatives.[12] The link between geographical and social isolation and polygamy continues today in the region. A few ex-Mormon or crypto-Mormon polygamous splinter sects left the church and persist in a pattern of family life that they explain as divine decree.[13]

The disadvantages and advantages of the mountain barriers were also economic.[14] Starvation was not an imaginary threat during the early years, with no external source of agricultural products within a 500-mile radius— or more. Costs of goods freighted overland were prohibitive, and Brigham Young soon rebelled against seeing Utah's scarce capital leaving the region through the import of "luxuries" like silk and sugar. He counseled the Mormons to begin a strict regimen of agricultural and manufacturing self-sufficiency. Its short-term legacy was a diversity of crops and cottage industries. In the "Dixie," or southern region of Zion that included Bunkerville, mild winters enabled cultivation of subtropical crops like cotton, sugar cane, and mulberries for silkworms. These rapidly disappeared from the Mormon landscape when improvements in transportation made imports more economical than local products.

With the discovery of gold in California in 1849, silver in Utah in 1869, and a general increase in migration to the Pacific Coast along the overland trail, Salt Lake City was ideally situated as a way station and service center for these new emigrants. Salt Lake City was the only urban source of services and supplies between the Colorado Front Range and California, as it is even today for high-order goods and services. Mormons also made money from local mining towns. The short growing season, unsuitable soils, and isolation of gentile mining communities in remote mountains meant ready markets for Mormon produce, draft animals, meat, dairy and poultry products, and even labor.

Despite the eventual disappearance of the early diversity of Mormon agricultural activity, an enduring legacy of the economic barriers imposed by geographic isolation in the nineteenth century is the Mormon commitment to self-sufficiency. Home gardening, fruit growing, canning, and maintaining a year's supply of provisions ("home storage") are still highly prized activities in both rural and urban Mormon households today.

Islands of Moisture

[The irrigation system] bore the same relation to our town that the circulatory system does to the body: the Big Ditch was the main artery from which all the laterals ran out, dividing and subdividing until the water reached the roots of every plant in the valley, every plant that was to survive.[15]

Mormon historiography makes much of its pioneers settling the desert and causing it "to bloom like the rose." It is safe to say that Mormon history would have been impossible without the region's major mountain ranges and high plateaus. In a settlement system where flat, dry valleys were the terrain of compact settlements, irrigated crops, and winter pastures, mountains provided the wood, water, and summer pasture that made Anglo-

American settlement possible. This fact is readily grasped by considering a transect beginning with the low point in a valley within the Mormon region, perhaps at 4,000 feet in elevation and with an average annual precipitation amount of under fifteen inches and sometimes under five. This is unquestionably a moisture-deficit environment. A modest elevation of 9,000 feet within an adjacent mountain range or high plateau might well have an average annual precipitation of forty inches, orographic precipitation falling mostly as winter and early spring snow, and a clear moisture surplus. The valleys before Mormon settlement supported xerophytic shrubs and bunch grasses; at most, some juniper, Gambel's oak, or Rocky Mountain Maple were found much higher on the benches.[16] The cool mountain canyons and slopes supported stands of aspens, commercial softwoods, mountain meadows, and permanent streams fed by the melting winter snow pack.

Mormons typically settled in compact, nucleated agricultural communities, located near the lower benches on gently sloping alluvial lands at the valley's edge, just below the foothills proper, where a permanent stream appeared from its mountain canyon into the valley. Streams provided water for households and agriculture within the valley, and power for gristmills or sawmills at the canyon's mouth or higher up the canyon. Most nuclei of Mormon communities, therefore, occurred within a band several miles wide along the valley perimeters, and tended to be larger and more frequent along the orographically favored west-facing slopes than along the drier, leeward east-facing slopes. Town elevations were normally low enough, however, to minimize the rocky soil and frost danger that increase with elevation in the benchlands of the Great Basin.

Not all mountain ranges in the region provide a full range of natural resources, however, particularly if the summits are below 9,000 feet, and if they are located far west or south of the principal Wasatch corridor of settlement. The Virgin Mountains, which begin about eight miles from Bunkerville, have wood, pasture, and springs, but the streams are ephemeral. For Bunkerville and neighboring communities, therefore, the principal source of water is not runoff from the local mountains but the headwaters of the Virgin River in the Pine Valley Mountains and high plateaus of southwest Utah, as much as one hundred miles away. The links between mountain runoff and valley cultivation are no less vital to such desert communities, even when the water source is not the local mountain range.

The spatial distribution of mountain water into the valleys depended on a variety of factors, including the population of irrigators, the agricultural economics of marginal farming, and the lay of the arable land over which the volume of available water could be expected to flow. Shortly after their establishment, each community dammed its creek, and dug one or more "Big Ditches" or canals from which smaller ditches could be diverted.[17] During the early decades, ditches running along the sides of streets were used for culinary water and for household gardens and orchards as well as for commercial agriculture.

The hamlet of Bunkerville diverted its water about three miles up river from the town and distributed it to fields all along that distance to several miles below the town, all within a narrow strip less than a mile wide, flanked by rugged desert country and the Virgin River channel.[18] The Bunkerville Ditch skirts the edge of the high river terrace to the southeast and is bled by numerous side ditches that water the house lots and fields, which slope slightly down toward the river channel. The flow of water in the farmer's ditches was normally controlled by small hand-operated head gates.

The early Mormon communities were laid out in a "foursquare" cardinally oriented grid pattern, with church and public buildings in the center, a pattern easily adapted to the subsequent introduction of the General Land Survey in 1869. Fields, on the other hand, had to be laid out according to the gravitational flow of water in a gently sloping terrain, and they had to be small enough to accommodate the labor-intensiveness of maintaining irrigated lands. Field patterns were thus geometrically irregular, and individual holdings were often as small as five to ten acres. Today much of the irrigation water runs through sprinkler systems and PVC pipes, but numerous examples of the traditional open-ditch system persist.

Mountain water in the early days irrigated a variety of food and fiber crops initiated under Brigham Young's self-sufficiency policy. From time to time, smaller areas of the Mormon region have attempted to specialize in irrigated crops, such as sugar beets or potatoes, or in specialty livestock, such as turkeys or minks. The fields that Brooks observed with her Sunday school class were more diversified in 1905 than fields today. Bunkerville's fields then included hay, alfalfa ("lucerne"), melons, corn, squash, and still some sugar cane and cotton. (The latter belonged to a farmer who took seriously his family's call to the Cotton Mission.) Pasture and forage crops for sheep and cattle garnered through the decades an increasing percentage of Utah's meager agricultural lands and are the principal crops today.

Town life enhanced both church activities and community maintenance of its irrigation system: indeed, these were hardly separate. The early water-diversion projects were all directed by the local church ward through voluntary (though expected) hand labor. The local bishop adjudicated water as well as spiritual conflicts. Water rights were allocated according to the dictates of first-come, first-serve, but "use it or lose it," and, ideally, according to each family's size. The daily functioning of the irrigation system was managed by a church-appointed water master, whose job was to make sure that farmers took only their allocated amount of water during their allocated time. The labor that Mormon men devoted to communal ditch digging and cleaning, as well as reconstruction of flash-flood-damaged irrigation works, was as subject to church directives as were doctrinal matters.

After 1880, water management increasingly passed into the hands of local semiprivate irrigation companies that issued shares in the supply of water. Such companies are quite viable today, and they administer not only agricultural irrigation water applied to the fields but also the remainder of such systems for house lots within some urban neighborhoods, including some sections of Salt Lake City. Water shares attached to house lots are still jealously guarded property in small towns and are used to water lawns and gardens.

Irrigation and water knit together the social life of the community. The annual cooperative clearing of the main ditch was a time for men to socialize. The family's barrel of drinking water was a center of home life, filled during hours when cattle would not sully the ditches. Neighborliness was defined by honoring another's water rights and by hauling another's drinking water when the main ditch was incapacitated by flash floods.

But if mountain moisture was a blessing and life-sustaining force in early Utah, it also harbored hidden death. Winter avalanches trapped Mormon men on lumber-hauling trips and constantly threatened gentile mining communities in the mountains. The nation's second oldest ski resort of Alta, Utah, was established on the site of a former mining community that had been flattened by avalanches.

Another threat came from dams which sometimes failed during violent flash floods. They were particularly dangerous for the desert river valley communities like Bunkerville, where canyon walls funneled with great force runoff that had nowhere else to go. Brooks recounts the panic of herself and young siblings trying desperately to round up the family's small dairy herd out of the pasture just ahead of a flood:

"It's a-coming'!" someone called, and everyone looked. A bank of
black debris advanced like a rolling wall some three feet high, behind
it trees, cottonwood and cedar, and the ridge of a barn bobbing

2. *"Old Mill on Way to City Creek Canyon, Salt Lake City." (Courtesy Special Collections Department, University of Utah Libraries, no. P0040 #33.)*

along, a church, a limp little calf, some squash swinging near the bank . . . . Fields before the cutting edge, where the flood whipped into the bank on our side, would melt away in chunks as big as houses, and where it swung away to cut into the opposite bank there would be a large extension of new sand deposited which could be farmed for years, or until the river changed its course again. So we would accept this. We would put the dam in again, and adjust as best we could.[19]

Areas of Concentrated Resources

The mountains of Zion stored additional resources used by the Saints. They provided water power sites, summer pasture, wood, pinon pine nuts, game, and minerals; the latter's wealth was usually exploited indirectly.

Swift-flowing creeks that could be dammed across their narrow, rocky banks provided the Mormons with many water power sites, even though the flows were seldom very large. Gristmills tended to be close to the canyon mouths, accessible to the agricultural communities (figure 2). Sawmills were sometimes located in town, but were often located in mountain canyons close to the source of timber.

Transhumance has been widely practiced throughout the Mountainous West, and the Mormon culture region is no exception.[20] The typical town-dwelling family raised a few dairy cattle and horses that grazed on the valley fields or surrounding benches. A few Mormons developed extensive ranches. Mountain moisture provided lush summer pastures for their range cattle and sheep, while valley lands provided winter pasture and a supply of hay and alfalfa for livestock feed. When Brooks was a young woman, her parents owned a homestead at a canyon mouth of the Virgin Mountains, where they tended dairy cattle, an orchard, and a garden during the summer. She also visited relatives who had a cattle ranch on Pine Valley Mountain in southwest Utah.

Overgrazing radically altered the vegetation and stream flow regimes of the entire region, typically by the 1870s and most severely during the height of the sheep industry, from 1890 to 1930 (figure 3).[21] Management of grazing allotments by the U.S. Forest Service and Bureau of Land Management has alleviated this problem—too little for environmentalists and too much for ranchers.

Mountain moisture also sustained commercial stands of subalpine conifers that had several effects on the traditional Mormon landscape. Mormons hauled the large timber out of the steep, roadless mountains and into the valley settlements: Mormon men under Brigham Young devised a system of canyon grants, whereby an individual entrepreneur willing to invest in building a road up a canyon for timber cutting was thereby entitled to the sawtimber, plus any tolls he might collect at the entry to his road.[22] Other families in the community, however, were entitled to collect firewood and fence poles along the grantee's route. Many canyons in Utah's mountains today still bear the name of the original entrepreneur. One example is Parley's Canyon, through which Interstate 80 passes today just east of Salt Lake City.

Wood nevertheless remained a critical shortage for Mormon settlements. The readily accessible timber might be cut over within a few decades, and forest fires, probably set by the new incursion of humans into the woods, decimated thousands of additional acres of trees. Timber was depleted in the Wasatch Mountains east of Salt Lake City by the 1870s. In response, the Mormons instituted policies of saving sawtimber for essential construction purposes and using other building materials, such as stone and adobe. One thinks of adobe houses primarily in connection with

3. *Sheep Shearing Camp in the Mountains, 1876. Note the extensive evidence of overgrazing. (Courtesy D. H. Christensen Collection, Special Collections Department, University of Utah Libraries, no. P0369.)*

the Hispanic Southwest, but the Mormon culture region also has a rich tradition of building in adobe as an ecological response to wood shortages, in light of the strong housing demands created by immigration and natural increase.[23] Juanita Brooks lived in a one-room adobe cabin as a small child. Many Mormon adobe homes exist today, although most are disguised after decades of being enlarged, remodeled, and sheathed.

Quarries, too, were typically located at the border zone between mountains or plateaus and valleys, where exposed stone was accessible to nearby communities for construction or lime kilns. Where good stone ("rock") was available, it was the preferred building material, considered to be more handsome and easier to maintain. Joseph Smith and Brigham Young taught that the Kingdom of God on earth was to be built of precious stone, and the rock churches and adobe cabins made a plausible linkage, at least more so than wood construction, between ecological necessity and eschatology.

Fencing, another important wood use, also faced critical shortages that were accommodated in a variety of ways.[24] Before the importation of barbed wire, mountain saplings provided horizontal fence poles. Early pioneers experimented with brush piles, woven willow hurdles, and even adobe walls (hence the expression "as ugly as a mud fence"). Juniper ("cedar"), a foothill species, became the typical source of posts for barbed wire fences; for corrals, a sort of rough paling or picket fence constructed of old boards, log edges, or small junipers can still be seen today.

Brigham Young encouraged the Mormons to grow trees of all kinds within their communities: for fruit, shade, beautification of the Kingdom, and hedging. Introduced Lombardy poplars and native cottonwoods were also grown to ease shortages of firewood. Few of the short-lived poplars survive today, but the cottonwoods and paling fences still demonstrate ingenuity in the face of resource scarcity.

Mining in Utah occurred predominantly in the mountains, but it was largely a non-Mormon activity.[25] Brigham Young feared the loss of Zion's Mormons to the California gold fields or to the silver and copper mines developed in Utah and Nevada after 1869. The Mormon vision was agrarian, and the lacustrine or alluvial valleys, rather than the hard rock mountain slopes and canyons, were the Mormons' preferred terrain. The mines of Alta, Park City, and Bingham Canyon in Utah yielded millions of dollars of wealth, mostly to "outsider" investors.

Yet Mormons benefited from the mountains' mineral wealth in important ways. The mining population of Zion peaked around 1900. Some Mormons, like Brooks's parents, raised and marketed fresh vegetables and poultry to provision the mining communities. Her mother's home production of food and her father's marketing for mining camps provided sufficient income to enable an enlargement of their home sufficient for their nine children. A few years later, her father supplemented his agricultural income by working as a freighter for nearby Nevada mining camps (figure 4). Young Mormon men of postpioneering generations who needed money to buy land and farming equipment could build up sufficient capital by saving a year of mine wages.

A notable exception to the Mormon nonmining rule was magnate Jesse Knight, who donated large sums from his silver mines near Eureka, Utah, to the capital improvement of Brigham Young University. Brigham Young also promoted the development of iron and coal, needed to fuel any kind of industry, and the Church actively proselytized Welsh miners to attract their expertise to Zion. Coalville, in Summit County, and Iron County,

4. *Team of Wagons and Horses Used for Freighting Suppliers to Mining Camps.*
Some Mormon men, such as Juanita Brooks's father, earned additional money by
freighting to mining camps in the mountains. (Courtesy Special Collections De-
partment, University of Utah Libraries, no. P0101 #30.)

Utah, are examples. But these woefully undercapitalized ventures ended
when rail transportation after 1869 made coal and iron cheaper to import
than to process locally; or when the railroads or independent entrepreneurs invested in mining and smelting.

Zones of Government Control

The principal landowner within the Mormon region today is not the
church nor private citizens, but Uncle Sam. Government holdings—
nearly 80 percent of Utah and over 90 percent of neighboring Nevada—are
principally in the form of National Forest and Bureau of Land Management
lands, carved from the public domain, with smaller percentages allocated
as Indian reservations, national parks, and state lands. Between the mountain slopes, canyon country, and alkaline deserts that comprise most of Deseret, only tiny slivers of valley lands were preempted and developed by

the Mormons. They nevertheless developed indigenous systems of rights for lumbering and grazing over a much wider area and saw no need for federal land management.

Early Mormon settlement in the West was, in part, a movement against secular government. The federal government that had failed to protect Mormon lives and property in the Middle West, that harassed plural families, and that established western army posts to monitor them was, needless to say, not a welcome institution in early Zion. Establishment of Utah Territory and the opening of tracts of land for homesteading in 1869 followed twenty-two years of indigenous rule, land-use systems, and a variety of social services.[26]

The federal presence added a layer of governance to Mormon institutions but did not affect their essential structure. In the Bunkerville of Brooks's youth, for example, land and water disputes were adjudicated by the bishop; an all-Mormon school board hired only Mormons in good standing to be public school teachers; high school classes were held in the church; and the bishop's and Relief Society storehouses served as church social service centers for the poor.[27]

The federal government did have an important role to play in Zion, however, in the diffusion of land conservation measures. For their toil in God's Vineyard, Mormon settlers sometimes created the Garden: lush strips of green pasture or orchards surrounding neat and stable towns, ringed by sandstone cliffs or mountain ranges. But other settlers reaped a landscape of barren, eroded fields, precious water lost through evaporation, deteriorating rangelands, and deforested slopes.[28] The latter outcome was, unfortunately, common. Mountains stripped of their trees and herbs delivered flash floods and landslides to the communities below. New dry-farming techniques on the benches brought impressive yields to some farmers, but ruinous soil erosion to others. Overgrazing combined with drought resulted in the classification of 60 percent of Utah's rangelands as severely overgrazed or eroded by 1934—in a state that has 85 percent of its land classified as rangeland, and only 4 percent as arable.[29] For a people who saw Mormon settlement of the Great Basin as a divine decree and fruitful fields as God's acknowledgment of their righteousness, environmental degradation must have been difficult to bear, but equally difficult to attribute to a Tragedy of the Commons.

It would be unjust to blame the Mormons for decades of deliberate landscape abuse: each primary industry was undertaken with little prior experience of environmental constraints, carrying capacity, and appropriate technologies.[30] Learning the bare rudiments of irrigation through trial and error gave few pioneers an understanding of irrigation engineering, appropriate amounts of water to apply on their fields, or the long-term dangers of surficial salt accumulation. Indeed, the deflation of soil during the Great Depression was caused in part by inappropriate dry-farming techniques promoted by the most advanced state and university extension advice of the day.

Federal management of mountain lands still in the public domain began with the establishment of national forests and parks in the early twentieth century, and Bureau of Land Management domains through the Taylor Grazing Act in 1934.[31] These generally honored preexisting land ownership, grazing, and mineral rights. One of the federal land management agencies' principal tasks was to correct decades of "mining" mountain renewable resources. The Forest Service's initial tasks in addressing mountain deterioration were to diminish the stocking of mountain rangelands, limit cutting of remaining timber, and protect the watershed for valley communities. Urban environmentalists today charge federal land managers with too little activity too oriented toward local livestock and timber interests; and that "Multiple Use" means multiple abuse. Longtime rural residents of the region are likely to charge too much government interference. Utah was prime ground for the "sagebrush rebellion" of the 1980s, a popular movement that sought to place public lands in private ownership.

As with "outsider" mining communities and ski resorts, federal agencies provide an important source of income for Mormons. Land management agencies provide payments to county governments in lieu of tax dollars. Direct benefits accrue to individuals employed by a variety of government offices, for which Salt Lake City is a major regional center; or indirectly through the service sector. Brooks's family also benefited from government employment when her father replaced his freighting job with a Postal Service contract to deliver Bunkerville's mail to the nearest rail station—a round trip of two days by horse and wagon.

Restorative Sanctuary

Mormons of the Mountain West have lived amidst some of the most spectacular scenery in the world: massive cordilleran peaks, deep powder slopes, secluded alpine lakes, burnished sandstone canyons, pastel badlands ("breaks"), steepled buttes, and freestanding stone arches. These are the terrains of internationally famous national parks and ski resorts. Viewing through modern, secular spectacles, one would imagine that the early Mormon settlers gloried in these landscapes' possibilities for recreation and relaxation as much as busloads of German, Japanese, and retired Midwestern tourists do today.

The historical record nevertheless reveals some surprises. Park Service history cites pioneer Ebenezer Bryce's comments on the land that became Bryce Canyon National Park: "It's a hell of a place to lose a cow." The initial Mormon settlers of Bluff, Utah, saw little restorative virtue in the scenic spectacle of the Grand Canyon as they grappled with the exhausting and dangerous challenge of lowering wagons down an 1,800-foot cliff to the one location where it was possible to ferry them across the Colorado River. Some early diarists thought the view of mountains was oppressive. The most restorative landscape emerging from the settlers' records was not the view of alpine wilderness, but the pleasures of one's own verdant valley-bottom pastures, orchards, and field crops.

The pioneers were not blind to the delights of subalpine recreation, however. The valley settlers certainly enjoyed trips to nearby mountains for picnics, buggy rides, Fourth of July celebrations, church outings, visits to friends on mountain ranches, and the like (figure 5). Practical trips for wood hauling and the gathering of pinon pine nuts often served double-duty as recreation. Desert dwellers like Brooks typically described the forested mountain canyons with relish and gratitude.

Perhaps most were simply too busy with the relentless hard work of tending large families and the labor-intensive system of farming marginal land to have much time to spend on relaxation in settings which, though scenic, formed the boundary of a lifeworld that focused on the Mormon town and the church. Common forms of recreation were community dances and talent shows in the meeting house, church organization meetings, and socializing with neighbors.[32] The sabbath day of rest was for church attendance, not recreation. Most other days were for the endless round of work. Utah's state emblem of the beehive seems apt indeed.

Latter-day Saint commitment to landscape development and improvement, as defined by an agrarian and urban society today, seems to pit Mormondom today against wilderness preservationists and those who would place strict limits on mountain development. The general Mormon response to mountains is thus one of recreational enjoyment, but, more importantly, one of economic development.

5. *An Outing to Brighton in the Wasatch Mountains above Salt Lake City in 1896.*
(Courtesy Special Collections Department, University of Utah Libraries, no. P0120
#108.)

Water-based recreation has always been welcomed by those with access
to it, however. A few eastern-style resorts were established near urban
areas in Zion during the late nineteenth century: Saltaire, on the Great Salt
Lake, and Saratoga (named after the eastern resort) at hot springs along
Utah Lake, were perhaps the most prominent, although their clientele was
largely local.[33] Customers were attracted to the resorts' water and amuse-
ments more than to alpine scenery: the latter seemed more or less ubiquitous, the former, a rare holiday.

Gentile impacts in the Mormon region's mountains grew over time as
mountains' recreational value became more apparent. Concessions within
national parks, ski resorts, and gambling across the Nevada border were financed by non-Mormon entrepreneurs, primarily for out-of-state tourists,
although local Mormon residents again supplied much of the labor needed
to staff these attractions and benefited from their wages.[34]

Conclusions

In a comparison of this volume's five themes with the experiences of Mormon settlers in general and one Mormon woman in particular, the correspondence of significance shared by the Mormon experience and the geographer's themes of isolation, moisture, and resources seems reasonably close. Mountains as a scenic or recreational destination was a less important concept than one would expect, and the concept of government domain in the early years was conspicuous by the means that the Latter-day Saints devised to avoid it.

I would add three additional and interrelated themes derived from Juanita Brooks's recollections, however: mountains as Zion, mountains as home, and mountains as metaphor. Any effort to understand the Mormon landscape begins with the realization that the meaning of this region for the people who lived in it was not as a case study of economic development nor as some abstract assemblage of survey patterns, house types, and other landscape elements. To Mormons, the mountains, deserts, and valleys were the Kingdom of Saints and the location of the millenium. It was also home.[35] And if mountains were the visible horizon of the Mormon homescape, then they, at least metaphorically, were also the vantage point to comprehend what lay beyond.

The concept of mountains as "restorative sanctuary" has had deep meaning, indeed, for Mormons in a theological rather than recreational sense. The religious purpose of economic development was to prepare a fitting home for Christ on His return to planet Earth. Old Testament prophets announced that the millenium would begin in Zion on the tops of mountains, referring to the location of Jerusalem atop the Judaean hills.[36] In transferring the concept of Zion from the Near East to America, Mormons felt especially validated in their choice of region by the surrounding highlands.[37] In Zion, God's Kingdom was to be restored and to be a sanctuary for His Saints. The geosophy was clear. Mountains figure prominently in Mormon hymns for this reason.[38] Critics of the church quibbled on physiographic grounds that Mormons actually settled in the valleys, not on mountaintops as the Bible specified. But most Mormons looked no further than the horizon to convince themselves that their Great Basin sanctuary literally matched scriptural descriptions of the place where Christ's kingdom was to be restored and the millennium would begin. This eschatology may help explain why incised desert canyon walls and buttes sometimes were named mountains by the early pioneers.[39] If it was meritorious in the eyes of the faithful to live among mountaintops, better to designate some out of the available terrain than to do without.

Yet such analysis is, after all, the perspective of the outsider. To Juanita Brooks and her co-religionists, the essential and consistent sectors of the Mormon scene were the location of house, family, neighbors, work, church, anecdotes, and daily trivia. These were not the object of the geographer's analysis: they were life.

If the personal landscape of home is too individualized for the geographer to investigate, however, it may be worthwhile to consider the patterns frequently presented by the daily Mormon scene. For a rural people geographically and socially isolated from the outside world, there was a pervasive spatial frame of reference. This geography was demonstrably ethnocentric. The community's ethnogeographic center was the meeting house of the local ward, or tabernacle or temple for large communities. Cardinally oriented numbered streets arrayed around the church building always indicated one's location relative to it, as names of wards (similar to parishes) often did where there was more than one in a community (North Ward, South Ward, etc.) The large fields were subdivided into individual landholdings and sometimes were named after cardinal directions oriented around the town center.

Mormon toponymy includes placenames even today not found on any topographic map; names that imply the village core and peripheral highlands. Even today, residents may simply refer to the open country or distant mountains surrounding the archetypal town and its fields as "the East Desert" or "the West Mountains."[40]

Just as Native Americans of the Southwest associated cardinal directions with colors and qualities, Mormon settlers described the northern valleys (Cache, Salt Lake, Utah) as being greener and more agriculturally productive and beneficent: to the south was the red rock desert, scantier precipitation, and greater hardship.[41] It was an ethnogeography that shared much in common with the T-in-O map of medieval Europe: a circumscribed habitable earth divided into a few sectors, with Jerusalem as its center.

Travels beyond the perimeter to places with other landscapes did not necessarily alter the basic ethnogeography. When pioneers were called to settle new communities, they expected to transplant the same landscape patterns. When Latter-day Saint men left Zion, they typically were missionaries for the church, and they anticipated a reabsorption into their old communities. External ideas of landscape planning were minimal. Non-

Mormons were such rare visitors in isolated Mormon communities a century ago that children took special notice of the first time they had ever seen one and recalled the circumstances decades later with clarity. During Brooks's childhood, any visitor who was neither a relative of a neighbor nor traveling on church business was such a rarity that crowds gathered around to stare. The church defined one's economy, acquaintances, recreation, education, and spiritual well-being. In such a lifeworld, Bunkerville and similar communities were the core of one's private geography: anyplace else, often including Salt Lake City, was beyond one's periphery of experience. Beyond Zion was Babylon.

But sometimes Latter-day Saints did alter their perceptions in reaching the familiar horizon, or sometimes the Outside broached the protective bulwarks and came to them. A variety of external influences were increasingly common after World War I, as automobiles and improved communications lessened rural isolation.

Brooks's autobiography suggests that, for her, the high ground that formed the circumference of her field of vision could become the vantage point for new understanding expected to lie beyond. As a child on her first Sunday school outing up the slope to the broad bench between Bunkerville and the Virgin Mountains, Brooks commented that having seen an enlarged vista on the "Wide, Wonderful World," she would never look at Bunkerville the same way again. A few years later, her first Outsider visited town and stayed briefly with her family (obviously Bunkerville had no hotel). He quoted Tennyson's *Ulysses* to her: "all experience is an arch wherethro' Gleams that untravell'd world, whose margin fades For ever and ever when I move." After he left town, Brooks rode her pony up to her favorite lookout point above town and vicariously understood through the Outsider that more of the "Wide, Wonderful World" existed than she previously imagined. Like many a small-town child planning a metamorphosis out of the cocoon, she wrote:

> I looked over my world here on the edge of the desert, its sun-blistered miles of rock and clay—a barren world full of emptiness. I knew that there were places where grass and trees and flowers grew just for the fun of it, without having to be nursed along by irrigation. . . . Or was it not the physical world at all to which the Outsider referred—but the world of thought, of knowledge? . . . [I] determined that I would see some of the world beyond the desert, that I would go to a college or university. . . . I would not wait for life to come to me; I would go out to meet it.[42]

Later in life, other views from mountain vistas had a similar emotionally liberating effect. Distant lands glimpsed or imagined from a viewpoint above one's familiar world became metaphors for expanding horizons of the landscape within.

The relationships between Mormons and mountains were varied and complex, ranging from the economic to the eschatological, from the public to the personal. Although some historical geographers have considered Mormons only as an example of desert colonization, serious settlement of arid lands using nineteenth-century Anglo-American technology could scarcely have been accomplished on a large scale without access to mountain resources. A belt or zone along the boundary between the valleys and mountains, only a few miles in width, probably accounts for the majority of early Mormon population and economic activity. The Mormons also integrated valleys and mountains through their religion, in which the righteous caused the desert "to bloom like the rose" and looked to the mountains for validation of their location and way of life. Integration of Zion's varied terrain was also an individual matter, where highlands comprised the farther reaches of the familiar landscape of home; perimeters on which one could stand in order to understand some of the geography of one's own consciousness.

Notes

1. Juanita Brooks, *Quicksand and Cactus: A Memoir of the Southern Mormon Frontier* (Salt Lake City: Howe Brothers, 1982); Levi S. Peterson, *Juanita Brooks, Mormon Woman Historian* (Salt Lake City, University of Utah Press, 1988). "Dixie" comprises southwest Utah and adjacent LDS communities of Nevada and Arizona. For some background works on this region, see Melvin T. Smith, "Forces That Shaped Utah's Dixie: Another Look," *Utah Historical Quarterly* 47 (1979): 110–29; Larry M. Logue, *A Sermon in the Desert: Belief and Behavior in Early St. George, Utah* (Urbana: University of Illinois Press, 1988); Deon C. Greer et al., *Atlas of Utah* (Provo: Brigham Young University Press, 1981). For a sample of autobiographies of other Mormon women, see Margaret Ward, ed. *A Fragment: The Autobiography of Mary Mount Tanner* (Salt Lake City: University of Utah Library, 1980); Annie Clark Tanner, *A Mormon Mother: An Autobiography* (Salt Lake City: University of Utah Press, 1969); Mary Ann Hafen, *Recollections of a Handcart Pioneer of 1860 with Some Account of Frontier Life in Utah and Nevada* (about Brooks's grandmother) (Lincoln: University of Nebraska Press, 1983);

Davis Bitton, *Guide to Mormon Diaries and Autobiographies* (Provo: Brigham Young University Press, 1977).

2. For some good overviews, see Leonard J. Arrington, Feramorz Y. Fox, and Dean L. May, *Building the City of God: Community and Cooperation among the Mormons* (Salt Lake City: Deseret Book Co., 1976); Leonard J. Arrington and Davis Bitton, *The Mormon Experience: A History of the Latter-day Saints* (New York: Alfred A. Knopf, 1979); Thomas G. Alexander, ed. *The Mormon People: Their Character and Traditions* (Provo: Brigham Young University Press, 1980); Klaus J. Hansen, *Mormonism and the American Experience* (Chicago: University of Chicago Press, 1981); Jan Shipps, *Mormonism: The Study of a New Religious Tradition* (Urbana: University of Illinois Press, 1985). A recent bibliography is found in Curt Bench, "Fifty Important Mormon Books," *Sunstone* 14, no.5 (1990): 54–58. Studies by historical geographers include Donald W. Meinig, "The Mormon Culture Region: Strategies and Patterns in the American West, 1847–1964," *Annals of the Association of American Geographers* 55 (1965): 191–220; Wayne L. Wahlquist, "A Review of Mormon Settlement Literature," *Utah Historical Quarterly* 45 (1977): 4–21; Richard H. Jackson, ed., *The Mormon Role in the Settlement of the West* (Provo: Brigham Young University Press, 1978); Richard V. Francaviglia, *The Mormon Landscape* (New York: AMS Press, 1979); Alan G. Noble, "Building Mormon Houses: A Preliminary Typology," *Pioneer America* 15 (1983): 55–66.

3. Jeanne Kay and Craig J. Brown, "Mormon Beliefs about Land and Natural Resources, 1847–1877," *Journal of Historical Geography* 11 (1985): 253–67; Donald H. Dyal, "Mormon Pursuit of the Agrarian Ideal," *Agricultural History* 63, no. 4 (1989): 19–35.

4. Brooks, *Quicksand and Cactus*, 157.

5. Brooks, *Quicksand and Cactus*, 112–13, 140.

6. Leonard Guelke, *Historical Understanding in Geography: An Idealist Approach* (Cambridge: Cambridge University Press, 1982).

7. Leonard J. Arrington, *Great Basin Kingdom: Economic History of the Latter-day Saints, 1830–1900* (Lincoln: University of Nebraska Press, 1958); Richard H. Jackson, "Mormon Perception and Settlement," *Annals of the Association of American Geographers* 68 (1978): 317–34.

8. Peter R. Hacker, "Shooting the Sheriff: A Look at Bernard DeVoto, Historian," *Utah Historical Quarterly* 58 (1990): 232–43; Fawn McKay Brodie, *No Man Knows My History: The Life of Joseph Smith, the Mormon Prophet* (New York: Alfred A. Knopf, 1971).

9. Wallace Stegner, *Mormon Country* (New York: Hawthorne Books, 1942); Stegner, *The Gathering of Zion: The Story of the Mormon Trail* (New York: McGraw-Hill, 1964); Gary B. Peterson and Lowell C. Bennion, *Sanpete Scenes: A Guide to Utah's Heart* (Eureka, Utah: Basin/Plateau Press, 1987); Edward Geary, *Goodbye to Pop-*

larhaven: Recollections of a Utah Boyhood (Salt Lake City: University of Utah Press, 1985); Brooks, *Quicksand and Cactus*.

10. Brooks, *Quicksand and Cactus*, 5–10.

11. Lawrence Foster, "Polygamy and the Frontier: Mormon Women in Early Utah," *Utah Historical Quarterly* 50 (1982): 268–89; Jessie L. Embry, *Mormon Polygamous Families: Life in the Principle* (Salt Lake City: University of Utah Press, 1987); Martha S. Bradley, "Changed Faces: The Official LDS Position on Polygamy, 1890–1990," *Sunstone* 14, no. 4 (1990): 26–33. There are also "insider" and "outsider" versions of Mormon women's history. Examples of the former, stressing acceptable feminine roles, are Kenneth W. Godfrey, Audrey M. Godfrey, and Jill Mulvay Derr, *Women's Voices: An Untold History of the Latter-day Saints* (Salt Lake City: Deseret Book Co., 1982); Maureen Ursenbach Beecher, "Women's Work on the Mormon Frontier," *Utah Historical Quarterly* 49 (1981): 276–90; Beecher and Lavina Fielding Anderson, *Sisters in Spirit: Mormon Women in Historical and Cultural Perspective* (Urbana: University of Illinois Press, 1987).

12. Brooks, *Quicksand and Cactus*, 42–50.

13. Paul Goeldner, "The Architecture of Equal Comforts: Polygamists in Utah," *Historic Preservation* 24 (1972).

14. Arrington, *Great Basin Kingdom*.

15. Brooks, *Quicksand and Cactus*, 107.

16. Benches are flat rims perched between the valley floors and foothills throughout the Great Basin. In the Mormon region, most are the ancient shorelines of postglacial Lake Bonneville, whose principal surviving remnant is the Great Salt Lake.

17. Leonard J. Arrington and Dean L. May, "A Different Mode of Life: Irrigation and Society in Nineteenth Century Utah," *Agricultural History* 49 (1975): 3–20.

18. U.S. Geological Survey, Mesquite and Flat Top Mesa, Nevada quadrangles, provisional editions (1985) 1:24,000.

19. Brooks, *Quicksand and Cactus*, 125.

20. Charles S. Peterson, "Grazing in Utah: A Historical Perspective," *Utah Historical Quarterly* 57 (1989): 300–319.

21. John Wesley Powell, *Report on the Lands of the Arid Region of the United States* (Washington, D.C., 1879; reprint, Cambridge, Mass.: Belknap Press of Harvard University Press, 1962), 121, 155–56.

22. Craig J. Brown, "The Allocation of Timber Resources within the Wasatch Mountains of Salt Lake County, Utah, 1847–70" (master's thesis, University of Utah, 1982).

23. Richard H. Jackson, "The Use of Adobe in the Mormon Cultural Region," *Journal of Cultural Geography* 1 (1980): 82–95; Thomas Carter and Peter Goss, *Utah's*

Historic Architecture, 1847–1940 (Salt Lake City: University of Utah Press, 1988). The Summer 1975 issue of the *Utah Historical Quarterly* is devoted to Mormon vernacular architecture.

24. Esther Ruth Truitt, "Enclosing a World," *Utah Historical Quarterly* 56 (1988): 352–59.

25. The Summer 1963 issue of the *Utah Historical Quarterly* is devoted to a history of mining in Utah.

26. Lawrence R. Linford, "Establishing and Maintaining Land Ownership in Utah prior to 1869," *Utah Historical Quarterly* 42 (1974): 126–43.

27. Albert L. Fisher, "Mormon Welfare Programs: Past and Present," *Social Science Journal* 15 (1978): 75–99.

28. John Wesley Powell, *Report on the Lands;* Walter P. Cottam and George Stewart, "Plant Succession as a Result of Grazing and Meadow Dessication by Erosion since Settlement in 1862," *Journal of Forestry* 38 (1940): 613–26; Richard H. Jackson, "Righteousness and Environmental Change: The Mormons and the Environment," Charles Redd Monograph in Western History no. 5 (Provo: Brigham Young University Press, 1975) 21–42; Brian Q. Cannon, "Struggle against Great Odds: Challenges in Utah's Marginal Agricultural Areas, 1925–39," *Utah Historical Quarterly* 54 (1986): 308–27; Peterson, "Grazing in Utah."

29. Greer, *Atlas of Utah,* 180–85; Peterson, "Grazing in Utah."

30. Dan L. Flores, "Zion in Eden: Phases of the Environmental History of Utah," *Environmental Review* 7 (1983): 325–44; Flores, "Agriculture, Mountain Ecology, and the Land Ethic: Phases of the Environmental History of Utah," in John R. Wunder, ed., *Working the Range: Essays on the History of Western Land Management and the Environment* (Westport, Conn.: Greenwood Press, 1985), 157–86.

31. Charles S. Peterson, "Natural Resource Utilization," in Richard D. Poll et al., eds., *Utah's History* (Provo: Brigham Young University Press, 1978), 651–68.

32. Joseph Heinerman, "The Mormon Meetinghouse: Reflections of Pioneer Religious and Social Life in Salt Lake City," *Utah Historical Quarterly* 50 (1982): 340–53.

33. Nancy D. McCormick and John S. McCormick, *Saltair* (Salt Lake City: University of Utah Press, 1985); Richard S. Van Wagoner, "Saratoga, Utah Lake's Oldest Resort," *Utah Historical Quarterly* 57 (1989): 108–24.

34. Nick Scrattish, "The Modern Discovery, Popularization, and Early Development of Bryce Canyon, Utah," *Utah Historical Quarterly* 49 (1981): 348–62.

35. On the importance of "home" for geographers, see Anne Buttimer, "Home, Reach, and the Sense of Place," in Anne Buttimer and David Seamon, eds., *The Human Experience of Space and Place* (New York: St. Martin's Press, 1980), 166–87; Yi-fu Tuan, "A View of Geography," *Geographical Review* 81 (1991): 99–107.

36. Joel 4:17–18, Isaiah 52:7–10, Ezekiel 36:1–12.

37. Steven L. Olsen, "Zion: The Structure of a Theological Revolution," *Sunstone* (1981): 21–27.

38. Samples from *Hymns of the Church of Jesus Christ of Latter-day Saints* (1985) include: "High on the Mountain Top," "Our Mountain Home So Dear," "O Ye Mountains High," "For the Strength of the Hills," "Zion Stands with Hills Surrounded."

39. Lady Mountain and Red Arch Mountain in Zion National Park are prominent examples.

40. Cf. Yi-fu Tuan, *Topophilia: A Study of Environmental Perception, Attitudes, and Values* (Englewood Cliffs, N.J.: Prentice-Hall, 1974), 30–44.

41. Richard H. Jackson, "Utah's Harsh Lands, Hearth of Greatness," *Utah Historical Quarterly* 49 (1981): 4–25.

42. Brooks, *Quicksand and Cactus*, 168–69.

Contributors

John L. Allen is a professor of geography at the University of Connecticut. He is the author of numerous books and articles on western historical geography and exploration.

John Dietz is a professor of geography at the University of Northern Colorado. He is a specialist on the economic development of Colorado, including an historical interest in the evolution of the San Luis Valley.

Lary M. Dilsaver is a professor of geography at the University of South Alabama. His widely published research focuses on the human geography of the Sierra Nevada and on the geography of the national parks.

Richard H. Jackson is a professor of geography at Brigham Young University. He publishes widely on the Mormons in the West and on the role of the federal government in shaping the human geography of the region.

John W. James is an associate professor of geography at the University of Nevada–Reno and has served as Nevada's state climatologist. His career includes a close monitoring of and participation in the evolution of regional planning in the Lake Tahoe area of the Sierra Nevada.

Jeanne Kay is dean of the Faculty of Environmental Sciences at the University of Waterloo in Ontario, Canada. She has published on the Mormons, Native Americans, and women on the frontier.

Cathy E. Kindquist is a doctoral candidate in geography at the University of British Columbia. A longtime resident of the Colorado high country, she has completed several studies and a book detailing the story of settlement in the region.

Victor Konrad is executive director of the Fulbright Program's Foundation for Educational Exchange between Canada and the United States in Ottawa. He has published numerous articles and books on the cultural and historical geography of North America.

Albert Larson is an assistant professor of geography at the University of Illinois at Chicago. He specializes in the study of the American cultural landscape.

Randall Rohe is an associate professor of geography at the University of Wisconsin at Waukesha. He publishes widely on the relationship between mining, the environment, and the cultural landscape of the American West.

Robert A. Sauder is a professor of geography at the University of New Orleans. He has written numerous publications on California's Owens Valley and on patterns of land disposal in the West.

Duane A. Smith is a professor of history at Fort Lewis College in Durango, Colorado. He is the author of numerous articles and books on the American West with an emphasis on the settlement and evolution of the Rocky Mountains.

Thomas R. Vale is a professor of geography at the University of Wisconsin at Madison. Both a biogeographer and a cultural geographer, he has published numerous books and articles on the physical and human geography of the Mountainous West.

Michael Williams is a reader in geography at Oxford University in England. His expertise on assessing human impacts upon the landscape has been demonstrated in settings around the world, including work on the evolution of South Australia and on the changing forests of North America.

William Wyckoff is an associate professor of geography in the Department of Earth Sciences at Montana State University in Bozeman. He is the author of numerous studies on the making of the American frontier, including work in western New York, Colorado, and Montana.

Index